Arabic For Dumm... Sheet

W9-DGP-653

Useful Questions

- **man** (*man;* who)
- **'ayna** (*ay-nah;* where)
- **mataa** (*mah-tah;* when)
- **kayfa** (*kay-fah;* how)
- **li maadhaa** (*lee mah-zah;* why)
- **kayf al-Haal?** (*kah-yef al-hal;* How are you?)
- **maa 'ismuka?** (*mah ees-moo-kah;* What's your name?) (MS)
- **maa 'ismuki?** (*mah ees-moo-kee;* What's your name?) (FS)

- **kam as-saa'a?** (*kam ah-sah-ah;* What time is it?)
- **bikam haadhaa?** (*bee-kam hah-zah;* How much is this?)
- **'ayna al-mirHaad?** (*ay-nah al-meer-had;* Where is the bathroom?)
- **hal tatakallam al-injliziya?** (*hal tah-tah-kah-lam al-een-jlee-zee-yah;* Do you speak English?)
- **hal yumkin 'an ta'id min faDlik?** (*hal yoom-keen an tah-eed meen fad-leek;* Could you please repeat that?)

Greetings, Goodbyes, and Other Expressions

- **'ahlan wa sahlan** (*ahel-lan wah sahel-lan;* hi)
- **'ahlan** (*ahel-lan;* hi) (informal)
- **'as-salaamu 'alaykum** (*ah-sah-lah-moo ah-lay-koom;* hello)
- **SabaaH al-khayr** (*sah-bah al-kah-yer;* good morning)
- **masaa' al-khayr** (*mah-sah al-kah-yer;* good evening)

- **'ilaa al-liqaa'** (*ee-lah ah-lee-kah;* see you soon)
- **'ilaa al-ghad** (*ee-lah al-rad;* see you tomorrow)
- **'afwan** (*af-wan;* excuse me)
- **shukran** (*shook-ran;* thank you)
- **shukran jaziilan** (*shook-ran jah-zee-lan;* thank you very much)

Days of the Week

- **al-'ithnayn** (*al-eeth-nah-yen;* Monday)
- **ath-thulathaa'** (*ah-too-lah-tah;* Tuesday)
- **al-'arbi'aa'** (*al-ar-bee-ah;* Wednesday)
- **al-khamiis** (*al-kah-mees;* Thursday)
- **al-jumu'a** (*al-joo-moo-ah;* Friday)
- **as-sabt** (*ah-sah-bet;* Saturday)
- **al-'aHad** (*al-ah-had;* Sunday)

For Dummies: Bestselling Book Series for Beginners

Arabic For Dummies®

Numbers

Arabic	Pronunciation	Translation
waaHid	wah-heed	1
'ithnayn	eet-nah-yen	2
thalaatha	tah-lah-tah	3
'arba'a	ar-bah-ah	4
khamsa	kam-sah	5
sitta	see-tah	6
sab'a	sab-ah	7
thamaaniya	tah-mah-nee-yah	8
tis'a	tees-ah	9
'ashra	ash-rah	10
'iHdaa 'ashar	ee-heh-dah ah-shar	11
'ithnaa 'ashar	ee-theh-nah ah-shar	12
thalaathata 'ashar	thah-lah-tha-tah ah-shar	13
'arba'ata 'ashar	ah-reh-bah-ah-tah ah-shar	14
khamsata 'ashar	khah-meh-sah-tah ah-shar	15
sittata 'ashar	see-tah-tah ah-shar	16
sab'ata 'ashar	sah-beh-ah-tah ah-shar	17
thamaaniyata 'ashar	thah-mah-nee-ya-tah ah-shar	18
tis'ata 'ashar	tee-seh-ah-tah ah-shar	19
'ishreen	ee-sheh-reen	20
thalaathiin	thah-lah-theen	30
'arba'iin	ah-reh-bah-een	40
khamsiin	khah-meh-seen	50
sittiin	see-teen	60
sab'iin	sah-beh-een	70
thamaaniin	thah-mah-neen	80
tis'iin	tee-seh-een	90
mi'a	mee-ah	100

For Dummies: Bestselling Book Series for Beginners

Arabic FOR DUMMIES®

by Amine Bouchentouf

Wiley Publishing, Inc.

Arabic For Dummies®

Published by
Wiley Publishing, Inc.
111 River St.
Hoboken, NJ 07030-5774
www.wiley.com

For general information on our other products and services, please contact our Customer Care Department within the U.S. at 800-762-2974, outside the U.S. at 317-572-3993, or fax 317-572-4002.

For technical support, please visit www.wiley.com/techsupport.

Wiley also publishes its books in a variety of electronic formats. Some content that appears in print may not be available in electronic books.

Library of Congress Control Number: 2006920607

ISBN-13: 978-0-471-77270-5

ISBN-10: 0-471-77270-4

Manufactured in the United States of America

10 9 8 7 6 5 4

1B/RT/QU/QW/IN

WILEY

About the Author

Amine Bouchentouf is a native English, Arabic, and French speaker born and raised in Casablanca, Morocco. Amine has been teaching Arabic and lecturing about relations between America and the Arab world in his spare time for over 4 years and has offered classes and seminars for students at Middlebury College, the Council on Foreign Relations, and various schools across the United States. He runs and maintains the Web site www.al-baab.com (which means "gateway" in Arabic).

Amine graduated from Middlebury College and has always been interested in promoting better relations between the West and the Middle East through dialogue and mutual understanding. Amine published his first book, *Arabic: A Complete Course* (Random House), soon after graduating college in order to help Americans understand Arabic language and culture. He has written *Arabic For Dummies* in an attempt to reach an even wider audience with the aim of fostering better relations through education.

He holds a degree in Economics from Middlebury and has extensive experience in the arena of international investing. He is a registered investment advisor and is a member of the National Association of Securities Dealers. Amine is currently working on his third book, *Investing in Commodities For Dummies* (Wiley Publishing).

Amine is an avid traveler and has visited over 15 countries across the Middle East, Europe, and North and South America. Aside from his interest in languages, business, and travel, Amine enjoys biking, rollerblading, playing guitar, chess, and golf. He lives in New York City.

Dedication

This book is dedicated to my greatest and most steadfast supporters — my family. To my mother for her infinite and unwavering support, and to my sister, Myriam, for her enthusiasm and passion — you are my greatest inspirations.

To my father and grandfather, may you rest in peace, thank you for instilling in me such a deep respect and awareness of my roots and culture. I am honored to be part of the Bouchentouf family.

And to my grandmother, who recently passed away, thanks for always believing in me.

Author's Acknowledgments

This book would not have been possible without the guidance and input from the wonderful folks at Wiley Publishing. It has been an honor to work with a team that adheres to the highest standards of professionalism.

First, I would like to thank Kathy Cox, my acquisitions editor, whose insight into the *Dummies* methodology has been invaluable to me, and for her tireless dedication to this book. To Tim Gallan, my project editor, for his patient, thorough and insightful guidance. And to my copy editor, Elizabeth Rea, for her detailed and meticulous review of the manuscript. Also, thanks to Courtney Allen who helped us get the ball rolling in the early stages of the project. I have thoroughly enjoyed working with such a wonderful team.

Special thanks to Ben Smith from Harvard University's Center for Middle Eastern Studies for agreeing to serve as technical reviewer of the text. His comments have ensured that the translation of the text adhered to the highest degree of linguistic accuracy.

I would also like to extend a special thanks to my agent, Mark Sullivan, whose dedication and hard work is exemplary. I'm proud to have someone so diligent and persistent representing me. Merci.

Also, thanks to my wonderful Arabic students at the Council on Foreign Relations: Mehlaqa, Danna, Mary, Mark, and Evan who helped me challenge myself and become a better communicator. And a special thanks to the hardworking folks at the ABC Language Exchange and to everyone at my alma mater, Middlebury College, for their enthusiasm and support of this project.

Finally, thank you to everyone who has supported me throughout this writing period. I would not have been able to do this without your precious support.

Publisher's Acknowledgments

We're proud of this book; please send us your comments through our Dummies online registration form located at www.dummies.com/register/.

Some of the people who helped bring this book to market include the following:

Acquisitions, Editorial, and Media Development

Senior Project Editor: Tim Gallan

Acquisitions Editor: Kathleen M. Cox

Copy Editor: Elizabeth Rea

Editorial Program Coordinator: Hanna K. Scott

Technical Editor: Benjamin Smith

Editorial Manager: Christine Meloy Beck

Editorial Assistants: Nadine Bell, Erin Calligan, David Lutton

Cartoons: Rich Tennant (www.the5thwave.com)

Composition Services

Project Coordinator: Adrienne Martinez

Layout and Graphics: Mary J. Gillot, Joyce Haughey, Stephanie D. Jumper, Melanee Prendergast, Julie Trippetti, Erin Zeltner

Proofreaders: Henry Lazarek, Joe Niesen, Christine Pingleton

Indexer: Steve Rath

Publishing and Editorial for Consumer Dummies

Diane Graves Steele, Vice President and Publisher, Consumer Dummies

Joyce Pepple, Acquisitions Director, Consumer Dummies

Kristin A. Cocks, Product Development Director, Consumer Dummies

Michael Spring, Vice President and Publisher, Travel

Kelly Regan, Editorial Director, Travel

Publishing for Technology Dummies

Andy Cummings, Vice President and Publisher, Dummies Technology/General User

Composition Services

Gerry Fahey, Vice President of Production Services

Debbie Stailey, Director of Composition Services

Contents at a Glance

Introduction *1*

Part I: Getting Started *7*
Chapter 1: You Already Know a Little Arabic 9
Chapter 2: The Nitty-Gritty: Basic Arabic Grammar 19
Chapter 3: 'as-salaamu 'alaykum!: Greetings and Introductions 49

Part II: Arabic in Action *59*
Chapter 4: Getting to Know You: Making Small Talk 61
Chapter 5: This Is Delicious! Eating In and Dining Out 81
Chapter 6: Going Shopping 99
Chapter 7: Around Town 121
Chapter 8: Enjoying Yourself: Recreation..143
Chapter 9: Talking on the Phone 155
Chapter 10: At the Office and Around the House...............................167

Part III: Arabic on the Go *187*
Chapter 11: Money, Money, Money..189
Chapter 12: Asking for Directions 205
Chapter 13: Staying at a Hotel...217
Chapter 14: Getting from Here to There: Transportation 239
Chapter 15: Planning a Trip..261
Chapter 16: Handling an Emergency 281

Part IV: The Part of Tens *293*
Chapter 17: Ten Ways to Pick Up Arabic Quickly...............................295
Chapter 18: Ten Things You Should Never Do in an Arab Country 299
Chapter 19: Ten Favorite Arabic Expressions.....................................305
Chapter 20: Ten Great Arabic Proverbs...311

Part V: Appendixes *315*
Appendix A: Verb Tables 317
Appendix B: Arabic-English Mini-Dictionary 331
Appendix C: Answer Key 345
Appendix D: About the CD 351

Index *353*

Table of Contents

Introduction *1*

About This Book...1
Conventions Used in This Book 2
What I Assume About You...3
How This Book Is Organized..3
   Part I: Getting Started 3
   Part II: Arabic in Action 4
   Part III: Arabic on the Go 4
   Part IV: The Part of Tens......................................4
   Part V: Appendixes 4
Icons Used in This Book...4
Where to Go from Here..5

Part 1: Getting Started *7*

Chapter 1: You Already Know a Little Arabic 9

Taking Stock of What's Familiar 9
Discovering the Arabic Alphabet................................11
   All about vowels..11
   All about consonants 14
Speaking Arabic Like a Native 18
Addressing Arabic Transcription................................18

Chapter 2: The Nitty-Gritty: Basic Arabic Grammar 19

Introducing Nouns, Adjectives, and Articles.............................19
   Getting a grip on nouns 20
   Identifying adjectives..21
   Discovering definite and indefinite articles
      (and the sun and moon).......................................24
   Understanding the interaction between nouns and adjectives 26
Creating Simple, Verb-Free Sentences 28
   To be or not to be: Sentences without verbs...................28
   Building sentences with common prepositions 30
   Using demonstratives and forming sentences 32
   Forming "to be" sentences using personal pronouns 34
   Creating negative "to be" sentences 36
   "To be" in the past tense 37
Working with Verbs 38
   Digging up the past tense 38
   Examining the present tense....................................41

Peeking into the future tense 44
Examining irregular verb forms 45

Chapter 3: 'as-salaamu 'alaykum!: Greetings and Introductions 49

Greetings! 49
You say hello 50
. . . I say goodbye 51
How are you doing? 51
I'm doing well! 52
Making Introductions 53
Asking "What's your name?" 54
Responding with the possessive "My name is . . ." 54
Saying "It's a pleasure to meet you!" 54
Talking About Countries and Nationalities 55
Asking "Where are you from?" 55
Telling where "I am from . . ." 55

Part II: Arabic in Action *59*

Chapter 4: Getting to Know You: Making Small Talk 61

Asking Key Questions 62
Talking About Yourself and Your Family 64
Making Small Talk on the Job 68
Talking About Hobbies 70
Shooting the Breeze: Talking About the Weather 71
Talking Numbers 74
Referring to Days and Months 76

Chapter 5: This Is Delicious! Eating In and Dining Out 81

All About Meals 81
Breakfast 82
Lunch 87
Dinner 92
Enjoying a Meal at Home 92
Dining Out 93
Perusing the menu 93
Placing your order 95
Finishing your meal and paying the bill 97

Chapter 6: Going Shopping 99

Going to the Store 99
Browsing the merchandise 100
Getting around the store 101
Getting to know the verb "to search" 104

Asking for a Particular Item 105
Comparing Merchandise 109
    Comparing two or more items..109
    Picking out the best item..111
More Than a Few Words About Buying and Selling.................114
Shopping for Clothes 116

Chapter 7: Around Town 121

Telling Time in Arabic...121
    Specifying the time of day 123
    Specifying minutes 124
Visiting Museums 128
Going to the Movies 135
Touring Religious Sites 138
    A few rules to keep in mind...138
    The Hajj..139

Chapter 8: Enjoying Yourself: Recreation 143

Starting Out with the Verbs fa'ala (Did) and yaf'alu (To Do).....143
Sporting an Athletic Side...145
Going to the Beach...149
Playing Musical Instruments 151
Popular Hobbies...152

Chapter 9: Talking on the Phone 155

Dialing Up the Basics 155
    Beginning a phone conversation.....................................156
    Asking to speak to someone 157
Making Plans Over the Phone..158
    Making social plans..158
    Making business appointments.......................................160
Leaving a Message 162
    Dealing with voice mail..162
    Leaving a message with a person....................................163

Chapter 10: At the Office and Around the House 167

Landing the Perfect Job...167
Managing the Office Environment...170
    Interacting with your colleagues.....................................172
    Giving orders...177
    Supplying your office 178
Life at Home...181

Part III: Arabic on the Go 187

Chapter 11: Money, Money, Money 189

At the Bank..189
Opening a bank account..190
Making deposits and withdrawals.............................198
Using the ATM...198
Exchanging Currency..199
Getting to know the currencies around the world.....199
Making exchanges 200

Chapter 12: Asking for Directions 205

Focusing on the "Where"..205
Asking "where" questions 205
Answering "where" questions.....................................206
Getting Direction About Directions 207
Asking for directions 207
Could you repeat that? 209
Using command forms 212
Discovering Ordinal Numbers 214

Chapter 13: Staying at a Hotel 217

Choosing the Right Accommodation....................................217
Discussing minor room details..................................220
Getting to know direct object pronouns 223
Making a Reservation 224
Figuring out the price 224
Indicating the length of your stay 228
Subjecting you to subjunctive verbs 230
Checking in to the Hotel...232
Checking Out of the Hotel..235

Chapter 14: Getting from Here to There: Transportation 239

Traveling by Plane 239
Making reservations..240
Getting some legwork out of the verb "to travel" 243
Registering at the airport 244
Boarding the plane 246
A brief departure on the verb "to arrive"..................248
Going through immigration and customs 249
Getting Around on Land..253
Hailing a taxi..254
Taking a bus 255
Boarding a train 257

Chapter 15: Planning a Trip 261

Choosing Your Destination 261
Picking the Right Time for Your Trip 269
    The months of the year 269
    Dates and ordinal numbers 270
Tackling Packing 273
Preparing Your Travel Documents 274
Using a Travel Agency 278

Chapter 16: Handling an Emergency 281

Shouting Out for Help 281
    A little help with the verb "to help" 283
    Lending a hand 284
Getting Medical Help 286
    Locating the appropriate doctor 286
    Talking about your body 286
    Explaining your symptoms 287
    Getting treatment 288
Acquiring Legal Help 290

Part IV: The Part of Tens 293

Chapter 17: Ten Ways to Pick Up Arabic Quickly 295

Watch Arabic Television 295
Use the Dictionary 296
Read Arabic Newspapers 296
Surf the Internet 297
Use a Language Tape or CD 297
Listen to Arabic Music 297
Make Arabic-Speaking Friends 298
Watch Arabic Movies 298
Eat at a Middle Eastern Restaurant 298
Sing Arabic Songs 298

**Chapter 18: Ten Things You Should Never Do
in an Arab Country** 299

Don't Shake Hands with a Firm Grip 299
Don't Enter a Room Full of People Without Saying
    "'as-salaamu 'alaykum" 300
Don't Start Eating Before Saying "bismi allah" 300
If You're Not Muslim, Don't Enter a Mosque Without Explicit
    Authorization 300
Don't Enter a Mosque with Your Shoes On .301
Don't Eat or Drink During Ramadan 301

Don't Drink Alcohol During Ramadan 302
Don't Drink Alcohol in Public 302
Don't Engage in Public Displays of Affection...................................302
Don't Refuse a Gift If One Is Offered to You 303

Chapter 19: Ten Favorite Arabic Expressions 305

marHaba bikum! 305
mumtaaz! 306
al-Hamdu li-llah...306
inshaa' allah 307
mabruk!..308
bi 'idni allah 308
bi SaHHa..308
taHiyyaat 309
muballagh...309
tabaaraka allah 309

Chapter 20: Ten Great Arabic Proverbs 311

al-'amthaal noor al-kalaam. 311
'a'mal khayr wa 'ilqahu fii al-baHr. 311
'uTlubuu al-'ilm min al-mahd 'ilaa al-laHd.......................................312
yad waaHida maa tusaffiq. 312
al-Harbaa' laa Yughaadir shajaratuh hattaa yakun mu'akkid
  'an shajara 'ukhraa. 312
khaTa' ma'roof 'aHsan min Haqiiqa ghayr ma'roofa.....................312
as-sirr mithel al-Hamaama: 'indamaa yughaadir yadii yaTiir. 313
al-'aql li an-niDHaar wa al-kalb li as-simaa'. 313
kul yawm min Hayaatuk SafHa min taariikhuk. 313
li faatik bi liila faatik bi Hiila. 314

Part V: Appendixes 315

Appendix A: Verb Tables 317

Appendix B: Mini-Dictionary 331

Appendix C: Answer Key 345

Appendix D: About the CD 351

Index 353

Introduction

Arabic, the official language of over 20 countries, is the mother tongue of over 300 million people. It's spoken throughout the Middle East, from Morocco to Iraq. Additionally, because Arabic is the language of the Koran and Islam, it's understood by more than 1.2 billion people across the world.

Due to recent geopolitical events, Arabic has catapulted to the top of the list of important world languages. Even in countries where Arabic isn't the official language, people are scrambling to master this important and vital global language.

For people in North America and Europe, at first glance Arabic seems like a difficult language to master; after all, it isn't a Romance language and doesn't use the Latin alphabet. However, like any other language, Arabic is governed by a set of rules, and when you master these rules, you're able to speak Arabic like a native speaker!

Arabic For Dummies is designed to identify and explain the rules that govern the Arabic language in the easiest and most interactive way possible. I organize each chapter in a straightforward and coherent manner and present the material in an interactive and engaging way.

About This Book

Unlike most books on the Arabic language, *Arabic For Dummies* is designed in a way that gives you the most accurate and in-depth information available on the composition of the language. The book is modular in nature; every chapter is organized in such a way that you don't have to read the whole book in order to understand the topic that's discussed. Feel free to jump through chapters and sections to suit your specific needs. Also, every grammatical and linguistic point is explained in plain English so that you can incorporate the concept immediately. I took great care to explain every concept clearly and succinctly.

To provide the best foundation and the widest usage for students of Arabic, *Arabic For Dummies* focuses on Modern Standard Arabic (MSA), which is the most widely used form of Arabic in the world. There are basically three different types of Arabic: Koranic Arabic, local dialects, and MSA.

✔ **Koranic Arabic** is the Arabic used to write the Koran, the holy book for Muslims. This form of Arabic is very rigid and hasn't changed much since the Koran was written approximately 1,500 years ago. Koranic Arabic is widely used in religious circles for prayer, discussions of Islamic issues, and serious deliberations. Its usage is limited primarily within a strict religious context. It's the equivalent of Biblical English.

✔ **The regional dialects** are the most informal type of Arabic. They tend to fall into three geographical categories: the North African dialect (Morocco, Algeria, Tunisia, and Libya); the Egyptian dialect (Egypt, parts of Syria, Palestine, and Jordan); and Gulf Arabic (Saudi Arabia, Kuwait, Iraq, Qatar, and the United Arab Emirates). Even though the words are pronounced differently and some of the everyday expressions differ dramatically from region to region, speakers from different regions can understand each other. The common denominator for the regional dialects is that they're all based on MSA.

✔ **Modern Standard Arabic (MSA)** is the most widely used and understood form of Arabic in the world. It's less rigid than Koranic Arabic but a bit more formal than the local dialects. MSA is the language that Arabic anchors use to present the news, professionals use to discuss business and technical issues, and friends and families use to socialize with one another.

Conventions Used in This Book

Throughout the book, each new Arabic word appears in **boldface,** followed by its proper pronunciation and its English equivalent in parentheses.

Because this is a language book, I include some sections to help you master the linguistic concepts with greater ease. Here's a description of the specialty sections you find in each chapter:

✔ **Talkin' the Talk dialogues:** Here's where you get to see Arabic in action. These common Arabic dialogues show you how to use important vocabulary words and terms you should be aware of. Select Talkin' the Talk dialogues have accompanying audio versions on the book's CD.

✔ **Words to Know blackboards:** An important part of mastering a new language is becoming familiar with important words and phrases. Key terms that I recommend you memorize are included in these sections, which present the transcription of the Arabic word, the pronunciation, and the translation.

✔ **Fun & Games activities:** The aim of *Arabic For Dummies* is to help you master the Arabic language in an interactive and engaging way. With that in mind, each chapter ends with a Fun & Games that lets you review the key concept covered in the chapter in a fun but effective way.

What I Assume About You

In writing *Arabic For Dummies*, I made the following assumptions about my likely readers:

✔ You've had very little exposure (or none at all) to the Arabic language.

✔ You're interested in mastering Arabic for either personal or professional reasons.

✔ You want to be able to speak a few words and phrases so that you can communicate basic information in Arabic.

✔ You've been exposed to Arabic but are interested in brushing up on your language skills.

✔ You're not looking for a dry book on Arabic grammar; you want to discover Arabic in a fun and engaging manner.

✔ You're looking for a practical course that will have you speaking basic Arabic in no time!

How This Book Is Organized

Arabic For Dummies is organized into five different parts, with each part divided into chapters. The following part descriptions give you a heads-up on what to expect in each part.

Part 1: Getting Started

The first part of *Arabic For Dummies* is a must-read if you've never been exposed to Arabic. I introduce the Arabic script and present the 28 letters of the Arabic alphabet before explaining the difference between consonants and vowels, which have a very peculiar relationship in Arabic. In addition, in this part you get a detailed and thorough overview of Arabic grammatical and linguistic constructs; for instance, you find out how nouns, verbs, and adjectives interact with each other to create phrases and sentences. Finally, you discover some of the most basic forms of greetings and are introduced to basic words and phrases.

Part II: Arabic in Action

This part exposes you to key words and phrases that allow you to interact with Arabic-speaking folks in a variety of different settings (such as in a restaurant, around town, at the office, or even at the mall). You discover how to make small talk and how to ask for basic information about people you speak to, such as their names, where they're from, and their occupations.

Part III: Arabic on the Go

This part gives you the tools you need to take Arabic on the road with you. Find out how to open a bank account, how to plan a trip, how to make a reservation at a hotel, and how to ask for directions.

Part IV: The Part of Tens

The chapters in this part share some of the nonverbal methods of communication that help you to better interact with Arabic-speaking people. For example, you discover ten of the greatest Arabic proverbs, and you find out proper ways to interact with people if you're in an Arabic-speaking country. I also share my recommendations on the best ways to acquire Arabic as quickly as possible.

Part V: Appendixes

This part is a useful reference if you need information quickly. One of the appendixes in this part is a detailed list of regular and irregular verbs to help you conjugate verbs in the past, present, and future tenses. I also include a mini-dictionary in both Arabic–English and English–Arabic formats for quick reference. Finally, you find an appendix that guides you through the audio tracks on the CD.

Icons Used in This Book

In order to help you get in and get out of this book easily and efficiently, I use icons (little pictures) that identify important pieces of information by category. The following icons appear in this book:

When you see this icon, make sure you read carefully. It points to information that will directly improve your Arabic language skills.

I use this icon to bring to your attention to information that you definitely want to keep in mind when studying and practicing Arabic.

Discovering a new language can be a wonderful experience. However, there are always potential pitfalls to avoid, whether grammatical, linguistic, or cultural. This icon points out important notions about Arabic that may trip you up.

Grammar is the glue that binds a language together. Even though this isn't a grammar book, it does include important grammar lessons you need to be aware of. This icon is attached to major grammar points that will help you master the Arabic language.

This icon points out nonverbal methods of communication common in Arabic-speaking countries and among Arabic speakers. I use this icon to fill the gap between language and culture so that you know the cultural contexts in which you can use newly discovered words and phrases.

Just about every chapter of this book contains Talkin' the Talk sections with real-world conversations and dialogues. Some of these dialogues are included as audio tracks on the CD that accompanies the book. When you come across this icon, pop in your CD and listen to the conversation as you read along.

Where to Go from Here

This book is organized so that you can jump around from topic to topic. You don't have to read the whole thing. Want to know how to ask for directions in Arabic? Jump to Chapter 12. Need to exchange money in an Arabic country? Check out Chapter 11. Care to venture into the realm of Arabic grammar? Chapter 2 is for you.

Part I
Getting Started

The 5th Wave — By Rich Tennant

"We're still learning our demonstrative pronouns, although most of what Dave says in Arabic is somewhat demonstrative."

In this part . . .

I introduce the Arabic script and present the 28 letters of the Arabic alphabet before explaining the difference between consonants and vowels, which have a very peculiar relationship in Arabic. In addition, in this part you get a detailed and thorough overview of Arabic grammatical and linguistic constructs. You find out how nouns, verbs, and adjectives interact with each other to create phrases and sentences. Finally, you discover some of the most basic forms of greetings and are introduced to basic words and phrases.

Chapter 1

You Already Know a Little Arabic

In This Chapter

▶ Discovering English words that come from Arabic

▶ Figuring out the Arabic alphabet

▶ Sounding like a native speaker

MarHaba (*mahr-hah-bah;* welcome) to the wonderful world of Arabic! Arabic is the official language of over 20 countries and is spoken by more than 300 million people across the globe! It's the language in which the Koran, the Holy Book in Islam, was revealed and written, and a large majority of the over 1.3 billion Muslims across the world study Arabic in order to read the Koran and to fulfill their religious duties. By speaking Arabic, you get access to people and places from Morocco to Indonesia. (For more on Arabic's role in history, see the sidebar "Arabic's historical importance.")

In this chapter, I ease you into Arabic by showing you some familiar English words that trace their roots to Arabic. You discover the Arabic alphabet and its beautiful letters, and I give you tips on how to pronounce those letters so that you can sound like a native speaker! Part of exploring a new language is discovering a new culture and a new way of looking at things, so in this first chapter of *Arabic For Dummies,* you begin your discovery of Arabic and its unique characteristics.

Taking Stock of What's Familiar

If English is your primary language, part of grasping a new **lougha** (*loo-rah;* language) is creating connections between the **kalimaat** (*kah-lee-maht;* words) of the **lougha,** in this case Arabic, and English. You may be surprised to hear that quite a few English words trace their origins to Arabic. For example, did you know that "magazine," "candy," and "coffee" are actually Arabic words? Table 1-1 lists some familiar English words with Arabic origins.

Arabic's historical importance

During the Middle Ages, when Europe was plunged into the Dark Ages, Arab scholars and historians translated and preserved most of the works of the Greek scholars, thereby preserving some of the greatest intellectual achievements that are the cornerstone of Western civilization!

Table 1-1	Arabic Origins of English Words	
English	*Arabic Origin*	*Arabic Meaning*
admiral	amir al-baHr	Ruler of the Sea
alcohol	al-kuHul	a mixture of powdered antimony
alcove	al-qubba	a dome or arch
algebra	al-jabr	to reduce or consolidate
almanac	al-manakh	a calendar
arsenal	daar As-SinaaH	house of manufacture
azure	al-azward	lapis lazuli
candy	qand	cane sugar
coffee	qahwa	coffee
cotton	quTun	cotton
elixir	al-iksiir	philosopher's stone
gazelle	ghazaal	gazelle
hazard	az-zahr	dice
magazine	al-makhzan	a storehouse; a place of storage
mattress	matraH	a place where things are thrown
ream	rizma	a bundle
saffron	za'fran	saffron
Sahara	SaHraa'	desert
satin	zaytuun	Arabic name for a Chinese city

English	Arabic Origin	Arabic Meaning
sherbet	sharaba	to drink
sofa	Sofaa	a cushion
sugar	sukkar	sugar
zero	Sifr	zero

As you can see from the table, Arabic has had a major influence on the English language. Some English words such as "admiral" and "arsenal" have an indirect Arabic origin, whereas others, such as "coffee" and "cotton," are exact matches! The influence runs the other way, too, especially when it comes to relatively contemporary terms. For example, the word **tilifizyuun** (*tee-lee-fee-zee-yoon;* television) comes straight from the word "television." As is often the case with languages, Arabic and English tend to influence each other, and that's what makes studying them so much fun!

Discovering the Arabic Alphabet

Unlike English and other Romance languages, you write and read Arabic from right to left. Like English, Arabic has both vowels and consonants, but the vowels in Arabic aren't actual letters. Rather, Arabic vowels are symbols that you place on top of or below consonants to create certain sounds. As for consonants, Arabic has 28 different consonants, and each one is represented by a letter. In order to vocalize these letters, you place a vowel above or below the particular consonant. For example, when you put a **fatHa,** a vowel representing the "ah" sound, above the consonant representing the letter "b," you get the sound "bah." When you take the same consonant and use a **kasra,** which represents the "ee" sound, you get the sound "bee."

All about vowels

Arabic has three main vowels. Luckily, they're very simple to pronounce because they're similar to English vowels. However, it's important to realize that Arabic also has vowel derivatives that are as important as the main vowels. These vowel derivatives fall into three categories: *double vowels, long vowels,* and *diphthongs.* In this section, I walk you through all the different vowels, vowel derivatives, and vowel combinations.

Main vowels

The three main Arabic vowels are:

- ✔ **fatHah:** The first main vowel in Arabic is called a **fatHa** *(feht-hah)*. A **fatHa** is the equivalent of the short "a" in "hat" or "cat." Occasionally, a **fatHa** also sounds like the short "e" in "bet" or "set." Much like the other vowels, the way you pronounce a **fatHa** depends on what consonants come before or after it. In Arabic script, the **fatHa** is written as a small horizontal line above a consonant. In English transcription, which I use in this book, it's simply represented by the letter "a," as in the words **kalb** (*kah-leb;* dog) or **walad** (*wah-lahd;* boy).

- ✔ **damma:** The second main Arabic vowel is the **damma** *(dah-mah)*. A **damma** sounds like the "uh" in "foot" or "book." In Arabic script, it's written like a tiny backward "e" above a particular consonant. In English transcription, it's represented by the letter "u," as in **funduq** (*foon-dook;* hotel) or **suHub** (*soo-hoob;* clouds).

- ✔ **kasra:** The third main vowel in Arabic is the **kasra** *(kahs-rah)*, which sounds like the long "e" in "feet" or "treat." The **kasra** is written the same way as a **fatHa** — as a small horizontal line — except that it goes underneath the consonant. In English transcription, it's written as an "i," as in **bint** (*bee-neht;* girl) or **'islaam** (*ees-lahm;* Islam).

Double vowels

One type of vowel derivative is the double vowel, which is known in Arabic as **tanwiin** *(tahn-ween)*. The process of **tanwiin** is a fairly simple one: Basically, you take a main vowel and place the same vowel right next to it, thus creating two vowels, or a double vowel. The sound that the double vowel makes depends on the main vowel that's doubled. Here are all possible combinations of double vowels:

- ✔ **Double fatHa: tanwiin** with **fatHa** creates the "an" sound, as in **'ahlan wa sahlan** (*ahel-an wah sahel-an;* Hi).

- ✔ **Double damma: tanwiin** with **damma** creates the "oun" sound. For example, **kouratoun** (*koo-rah-toon;* ball) contains a double **damma**.

- ✔ **Double kasra: tanwiin** with **kasra** makes the "een" sound, as in **SafHatin** (*sahf-hah-teen;* page).

Long vowels

Long vowels are derivatives that elongate the main vowels. Seeing as Arabic is a very poetic and musical language, I believe a musical metaphor is in order here! Think of the difference between long vowels and short (main) vowels in terms of a musical beat, and you should be able to differentiate between them much easier. If a main vowel lasts for one beat, then its long vowel equivalent lasts for two beats. Whereas you create double vowels by writing two main vowels next to each other, you create long vowels by adding a letter to one of the main vowels. Each main vowel has a corresponding consonant that elongates it. Here are a few examples to help you get your head around this long-vowel process:

- ✔ To create a long vowel form of a **fatHa**, you attach an **'alif** to the consonant that the **fatHa** is associated with. In English transcription, the long **fatHa** form is written as "aa," such as in **kitaab** (*kee-taab;* book) or **baab** (*bahb;* door). The "aa" means that you hold the vowel sound for two beats as opposed to one.

- ✔ The long vowel form of **damma** is obtained by attaching a **waaw** to the consonant with the **damma**. This addition elongates the vowel "uh" into a more pronounced "uu," such as in **nuur** (*noohr;* light) or **ghuul** (*roohl;* ghost). Make sure you hold the "uu" vowel for two beats and not one.

- ✔ To create a long vowel form of a **kasra**, you attach a **yaa'** to the consonant with the **kasra**. Just as the **'alif** elongates the **fatHa** and the **waaw** elongates the **damma**, the **yaa'** elongates the **kasra**. Some examples include the "ii" in words like **kabiir** (*kah-beer;* big) and **Saghiir** (*sah-reer;* small).

The Arabic characters for the long vowels are shown in Table 1-2.

Table 1-2	Arabic Vowel Characters	
Arabic Character	*Name of the Character*	*Explanation*
ا	'alif	To create a long vowel form of a fatHa
و	waaw	To create a long vowel form of a damma
ي	yaa'	To create a long vowel form of a kasra

Diphthongs

Diphthongs in Arabic are a special category of vowels because, in essence, they're monosyllabic sounds that begin with one vowel and "glide" into another vowel. A common example in English is the sound at the end of the word "toy." Fortunately, Arabic has only two diphthong sounds used to distinguish between the **yaa'** (ي) and the **waaw** (و) forms of long vowels. When you come across either of these two letters, one of the first questions to ask yourself is: "Is this a long vowel or a diphthong?" There's an easy way to determine which is which: When either the **yaa'** or the **waaw** is a diphthong, you see a **sukun** (*soo-koon*) above the consonant. A **sukun** is similar to the main vowels in that it's a little symbol (a small circle) that you place above the consonant. However, unlike the vowels, you don't vocalize the **sukun** — it's almost like a "silent" vowel. So when a **waaw** or **yaa'** has a **sukun** over it, you know that the sound is a diphthong! Here are some examples:

- ✔ **waaw** diphthongs: **yawm** (*yah-oom;* day); **nawm** (*nah-oom;* sleep); **Sawt** (*sah-oot;* noise)

- ✔ **yaa'** diphthongs: **bayt** (*bah-yet;* house); **'ayn** (*ah-yen;* eye); **layla** (*lah-ye-lah;* night)

All about consonants

Arabic uses 28 different consonants, and each consonant is represented by a different letter. Because the Arabic alphabet is written in cursive, most of the letters connect with each other. For this reason, every single letter that represents a consonant actually can be written four different ways depending on its position in a word — whether it's in the initial, medial, or final positions, or whether it stands alone. In English transcription of the Arabic script, all letters are case-sensitive.

Thankfully, most of the consonants in Arabic have English equivalents. Unfortunately, a few Arabic consonants are quite foreign to nonnative speakers. Table 1-3 shows all 28 Arabic consonants, how they're written in Arabic, how they're transcribed in English, and how they sound. This table can help you pronounce the letters so that you sound like a native speaker!

Table 1-3		Arabic Consonants		
Arabic Character	**Name of the Letter**	**Pronunciation**	**Sounds Like . . .**	**Example**
ا	'alif ('a)	ah-leef	Sounds like the "a" in "apple"	'ab (*ah-b;* father)
ب	baa' (b)	bah	Sounds like the "b" in "boy"	baab (*bahb;* door)
ت	taa' (t)	tah	Sounds like the "t" in "table"	tilmiidh (*teel-meez;* student)
ث	thaa' (th)	thah	Sounds like the "th" in "think"	thalaatha (*thah-lah-thah;* three)

Arabic Character	Name of the Letter	Pronunciation	Sounds Like . . .	Example
ج	jiim (j)	jeem	Sounds like the "j" in "measure"	jamiil (jah-meel; pretty)
ح	Haa' (H)	hah	No equivalent in English; imagine the sound you make when you want to blow on your reading glasses to clean them; that soft, raspy noise that comes out is the letter Haa'.	Harr (*hah-r;* hot)
خ	khaa' (kh)	khah	Sounds a lot like "Bach" in German or "Baruch" in Hebrew	khuukh (*kh-oo-kh;* peach)
د	daal (d)	dahl	Sounds like the "d" in dog	daar (*dah-r;* house)
ذ	dhaal (dh)	dhahl	Sounds like the "th" in "those"	dhahab (*thah-hab;* gold)
ر	raa' (r)	rah	Like the Spanish "r," rolled really fast	rajul (*rah-jool;* man)
ز	zaay (z)	zay	Sounds like the "z" in "zebra"	zawja (*zah-oo-ja;* wife)
س	siin (s)	seen	Sounds like the "s" in "snake"	samak (*sah-mahk;* fish)
ش	shiin (sh)	sheen	Sounds like the "sh" in "sheep"	shams (*shah-mes;* sun)
ص	Saad (S)	sahd	A very deep "s" sound you can make if you open your mouth really wide and lower your jaw	Sadiiq (*sah-deek;* friend)

(continued)

Table 1-3 *(continued)*

Arabic Character	Name of the Letter	Pronunciation	Sounds Like . . .	Example
ض	Daad (D)	dahd	A very deep "d" sound; the exact same sound as a Saad except that you use a "d" instead of an "s"	Dabaab (*dah-bahb;* fog)
ط	Taa' (T)	tah	A deep "t" sound; start off by saying a regular "t" and then lower your mouth to make it rounder	Tabiib (*tah-beeb;* doctor)
ظ	DHaa' (DH)	dhah	Take the "th" as in "those" and draw it to the back of your throat	DHahr (*dha-her;* back)
ع	'ayn (')	ayen	No equivalent in any of the Romance languages; produced at the very back of the throat. Breathe heavily and consistently through your esophagus and then intermittently choke off the airflow so that you create a staccato noise	iraaq (*ee-rahk;* Iraq)
غ	ghayn (gh)	ghayen	Sounds like the French "r" in "rendezvous"; it's created at the back of the throat	ghariib (*rah-reeb;* strange)
ف	faa' (f)	fah	Sounds like the "f" in "Frank"	funduq (*foon-dook;* hotel)
ق	qaaf (q)	qahf	Similar to the letter "k," but produced much farther at the back of the throat; you should feel airflow being constricted at the back of your throat	qahwa (*kah-wah;* coffee)

Arabic Character	Name of the Letter	Pronunciation	Sounds Like . . .	Example
ك	kaaf (k)	kahf	Sounds like the "k" in "keeper"	kutub (*koo-toob*; books)
ل	laam (l)	lahm	Sounds like the "l" in "llama"	lisaan (*lee-sahn*; tongue)
م	miim (m)	meem	Sounds like the "m" in "Mary"	Makhzan (*mah-khzan*; storehouse)
ن	nuun (n)	noon	Sounds like the "n" in "no"	naDHiif (*nah-dheef*; clean)
ه	haa' (h)	haah	Created by exhaling heavily; very different from the Haa' earlier in the list. (Think of yourself as a marathon runner who's just finished a long race and is breathing heavily through the lungs to replenish your oxygen.)	huwa (*hoo-wah*; him)
و	waaw (w)	wahw	Sounds like the "w" in "winner"	waziir (*wah-zeer*; minister)
ي	yaa' (y)	yaah	Sounds like the "y" in "yes"	yamiin (*yah-meen*; right)

So there you have it — all 28 different consonants in the Arabic alphabet! To sound as fluent as possible, memorize as many of the letters as you can and try to associate each letter with the Arabic words in which it appears. The trick to getting the pronunciation of some of these more exotic Arabic sounds is repetition, repetition, and even more repetition! That old saying, "Practice makes perfect" certainly applies to Arabic.

Speaking Arabic Like a Native

In this section, I share a couple of tricks to help you focus on pronunciation of difficult letters that, if you can master, are sure to make you sound like a native speaker! Here are some difficult letters and some related words you should familiarize yourself with:

- **Haa': Hamraa'** (*hahm-raah;* red); **Hassan** (*hah-san;* man's name); **Hiwaar** (*hee-war;* conversation); **Haziin** (*hah-zeen;* sad)

- **'ayn: 'ajiib** (*ah-jeeb;* amazing); **'aziima** (*ah-zee-mah;* determination); **'ariiD** (*ah-reed;* wide)

- **qaaf: qif** (*kee-f;* stop); **qird** (*kee-red;* monkey); **qaws** (*kah-wes;* bow)

- **ghayn: ghaDbaan** (*rad-bahn;* angry); **ghurfa** (*goor-fah;* room); **ghadan** (*rah-dan;* tomorrow)

The difference between native Arabic speakers and nonnatives is enunciation. If you can enunciate your letters clearly — particularly the more difficult ones — you'll sound like you're fluent! Practice these words over and over until you feel comfortable repeating them really quickly and very distinctly. With practice, you'll sound more like a native and less like someone who's just trying to pick up the language! Plus, memorizing these words not only helps with your pronunciation but also helps build your vocabulary!

Addressing Arabic Transcription

The transcription I use in this book is a widely used and universally recognized method of transcribing Arabic to English. Students of Arabic across the United States and around the world use this method. It's very helpful for beginners because it allows you to speak the language without actually knowing how to read Arabic script.

In the transcription method used in this book, every letter in Arabic is represented by a letter in Roman script. It's important to note that this method is case-sensitive, which means that a lowercase Roman letter represents a different letter in the Arabic script than a capital Roman letter.

Transcription is a very helpful tool for beginners, but it's recommended that intermediate and advanced students of Arabic master the fundamentals of the Arabic script.

Chapter 2

The Nitty-Gritty: Basic Arabic Grammar

In This Chapter

▶ Playing around with nouns and adjectives

▶ Getting specific with definite and indefinite articles

▶ Forming simple sentences

▶ Getting to know Arabic verbs

Grammar is the foundation of any language. It's the glue that binds all the different elements of language together and allows us to communicate using a defined set of rules. Because grammar is so important, this chapter gives you an overview of the major grammatical concepts in the Arabic language, from the basic parts of speech (nouns, adjectives, articles, and verbs) to instructions on how to build both simple and descriptive sentences using common regular and irregular verbs. In addition, I introduce prepositions, demonstratives, and other parts of speech that will help you create phrases and sentences and, in general, express yourself in Arabic.

As you work through different chapters and sections of *Arabic For Dummies*, if you're ever unsure of how to proceed with a sentence formation, simply flip back to this chapter and review the grammar details that apply to your question. You'll be all set!

Introducing Nouns, Adjectives, and Articles

Nouns and adjectives are two of the most essential elements in any language. Nouns in Arabic, much like in English and other Romance languages, are the parts of speech used to name a person, place, thing, quality, or action.

Adjectives, on the other hand, are the parts of speech that modify nouns. Although nouns and adjectives go hand in hand, the best way to understand how they work in Arabic is to address each one separately.

Getting a grip on nouns

In Arabic, every noun has a masculine, feminine, singular, and plural form. Table 2-1 lists some common Arabic nouns. You'll notice that I've listed both singular and plural forms of some nouns as well as masculine (M) and feminine (F) forms of others.

Table 2-1	Common Nouns in Arabic	
Arabic	*Pronunciation*	*Translation*
walad	wah-lad	boy
'awlaad	aw-lad	boys
bint	bee-net	girl
banaat	bah-nat	girls
rajul	rah-jool	man
rijaal	ree-jal	men
'imra'a	eem-rah-ah	woman
nisaa'	nee-sah	women
tilmiidh	teel-meez	student (M)
tilmiidha	teel-mee-zah	student (F)
mudarris	moo-dah-rees	teacher (M)
mudarrisa	moo-dah-ree-sah	teacher (F)
Taalib	tah-leeb	college student (M)
Taaliba	tah-lee-bah	college student (F)
'ustaadh	oos-taz	professor (M)
'ustaadha	oos-tah-zah	professor (F)
madrasa	mad-rah-sah	school
jaami'a	jah-mee-ah	university
kulliyya	koo-lee-yah	college

Arabic	Pronunciation	Translation
kitaab	kee-tab	book
Taawila	tah-wee-lah	table
sayyaara	sah-yah-rah	car

Identifying adjectives

In Arabic, an adjective must be in agreement with the noun it modifies in both gender and plurality. Table 2-2 presents some common adjectives in both the feminine and masculine forms.

Table 2-2	Common Adjectives in Arabic	
Arabic	**Pronunciation**	**Translation**
kabiir	kah-beer	big (M)
kabiira	kah-bee-rah	big (F)
Saghiir	sah-geer	small (M)
Saghiira	sah-gee-rah	small (F)
Tawiil	tah-weel	tall (M)
Tawiila	tah-wee-lah	tall (F)
qaSiir	kah-seer	short (M)
qaSiira	kah-see-rah	short (F)
jamiil	jah-meel	beautiful/handsome (M)
jamiila	jah-mee-lah	beautiful/pretty (F)
qawiiy	kah-wee	strong (M)
qawiiya	kah-wee-yah	strong (F)
Da'iif	dah-eef	weak (M)
Da'iifa	dah-ee-fah	weak (F)
SaHiiH	sah-heeh	healthy (M)
SaHiiHa	sah-hee-hah	healthy (F)

(continued)

Table 2-2 *(continued)*

Arabic	Pronunciation	Translation
mariiD	mah-reed	sick (M)
mariiDa	mah-ree-dah	sick (F)
dakiiy	dah-kee	smart (M)
dakiiya	dah-kee-yah	smart (F)
ghabiiy	gah-bee	dumb (M)
ghabiiya	gah-bee-yah	dumb (F)
sarii'	sah-reeh	fast (M)
sarii'a	sah-ree-ah	fast (F)
baTii'	bah-teeh	slow (M)
baTii'a	bah-tee-ah	slow (F)
thaqiil	tah-keel	heavy (M)
thaqiila	tah-kee-lah	heavy (F)
khafiif	kah-feef	light (M)
khafiifa	kah-fee-fah	light (F)
Sa'b	sahb	difficult (M)
Sa'ba	sah-bah	difficult (F)
sahl	sah-hel	easy (M)
sahla	sah-lah	easy (F)
laTiif	lah-teef	nice/kind (M)
laTiifa	lah-tee-fah	nice/kind (F)
qabiiH	kah-beeh	ugly (M)
qabiiHa	kah-bee-hah	ugly (F)
'ajiib	ah-jeeb	amazing (M)
'ajiiba	ah-jee-bah	amazing (F)
ladhiidh	lah-zeez	delicious (M)
ladhiidha	lah-zee-zah	delicious (F)

Notice that the masculine forms of the adjectives in Table 2-2 are manipulated slightly to achieve the feminine adjective forms; essentially, all you do is add the suffix **-a** to the masculine adjective to obtain its feminine form. This rule applies to all regular adjective forms.

However, in addition to the regular adjective forms, another category of adjectives exists in which the masculine and feminine forms are completely different from each other. This is the *irregular adjective form*.

Fortunately, *all* irregular adjectives fall in the same category: color words; and *every* color word is an irregular adjective. Put simply, **'alwaan** (*al-wan;* colors) in Arabic are all irregular adjectives because the masculine color form is radically different than its feminine version. Table 2-3 lists the most common irregular adjectives.

Table 2-3	Irregular Adjectives: Colors	
Arabic	*Pronunciation*	*Translation*
'abyaD	ab-yad	white (M)
bayDaa'	bay-dah	white (F)
'aswad	ass-wad	black (M)
sawdaa'	saw-dah	black (F)
'azraq	az-rak	blue (M)
zarqaa'	zar-kah	blue (F)
'akhDar	ak-dar	green (M)
khaDraa'	kad-rah	green (F)
'aHmar	ah-mar	red (M)
Hamraa'	ham-rah	red (F)
'aSfar	ass-far	yellow (M)
Safraa'	saf-rah	yellow (F)
'asmar	ass-mar	brown (M)
samraa'	sam-rah	brown (F)
'urjuwaaniiy	oor-joo-wah-nee	purple (M)
jurwaaniiya	joor-wah-nee-yah	purple (F)

Every **lawn** (*lah-wen;* color) in Table 2-3 (as well as the **lawn** I didn't have space to list) must agree in gender with the noun it describes.

One of the biggest differences between adjective and noun interactions in the English and Arabic languages is that nouns in Arabic come *before* the adjectives. In English, nouns always come *after* their adjectives.

Discovering definite and indefinite articles (and the sun and moon)

A common trait that nouns and adjectives share in the Arabic language is that both can be modified using definite article prefixes. To refresh your memory, an *article* is a part of speech that you use to indicate nouns or adjectives and specify their applications. In English, there are two types of articles: indefinite and definite articles. The indefinite articles in English are "a" and "an," such as in "a book" or "an umbrella." The definite article is the word "the," as in "the book" or "the umbrella."

Unlike English, Arabic has no outright indefinite article; instead, the indefinite article in Arabic is always implied. For example, when you say **kitaab** (*kee-tab;* book), you mean both "book" and "a book." Similarly, **madrasa** (*mad-rah-sah;* school) means both "school" and "a school." However, Arabic does employ a definite article, which is the prefix you attach to either the noun or the adjective you want to define.

The rule

The definite article in Arabic is the prefix **al-.** When you want to define a noun or adjective, you simply attach this prefix to the word. For example, "the book" is **al-kitaab,** and "the school" is **al-madrasa.**

The inevitable exceptions

In the examples **al-kitaab** and **al-madrasa,** the prefix **al-** retains its original form. However, there are exceptions to this rule. Sometimes, the "l" in the prefix **al-** drops off and is replaced by a letter similar to the first letter of the word being defined. For example, the word **nuur** (*noor*) means "light" in Arabic. If you want to say "the light," you may assume that you simply attach the prefix **al-** and get **al-nuur.** However, that's not quite right. Instead, the appropriate way of saying "the light" in Arabic is **an-nuur** (*ah-noor*), where you replace the "l" in **al-** with the first letter of the definite word, which in this case is "n." Another example of this definite article exception is the word **SabaaH** (*sah-bah*), which means "morning." When you define it, the resulting word is **aS-SabaaH** (*ah-sah-bah;* the morning) and not **al-SabaaH.**

So how do you know whether to use **al-** or another definite article prefix format? The answer's actually quite simple and has something to do with a really cool concept. Every single letter in Arabic falls into one of two categories: sun letters and moon letters. Put simply, every word that begins with a moon letter gets the prefix **al-,** and every word that begins with a sun letter gets the prefix **a-** followed by its sun letter. Table 2-4 lists all the sun letters. Every other letter in Arabic is automatically a moon letter.

Table 2-4	The Sun Letters	
Arabic	*Pronunciation*	*Translation*
ت	taa	t
ث	thaa	th
د	daal	d
ذ	dhaal	dh
ر	raa	r
ز	zay	z
س	siin	s
ش	shiin	sh
ص	Saad	S
ض	Daad	D
ط	Taa	T
ظ	Dhaa	DH
ن	nuun	n

Table 2-5 lists some common nouns and adjectives that are defined. Notice the difference between the words that begin with sun letters and moon letters.

Table 2-5	Common Definite Nouns and Articles	
Arabic	*Pronunciation*	*Translation*
al-kitaab	al-kee-tab	the book
al-madrasa	al-mad-rah-sah	the school
al-walad	al-wah-lad	the boy

(continued)

Table 2-5 *(continued)*		
al-bint	al-bee-net	the girl
ar-rajul	ah-rah-jool	the man
al-'imra'a	al-eem-rah-ah	the woman
aS-SabaaH	ah-sah-bah	the morning
ash-sham	ah-shah-mes	the sun
al-qamar	al-kah-mar	the moon
al-kabiir	al-kah-beer	the big (one) (M)
aS-Saghiir	ah-sah-geer	the small (one) (M)
as-sarii'	ah-sah-reeh	the fast (one) (M)
al-'azraq	al-az-rak	the blue (one) (M)
az-zarqaa'	ah-zar-kah	the blue (one) (F)
aS-Safraa'	ah-saf-rah	the yellow (one) (F)
aS-Samraa'	ah-sam-rah	the brown (one) (F)
al-ladhiidh	ah-lah-zeez	the delicious (one) (M)

Understanding the interaction between nouns and adjectives

Nouns and adjectives go hand in hand. In this section, I show you how you can manipulate nouns and adjectives to create little phrases. Recall that unlike in the English language, nouns in Arabic always come *before* the adjective.

You can create three types of phrases by manipulating nouns and adjectives. This section examines the ways you can pair up nouns and adjectives to create definite and indefinite phrases. (Later in the chapter, I show you how to create a complete sentence by simply using a noun and an adjective.)

Indefinite phrases

One of the most important things to remember about nouns and adjectives in Arabic is that they can be both defined and undefined using the definite article prefix **al-**. Hence, to create an indefinite phrase, all you do is take an undefined noun and add to it an undefined adjective. For example, to say "a big book" or "big book," you add the adjective **kabiir** (*kah-beer;* big) to the noun **kitaab** (*kee-tab;* book). So the phrase **kitaab kabiir** means "a big book" in Arabic. Here are some other examples of indefinite phrases featuring undefined nouns and adjectives:

- ✓ **walad Tawiil** (*wah-lad tah-weel;* a tall boy)
- ✓ **bint jamiila** (*bee-net jah-mee-lah;* a pretty girl)
- ✓ **rajul qawiiy** (*rah-jool kah-wee;* a strong man)
- ✓ **'imra'a laTiifa** (*eem-rah-ah lah-tee-fah;* a nice woman)
- ✓ **madrasa Saghiira** (*mad-rah-sah sah-gee-rah;* a small school)
- ✓ **Taawila Hamraa'** (*tah-wee-lah ham-rah;* a red table)

Notice that the adjectives agree with their corresponding nouns in gender. For example, you say **bint jamiila** and *not* **bint jamiil.**

Adding more descriptive words to the noun is very simple: Because adjectives follow the noun in Arabic, you just add an extra adjective and you're done! But don't forget to add the conjunction **wa** (*wah;* and) between the adjectives. Check out some examples:

- ✓ **walad Tawiil wa kabiir** (*wah-lad tah-weel wah kah-beer;* a tall and big boy)
- ✓ **bint Tawiila wa jamiila** (*bee-net tah-wee-lah wah jah-mee-lah;* a tall and pretty girl)
- ✓ **rajul qawiiy wa sarii'** (*rah-jool kah-wee wah sah-reeh;* a strong and fast man)
- ✓ **'imra'a laTiifa wa qawiiya** (*eem-rah-ah lah-tee-fah wah kah-wee-yah;* a nice and strong woman)
- ✓ **madrasa Saghiira wa bayDaa'** (*mad-rah-sah sah-gee-rah wah bay-dah;* a small and white school)
- ✓ **Taawila Hamraa' wa qaSiira** (*tah-wee-lah ham-rah wah kah-see-rah;* a red and short table)

Definite phrases

The biggest difference between creating an indefinite phrase and a definite phrase is the use of the definite article prefix **al-**. Both noun and adjective must be defined using the definite article prefix. For example, to say "the big book," you say **al-kitaab al-kabiir.** Here are some examples of definite phrases:

- ✓ **al-walad aT-Tawiil** (*al-wah-lad ah-tah-weel;* the big boy)
- ✓ **al-bint al-jamiila** (*al-bee-net al-jah-mee-lah;* the pretty girl)
- ✓ **ar-rajul al-qawiiy** (*ah-rah-jool al-kay-wee;* the strong man)

- ✔ **al-'imra'a al-laTiifa** (*al-eem-rah-ah ah-lah-tee-fah;* the nice woman)
- ✔ **al-madrasa aS-Saghiira** (*al-mad-rah-sah ah-sah-gee-rah;* the small school)
- ✔ **aT-Taawila al-Hamraa'** (*ah-tah-wee-lah al-ham-rah;* the red table)

Using similar patterns, you can create a defined phrase using multiple adjectives. Just like in indefinite phrases, make sure you use the conjunction **wa** in between adjectives:

- ✔ **al-walad aT-Tawiil wa al-kabiir** (*al-wah-lad ah-tah-weel wah al-kah-beer;* the tall and big boy)
- ✔ **al-bint aT-Tawiila wa al-jamiila** (*al-bee-net ah-tah-wee-lah wah al-jah-mee-lah;* the tall and pretty girl)
- ✔ **ar-rajul al-qawiiy wa as-sarii'** (*ah-rah-jool al-kah-wee wah ah-sah-reeh;* the strong and fast man)
- ✔ **al-'imra'a al-laTiifa wa al-qawiiya** (*al-eem-rah-ah al-lah-tee-fah wah al-kah-wee-yah;* the nice and strong woman)
- ✔ **al-madrasa aS-Saghiira wa al-bayDaa'** (*al-mad-rah-sah ah-sah-gee-rah wah al-bay-dah;* the small and white school)
- ✔ **aT-Taawila al-Hamraa' wa al-qaSiira** (*ah-tah-wee-lah al-ham-rah wah al-kah-see-rah;* the red and short table)

Creating Simple, Verb-Free Sentences

There are two ways to form sentences in Arabic: You can manipulate definite and indefinite nouns and adjectives, or you can pull together nouns, adjectives, and verbs. In Arabic, it's possible to create a complete sentence with a subject, object, and verb without actually using a verb! This concept may seem a little strange at first, but this section helps you quickly see the logic and reasoning behind such a structure.

To be or not to be: Sentences without verbs

Before you can construct verb-free sentences, you need to know that there's actually no "to be" verb in the Arabic language. The verb "is/are" as a proper verb simply doesn't exist. That's not to say that you can't create an "is/are" sentence in Arabic — you can. "Is/are" sentences are created without the use of an actual verb. In other words, you create "to be" sentences by manipulating indefinite and definite nouns and adjectives, similar to what I cover in the section "Understanding the interaction between nouns and adjectives" earlier in this chapter.

When you put an indefinite noun with an indefinite adjective, you create an indefinite phrase. Similarly, when you add a definite adjective to a definite noun, you end up with a definite phrase. So what happens when you combine a definite noun with an indefinite adjective? This combination — defined noun and undefined adjective — produces an "is/are" sentence similar to what you get when you use the verb "to be" in English.

For example, take the defined noun **al-kitaab** (the book) and add to it the indefinite adjective **kabiir** (big). The resulting phrase is **al-kitaab kabiir,** which means "The book is big." Here are some more examples to illustrate the construction of "is/are" sentences:

- ✔ **al-walad mariiD.** (*al-wah-lad mah-reed;* The boy is sick.)

- ✔ **al-bint SaHiiHa.** (*al-bee-net sah-hee-hah;* The girl is healthy.)

- ✔ **as-sayyaara khadraa'.** (*ah-sah-yah-rah kad-rah;* The car is green.)

- ✔ **aT-Taaliba dakiiya.** (*ah-tah-lee-bah dah-kee-yah;* The student is smart.) (F)

- ✔ **al-mudarris qaSiir.** (*al-moo-dah-rees kah-seer;* The teacher is short.) (M)

- ✔ **al-'ustaadh Tawiil.** (*al-oos-taz tah-weel;* The professor is tall.) (M)

If you want to use additional adjectives in these verb-free sentences, you simply add the conjunction **wa.** Here are some examples of "is/are" sentences with multiple adjectives:

- ✔ **al-walad mariiD wa Da'iif.** (*al-wah-lad mah-reed wah dah-eef;* The boy is sick and weak.)

- ✔ **al-bint SaHiiHa wa qawiiya.** (*al-bee-net sah-hee-hah wah kah-wee-yah;* The girl is healthy and strong.)

- ✔ **as-sayyaara khadraa' wa sarii'a.** (*ah-sah-yah-rah kad-rah wah sah-ree-ah;* The car is green and fast.)

- ✔ **aT-Taaliba dakiiya wa laTiifa.** (*ah-tah-lee-bah dah-kee-yah wah lah-tee-fah;* The student is smart and nice.) (F)

- ✔ **al-mudarris qaSiir wa dakiiy.** (*al-moo-dah-rees kah-seer wah dah-kee;* The teacher is short and smart.) (M)

- ✔ **al-'ustaadh Tawiil wa Sa'b.** (*al-oos-taz tah-weel wah sahb;* The professor is tall and difficult.) (M)

This construct is fairly flexible, and if you change the nature of one of the adjectives, you radically alter the meaning of the **jumla** (*joom-lah;* sentence). For instance, the examples all show a defined noun with two indefinite adjectives. What happens when you mix things up and add an indefinite noun to an indefinite adjective and a definite adjective?

Consider the example **al-bint SaHiiHa wa qawiiya** (The girl is healthy and strong). Keep **al-bint** as a definite noun but change the indefinite adjective **SaHiiHa** into its definite version, **aS-SaHiiHa**; also, drop the **wa,** and keep **qawiiya** as an indefinite adjective. The resulting phrase is **al-bint aS-SaHiiHa qawiiya,** which means "The healthy girl is strong."

You can grasp what's going on here by dividing the terms into clauses: The first clause is the definite noun/definite adjective combination **al-bint aS-SaHiiHa** (the healthy girl); the second clause is the indefinite adjective **qawiiya** (strong). Combining these clauses is the same as combining a definite noun with an indefinite adjective — the result is an "is/are" sentence. Here are more examples to help clear up any confusion you have regarding this concept:

- **al-walad al-mariiD Da'iif.** (*al-wah-lad al-mah-reed dah-eef;* The sick boy is weak.)

- **as-sayyaara al-khadraa' sarii'a.** (*ah-sah-yah-rah al-kad-rah sah-ree-ah;* The green car is fast.)

- **aT-Taaliba ad-dakiiya laTiifa.** (*ah-tah-lee-bah ah-dah-kee-yah lah-tee-fah;* The smart student is nice.) (F)

- **al-mudarris al-qaSiir dakiiy.** (*al-moo-dah-rees al-kah-seer dah-kee;* The short teacher is smart.) (M)

- **al-'ustaadh aT-Tawiil Sa'b.** (*al-oos-taz ah-tah-weel sahb;* The tall professor is difficult.) (M)

Notice that a simple change in the definite article changes the meaning of the phrase or sentence. For example, when the noun is defined and both adjectives are indefinite, you create an "is" sentence, as in "The boy is big." On the other hand, when both noun and adjective are defined, the adjective affects the noun directly, and you get "the big boy."

Building sentences with common prepositions

In grammatical terms, *prepositions* are words or small phrases that indicate a relationship between substantive and other types of words, such as adjectives, verbs, nouns, or other substantives. In both English and Arabic, prepositions are parts of speech that are essential in the formation of sentences. You can add them to "is/are" sentences to give them more specificity. Table 2-6 lists the most common prepositions you're likely to use in Arabic.

Table 2-6	Common Prepositions	
Arabic	*Pronunciation*	*Translation*
min	meen	from
fii	fee	in
'ilaa	ee-lah	to
ma'a	mah-ah	with
'alaa	ah-lah	on
qariib min	kah-reeb meen	close to
ba'iid min	bah-eed meen	far from
'amaama	ah-mah-mah	in front of
waraa'a	wah-rah-ah	behind
taHta	tah-tah	underneath
fawqa	faw-kah	above
bijaanibi	bee-jah-nee-bee	next to

You can use these prepositions to construct clauses and phrases using both indefinite and definite nouns and adjectives. Here are some examples:

✔ **al-bint 'amaama al-madrasa.** (*al-bee-net ah-mah-mah al-mad-rah-sah;* The girl is in front of the school.)

✔ **aT-Taawila fii al-ghurfa.** (*ah-tah-wee-lah fee al-goor-fah;* The table is in the room.)

✔ **al-'ustaadha fii al-jaami'a.** (*al-oos-tah-zah fee al-jah-mee-ah;* The professor is in the university.) (F)

✔ **al-maT'am bijaanibi al-funduq.** (*al-mat-ham bee-jah-nee-bee al-foon-dook;* The restaurant is next to the hotel.)

✔ **ar-rajul min 'amriika.** (*ah-rah-jool meen am-ree-kah;* The man is from America.)

✔ **al-madiina qariiba min ash-shaaTi'.** (*al-mah-dee-nah kah-ree-bah meen ah-shah-teeh;* The city is close to the beach.)

- ✔ **as-sayyaara al-bayDaa' waraa'a al-manzil.** (*ah-sah-yah-rah al-bay-dah wah-rah-ah al-man-zeel;* The white car is behind the house.)

- ✔ **al-walad al-laTiif ma'a al-mudarris.** (*al-wah-lad ah-lah-teef mah-ah al-moo-dah-rees;* The nice boy is with the teacher.)

In addition, you can use multiple adjectives with both the subject and object nouns:

- ✔ **al-'imra'a al-jamiila fii as-sayyaara as-sarii'a.** (*al-eem-rah-ah al-jah-mee-lah fee ah-sah-yah-rah ah-sah-ree-ah;* The beautiful woman is in the fast car.)

- ✔ **al-mudarissa ad-dakiyya 'amaama al-madrasa al-bayDaa'.** (*al-moo-dah-ree-sah ah-dah-kee-yah ah-mah-mah al-mad-rah-sah al-bay-dah;* The smart teacher is in front of the white school.) (F)

- ✔ **al-kursiiy aS-Saghiir waraa'a aT-Taawila al-kabiira.** (*al-koor-see ah-sah-geer wah-rah-ah ah-tah-wee-lah al-kah-bee-rah;* The small chair is behind the big table.)

Using demonstratives and forming sentences

A *demonstrative* is the part of speech that you use to indicate or specify a noun that you're referring to. Common demonstratives in English are the words "this" and "that." In English, most demonstratives are gender-neutral, meaning that they can refer to nouns that are both feminine and masculine. In Arabic, however, some demonstratives are gender-neutral whereas others are gender-specific.

How do you know whether a demonstrative is gender-neutral or gender-specific? Here's the short answer: If a demonstrative refers to a number of objects (such as "those" or "these"), it's gender-neutral and may be used for both masculine and feminine objects. If, on the other hand, you're using a singular demonstrative ("this" or "that"), it must be in agreement with the gender of the object being singled out.

Following are demonstratives in the singular format:

- ✔ **haadhaa** (*hah-zah;* this) (M)

- ✔ **haadhihi** (*hah-zee-hee;* this) (F)

- ✔ **dhaalika** (*zah-lee-kah;* that) (M)

- ✔ **tilka** (*teel-kah;* that) (F)

Here are the plural demonstratives, which are gender-neutral:

- **haa'ulaa'i** (*hah-oo-lah-ee;* these)
- **'ulaa'ika** (*oo-lah-ee-kah;* those)

You can combine demonstratives with both definite and indefinite nouns and adjectives. For example, to say "this boy," add the definite noun **al-walad** (boy) to the demonstrative **haadhaa** (this; M); because demonstratives always come before the nouns they identify, the resulting phrase is **haadhaa al-walad.** Here are more examples of this construct:

- **haadhihi al-bint** (*hah-zee-hee al-bee-net;* this girl)
- **'ulaa'ika al-banaat** (*oo-lah-ee-kah al-bah-nat;* those girls)
- **haa'ulaa'i al-'awlaad** (*hah-oo-lah-ee al-aw-lad;* these boys)
- **tilka al-'ustaadha** (*teel-kah al-oos-tah-zah;* that professor) (F)
- **dhaalika al-kitaab** (*zah-lee-kah al-kee-tab;* that book)

When you use a demonstrative, which is, in essence, a definite article, the meaning of the phrase changes depending on whether the object is defined or undefined. When a demonstrative is followed by a defined noun, you get a definite clause, as in the examples in the preceding list. However, when you attach an indefinite noun to a demonstrative, the result is an "is/are" sentence. For instance, if you add the demonstrative **haadhaa** to the indefinite subject noun **walad,** you get **haadhaa walad** (*hah-zah wah-lad;* This is a boy). Using the examples from the preceding list, I show you what happens when you drop the definite article from the subject noun in a demonstrative clause:

- **haadhihi bint.** (*hah-zee-hee bee-net;* This is a girl.)
- **'ulaa'ika banaat.** (*oo-lah-ee-kah bah-nat;* Those are girls.)
- **haa'ulaa'i 'awlaad.** (*hah-oo-lah-ee aw-lad;* These are boys.)
- **tilka 'ustaadha.** (*teel-kah oos-tah-zah;* That is a professor.) (F)
- **dhaalika kitaab.** (*zah-lee-kah kee-tab;* That is a book.)

When you combine a demonstrative clause with a definite subject noun and an indefinite adjective, the resulting phrase is a more descriptive "is/are" sentence:

- **haadhihi al-bint jamiila.** (*hah-zee-hee al-bee-net jah-mee-lah;* This girl is pretty.)
- **'ulaa'ika al-banaat Tawiilaat.** (*oo-lah-ee-kah al-bah-nat tah-wee-lat;* Those girls are tall.)
- **tilka al-madrasa kabiira.** (*teel-kah al-mad-rah-sah kah-bee-rah;* That school is big.)

Conversely, when you combine a demonstrative clause with a definite subject noun and a definite adjective, you get a regular demonstrative phrase:

- ✔ **haadhaa ar-rajul al-jamiil** (*hah-zah ah-rah-jool al-jah-meel;* that handsome man)

- ✔ **dhaalika al-kitaab al-'ajiib** (*zah-lee-kah al-kee-tab al-ah-jeeb;* that amazing book)

- ✔ **tilka al-madiina aS-Saghiira** (*teel-kah al-mah-dee-nah ah-sah-gee-rah;* that small city)

Forming "to be" sentences using personal pronouns

Every language has *personal pronouns,* the parts of speech that stand in for people, places, things, or ideas. Arabic is no different, except that personal pronouns in Arabic are a lot more comprehensive and specific than personal pronoun structures in other languages, such as English. Table 2-7 presents all the major personal pronouns in the Arabic language.

In the translation and conjugation tables in this section and throughout *Arabic For Dummies,* in addition to singular and plural denotations, you see a form labeled *dual.* This number form, which describes a pair or two of an item, doesn't exist in English.

Table 2-7	Personal Pronouns	
Arabic	*Pronunciation*	*Translation*
'anaa	ah-nah	I/me
'anta	an-tah	you (MS)
'anti	an-tee	you (FS)
huwa	hoo-wah	he/it
hiya	hee-yah	she/it
naHnu	nah-noo	we
'antum	an-toom	you (MP)
'antunna	an-too-nah	you (FP)
hum	hoom	they (MP)

Arabic	Pronunciation	Translation
hunna	hoo-nah	they (FP)
'antumaa	an-too-mah	you (dual)
humaa	hoo-mah	they (M/dual)
humaa	hoo-mah	they (F/dual)

In addition to the personal pronouns common in English and other languages, Arabic makes a gender distinction with "you" in the singular and masculine forms. Furthermore, Arabic includes special pronouns reserved for describing two items (no more, no less). So all in all, personal pronouns in Arabic may describe one thing, two things, and three or more things.

The personal pronoun always comes before the predicate noun that it designates, and it also creates an "is/are" sentence. For instance, when you say **hiya bint** *(hee-yah bee-net)*, you mean "She is a girl." Similarly, **huwa walad** *(hoo-wah wah-lad)* means "He is a boy." The meaning changes slightly when the subject noun is defined. For example, **hiya al-bint** means "She is the girl," and **huwa al-walad** means "He is the boy." Here are some more examples to familiarize you with this concept:

- **'anaa rajul.** *(ah-nah rah-jool;* I am a man.)
- **'anaa ar-rajul.** *(ah-nah ah-rah-jool;* I am the man.)
- **hum 'awlaad.** *(hoom aw-lad;* They are boys.)
- **hiya al-'imra'a.** *(hee-yah al-eem-rah-ah;* She is the woman.)
- **'anta kabiir.** *(an-tah kah-beer;* You are big.) (MS)
- **'anti jamiila.** *(an-tee jah-mee-lah;* You are beautiful.) (FS)
- **'antum su'adaa'.** *(an-toom soo-ah-dah;* You are happy.) (MP)
- **'anti bint jamiila.** *(an-tee bee-net jah-mee-lah;* You are a pretty girl.)
- **'anta al-walad al-kabiir.** *(an-tah al-wah-lad al-kah-beer;* You are the big boy.)
- **hunna 'an-nisaa' al-laTiifaat.** *(hoo-nah ah-nee-sah ah-lah-tee-fat;* They are the nice women.)
- **hunna nisaa' laTiifaat.** *(hoo-nah nee-sah lah-tee-fat;* They are nice women.)
- **huwa rajul qawiiy.** *(hoo-wah rah-jool kah-wee;* He is a strong man.)
- **huwa ar-rajul al-qawiiy.** *(hoo-wah ah-rah-jool al-kah-wee;* He is the strong man.)

Creating negative "to be" sentences

Although Arabic doesn't have a "to be" regular verb to create "I am" or "you are" phrases, it does have a verb you use to say "I am not" or "you are not." This special irregular verb **laysa** *(lay-sah)* creates negative "to be" sentences. The following table shows **laysa** conjugated using all the personal pronouns.

Form	Pronunciation	Translation
'anaa lastu	ah-nah las-too	I am not
'anta lasta	an-tah las-tah	You are not (MS)
'anti lasti	an-tee las-tee	You are not (FS)
huwa laysa	hoo-wah lay-sah	He is not
hiya laysat	hee-yah lay-sat	She is not
naHnu lasnaa	nah-noo las-nah	We are not
'antum lastum	an-toom las-toom	You are not (MP)
'antunna lastunna	an-too-nah las-too-nah	You are not (FP)
hum laysuu	hoom lay-soo	They are not (MP)
hunna lasna	hoo-nah las-nah	They are not (FP)
antumaa lastumaa	an-too-mah las-too-mah	You are not (dual/MP/FP)
humaa laysaa	hoo-mah lay-sah	They are not (dual/MP)
humaa laysataa	hoo-mah lay-sah-tah	They are not (dual/FP)

Following are some examples of negative "to be" sentences using the verb **laysa.**

- **'anaa lastu Taalib.** (*ah-nah las-too tah-leeb;* I am not a student.)

- **'anta lasta mariiD.** (*an-tah las-tah mah-reed;* You are not sick.) (M)

- **naHnu lasnaa fii al-madrasa.** (*nah-noo las-nah fee al-mad-rah-sah;* We are not in the school.)

- **al-kura laysat taHta as-sayyaara.** (*al-koo-rah lay-sat tah-tah ah-sah-yah-rah;* The ball is not under the car.)

- **al-maT'am laysa bijaanibi al-funduq.** (*al-mat-ham lay-sah bee-jah-nee-bee al-foon-dook;* The restaurant is not next to the hotel.)

- **al-madrasa laysat kabiira.** (*al-mad-rah-sah lay-sat kah-bee-rah;* The school is not big.)

- **'anta lasta al-walad aS-Saghiir.** (*an-tah las-tah al-wah-lad ah-sah-geer;* You are not the small boy.) (MS)

- **al-bint aT-Tawiila laysat Da'iifa.** (*al-bee-net ah-tah-wee-lah lay-sat dah-ee-fah;* The tall girl is not weak.)

"To be" in the past tense

Arabic's verb for "was/were" (in other words, "to be" in the past tense) is **kaana** (*kah-nah;* was/were). Similar to the negative form of "to be," the past form is an irregular verb form conjugated using all the personal pronouns.

Form	Pronunciation	Translation
'anaa kuntu	ah-nah koon-too	I was
'anta kunta	an-tah koon-tah	You were (MS)
'anti kunti	an-tee koon-tee	You were (FS)
huwa kaana	hoo-wah kah-nah	He was
hiya kaanat	hee-yah kah-nat	She was
naHnu kunnaa	nah-noo koo-nah	We were
'antum kuntum	an-toom koon-toom	You were (MP)
'antunna kuntunna	an-too-nah koon-too-nah	You were (FP)
hum kaanuu	hoom kah-noo	They were (MP)
hunna kunna	hoo-nah koo-nah	They were (FP)
antumaa kuntumaa	an-too-mah koon-too-mah	You were (dual/MP/FP)
humaa kaanaa	hoo-mah kah-nah	They were (dual/MP)
humaa kaanataa	hoo-mah kah-nah-tah	They were (dual/FP)

Here are some sentences featuring **kaana:**

- ✔ **'anaa kuntu mariiD.** (*ah-nah koon-too mah-reed;* I was sick.)

- ✔ **'anta kunta fii al-maktaba.** (*an-tah koon-tah fee al-mak-tah-bah;* You were in the library.)

- ✔ **hiya kaanat qariiba min al-manzil.** (*hee-yah kah-nat kah-ree-bah meen al-man-zeel;* She was close to the house.)

- ✔ **naHnu kunnaa fii al-masbaH.** (*nah-noo koo-nah fee al-mas-bah;* We were in the swimming pool.)

- ✔ **al-madrasa kaanat 'amaama al-maT'am.** (*al-mad-rah-sah kah-nat ah-mah-mah al-mat-ham;* The school was close to the restaurant.)

- ✔ **al-kitaab al-'azraq kaana fawqa aT-Taawila aS-Saghiira.** (*al-kee-tab al-az-rak kah-nah faw-kah ah-tah-wee-lah ah-sah-gee-rah;* The blue book was on top of the small table.)

- ✔ **al-'imra'a wa ar-rajul kaanaa fii al-Hubb.** (*al-eem-rah-ah wah ah-rah-jool kah-nah fee al-hoob;* The woman and the man were in love.)

✔ **al-'awlaad kaanuu qariib min al-banaat.** (*al-aw-lad kah-noo kah-reeb meen al-bah-nat;* The boys were close to the girls.)

✔ **aT-Ta'aam kaana ladhiidh.** (*ah-tah-am kah-nah lah-zeez;* The food was delicious.)

Working with Verbs

You'll be very pleased to know that verb tenses in Arabic, when compared to other languages, are fairly straightforward. Basically, you only need to be concerned with two proper verb forms: the past and the present. A future verb tense exists, but it's a derivative of the present tense that you achieve by attaching a prefix to the present tense of the verb.

In this section, I tell you everything you need to know about **'af'aal** (*af-al;* verbs) in Arabic! I examine the past tense followed by the present and future tenses, and then I show you irregular verb forms for all three tenses.

Digging up the past tense

The structural form of the past tense is one of the easiest grammatical structures in the Arabic language. Basically, every regular verb that's conjugated in the past tense follows a very strict pattern. First, you refer to all regular verbs in the past tense using the **huwa** (*hoo-wah;* he) personal pronoun. Second, the overwhelming majority of verbs in **huwa** form in the past tense have three consonants that are accompanied by the same vowel: the **fatHa** (*fat-hah).* The **fatHa** creates the "ah" sound.

For example, the verb "wrote" in the past tense is **kataba** (*kah-tah-bah);* its three consonants are "k," "t," and "b." Here are some common verbs you may use while speaking Arabic:

✔ **'akala** (*ah-kah-lah;* ate)

✔ **fa'ala** (*fah-ah-lah;* did)

✔ **dhahaba** (*zah-hah-bah;* went)

✔ **qara'a** (*kah-rah-ah;* read)

✔ **ra'a** (*rah-ah;* saw)

The following table shows the verb **kataba** (*kah-tah-bah;* wrote) conjugated using all the personal pronouns. Note that the first part of the verb remains constant; only its suffix changes depending on the personal pronoun used.

Form	Pronunciation	Translation
'anaa katabtu	ah-nah kah-tab-too	I wrote
'anta katabta	an-tah kah-tab-tah	You wrote (MS)
'anti katabtii	an-tee kah-tab-tee	You wrote (FS)
huwa kataba	hoo-wah kah-tah-bah	He wrote
hiya katabat	hee-yah kah-tah-bat	She wrote
naHnu katabnaa	nah-noo kah-tab-nah	We wrote
'antum katabtum	an-toom kah-tab-toom	You wrote (MP)
'antunna katabtunna	an-too-nah kah-tab-too-nah	You wrote (FP)
hum katabuu	hoom kah-tah-boo	They wrote (MP)
hunna katabna	hoo-nah kah-tab-nah	They wrote (FP)
antumaa katabtumaa	an-too-mah kah-tab-too-mah	You wrote (dual/MP/FP)
humaa katabaa	hoo-mah kah-tah-bah	They wrote (dual/MP)
humaa katabataa	hoo-mah kah-tah-bah-tah	They wrote (dual/FP)

Now here's the verb **darasa** (*dah-rah-sah;* studied) conjugated using all the personal pronouns.

Form	Pronunciation	Translation
'anaa darastu	ah-nah dah-ras-too	I studied
'anta darasta	an-tah dah-ras-tah	You studied (MS)
'anti darastii	an-tee dah-ras-tee	You studied (FS)
huwa darasa	hoo-wah dah-rah-sah	He studied
hiya darasat	hee-yah dah-rah-sat	She studied
naHnu darasnaa	nah-noo dah-ras-nah	We studied
'antum darastum	an-toom dah-ras-toom	You studied (MP)
'antunna darastunna	an-too-nah dah-ras-too-nah	You studied (FP)
hum darasuu	hoom dah-rah-soo	They studied (MP)
hunna darasna	hoo-nah dah-ras-nah	They studied (FP)
antumaa darastumaa	an-too-mah dah-ras-too-mah	You studied (dual/MP/FP)
humaa darasaa	hoo-mah dah-rah-sah	They studied (dual/MP)
humaa darasataa	hoo-mah dah-rah-sah-tah	They studied (dual/FP)

Compare the conjugations of **darasa** and **kataba** and you probably see a clear pattern emerge: Every personal pronoun has a corresponding suffix used to conjugate and identify the verb form in its specific tense. Table 2-8 outlines these specific suffixes.

Table 2-8	Personal Pronoun Suffixes for Verbs in the Past Tense		
Arabic Pronoun	**Pronunciation**	**Translation**	**Verb Suffix**
'anaa	ah-nah	I/me	-tu
'anta	an-tah	you (MS)	-ta
'anti	an-tee	you (FS)	-tii
huwa	hoo-wah	he/it	-a
hiya	hee-yah	she/it	-at
naHnu	nah-noo	we	-naa
'antum	an-toom	you (MP)	-tum
'antunna	an-too-nah	you (FP)	-tunna
hum	hoom	they (MP)	-uu
hunna	hoo-nah	they (FP)	-na
'antumaa	an-too-mah	you (dual)	-tumaaa
humaa	hoo-mah	they (M/dual)	-aa
humaa	hoo-mah	they (F/dual)	-ataa

Anytime you come across a regular verb you want to conjugate in the past tense, use these verb suffixes with the corresponding personal pronouns.

At this stage, you should know that not all regular verbs in the past tense have three consonants. Some regular verbs have more than three consonants, such as:

✔ **tafarraja** (*tah-fah-rah-jah;* watched)

✔ **takallama** (*tah-kah-lah-mah;* spoke)

Even though these verbs have more than three consonants, they're still considered regular verbs. To conjugate them, you keep the first part of the word constant and only change the last consonant of the word using the corresponding suffixes to match the personal pronouns. To get a better sense of this conversion, take a look at the verb **takallama** (spoke) conjugated in the past tense. Notice that the first part of the word stays the same; only the ending changes.

Form	Pronunciation	Translation
'anaa takallamtu	ah-nah tah-kah-lam-too	I spoke
'anta takallamta	an-tah tah-kah-lam-tah	You spoke (MS)
'anti takallamtii	an-tee tah-kah-lam-tee	You spoke (FS)
huwa takallama	hoo-wah tah-kah-lah-mah	He spoke
hiya takallamat	hee-yah tah-kah-lah-mat	She spoke
naHnu takallamnaa	nah-noo tah-kah-lam-nah	We spoke
'antum takallamtum	an-toom tah-kah-lam-toom	You spoke (MP)
'antunna takallamtunna	an-too-nah tah-kah-lam-too-nah	You spoke (FP)
hum takallamuu	hoom tah-kah-lah-moo	They spoke (MP)
hunna takallamna	hoo-nah tah-kah-lam-nah	They spoke (FP)
antumaa takallamtumaa	an-too-mah tah-kah-lam-too-mah	You spoke (dual/MP/FP)
humaa takallamaa	hoo-mah tah-kah-lah-mah	They spoke (dual/MP)
humaa takallamataa	hoo-mah tah-kah-lah-mah-tah	They spoke (dual/FP)

When you know how to conjugate verbs in the past tense, your sentence-building options are endless. Here are some simple sentences that combine nouns, adjectives, and verbs in the past tense:

- ✔ **'al-walad dhahaba 'ilaa al-madrasa.** (*al-wah-lad zah-hah-bah ee-lah al-mad-rah-sah;* The boy went to the school.)

- ✔ **al-bint takallamat fii al-qism.** (*al-bee-net tah-kah-lah-mat fee al-kee-sem;* The girl spoke in the classroom.)

- ✔ **'akalnaa Ta'aam ladhiidh.** (*ah-kal-nah tah-am lah-zeez;* We ate delicious food.)

- ✔ **dhahaba ar-rajul 'ilaa al-jaami'a fii as-sayaara.** (*zah-hah-bah ah-rah-jool ee-lah al-jah-mee-ah fee ah-sah-yah-rah;* The man went to the school in the car.)

Examining the present tense

Conjugating verbs in the past tense is relatively straightforward, but conjugating verbs in the present tense is a bit trickier. Instead of changing only the ending of the verb, you must also alter its beginning. In other words, you need to be familiar not only with the suffix but also the prefix that corresponds to each personal pronoun.

To illustrate the difference between past and present tense, the verb **kataba** (wrote) is conjugated as **yaktubu** (*yak-too-boo;* to write), whereas the verb **darasa** (studied) is **yadrusu** (*yad-roo-soo;* to study).

Here's the verb **yaktubu** (to write) conjugated using all the personal pronouns. Notice how both the suffixes and prefixes change in the present tense.

Form	Pronunciation	Translation
'anaa 'aktubu	ah-nah ak-too-boo	I am writing
'anta taktubu	an-tah tak-too-boo	You are writing (MS)
'anti taktubiina	an-tee tak-too-bee-nah	You are writing (FS)
huwa yaktubu	hoo-wah yak-too-boo	He is writing
hiya taktubu	hee-yah tak-too-boo	She is writing
naHnu naktubu	nah-noo nak-too-boo	We are writing
'antum taktubuuna	an-toom tak-too-boo-nah	You are writing (MP)
'antunna taktubna	an-too-nah tak-toob-nah	You are writing (FP)
hum yaktubuuna	hoom yak-too-boo-nah	They are writing (MP)
hunna yaktubna	hoo-nah yak-toob-nah	They are writing (FP)
antumaa taktubaani	an-too-mah tak-too-bah-nee	You are writing (dual/MP/FP)
humaa yaktubaani	hoo-mah yak-too-bah-nee	They are writing (dual/MP)
humaa taktubaani	hoo-mah tak-too-bah-nee	They are writing (dual/FP)

As you can see, you need to be familiar with both the prefixes and suffixes to conjugate verbs in the present tense. Table 2-9 includes every personal pronoun with its corresponding prefix and suffix for the present tense.

Table 2-9   Personal Pronoun Prefixes and Suffixes for Verbs in the Present Tense

Arabic Pronoun	Pronunciation	Translation	Verb Prefix	Verb Suffix
'anaa	ah-nah	I/me	'a-	-u
'anta	an-tah	you (MS)	ta-	-u
'anti	an-tee	you (FS)	ta-	-iina
huwa	hoo-wah	he/it	ya-	-u
hiya	hee-yah	she/it	ta-	-u

Arabic Pronoun	Pronunciation	Translation	Verb Prefix	Verb Suffix
naHnu	nah-noo	we	na-	-u
'antum	an-toom	you (MP)	ta-	-uuna
'antunna	an-too-nah	you (FP)	ta-	-na
hum	hoom	they (MP)	ya-	-uuna
hunna	hoo-nah	they (FP)	ya-	-na
'antumaa	an-too-mah	you (dual)	ta-	-aani
humaa	hoo-mah	they (M/dual)	ya-	-aani
humaa	hoo-mah	they (F/dual)	ta-	-aani

Aside from prefixes and suffixes, another major difference between the past and present tenses in Arabic is that every verb in the present tense has a dominant vowel that's unique and distinctive. For example, the dominant vowel in **yaktubu** is a **damma** (*dah-mah;* "ooh" sound). However, in the verb **yaf'alu** (*yaf-ah-loo;* to do), the dominant vowel is the **fatHa** (*fat-hah;* "ah" sound). This means that when you conjugate the verb **yaf'alu** using the personal pronoun **'anaa,** you say **'anaa 'af'alu** and *not* **'anaa 'af'ulu.** For complete coverage of Arabic vowels (**damma, fatHa,** and **kasra**), check out Chapter 1.

The dominant vowel is always the middle vowel. Unfortunately, there's no hard rule you can use to determine which dominant vowel is associated with each verb. The best way to identify the dominant vowel is to look up the verb in the **qaamuus** (*kah-moos;* dictionary).

In this list, I divided up some of the most common Arabic verbs according to their dominant vowels:

✔ **damma**

- **yaktubu** (*yak-too-boo;* to write)
- **yadrusu** (*yad-roo-soo;* to study)
- **ya'kulu** (*yah-koo-loo;* to eat)
- **yaskunu** (*yas-koo-noo;* to live)

✔ **fatHa**

- **yaf'alu** (*yaf-ah-loo;* to do)
- **yaqra'u** (*yak-rah-oo;* to read)
- **yadhhabu** (*yaz-hah-boo;* to go)
- **yaftaHu** (*yaf-tah-hoo;* to open)

✔ **kasra**

- **yarji'u** (*yar-jee-oo;* to return)
- **ya'rifu** (*yah-ree-foo;* to know)

When you conjugate a verb in the present tense, you must do two things:

1. **Identify the dominant vowel that will be used to conjugate the verb using all personal pronouns.**
2. **Isolate the prefix and suffix that correspond to the appropriate personal pronouns.**

Peeking into the future tense

Although Arabic grammar has a future tense, you'll be glad to know that the tense has no outright verb structure. Rather, you achieve the future tense by adding the prefix **sa-** to the existing present tense form of the verb. For example, **yaktubu** means "to write." Add the prefix **sa-** to **yaktubu** and you get **sayaktubu,** which means "he will write."

To illustrate the future tense, here's the verb **yaktubu** conjugated in the future tense.

Form	*Pronunciation*	*Translation*
'anaa sa'aktubu	ah-nah sah-ak-too-boo	I will write
'anta sataktubu	an-tah sah-tak-too-boo	You will write (MS)
'anti sataktubiina	an-tee sah-tak-too-bee-nah	You will write (FS)
huwa sayaktubu	hoo-wah sah-yak-too-boo	He will write
hiya sataktubu	hee-yah sah-tak-too-boo	She will write
naHnu sanaktubu	nah-noo sah-nak-too-boo	We will write
'antum sataktubuuna	an-toom sah-tak-too-boo-nah	You will write (MP)
'antunna sataktubna	an-too-nah sah-tak-toob-nah	You will write (FP)
hum sayaktubuuna	hoom sah-yak-too-boo-nah	They will write (MP)
hunna sayaktubna	hoo-nah sah-yak-toob-nah	They will write (FP)
antumaa sataktubaani	an-too-mah sah-tak-too-bah-nee	You will write (dual/MP/FP)

Form	Pronunciation	Translation
humaa sayaktubaani	hoo-mah sah-yak-too-bah-nee	They will write (dual/MP)
humaa sataktubaani	hoo-mah sah-tak-too-bah-nee	They will write (dual/FP)

Examining irregular verb forms

Arabic uses both regular and irregular verbs. Regular verbs have a specific pattern and follow a specific set of rules, but irregular verbs do not. Because these irregular forms include some of the most common verbs in the language (such as "to buy," "to sell," and "to give"), you should examine them separately. This section looks at some of the most common irregular verbs in the Arabic language.

The verb "to sell" is conjugated as **baa'a** (*bah-ah;* sold) in the past tense. In the conjugation that follows, notice that unlike regular verbs, **baa'a** has only two consonants (the **baa'** and the **'ayn**).

Form	Pronunciation	Translation
'anaa bi'tu	ah-nah beeh-too	I sold
'anta bi'ta	an-tah beeh-tah	You sold (MS)
'anti bi'tii	an-tee beeh-tee	You sold (FS)
huwa baa'a	hoo-wah bah-ah	He sold
hiya baa'at	hee-yah bah-at	She sold
naHnu bi'naa	nah-noo beeh-nah	We sold
'antum bi'tum	an-toom beeh-toom	You sold (MP)
'antunna bi'tunna	an-too-nah beeh-too-nah	You sold (FP)
hum baa'uu	hoom bah-ooh	They sold (MP)
hunna bi'na	hoo-nah beeh-nah	They sold (FP)
antumaa bi'tumaa	an-too-mah beeh-too-mah	You sold (dual/MP/FP)
humaa baa'aa	hoo-mah bah-ah	They sold (dual/MP)
humaa baa'ataa	hoo-mah bah-ah-tah	They sold (dual/FP)

In order to conjugate the verb **baa'a** in the present tense, use the form **yabi-i'u** (*yah-bee-ooh;* to sell).

Form	Pronunciation	Translation
'anaa 'abii'u	ah-nah ah-bee-ooh	I am selling
'anta tabii'u	an-tah tah-bee-ooh	You are selling (MS)
'anti tabii'iina	an-tee tah-bee-ee-nah	You are selling (FS)
huwa yabii'u	hoo-wah yah-bee-ooh	He is selling
hiya tabii'u	hee-yah tah-bee-ooh	She is selling
naHnu nabii'u	nah-noo nah-bee-ooh	We are selling
'antum tabii'uuna	an-toom tah-bee-oo-nah	You are selling (MP)
'antunna tabi'na	an-too-nah tah-beeh-nah	You are selling (FP)
hum yabii'uuna	hoom yah-bee-oo-nah	They are selling (MP)
hunna yabi'na	hoo-nah yah-bee-nah	They are selling (FP)
antumaa tabii'aani	an-too-mah tah-bee-ah-nee	You are selling (dual/MP/FP)
humaa yabii'aani	hoo-mah yah-bee-ah-nee	They are selling (dual/MP)
humaa tabii'aani	hoo-mah tah-bee-ah-nee	They are selling (dual/FP)

For the future tense, simply add the prefix **sa-** to the present form to get **sayabii'u** (*sah-yah-bee-ooh;* he will sell).

Form	Pronunciation	Translation
'anaa sa'abii'u	ah-nah sah-ah-bee-ooh	I will sell
'anta satabii'u	an-tah sah-tah-bee-ooh	You will sell (MS)
'anti satabii'iina	an-tee sah-tah-bee-ee-nah	You will sell (FS)
huwa sayabii'u	hoo-wah sah-yah-bee-ooh	He will sell
hiya satabii'u	hee-yah sah-tah-bee-ooh	She will sell
naHnu sanabii'u	nah-noo sah-nah-bee-ooh	We will sell
'antum satabii'uuna	an-toom sah-tah-bee-oo-nah	You will sell (MP)
'antunna satabi'na	an-too-nah sah-tah-beeh-nah	You will sell (FP)

Form	Pronunciation	Translation
hum sayabii'uuna	hoom sah-yah-bee-oo-nah	They will sell (MP)
hunna sayabi'na	hoo-nah sah-yah-bee-nah	They will sell (FP)
antumaa satabii'aani	an-too-mah sah-tah-bee-ah-nee	You will sell (dual/MP/FP)
humaa sayabii'aani	hoo-mah sah-yah-bee-ah-nee	They will sell (dual/MP)
humaa satabii'aani	hoo-mah sah-tah-bee-ah-nee	They will sell (dual/FP)

Here are some other common irregular verbs:

- ✔ **waSala/yaSilu** (*wah-sah-lah/yah-see-loo;* arrived/to arrive)
- ✔ **zaara/yazuuru** (*zah-rah/yah-zoo-roo;* visited/to visit)
- ✔ **mashaa/yamshii** (*mah-shah/yam-shee;* walked/to walk)
- ✔ **'ishtaraa/yashtarii** (*eesh-tah-rah/yash-tah-ree;* bought/to buy)
- ✔ **radda/yaruddu** (*rah-dah/yah-roo-doo;* answered/to answer)
- ✔ **jaa'a/yajii'u** (*jah-ah/yah-jee-ooh;* came/to come)
- ✔ **ra'aa/yaraa** (*rah-ah/yah-rah;* saw/to see)
- ✔ **'a'Taa/yu'Tii** (*ah-tah; yah-tee;* gave/to give)

Fun & Games

Match the personal pronouns on the left column with their Arabic equivalents on the right.

you (MS)   huwa

we   'anta

they (FP)   'anaa

you (FS)   naHnu

he   'anti

I   hunna

The answers are in Appendix C.

Chapter 3

'as-salaamu 'alaykum!: Greetings and Introductions

In This Chapter

▶ Handling pleasantries

▶ Using common introductions

▶ Referring to countries and nationalities

In Arabic culture, you can't underestimate the importance of greetings. First impressions in the Middle East are crucial, and knowing both the verbal and nonverbal nuances of greeting people is one of the most important aspects of mastering Arabic.

In this chapter, I show you how to greet people in Arabic, how to respond to basic greetings, and how to interact with native Arabic speakers. You find out when it's appropriate to use formal and informal terms, how to make small talk, and how to introduce yourself. **HaDHan sa'iidan!** (*had-dan sa-ee-dan;* Good luck!)

Greetings!

In Arabic, you have to choose between formal and informal ways of greeting people. The greeting you use depends on whom you're addressing: If you're greeting someone you don't know for the very first time, you must use the more formal greetings. On the other hand, if you're greeting an old family friend or a colleague you know well, feel free to use the more informal forms of greeting. If you're not sure which form to use, you're better off going formal. I cover both types of greetings as well as some other handy pleasantries in this section.

You say hello . . .

The formal way of greeting someone in Arabic is **'as-salaamu 'alaykum** (*ass-sa-laam-ou a-lai-koum*). Even though it translates into English as "hello," it literally means "May peace be upon you." Arabic is a very poetic language, so you're going to have to get used to the fact that a lot of the phrases used in everyday life are very descriptive!

Using **'as-salaamu 'alaykum** is appropriate when

  ✔ You're greeting a potential business partner.

  ✔ You're at a formal event, dinner, or gala.

  ✔ You're meeting someone for the first time.

The most common reply to **'as-salaamu 'alaykum** is **wa 'alaykum 'as-salaam** (*wa a-lai-koum ass-sa-laam;* and upon you peace).

The phrase **'ahlan wa sahlan** (*ahel-an wah sah-lan*) is a very informal way of greeting a person or group of people. Translated into English, it resembles the more informal "hi" as opposed to "hello." When someone says **'ahlan wa sahlan,** you should also reply **'ahlan wa sahlan.**

Using the informal **'ahlan wa sahlan** is appropriate when

  ✔ You're greeting an old friend.

  ✔ You're greeting a family member.

  ✔ You're greeting someone at an informal gathering, such as a family lunch.

Although **'ahlan wa sahlan** is one of the friendliest and most informal greetings in Arabic, you can actually greet someone you know very well, such as a close friend or family member, by simply saying **'ahlan!** Because it's the most informal way of greeting someone in Arabic, make sure that you use **'ahlan** only with people you're very comfortable with; otherwise you may appear disrespectful even if you're trying to be friendly! (Nonverbal signs may also convey disrespect; see the sidebar "Sending the right nonverbal message.")

Kinship, family relations, and tribal connections are extraordinarily important to people from the Middle East. In the early period of Islam when traders and nomads roamed the Arabian Peninsula, they identified themselves as members of one nation — the **'ahl al-islaam** (*ah-el al-is-laam;* kinship of Islam). They greeted each other by identifying themselves as part of the **'ahl** (*ah-el;* kin) by saying **'ahlan.** This is how the phrase **'ahlan wa sahlan** originated, although today it's simply a friendly way of greeting people.

. . . I say goodbye

Saying goodbye in Arabic is a little more straightforward than greetings because, even though there are different ways of saying goodbye, they aren't divided into formal or informal options. Here are the most common ways of saying goodbye in Arabic:

- ✔ **ma'a as-salaama** (*ma-a ass-sa-laa-ma;* go with peace, or goodbye)
- ✔ **'ilaa al-liqaa'** (*ee-laa al-li-kaa;* until next time)
- ✔ **'ilaa al-ghad** (*ee-laa al-gad;* see you tomorrow)

How are you doing?

After you've greeted someone by saying **'ahlan wa sahlan** or **'as-salaamu 'alaykum,** the next part of an Arabic greeting is asking how the person's doing.

The most common way of asking someone how he's doing is **kayf al-Haal?** *(ka-yef al-haal).* When you break down the phrase, you discover that **Haal** means "health" and **kayf** means "how." (The prefix **al-** attached to **Haal** is a definite article, so **al-Haal** means "the health.") Therefore, the phrase **kayf al-Haal?** literally means "How is the health?," but for all intents and purposes, you can translate it into English as "How are you?"

kayf al-Haal is a gender-neutral phrase for asking people how they're doing, but you should also be aware of gender-defined greeting terms, which are derivatives of the **kayf al-Haal** phrase:

- ✔ When addressing a man, use **kayf Haaluka** *(ka-yef haa-lou-ka).*
- ✔ When addressing a woman, use **kayf Haaluki** *(ka-yef haa-lou-kee).*

Another variation of **kayf al-Haal** is **kayf Haalak?** *(ka-yef haa-lak;* How is your health?). You can use either greeting, but **kayf al-Haal** is preferred when you're meeting someone for the first time because **kayf Haalak** is a bit more personal and informal.

I'm doing well!

When someone asks you how you're doing, if you're doing just fine, the typical response is **al-Hamdu li-llah** *(al-ham-dou lee-lah).* **al-Hamdu li-llah** literally means "Praise to God," but in this context, it translates to "I'm doing well." Typically, after you say **al-Hamdu li-llah,** you follow up by saying **shukran** *(shouk-ran;* thank you). As you expose yourself to more and more

Arabic phrases and terms, you'll notice that the reference to Allah is widespread. Modern Arabic evolved from the Koran, and many everyday phrases still contain religious references. That's why a phrase as mundane as "I'm doing well" takes on religious overtones.

A greeting wouldn't be complete if both sides didn't address each other. So after you say **al-Hamdu li-llah, shukran,** you need to ask the other person how he or she is doing:

- ✔ If you're speaking with a man, you say **wa 'anta kayf al-Haal** (*wa an-ta ka-yef al-haal;* And you, how are you?).

- ✔ If you're speaking with a woman, you say **wa 'anti kayf al-Haal** (*wa an-tee ka-yef al-haal;* And you, how are you?).

Talkin' the Talk

Myriam and Lisa, who are both students at the university, greet each other at the school entrance.

Myriam:	**as-salaamu 'alaykum!** *as-salaam-ou a-lai-koum!* Hello!
Lisa:	**wa 'alaykum as-salaam!** *wah a-lai-koum as-salaam!* Hello!
Myriam:	**kayf al-Haal?** *ka-yef al-haal?* How are you?
Lisa:	**al-Hamdu li-llah, shukran. wa 'anti, kayf al-Haal?** *al-ham-dou lee-lah, shouk-ran. wah an-tee,* *ka-yef al-haal?* I'm doing well, thank you. And you, how are you?
Myriam:	**al-Hamdu li-llah, shukran.** *al-ham-dou lee-lah, shouk-ran.* I'm doing well, thank you!
Lisa:	**'ilaa al-ghad!** *ee-laa al-gad!* I'll see you tomorrow!
Myriam:	**'ilaa al-ghad!** *ee-laa al-gad!* I'll see you tomorrow!

CULTURAL WISDOM

Sending the right nonverbal message

Although familiarizing yourself with the language is the first step to interacting with people from the Middle East, you also need to understand some of the nonverbal signs that can be as meaningful as words in communicating with native speakers. For example, when shaking someone's hand, be sure to avoid pressing the person's palm with too much force. In the United States, a firm and strong handshake is encouraged in order to display a healthy dose of confidence. In most Arab countries, however, a forceful handshake is viewed as an openly hostile act! The reasoning is that you use force against people whom you don't consider friends, so a forceful handshake indicates that you don't consider that person a friend. Therefore, the most acceptable way to shake hands in the Arab world is to present a friendly, not-too-firm grip.

Making Introductions

Carrying on a conversation with someone you haven't exchanged names with is awkward, to say the least. But it's an awkwardness that's easy enough to remedy when you know a few key phrases. This section explains how to ask people for their names and how to share your name using the possessive form, which may be one of the easiest grammar lessons and linguistic concepts you'll encounter in Arabic!

Asking "What's your name?"

After you go through the basic greeting procedure, which is covered in the preceding section, you're ready to ask people their names. This task is relatively easy given that you only need to know two words: **'ism** (name) and **maa** (what). If you're addressing a man, you ask **maa 'ismuka?** (*maa ees-moo-ka;* What's your name?) (M). When addressing a woman, you ask **maa 'ismuki?** (*maa ees-moo-kee;* What's your name?) (F).

TIP

If you say **maa 'ismuk** without using the suffixes **–a** or **–i** at the end of **'ismuk,** you're actually using a gender-neutral form, which is perfectly acceptable. You can address both men and women by saying **maa 'ismuk?** (*maa ees-mook;* What's your name?) (GN).

Responding with the possessive "My name is . . ."

The possessive form is one of Arabic's easiest grammatical lessons: All you do is add the suffix **–ii** (pronounced *ee*) to the noun, and — voila! — you have the possessive form of the noun. For example, to say "my name," you add **–ii** to **'ism** and get **'ismii** (*ees-mee;* my name). So to say "My name is Amine," all you say is **'ismii amiin.** It's that simple!

Saying "It's a pleasure to meet you!"

When someone introduces himself or herself, a polite response is **tasharraf-naa.** (*tah-shah-raf-nah;* It's a pleasure to meet you.) **tasharrafnaa** is a formal response, whereas **'ahlan wa sahlan** (*ahel-an wah sah-lan;* Nice to meet you.) is much more informal.

sharafa is the Arabic term for "honor," which means that **tasharrafnaa** literally translates to "We're honored." In English, it's the equivalent of "It's a pleasure to meet you."

'ahlan wa sahlan is a phrase with a dual role: When used at the beginning of a dialogue, it means "hi" (see the section "You say hello . . ." earlier in this chapter for further explanation). When used right after an introduction, you're informally saying "Nice to meet you."

Talkin' the Talk

Amine walks into a coffee shop in downtown Casablanca and greets Alex.

Amine:	**'ahlan wa sahlan!**
	ahel-an wah sah-lan!
	Hi!

Alex:	**'ahlan wa sahlan!**
	ahel-an wah sah-lan!
	Hi!

Amine:	**'ismii amiin. wa 'anta, maa ismuka?**
	ees-mee a-mii-n. wah an-ta maa ees-moo-ka?
	My name is Amine. And you, what's your name?

Alex:	**'ismii aleks.**
	ees-mee aleks.
	My name is Alex

Amine:	**tasharrafnaa!**
	tah-shah-raf-nah!
	It's a pleasure to meet you!
Alex:	**tasharrafnaa!**
	tah-shah-raf-nah!
	It's a pleasure to meet you!

Talking About Countries and Nationalities

With the growing internationalism of the modern world, when you meet someone for the first time, you may want to know what country he or she is from. Fortunately for English speakers, the names of countries in Arabic are very similar to their names in English. Even more good news is the fact that the terms for nationalities are derivatives of the country names.

Asking "Where are you from?"

If you're speaking with a man and want to ask him where he's from, you use the phrase **min 'ayna 'anta** *(min ay-na ann-ta)*. Similarly, if you want to ask a woman "Where are you from?," you say **min 'ayna 'anti?** *(min ay-na ann-tee)*.

If you want to ask if a man is from a certain place — for example, America — you say **hal 'anta min 'amriikaa?** *(hal ann-ta min am-ree-kaa;* Are you from America?) (M). If you're speaking with a woman, you simply replace **'anta** with **'anti.**

Telling where "I am from . . ."

To say "I am from . . .," you use the preposition **min** (from) and the personal pronoun **'anaa** (I/me). Therefore, "I'm from America" is **'anaa min 'amriikaa.** It's that simple!

To help you both understand responses to the question "Where are you from?" (see the preceding section) and give your own response to such questions, Table 3-1 lists the names of various countries and corresponding nationalities in Arabic.

Table 3-1   Country Names and Nationalities in Arabic

Country/Nationalities	Pronunciation	Translation
al-maghrib	al-magh-rib	Morocco
maghribii	magh-ree-bee	Moroccan (M)
maghribiiyya	magh-ree-bee-ya	Moroccan (F)
al-jazaa'ir	al-jah-zah-eer	Algeria
jazaa'irii	ja-zaa-ee-ree	Algerian (M)
jazaa'iriiyya	ja-zaa-ee-ree-ya	Algerian (F)
tuunis	tuu-nis	Tunisia
tuunisii	tuu-nee-see	Tunisian (M)
tuunisiiyya	tuu-nee-see-ya	Tunisian (F)
miSr	mee-sar	Egypt
miSrii	mees-ree	Egyptian (M)
miSriiyya	mees-ree-ya	Egyptian (F)
al-'iraaq	al-i-raa-q	Iraq
'iraaqii	ee-raa-qee	Iraqi (M)
'iraaqiiyya	ee-raa-qee-ya	Iraqi (F)
as-sa'uudiiyya	as-sa-uu-dee-ya	Saudi Arabia
sa'uudii	sa-uu-dee	Saudi (M)
sa'uudiiyya	sa-uu-dee-ya	Saudi (F)
'amriikaa	am-ree-kaa	America/USA
'amriikii	am-ree-kee	American (M)
'amriikiiyya	am-ree-kee-ya	American (F)

To tell someone "I am from Morocco," you say **'anaa min al-maghrib** (*ann-aa min al-magh-rib*). Alternatively, you may also say **'anaa maghribii** (*ann-aa magh-ree-bee;* I am Moroccan) (M).

Words to Know

wa 'alaykum as-salaam	wa 'a-lai-koum ass-sa-laam	hello (reply to as-salaamu 'alaykum)
'ahlan wa sahlan	ahel-an wa sah-lan	hi; or nice to meet you, depending on the context
al-Hamdu li-llah	al-ham-dou lee-llah	I'm doing well (Praise to God)
'ism	ee-ssam	name
'ismii	ees-mee	my name
'anaa	ann-aa	personal pronoun "me" or "I"
'anta	ann-ta	personal pronoun "you" (M)
'anti	ann-tee	personal pronoun "you" (F)
SabaaH al-khayr	sa-baah al-kha-yer	good morning
masaa' al-khayr	ma-saa al-kha-yer	good evening
tasbaH 'alaa khayr	tas-bah 'a-la kha-yer	good night
'ilaa al-liqaa'	ee-laa al-li-qaa	until next time

Fun & Games

Fill in the missing words below in the dialogue between a teacher and his student.

Teacher	'as-salaamu 'alaykum.
Student	wa _____.
Teacher	kayf _____?
Student	al-Hamdu li-llah, shukran. Wa _____?
Teacher	al-Hamdu li-llah, shukran. Maa _____?
Student	_____ Mark. Wa 'anti, maa _____?
Teacher	_____ Layla.
Student	tasharrafnaa!
Teacher	_____
Student	min _____ 'anta?
Teacher	'anaa _____ 'amriikaa. Wa 'anta?
Student	'anaa _____ 'amriikaa.
Teacher	'ilaa _____.
Student	'ilaa al-ghad.

The answers are in Appendix C.

Part II
Arabic in Action

The 5th Wave   By Rich Tennant

"There are several regional dialects to the Arabic language. Right now we're learning the falafel sandwich shop dialect."

In this part . . .

Y ou get to know key words and phrases that allow you to interact with Arabic-speaking folks in a variety of different settings (such as in a restaurant, around town, at the office, or even at the mall). You discover how to make small talk and how to ask for basic information about people you speak to, such as their names, where they're from, and their occupations.

Chapter 4

Getting to Know You: Making Small Talk

In This Chapter

▶ Asking simple questions

▶ Talking about your family, job, and hobbies

▶ Commenting on the weather

▶ Discovering the Arabic number system

▶ Sorting out words for days and months

kalaam khafiif (*kah-laah-m khah-feef;* small talk, literally "light talk") plays an important role during interactions with Arabic speakers. Sometimes you need to engage in **kalaam khafiif** when you meet people for the first time; you may know their **'ism** (*ee-sehm;* name), but you want to find out more about them, such as where they're from and what they do. **kalaam khafiif** allows you to find out more about the person you're interacting with as well as lets you tell a little bit about yourself. **kalaam khafiif** may also take place between people who know each other but prefer to make small talk in order to avoid awkward silence! Whatever the case, the ability to engage in **kalaam khafiif** is important.

You need to be aware of a number of rules when you make small talk in Arabic. Some cultural, social, and personal topics are off-limits, and you may offend someone unnecessarily if you don't know what topics to avoid. This chapter explains how to make **kalaam khafiif** in Arabic, including how to ask simple questions to find out more about the person or people you're talking to. I review how to talk about your **'usra** (*oos-rah;* family), your **mihna** (*meeh-nah;* job), and your **hiwaayaat** (*hee-waa-yat;* hobbies). I also share how to chat about **aT-Taqs** (*aht-tah-kes;* the weather). Finally, you discover key words that will allow you to engage in **kalaam khafiif** like a native speaker!

Asking Key Questions

One of the best ways to start a conversation is to ask a **su'aal** (*soo-aahl;* question). To get you started, here are some key question words in Arabic:

- **man?** (*meh-n;* Who?)
- **'ayna?** (*eh-yeh-nah;* Where?)
- **mataa?** (*mah-taah;* When?)
- **maa?** (*maah;* What?)
- **maadhaa?** (*maah-zaah;* What?) (used with verbs)
- **lii maadhaa?** (*lee maah-zaah;* Why?)
- **kayfa?** (*keh-yeh-fah;* How?)
- **bikam?** (*bee-kah-m;* How much?)
- **kam min?** (*kam meen;* How many?)

You may use these question words to ask more elaborate and detailed questions. Here are some examples:

- **maa 'ismuka?** (*maah ees-moo-kah;* What's your name?) (MS)
- **maa 'ismuki?** (*maah ees-moo-kee;* What's your name?) (FS)
- **maa mihnatuka?** (*maah meeh-nah-too-kah;* What do you do?; literally "What is your job?") (MS)
- **maa mihnatuki?** (*maah meeh-nah-too-kee;* What do you do?; literally "What is your job?") (FS)
- **maadha taf'al?** (*maah-zaah tah-feh-al;* What are you doing?) (MS)
- **maadha taf'aliina?** (*maah-zaah tah-feh-alee-nah;* What are you doing?) (FS)
- **min 'ayna 'anta?** (*meh-n eh-yeh-nah ahn-tah;* Where are you from?) (MS)
- **min 'ayna 'anti?** (*meh-n eh-yeh-nah ahn-tee;* Where are you from?) (FS)
- **maadha yaktubu?** (*maah-zaah yah-keh-too-boo;* What is he writing?)
- **hal tuHibbu al-qiraa'a?** (*hal too-hee-buh al-kee-raa-ah;* Do you like to read?) (MS)
- **hal haadhaa kitaabuka?** (*hal hah-zah kee-tah-boo-kah;* Is this your book?)
- **'ayna maHaTTatu al-qiTaar?** (*eh-yeh-nah mah-hah-tah-too al-kee-taar;* Where is the train station?)
- **mataa satadhhab 'ilaa al-maTaar?** (*mah-taah sa-taz-hab ee-laah al-mah-taar;* When did she go to the airport?)
- **'ayna 'aHsan maT'am?** (*eh-yeh-nah ah-sah-n mah-tam;* Where is the best restaurant?)

✔ **lii maadhaa dhahabta 'ilaa as-suuq?** *(lee maah-zaah za-hab-tah ee-laah ass-sook;* Why did you go to the market?) (MS)

Notice that some of the questions above refer to either masculine or feminine subjects. When you ask a question in Arabic, you choose the gender of the subject by modifying the gender suffix of the noun in question. For example, **kitaab** *(kee-tab)* means "book," but **kitaabuka** *(kee-tah-boo-kah)* means "your book" (M), and **kitaabuki** *(kee-tah-boo-kee)* means "your book" (F). So if you want to ask a man for his book, you use **kitaabuka**.

Talkin' the Talk

Yassin and Youssef are both incoming freshmen at al-azhar University in Cairo, Egypt. They strike up a friendly conversation outside the cafeteria.

Yassin:	**'afwan. hal 'anta Taalib fii al-jaami'a?** *ah-feh-wan. hal ahn-tah tah-leeb fee al-jah-mee-ah?* Excuse me. Are you a student at the university?
Youssef:	**na'am. 'anaa fii as-sana al-'uulaa. wa 'anta?** *nah-am. an-nah fee ass-sah-nah al-oo-lah.* *wah ahn-tah?* Yes. I'm in the freshman class. And you?
Yassin:	**'anaa fii as-sana al-uulaa 'ayDan!** *an-nah fee ass-sah-nah al-oo-lah ah-yeh-dan!* I'm also in the freshman class!
Youssef:	**mumtaaz! hal 'anta fii binaayat al-jaami'a?** *moom-taz! hal ahn-tah fee bee-nah-yat al-jah-mee-ah?* Excellent! Are you living on campus?
Yassin:	**na'am. 'anaa fii binaayat 'aHmed.** *nah-am. ah-nah fee bee-nah-yat ah-med.* Yes. I'm in the Ahmed dorms.
Youssef:	**'anaa fii binaayat faySal.** *ah-nah fee bee-nah-yat fay-sal.* I'm in the Faysal dorms.
Yassin:	**'ilaa al-liqaa'.** *ee-lah ah-lee-kah.* See you around.
Youssef:	**'ilaa al-liqaa'.** *ee-lah ah-lee-kah.* See you around.

Words to Know

Taalib	tah-leeb	college student (M)
tilmiidh	teel-meez	student (M)
'ustaadh	oos-taa-z	professor (M)
mudarris	moo-dah-rees	teacher (M)
jaami'a	jah-mee-ah	university
kulliya	koo-lee-yah	college
sana	sah-nah	year/class
'awwal	ah-wall	first (M)
'uulaa	oo-lah	first (F)
sana 'uulaa	sah-nah ooh-lah	first year/ freshman

Talking About Yourself and Your Family

When you meet someone for the first time, you want to get to know a little more about them. One of the best ways to get acquainted with the person you're talking to is by finding out more about his or her **'usra** (*oos-rah;* the family). The **'usra** is one of the best topics of conversation because it generates a lot of interest and endless conversation. Table 4-1 lists some important members of the **'usra** who may come up in casual conversation.

Table 4-1	All in the Family	
Arabic	*Pronunciation*	*Translation*
'ab	ah-b	father
'um	oo-m	mother
waalidayn	wah-lee-day-en	parents

Arabic	Pronunciation	Translation
'ibn	ee-ben	son
bint	bee-net	daughter
'abnaa'	ah-ben-aah	children
zawj	zah-weh-j	husband
zawja	zah-weh-jah	wife
'akh	ah-kh-eh	brother
'ukht	oo-khe-t	sister
jadd	jah-d	grandfather
jadda	jah-dah	grandmother
Hafiid	hah-feed	grandson
Hafiida	hah-fee-dah	granddaughter
'amm	ahm	paternal uncle (father's brother)
'amma	ah-mah	paternal aunt (father's sister)
khaal	kah-l	maternal uncle (mother's brother)
khaala	kah-lah	maternal aunt (mother's sister)
zawj al-'amma	zah-weh-j al-ah-mah	paternal aunt's husband
zawjat al-'amm	zah-weh-jaht al-ahm	paternal uncle's wife
zawj al-khaala	zah-weh-j al-kah-lah	maternal aunt's husband
zawjat al-khaal	zah-weh-jaht al-kah-l	maternal uncle's wife
'ibn al-'amm	ee-ben al-ahm	male cousin from the father's side
bint al-'amm	bee-net al-ahm	female cousin from the father's side
'ibn al-khaal	ee-ben al-kah-l	male cousin from the mother's side
'ibn al-khaala	bee-net al-kah-lah	female cousin from the mother's side

(continued)

Table 4-1 *(continued)*

Arabic	Pronunciation	Translation
'ahl az-zawj	ahel az-zah-weh-j	in-laws (M; collective)
'ahl az-zawja	ahel az-zah-weh-jah	in-laws (F; collective)
Hamou	hah-mooh	father-in-law
Hamaat	hah-maht	mother-in-law
silf	see-lef	brother-in-law
silfa	see-leh-fah	sister-in-law
rabboun	rah-boon	stepfather
rabba	rah-bah	stepmother
'akh min al-'ab	ah-kh-eh min al-ah-b	stepbrother from the father's side
'ukht min al-'ab	oo-khe-t min al-ah-b	stepsister from the father's side
'akh min al-'umm	ah-kh-eh min al-oo-m	stepbrother from the mother's side
'ukht min al-'umm	oo-khe-t min al-oo-m	stepsister from the mother's side

CULTURAL WISDOM

The role of family in Arab culture

The **'usra** plays a very important role in Arab life, society, and culture, and the Arab **'usra** structure is very different than the Western family unit. The notion of the **'usra** is much more comprehensive and reinforced in the Arab world and the Middle East than it is in America or other Western countries. The family unit most prevalent in the West is the nuclear family — generally comprised of two parents and their children — but the **'usra** in the Arab world is an extended, close-knit family network made up of parents, children, grandparents, aunts, uncles, and cousins.

It's not uncommon to find an Arab household in which children live not only with their parents but also with their aunts and uncles, cousins, and grandparents. In Arab culture, the idea of the immediate family extends to second- and even third-degree cousins! In addition, lineage is important, and the terms for family relatives are specifically designed to differentiate between cousins from the mother's side (**'ibn al-khaal**) and cousins from the father's side (**'ibn al-'amm**). Thus, if you're talking to an Arab about his or her family, you can be sure that you'll have a lot to talk about!

Talkin' the Talk

Hassan is on a flight to New York from Casablanca, Morocco. He strikes up a conversation with Alexandra, who is sitting next to him.

Hassan: **'afwan. hal 'anti 'amriikiiyya?**
ah-feh-wan. hal ahn-tee am-ree-kee-yah?
Excuse me. Are you American?

Alexandra: **na'am 'anaa 'amriikiiyya. wa 'anta?**
nah-am ah-nah am-ree-kee-yah. wah ahn-tah?
Yes, I'm American. And you?

Hassan: **'anaa maghriibii. hal zurti 'usra fii al-maghrib?**
ah-nah mah-gree-bee. hal zoo-reh-tee oos-rah fee al-mah-rib?
I'm Moroccan. Were you visiting family in Morocco?

Alexandra: **na'am. khaalatii fii Tanja. 'ayna sa-tadh-hab fii 'amriikaa?**
nah-am. kah-lah-tee fee tah-neh-jah. eh-yeh-nah sah-tah-zeh-hab fee am-ree-kah?
Yes. My aunt lives in Tangiers. What part of the United States are you visiting?

Hassan: **sa-'azuuru 'akhii fii nyuu yoork.**
sah-ah-zuu-ru ah-kee fee noo york.
I'm going to visit my brother in New York.

Alexandra: **Safar sa'eed.**
sah-far sah-eed.
Have a safe trip.

Hassan: **kadhaalika 'anti.**
kah-zah-lee-kah ahn-tee.
Same to you.

Words to Know

ziyaara	zee-yah-rah	visit
'azuuru	ah-zoo-roo	I visit
safar	sah-far	trip
kadhaalika	kah-zah-lee-kah	same/similar
sa'eed	sah-eed	safe/happy

Making Small Talk on the Job

You can generally find out a lot about a person based on his or her **mihna** (*meeh-nah;* job). A lot of people identify themselves with their occupations, so being able to make small talk about jobs is essential.

Professions in Arabic always have a gender distinction. If you want to ask someone about his or her profession, you have two options:

✔ **maa mihnatuka?** (*maah meeh-nah-too-kah;* What is your job?; literally "What do you do?") (M)

✔ **maa mihnatuki?** (*maah meeh-nah-too-kee;* What is your job?; literally "What do you do?") (F)

✔ **'ayna ta'mal?** (*eh-yeh-nah tah-mal;* Where do you work?) (M)

✔ **'ayna ta'maliina?** (*eh-yeh-nah tah-mah-lee-nah;* Where do you work?) (F)

Table 4-2 contains some important words relating to different occupations.

Table 4-2		Professions
Arabic	**Pronunciation**	**Translation**
maSrafii	mah-srah-fee	banker (M)
SaHafii	sah-hah-fee	journalist (M)
kaatib	kah-teeb	writer (M)

Arabic	Pronunciation	Translation
mumathil	moo-mah-theel	actor (M)
muhandis	moo-han-dees	architect (M)
Tabiib	tah-beeb	doctor (M)
fannaan	fah-nan	artist (M)
mughannii	moo-gah-nee	singer (M)
mutarjim	moo-tar-jeem	translator (M)
mumarriD	moo-mah-reed	nurse (M)
muHaamii	moo-hah-mee	lawyer (M)
Tabbaakh	tah-bah-kh	cook (M)
taajir	tah-jeer	merchant (M)
muHaasib	moo-hah-seeb	accountant (M)
simsaar	seem-sahr	broker (M)
Hallaaq	hah-lahk	barber (M)
fallaaH	fah-lah	farmer (M)
raaqiS	rah-kees	dancer (M)
shurTii	shoor-tee	police officer (M)
'iTfaa'ii	eet-fah-ee	fireman
rajul 'a'maal	rah-jool ah-maal	businessman

Table 4-2 gives the masculine forms of professions. You'll be pleased to know that converting the masculine forms of professions into the feminine forms involves simply adding a **fatHa** to the end of the masculine profession. For example, to say "translator" in the feminine, you add a **fatHa** to **muTarjim** to get **muTarjima** (*moo-tar-jee-mah;* translator) (F).

Talkin' the Talk

Hassan and Amanda, two passengers on a plane from Casablanca to New York, are talking about their respective jobs.

Alexandra:	**maa mihnatuka?** *maah meeh-nah-too-kah?* What do you do?
Hassan:	**'anaa muhandis fii dar al-baydaa'.** *ah-nah moo-han-dees fee dar al-bay-dah.* I'm an architect in Casablanca.
Alexandra:	**haadhaa mumtaaz!** *hah-zah moom-taz!* That's excellent!
Hassan:	**wa 'anti, 'ayna ta'maliina?** *wah ahn-tee, eh-yeh-nah tah-mah-lee-nah* And you, where do you work?
Alexandra:	**'anaa SaHafiyya.** *ah-nah sah-hah-fee-yah.* I'm a journalist.
Hassan:	**ma'a 'ayy jariida?** *mah-ah ay jah-ree-dah?* With which newspaper?
Alexandra:	**ma'a nyuu yoork taymz.** *mah-ah noo-york tie-mez.* With *The New York Times*.

Talking About Hobbies

hiwaayaat (*hee-wah-yat;* hobbies) are a really great topic for **kalaam khafiif.** Almost everyone has a hobby, and because a hobby, by definition, is an activity that a person is really passionate about, you can be sure that he or she will enjoy talking about it! People really like to talk about their hobbies, so knowing how to engage in **kalaam khafiif** related to **hiwaayaat** is important. Here are some activities that may be considered **hiwaayaat:**

- **raqS** (*rah-kes;* dancing)
- **ghinaa'** (*ree-nah;* singing)

✔ **kurat al-qadam** (*koo-raht al-kah-dam;* soccer)

✔ **qiraa'a** (*kee-rah-ah;* reading)

✔ **darraaja** (*dah-rah-jah;* bicycling)

✔ **Tayyaarat waraq** (*tah-yah-raht wah-rak;* kite flying)

Talkin' the Talk

Yassin and Youssef, two freshmen students at al-azhar University, find that they have a hobby in common.

Yassin:	**maa hiya hiwaayatuka?**
	mah hee-ya hee-wah-yah-too-kah?
	What is your hobby?
Youssef:	**'anaa 'uHibbu kurat al-qadam.**
	an-nah oo-hee-boo koo-raht al-kah-dam.
	I like soccer.
Yassin:	**'anaa 'uHibbu kurat al-qadam 'ayDan!**
	an-nah oo-hee-boo koo-raht al-kah-dam ay-dan!
	I also like soccer!
Youssef:	**yajib 'an nal'abahaa!**
	yah-jeeb ahn nah-luh-aba-haa!
	We must play sometime!
Yassin:	**Taba'an!**
	Tah-bah-an!
	Definitely!

Shooting the Breeze: Talking About the Weather

If you want to engage in **kalaam khafiif,** shoot the breeze, or chitchat with a friend or stranger, talking about **Taqs** (*tah-kes;* weather) is a pretty safe topic. In conversations about **Taqs,** you're likely to use some of the following words:

- **shams** (*shah-mes;* sun)

- **maTar** (*mah-tar;* rain)

- **ra'd** (*rah-ed;* thunder)

- **barq** (*bah-rek;* lightning)

- **suHub** (*soo-hoob;* clouds)

- **Harara** (*hah-rah-rah;* temperature)

- **daraja** (*dah-rah-jah;* degrees)

- **bard** (*bah-red;* cold)

- **sukhoun** (*suh-koon;* hot)

- **ruTuuba** (*roo-too-bah;* humidity)

- **riiH** (*ree-eh;* wind)

- **'aaSifa** (*ah-tee-fah;* storm)

- **thalj** (*thah-lej;* snow)

- **qawsu quzaH** (*kah-wuh-suh koo-zah;* rainbow)

If you want to express the temperature, as in "It's *x* degrees," you must use the following construct: **al-Harara (insert number) daraja.** So, **al-Harara 35 daraja** means "It's 35 degrees."

Because the weather is a quasi-universal topic that interests almost everyone, here are some expressions you can use to start talking about **Taqs:**

- **hal sayakun maTar al-yawm?** (*hal sah-yah-koon mah-tar al-yah-oum;* Is it going to rain today?)

- **yawm sukhoun, na'am?** (*yah-oum suh-koon, nah-am;* Hot day, isn't it?)

- **'inna yahubbu al-bard faj'atan.** (*ee-nah yah-hoo-boo al-bah-red fah-jeh-ah-tan;* It's gotten cold all of a sudden.)

- **hal sayabqaa aT-Taqs haakadhaa kul al-usbuu'?** (*hal sah-yab-kah at-tah-kes hah-kah-zah kool al-oos-boo;* Will the weather remain like this all week?)

It would be difficult to chat about the weather without mentioning the **fuSuul** (*fuh-sool;* seasons):

- **Sayf** (*sah-yef;* summer)

- **khariif** (*kah-reef;* fall)

- **shitaa'** (*shee-tah;* winter)

- **rabii'** (*rah-beeh;* spring)

Temperatures in the majority of the Middle Eastern countries are stated in Celsius and not Fahrenheit. If you hear someone say that **al-harara 25 daraja** (*al-hah-rah-rah 25 dah-rah-jah;* It's 25 degrees), don't worry that you're going to freeze! They actually mean that it's almost 80 degrees Fahrenheit. To convert degrees from Celsius to Fahrenheit, use the following formula:

(Celsius × 1.8) + 32 = Degrees Fahrenheit

Talkin' the Talk

Alexandra and Hassan are talking about the weather.

Hassan: **kayfa aT-Taqs fii nyuu yoork?**
keh-yeh-fah ah-tah-kes fii noo york?
How's the weather in New York?

Alexandra: **aT-Taqs mumtaaz al-'aan!**
ah-tah-kes moom-taz al-ahn!
The weather is excellent right now!

Hassan: **hal satakun shams?**
hal sah-tah-koon shah-mes?
Is it going to be sunny?

Alexandra: **satakun shams kul al-'usbuu'.**
sah-tah-koon shah-mes kool al-oos-boo.
It's going to be sunny all week long.

Hassan: **wa ba'da dhaalika?**
wah bah-dah zah-lee-kah?
And after that?

Alexandra: **laa 'a'rif.**
lah ah-reef.
I don't know.

Hurray, it's raining!

One of the happiest times of the year for people of the Middle East is when the rain comes. After all, these hot desert countries get very little rainfall. You will almost never hear anyone complaining about rain in Arabic — there are no equivalent expressions for "rain, rain, go away." Actually, the opposite is true! There's a song that farmers, students, and children sing when the rain starts falling: **ah shta-ta-ta-ta-ta / 'awlaad al-Harata; Sabbi, Sabbi, Sabbi / al-'awlad fii qubbi** (*ah-sheh-tah-tah-tah-tah-tah / ah-ou-lad al-hah-rah-tah;*

sah-bee, sah-bee, sah-bee / al-ah-ou-lad fee koobee; Oh rain, rain, rain, rain, rain / Children of the plowman; Pour, pour, pour / The children are in the hood of my jellaba). A *jellaba* is a long, flowing garment worn by farmers in the Middle East. It has a big hood in which the farmer puts objects. Of course, children can't fit in the hood of the jellaba, but the hood is big enough that it symbolizes protection against the rain. This is a happy song that expresses people's joy when it rains!

Talking Numbers

Knowing how to express numbers in Arabic is a basic language lesson. You're bound to encounter Arabic numbers in all sorts of settings, including **kalaam khafiif.** For example, when you're talking with someone about the weather, you need to know your numbers in order to reference the temperature or understand a reference if the other person makes one. In this section, I introduce you to the Arabic **'arqaam** (*ah-reh-kam;* numbers). (The singular form of **'arqaam** is **raqm** (*rah-kem;* number).)

Arabic **'arqaam** are part of one of the earliest traditions of number notation. Even though the Western world's number system is sometimes referred to as "Arabic numerals," actual Arabic **'arqaam** are written differently than the ones used in the West. One of the most important aspects of Arabic numbers to keep in mind is that you read them from left to right. That's right! Even though you read and write Arabic from right to left, you read and write Arabic numbers from left to right! Table 4-3 lays out the Arabic **'arqaam** from 0 to 10.

Table 4-3	Arabic Numerals 0–10	
Arabic	*Pronunciation*	*Translation*
Sifr	seh-fer	0
waaHid	wah-eed	1
'ithnayn	eeth-nah-yen	2
thalaatha	thah-lah-thah	3

Arabic	Pronunciation	Translation
'arba'a	ah-reh-bah-ah	4
khamsa	khah-meh-sah	5
sitta	see-tah	6
sab'a	sah-beh-ah	7
thamaaniya	thah-mah-nee-yah	8
tis'a	tee-seh-ah	9
'ashra	ah-she-rah	10

'arqaam are important not only for discussing the weather but also for telling time, asking about prices, and conducting everyday business. Table 4-4 contains the **'arqaam** from 11 to 20.

Table 4-4	Arabic Numerals 11–20	
Arabic	**Pronunciation**	**Translation**
'iHdaa 'ashar	ee-heh-dah ah-shar	11
'ithnaa 'ashar	ee-theh-nah ah-shar	12
thalaathata 'ashar	thah-lah-tha-tah ah-shar	13
'arba'ata 'ashar	ah-reh-bah-ah-tah ah-shar	14
khamsata 'ashar	khah-meh-sah-tah ah-shar	15
sittata 'ashar	see-tah-tah ah-shar	16
sab'ata 'ashar	sah-beh-ah-tah ah-shar	17
thamaaniyata 'ashar	thah-mah-nee-ya-tah ah-shar	18
tis'ata 'ashar	tee-seh-ah-tah ah-shar	19
'ishreen	ee-sheh-reen	20

The **'arqaam** from **'iHdaa 'ashar** (11) to **tis'ata 'ashar** (19) are obtained by combining a derivative form of the number **'ashra** (10) — specifically **'ashar** (tenth) — with a derivative form of the singular number. In the case of the **'arqaam** from **thalaathata 'ashar** (13) through **tis'ata 'ashar** (19), all you do is add the suffix **-ta** to the regular number and add the derivative form **'ashar!** After you're familiar with this pattern, remembering these **'arqaam** is much easier.

Table 4-5 shows the **'arqaam** in increments of 10 from 20 to 100.

Table 4-5	Arabic Numerals 20–100	
Arabic	*Pronunciation*	*Translation*
'ishriin	ee-sheh-reen	20
thalaathiin	thah-lah-theen	30
'arba'iin	ah-reh-bah-een	40
khamsiin	khah-meh-seen	50
sittiin	see-teen	60
sab'iin	sah-beh-een	70
thamaaniin	thah-mah-neen	80
tis'iin	tee-seh-een	90
mi'a	mee-ah	100

In English, you add the suffix **-ty** to get thirty, forty, and so on. In Arabic, the suffix **-iin** plays that role, as in **'arba'iin** (40) or **khamsiin** (50).

Referring to Days and Months

When you're engaged in **kalaam khafiif,** you may find that you need to refer to certain days of the week or months. Fortunately the days of the **'usbuu'** (*ooh-seh-booh;* week) are number derivatives — that is, they're derived from Arabic numbers. So recognizing the roots of the words for days of the week is key:

- ✔ **al-'aHad** (*al-ah-had;* Sunday)
- ✔ **al-'ithnayn** (*al-eeth-nah-yen;* Monday)
- ✔ **ath-thulathaa'** (*ah-thoo-lah-thah;* Tuesday)
- ✔ **al-'arbi'aa'** (*al-ah-reh-bee-ah;* Wednesday)
- ✔ **al-khamiis** (*al-khah-mees;* Thursday)
- ✔ **al-jumu'a** (*al-joo-moo-ah;* Friday)
- ✔ **as-sabt** (*ass-sah-bet;* Saturday)

Notice that **'aHad** (Sunday) is derived from **waaHid** (1); **al-'ithnayn** (Monday) from **'ithnayn** (2); **ath-thulathaa'** (Tuesday) from **thalaatha** (3); **al-'arbi'aa'** (Wednesday) from **'arba'a** (4); and **al-khamiis** (Thursday) from **khamsa** (5). In the Islamic calendar, Sunday is the first day, Monday the second day, and so on.

al-jumu'a gets its name from **jumu'a,** which means "to gather;" it's the day when Muslims gather around the mosque and pray. Similarly, **as-sabt** is the day of rest, similar to the Jewish Sabbath.

Arabs use three different types of calendars to note the passage of time.

- ✔ The **Gregorian calendar** is basically the same calendar as the one used throughout the Western world.

- ✔ The **Islamic calendar** is partly based on the lunar cycle and has radically different names for the months than its Western counterpart.

- ✔ The **lunar calendar** is based entirely on the moon's rotations and is used to identify specific religious holidays, such as the end and beginning of the holy month of Ramadan, in which Muslims fast from the break of dawn until dusk.

Tables 4-7 and 4-8 show the **ash-hur** (*ah-shuh-hur;* months) in the Gregorian and Islamic calendars, because they're the most widely used calendars.

Table 4-7	Gregorian Calendar	
Arabic	*Pronunciation*	*Translation*
yanaayir	yah-nah-yeer	January
fibraayir	feeb-rah-yeer	February
maaris	mah-rees	March
'abriil	ah-beh-reel	April
maayuu	mah-yoo	May
yunyu	yoo-neh-yoo	June
yulyu	yoo-leh-yoo	July
'aghusTus	ah-goo-seh-toos	August
sibtambar	see-beh-tam-bar	September
'uktuubar	oo-key-too-bar	October
nufambar	noo-fahm-bar	November
disambar	dee-sahm-bar	December

The Arabic names of the Gregorian months are similar to the names in English. However, the names of the Islamic calendar are quite different.

Table 4-8	Islamic Calendar
Arabic	*Pronunciation*
muHarram	moo-hah-ram
Safar	sah-far
rabii' al-awwal	rah-bee al-ah-wall
rabii' ath-thaanii	rah-bee ah-thah-nee
jumaada al-awwal	joo-mah-dah al-ah-wall
jumaada ath-thaanii	joo-mah-dah ah-thah-nee
rajab	rah-jab
sha'baan	sha-huh-ban
ramaDaan	rah-mah-dan
shawwaal	shah-wuh-al
dhuu al-qaa'ida	zoo al-kah-ee-dah
dhuu al-Hijja	zoo al-hee-jah

Because the Islamic calendar is partly based on the lunar cycle, the months don't overlap with the Gregorian calendar, making it difficult to match the months with the Gregorian ones.

Fun & Games

'udhkur al-fuSl. (Name the season.)

A. _____

B. _____

C. _____

D. _____

The answers are in Appendix C.

Chapter 5

This Is Delicious! Eating In and Dining Out

In This Chapter

▶ Covering breakfast, lunch, and dinner
▶ Finding your way around the kitchen
▶ Eating at home
▶ Dining at a restaurant

Ta'aam (*tah-am;* food) is a great way to explore a new culture. You can find out a lot about a people by exploring what they eat, how they eat it, and how they prepare it. Like in many other cultures, **Ta'aam** plays a central role in Arabic culture. In this chapter, you expand your vocabulary with the Arabic words for some popular meals and foods, and you find out how to place an order at a restaurant and how to interact appropriately with your waiter or waitress.

All About Meals

The three basic **wajbaat** (*waj-bat;* meals) in Arabic are:

✔ **fuTuur** (*foo-toor;* breakfast)
✔ **ghidaa'** (*gee-dah;* lunch)
✔ **'ashaa'** (*ah-ashaa;* dinner)

Sometimes when you're feeling a little **jaai'** (*jah-eeh;* hungry) but aren't ready for a full course **wajba**, you may want a small **wajba khafiifa** (*waj-bah kah-fee-fah;* snack) instead.

Breakfast

I'm sure you've heard it before, but **fuTuur** is the most important **wajba** of the day: When you start your day on a full stomach, you feel better and accomplish more. In the mornings, I like to start my day with a cup of **qahwa** (*kah-wah;* coffee). I usually like to drink it **kaHla** (*kah-lah;* black), but sometimes I add a little **Haliib** (*hah-leeb;* milk) and some **sukkar** (*soo-kar;* sugar) to give it a bit of flavor. Some days, I prefer to drink **shay** (*shay;* tea) instead of **qahwa.** My favorite accompaniments for my **qahwa** or **shay** are **khubz** (*koo-bez;* bread) and **mu'ajjanaat** (*moo-ah-jah-nat;* pastries).

Here are some other things you can expect in a regular **fuTuur:**

- ✔ **'asal** (*ah-sal;* honey)
- ✔ **qahwa bi Haliib** (*kah-wah bee hah-leeb;* coffee with milk)
- ✔ **qahwa bi sukkar** (*kah-wah bee soo-kar;* coffee with sugar)
- ✔ **qahwa bi Haliib wa sukkar** (*kah-wah bee hah-leeb wah soo-kar;* coffee with milk and sugar)
- ✔ **shay bi 'asal** (*shay bee ah-sel;* tea with honey)
- ✔ **khubz muHammar** (*koo-bez moo-hah-mar;* toasted bread)
- ✔ **khubz bi zabda** (*koo-bez bee zab-dah;* bread with butter)
- ✔ **khubz bi zabda wa 'asal** (*koo-bez bee zab-dah wah ah-sal;* bread with butter and honey)
- ✔ **shefanj** (*sheh-fanj;* donuts)
- ✔ **Hubuub al-fuTuur** (*hoo-boob al-foo-toor;* breakfast cereal)
- ✔ **bayD** (*bah-yed;* eggs)

Having **fuTuur fii al-manzil** (*foo-toor fee al-man-zeel;* breakfast at home) is a nice, relaxing way to start the day.

Talkin' the Talk

Fatima prepares breakfast for her daughter Nadia at home before sending her off to school.

Fatima: **hal turiidiina 'aSiir haadha aS-SabaaH?**
hal too-ree-dee-nah ah-seer hah-zah ah-sah-bah?
Would you like juice this morning?

Nadia: **na'am ya 'ummii.**
nah-am yah oo-mee.
Yes mommy.

Fatima: **'ay naw' min 'aSiir: 'aSiir al-burtuqaal, 'aSiir at-tuffaah, 'aSiir al-jazar?**
ay nah-weh meen ah-seer: ah-seer al-boor-too-kal, ah-seer ah-too-fah, ah-seer al-jah-zar.
What kind of juice do you want: orange juice, apple juice, or carrot juice?

Nadia: **'uriidu 'aSiir al-burtuqaal.**
oo-ree-doo ah-seer al-boor-too-kal.
I want orange juice.

Fatima: **mumtaaz! haadhaa raai' li aS-SaHa. wa hal turiidiina Hubuub al-fuTuur 'ayDan?**
moom-taz! hah-zah rah-eeh lee ah-sah-hah. wah hal too-ree-dee-nah hoo-boob al-foo-toor ay-zan?
Excellent! It's great for your health. And do you want cereal as well?

Nadia: **na'am, wa fiih Haliib kathiir.**
nah-am wah feeh hah-leeb kah-theer.
Yes, and with lots of milk.

Fatima: **wa haa huwa al-khubz bi zabda.**
wah hah hoo-wah al-koo-bez bee zab-dah.
And here's some bread with butter.

Nadia: **shukran. sa-'adhhabu 'ilaa al-madrasa al-'aan.**
shook-ran. sah-az-hah-boo ee-lah al-mad-rah-sah al-an.
Thank you. I'm going to go to school now.

Fatima: **laHdha. nasaytii al-mawza.**
lah-zah. nah-say-tee al-maw-zah.
One moment. Don't forget the banana.

Nadia: **Tab'an! shukran.**
tah-bah-an! shook-ran.
Of course! Thank you.

Words to Know

'aSiir	ah-seer	juice
'aSiir al-burtuqaal	ah-seer al-boor-too-kal	orange juice
'aSiir at-tuffaaH	ah-seer ah-too-fah	apple juice
'aSiir al-jazar	ah-seer al-jah-zar	carrot juice
burtuqaala	boor-too-kal	orange
tufaaHa	too-fah-hah	apple
jazar	jah-zah-rah	carrots
mawza	maw-zah	banana
SaHa	sah-hah	health
Haliib	hah-leeb	milk
al-'aan	al-an	now
laHdha	lah-zah	one moment
nasaa	nah-sah	forgot
yansaa	yan-sah	to forget
nasayti	nah-say-tee	you forgot (FS)
nasayta	nah-say-tah	you forgot (MS)

If you're on the go, stopping by a **qahwa** (*kah-wah;* coffee shop) in the **SabaaH** (*sah-bah;* morning) is a good alternative to getting your **fuTuur** at home. (***Note:*** The word **qahwa** denotes both the beverage as well as the coffee shop. Remember this distinction so that you don't get confused unnecessarily!)

Talkin' the Talk

 Laura stops by the local coffee shop in the morning to order breakfast from Ahmed.

Laura:	**SabaaH al-khayr 'aHmad.**
	sah-bah al-kah-yer ah-mad.
	Good morning Ahmed.

Ahmed:	**SabaaH an-nuur lora. maadhaa tuHibbiina haadha aS-SabaaH?**
	sah-bah ah-noor loh-rah. mah-zah too-hee-bee-nah hah-zah ah-sah-bah?
	Good morning Laura. What would you like this morning?

Laura:	**al-'aadii.**
	al-ah-dee.
	The usual.

Ahmed:	**fawran. qahwa wa Haliib, na'am?**
	faw-ran. kah-wah wah hah-leeb.
	Right away. Coffee with milk, right?

Laura:	**na'am.**
	nah-am.
	Yes.

Ahmed:	**kam min mil'aqat as-sukkar?**
	kam meen meel-ah-kat ah-soo-kar?
	How many spoons of sugar?

Laura:	**mil'aqatayn.**
	meel-ah-kah-tayn.
	Two spoons.

Ahmed:	**hal tuHibbiina al-qahwa Saghiira 'aadiya 'aw kabiira?**
	hal too-hee-bee-nah al-kah-wah sah-gee-rah ah-dee-yah aw kah-bee-rah?
	Would you like a small, medium, or large coffee?

Laura:	**'uHibbu qahwa kabiira al-yawm.**
	oo-hee-boo kah-wah kah-bee-rah al-yah-oum.
	I'd like a large coffee today.

Ahmed:	**wa hal turiidiina shay'un li al-'akl?**
	wah hal too-ree-dee-nah shay-oon lee al-ah-kel?
	And would you like anything to eat?

Laura:	**hal 'indaka shefanj?**
	hal een-dah-kah sheh-fanj?
	Do you have donuts?

Ahmed:	**na'am. kam min shefanja turiidiina?**
	nah-am. kam meen sheh-fan-jah too-ree-dee-nah?
	Yes. How many donuts do you want?

Laura:	**'uriidu thalaathat shefanja min faDlik.**
	oo-ree-doo thah-lah-that sheh-fan-jah meen fad-leek.
	I'd like three donuts please.

Words to Know

'aadii	ah-dee	regular
mil'aqa	meel-ah-kah	spoon
Saghiir	sah-geer	small (M)
Saghiira	sah-gee-rah	small (F)
'aadii	ah-dee	medium (M)
'aadiya	ah-dee-yah	medium (F)
kabiir	kah-beer	large (M)
kabiirah	kah-bee-rah	large (F)
al-'akl	al-ah-kel	to eat
shefanja	sheh-fan-jah	donut

Having a piece of **faakiha** (*fah-kee-hah;* fruit) such as a **burtuqaala** (orange) or **tuffaaHa** (apple) is a healthy addition to any **fuTuur**. Because **fawaakih** (*fah-wah-keeh;* fruits) play an important role in any healthy meal, here are some of the more common **fawaakih**:

- **tuuta** (*too-tah;* strawberry)
- **'ijaaS** (*ee-jas;* pear)
- **dallaaHa** (*dah-lah-hah;* watermelon)
- **baTTiikh** (*bah-teek;* cantaloupe)
- **khawkha** (*kaw-kah;* peach)
- **'inab** (*ee-nab;* grapes)
- **laymoon** (*lay-moon;* lemon)
- **laymoon hindii** (*lay-moon heen-dee;* grapefruit)
- **laymoon maaliH** (*lay-moon mah-leeh;* lime)
- **al-anbaj** (*al-ann-baj;* mango)

Lunch

Eating your **fuTuur** keeps you **shab'aan** (*shab-an;* satisfied) for a few hours — time to get some work done and remain productive. Later, though, you're bound to get **jaai'** (*jah-eeh;* hungry) again. Perhaps a piece of **faakiha** will keep you going until it's time for **al-ghidaa'** (*al-gee-dah;* lunch).

al-ghidaa' is a very important **wajba**. In most Middle Eastern countries, workers don't sit in their cubicles and eat their **ghidaa'**. Rather, most offices close and employees get two hours or more for **al-ghidaa'**!

Unlike **fuTuur**, the **Ta'aam** during the **ghidaa'** is quite different. Here are some of the common **Ta'aam** you can expect during the **ghidaa'**:

- **laHam** (*lah-ham;* meat)
- **laHam al-baqar** (*lah-ham al-bah-kar;* beef)
- **laHam al-ghanam** (*lah-ham al-gah-nam;* lamb)
- **laHam al-'ajal** (*lah-ham al-ah-jel;* veal)
- **samak** (*sah-mak;* fish)
- **dajaaj** (*dah-jaj;* chicken)
- **ruz** (*rooz;* rice)

Sometimes, your **ghidaa'** may consist of a simple **sandwiish** (*sand-weesh;* sandwich). Other times, you may prefer a nice, healthy **shalada** (*shah-lah-dah;* salad). I'm convinced that **khudar** (*koo-dar;* vegetables) make or break the **shalada.** Here are some **khudar** to help you make your **shalada ladhiidha** (*lah-zee-zah;* delicious):

- **khass** (*kass;* lettuce)

- **TamaaTim** (*tah-mah-teem;* tomatoes)

- **khurshuuf** (*koor-shoof;* artichokes)

- **baTaaTis** (*bah-tah-tees;* potatoes)

- **hilyoon** (*heel-yoon;* asparagus)

- **'afookaat** (*ah-foo-kat;* avocado)

- **qarnabiiT** (*kar-nah-beet;* broccoli)

- **qunnabiiT** (*koo-nah-beet;* cauliflower)

- **dhurra** (*zoo-rah;* corn)

- **khiyaar** (*kee-yar;* cucumber)

- **fuul** (*fool;* beans)

- **'ayshu al-ghuraab** (*ay-shoo al-goo-rab;* mushrooms)

- **baSla** (*bass-lah;* onions)

- **baziilya** (*bah-zee-lee-yah;* peas)

- **'isfaanaakh** (*ees-fah-nak;* spinach)

In order to make a **sandwiish** even more delicious, add some of the following **Tawaabil** (*tah-wah-beel;* condiments):

- **SalSa min aT-TamaaTim** (*sal-sah meen at-tah-mah-teem;* ketchup)

- **khardal** (*kar-dal;* mustard)

- **miiyooniiz** (*mee-yoo-neez;* mayonnaise)

- **mukhallalaat** (*moo-kah-lah-lat;* pickles)

Talkin' the Talk

Matt is on his lunch break and decides to stop by the local cafeteria to order a sandwich. Nawal takes his order.

Nawal: **'ahlan. kayfa yumkin 'an 'usaa'iduka?**
ahel-an. kay-fah yoom-keen an oo-sah-ee-doo-kah?
Hi. How may I help you?

Matt: **'uriidu 'an 'aTlub sandwiish min faDlik.**
oo-ree-doo an at-loob sand-weesh meen fad-leek.
I would like to order a sandwich please.

Nawal: **'ay Hajem sandwiish turiid: kabiir 'aw Saghiir?**
ay hah-jem sand-weesh too-reed: kah-beer aw sah-geer?
What size sandwich do you want: large or small?

Matt: **as-sandwiish al-kabiir.**
ah-sand-weesh al-kah-beer.
The large sandwich.

Nawal: **'ay naw' min khubz tuHibb: khubz 'abyaD 'aw khubz az-zara'?**
ay nah-ouh meen koo-bez too-heeb: koo-bez ab-yad aw koo-bez ah-zah-rah?
What type of bread would you like: white bread or whole wheat bread?

Matt: **khubz 'abyaD.**
koo-bez ab-yad.
White bread.

Nawal: **'indanaa jamii' al-alHaam: laHam al-ghanam, laHam al-baqar wa laHam al-'ajal. wa 'indanaa dajaaj 'ayDan. 'ay laHam turiid fii as-sandwiish?**
een-dah-nah jah-meeh al-al-ham: lah-ham al-gah-nam, lah-ham al-bah-kar wah lah-ham al-ah-jal. wah een-dah-nah dah-jaj ay-zan. ay lah-ham too-reed fee ah-sand-weesh?
We have all sorts of meat: lamb, beef, and veal. And we also have chicken. What kind of meat do you want in the sandwich?

Matt: **dajaaj min faDlik.**
dah-jaj meen fad-leek.
Chicken please.

Nawal: **wa hal tuHibb khudar fii as-sandwiish?**
wah hal too-heeb koo-dar fee ah-sand-weesh?
And would you like any vegetables in your sandwich?

Matt: **na'am. hal 'indakum TamaaTim?**
nah-am. hal een-dah-koom tah-mah-teem?
Yes. Do you have any tomatoes?

Nawal: **na'am. shay' 'aakhar?**
nah-am. shay ah-kar?
Yes. Anything else?

Matt:	**khass, qarnabiiT wa baSla.**
	kass, kar-nah-beet wah bas-lah.
	Lettuce, broccoli, and onions.

Nawal:	**'afwan, lam 'indanaa qarnabiiT.**
	af-wan, lam een-dah-nah kar-nah-beet.
	I apologize, we don't have any broccoli.

Matt:	**Tayyib. khasswa TamaaTim faqat.**
	tah-yeeb. kass, wah tah-mah-teem fah-kat.
	That's okay. Lettuce and tomatoes will do.

Nawal:	**wa hal turiid Tawaabil?**
	wah hal too-reed tah-wah-beel?
	And do you want condiments?

Matt:	**mukhallalaat faqat. shukran.**
	moo-kah-lah-lat fah-kat. shook-ran.
	Pickles only. Thank you.

Words to Know

'aTlub	at-loob	order
Hajem	hah-jem	size
naw'	nah-ouh	type
khubz 'abyaD	koo-bez ab-yad	white bread
khubz az-zara'	koo-bez ah-zah-rah	whole wheat bread
jamii'	jah-meeh	all sorts
faqat	fah-kat	only

The most important **fi'l** (*fee-al;* verb) you should know relating to **Ta'aam** is the verb **'akala** (*ah-kah-lah*), which means "ate" in the **maaDii**. In the **muDaari'**, it's conjugated as **ya'kulu** (*yah-koo-loo;* to eat).

Here is the verb **'akala** conjugated in the **maaDii** form:

Form	Pronunciation	Translation
'anaa 'akaltu	ah-nah ah-kal-too	I ate
'anta 'akalta	ahn-tah ah-kal-tah	You ate (MS)
'anti 'akalti	ahn-tee ah-kal-tee	You ate (FS)
huwa 'akala	hoo-wah ah-kah-lah	He ate
hiya 'akalat	hee-yah ah-kah-lat	She ate
naHnu 'akalnaa	nah-noo ah-kal-nah	We ate
'antum 'akaltum	ahn-toom ah-kal-toom	You ate (MP)
'antunna 'akaltunna	ahn-too-nah ah-kal-too-nah	You ate (FP)
hum 'akaluu	hoom ah-kah-loo	They ate (MP)
hunna 'akalna	hoo-nah ah-kal-nah	They ate (FP)
antumaa 'akaltumaa	ahn-too-mah ah-kal-too-mah	You ate (dual/MP/FP)
humaa 'akalaa	hoo-mah ah-kah-lah	They ate (dual/MP)
humaa 'akalataa	hoo-mah ah-kah-lah-tah	They ate (dual/FP)

Because "to eat" is a regular verb, you conjugate it using the form **ya'kulu** in the **muDaari'**:

Form	Pronunciation	Translation
'anaa 'a'kulu	ah-nah ah-koo-loo	I am eating
'anta ta'kulu	ahn-tah tah-koo-loo	You are eating (MS)
'anti ta'kuliina	ahn-tee tah-koo-lee-nah	You are eating (FS)
huwa ya'kulu	hoo-wah yah-koo-loo	He is eating
hiya ta'kulu	hee-yah tah-koo-loo	She is eating
naHnu na'kulu	nah-noo nah-koo-loo	We are eating
'antum ta'kuluuna	ahn-toom tah-koo-loo-nah	You are eating (MP)
'antunna ta'kulna	ahn-too-nah tah-kool-nah	You are eating (FP)
hum ya'kuluuna	hoom yah-koo-loo-nah	They are eating (MP)
hunna ya'kulna	hoo-nah yah-kool-nah	They are eating (FP)
antumaa ta'kulaani	ahn-too-mah tah-koo-lah-nee	You are eating (dual/MP/FP)
humaa ya'kulaani	hoo-mah yah-koo-lah-nee	They are eating (dual/MP)
humaa ta'kulaani	hoo-mah tah-koo-lah-nee	They are eating (dual/FP)

Dinner

'ishaa' (*eeh-shah*; dinner) is an important meal in the course of the day. In most Arab countries, **'ishaa'** is usually eaten very late, around 9 p.m. or even 10 p.m. Because **ghidaa'** and **fuTuur** are the meals at which people eat a lot and because of the traditionally late hour of **'ishaa'**, most people in the Arab world have light meals during **'ishaa'**.

A typical **'ishaa'** usually consists of some sort of **samak** (*sah-mak*; fish), **dajaaj** (*dah-jaj*; chicken), or other kind of **laHm** (*lah-hem*; meat).

Enjoying a Meal at Home

Grabbing a quick bite on the go is often convenient if you have a busy schedule, but there's nothing like a home-cooked meal. This section covers the key terms to help you prepare and set the table for a **wajba ladhiida fii al-manzil** (*waj-bah lah-zee-zah fee al-man-zeel*; a delicious home-cooked meal)!

Here are some common items you might find in your **maTbakh** (*mat-bak*; kitchen):

- **farraan** (*fah-ran*; oven)
- **thallaaja** (*thah-la-jah*; refrigerator)
- **maghsala** (*mag-sah-lah*; sink)
- **khizaanaat** (*kee-zah-nat*; cupboards)
- **milH** (*mee-leh*; salt)
- **fulful** (*fool-fool*; pepper)
- **zayt az-zaytuun** (*zah-yet ah-zay-toon*; olive oil)

When you're done **Tibaakha** (*tee-bah-kah*; cooking) **daakhil** (*dah-keel*; inside) the **maTbakh**, you're ready to step into the **ghurfat al-'akel** (*goor-fat al-ah-kel*; dining room) and set up the **Ta'aam** on top of the **maa'ida** (*mah-ee-dah*; dining table). Here are some items you may find on your **maa'ida**:

- **'aS-SHaan** (*ass-han*; plates)
- **'aTbaaq** (*at-bak*; dishes)
- **ku'uus** (*koo-oos*; glasses)
- **'akwaab** (*ak-wab*; tumblers)
- **'awaan fiDDiyya** (*ah-wan fee-dee-yah*; silverware)
- **shawkaat** (*shaw-kat*; forks)

✔ **malaa'iq** (*mah-lah-eek;* spoons)

✔ **sakaakiin** (*sah-kah-keen;* knives)

✔ **manaadil** (*mah-nah-deel;* napkins)

Dining Out

Going to a nice **maT'am** (*mat-am;* restaurant) is one of my favorite things to do. I enjoy interacting with the **khaadim al-maT'am** (*kah-deem al-mat-am;* waiter) and the **khaadimat al-maT'am** (*kah-dee-maht al-mat-am;* waitress), and I like taking my time picking and choosing from the **qaa'imat aT-Ta'aam** (*kah-ee-mah ah-tah-am;* menu). In this section, you find out how to make your trip to the **maT'am** as enjoyable as possible, from interacting with the **khaadim al-maT'am** to displaying proper dining etiquette and choosing the best food from the **qaa'imat aT-Ta'aam.**

The dining experience in most restaurants in the Middle East, as well as in Middle Eastern restaurants all over the world, is truly an enchanting and magical experience. The décor is usually very ornate and sumptuous, with oriental patterns and vivid colors adorning the rooms. The wait staff usually wears traditional **jellaba** *(jeh-lah-bah),* which are long, flowing garments that are pleasing to the eye, and the food is very exotic, spicy, and delicious. When you go to a Middle Eastern restaurant, allow at least a couple of hours for the dining experience — don't be surprised if you end up savoring a five- or even seven-course meal!

Perusing the menu

As in other restaurants, the **qaa'imat aT-Ta'aam** in Middle Eastern restaurants is usually divided into three sections:

✔ **muqabbilaat** (*moo-kah-bee-lat;* appetizers)

✔ **Ta'aam ra'iisii** (*tah-am rah-ee-see;* main course/entrees)

✔ **taHliya** (*tah-lee-yah;* dessert)

Appetizers

In the **muqabbilaat** section of the menu, you find some **Ta'aam khafiif** (*tah-am kah-feef;* light food) to help build your appetite. Here are some common **muqabbilaat:**

✔ **rubyaan** (*roob-yan;* shrimp)

✔ **baadhinjaan** (*bah-zeen-jan;* eggplant)

- **kam'a** (*kam-ah;* truffles)
- **thuum muHammar** (*toom moo-hah-mar;* roasted garlic)
- **waraq 'ay-nab** (*wah-rak ay-nab;* stuffed vine leaves)
- **'adas** (*ah-das;* lentils)
- **Hasaa'** (*hah-sah;* soup)
- **Hariira** (*hah-ree-rah;* Middle Eastern soup)

Entrees

The **Ta'aam ra'iisii** consist of dishes featuring **dajaaj** (chicken), various other **laHam** (meat), and **samak** (fish). **samak** is usually a very popular dish because it's tasty, healthy, and light. Most restaurants have a pretty extensive selection of **samak,** including:

- **salmoon** (*sal-moon;* salmon)
- **al-qood** (*al-kood;* cod)
- **tuun** (*toon;* tuna)
- **al-'uTruuT** (*al-oot-root;* trout)
- **'isqoomrii** (*ees-koom-ree;* mackerel)
- **shabbooT** (*shah-boot;* carp)
- **moosaa** (*moo-sah;* sole)
- **qirsh** (*kee-resh;* shark)

Desserts

Like a lot of people, my favorite part of a restaurant menu is, of course, the **taHliya!** The **taHliya** is a great way to wrap up a nice **wajba.** I like the **taHliya** because there are a lot of **Halawiyyaat** (*hah-lah-wee-yat;* sweets) to choose from. Here are some popular **taHliya:**

- **ka'k** (*kahk;* cake)
- **ka'k ash-shuukuulaat** (*kahk ah-shoo-koo-lat;* chocolate cake)
- **Halwa al-jaliidiiya** (*hal-wah jah-lee-dee-yah;* ice cream)
- **'aTbaaq** (*at-bak;* pudding)
- **al-jubun** (*al-joo-boon;* cheese)

Beverages

In addition to **Ta'aam,** you may also notice a portion of the menu — or an entirely different menu — introducing different kinds of **mashruubaat** (*mash-roo-bat;* drinks). The following are some **mashruubaat** you may come across in the **qaa'imat aT-Ta'aam:**

✔ **maa'** (*mah;* water)

✔ **maa' ghaaziya** (*mah gah-zee-yah;* soda water)

✔ **'aSiir al-laymoon** (*ah-seer ah-lay-moon;* lemonade)

✔ **al-khamer** (*al-kah-mer;* alcohol)

✔ **biirra** (*bee-rah;* beer)

✔ **nabiidh** (*nah-beez;* wine)

✔ **nabiidh 'aHmar** (*nah-beez ah-mar;* red wine)

✔ **nabiidh 'abyaD** (*nah-beez ab-yad;* white wine)

Placing your order

After you peruse the **qaa'imat aT-Ta'aam,** you're ready to place your order with the **khaadim al-maT'am** (waiter) or **khaadimat al-maT'am** (waitress). **maT'am** staff are usually highly trained individuals who know the ins and outs of the **Ta'aam** that the **maT'am** serves, so don't be afraid of asking lots of **'as'ila** (*ass-ee-lah;* questions) about things on the **qaa'imat aT-Ta'aam** that sound good to you.

Talkin' the Talk

Sam and Atika go to Restaurant Atlas for a romantic dinner for two. They place their drink orders with their waitress.

Waitress:	**marHaba bikum 'ilaa maT'am 'aTlas. kayfa yumkin 'an 'usaa'idukum?** *mar-hah-bah bee-koom ee-lah mat-ham at-las. kay-fah yoom-keen an oo-sah-ee-doo-koom?* Welcome to Restaurant Atlas. How may I help you?
Sam:	**'ay mashruubaat 'indakum?** *ay mash-roo-bat een-dah-koom?* What do you have to drink?
Waitress:	**'indanaa maa', maa' ghaaziya wa 'aSiir al-laymoon.** *een-dah-nah mah, mah gah-zee-yah wah ah-seer ah-lay-moon.* We have water, soda water, and lemonade.
Sam:	**sa-nabda' bi maa' min faDlik.** *sah-nab-dah bee mah meen fad-leek.* We'll start with water please.

Waitress:	**turiidaani maa' Tabi'ii 'aw maa' 'aadii?** *too-ree-dah-nee mah tah-bee-eey aw mah ah-dee?* Do you want mineral (bottled) water or regular (tap) water?
Sam:	**maa' Tabi'ii.** *mah tah-bee-eey.* Mineral water.
Waitress:	**fawran. hal turiidaani khamer 'ayDan?** *faw-ran. hal too-ree-dah-nee kah-mer ay-zan?* Right away. And would you like any alcoholic drinks as well?
Atika:	**hal 'indakum nabiidh?** *hal een-dah-koom nah-beez?* Do you have any wine?
Waitress:	**na'am. 'indanaa nabiidh 'abyaD wa nabiidh 'aHmar.** *nah-am. een-dah-nah nah-beez ab-yad wah nah-beez ah-mar.* Yes. We have white wine and red wine.
Atika:	**sa-na'khudh nabiidh 'aHmar min faDlik.** *sah-nah-kooz nah-beez ah-mar meen fad-leek.* We'll have red wine please.
Waitress:	**mumtaaz. sa 'a'Tiikum waqt li-taqra'aani al-qaa'ima.** *moom-taz. sah ah-tee-koom wah-ket lee-tak-rah-ah-nee al-kah-ee-mah.* Excellent. I'll give you some time to read through the menu.
Sam:	**shukran.** *shook-ran.* Thank you.

After Sam and Atika peruse the menu, they're ready to place their order.

Waitress:	**hal 'antumaa musta'idaani li-'iTlaab aT-Ta'aam?** *hal an-too-mah moos-tah-ee-dah-nee lee-eet-lab ah-tah-am?* Are you ready to place your order?
Atika:	**na'am. li al-muqabbilaat sa-nabda' bi rubyaan wa kam'a.** *nah-am. lee al-moo-kah-bee-lat sah-nab-dah bee roob-yan wah kam-ah.* Yes. For appetizers, we'd like shrimp and truffles.

Waitress:	**'ikhtiyaar mumtaaz.** *eek-tee-yar moom-taz.* Excellent selection.
Sam:	**wa ba'da dhaalika sa-na'khudh salmoon.** *wah bah-dah zah-lee-kah sa-nah-kooz sal-moon.* And after that we'd like to have salmon.
Waitress:	**shay' 'aakhar?** *shay ah-kar?* Anything else?
Atika:	**nuriid ka'k ash-shuukuulaat li at-taHliya.** *noo-reed kahk ah-shoo-koo-lat lee ah-tah-lee-yah.* We'd like the chocolate cake for dessert.

Words to Know

maa' Tabii'ii	mah tah-bee-eey	mineral water
maa' 'aadii	mah ah-dee	tap water
musta'id	moos-tah-eed	ready
'ikhtiyaar	eek-tee-yar	selection

Finishing your meal and paying the bill

When you finish your meal, you're ready to leave the **maT'am**. But before you do, you need to take care of your **Hisaab** (*hee-sab;* bill). You may ask your waiter for the bill by saying **al-Hisaab min faDlik** (*al-hee-sab meen fad-leek;* the bill please). Another option is to ask the waiter or waitress **kam al-kaamil?** (*kam al-kah-meel;* What's the total?).

Like in the United States, tipping your waiter or waitress is customary in Arabic-speaking countries and Middle Eastern restaurants. The amount of the **baqsheeh** (*bak-sheesh;* tip) depends on the kind of service you received, but usually 15 to 20 percent is average.

Fun & Games

Identify the **fawaakih** (fruits) and **khudar** (vegetables) in the picture below:

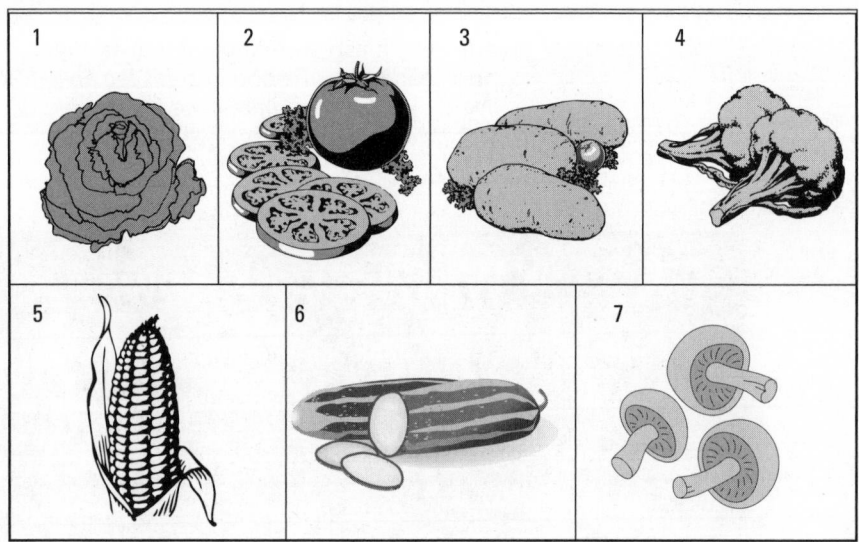

1.

2.

3.

4.

5.

6.

7.

Answers are in Appendix C.

Chapter 6

Going Shopping

. . . .

In This Chapter

▶ Browsing inside the store

▶ Comparing items and costs

▶ Identifying clothing sizes and colors

. . . .

Whether you're in a foreign country or at the local mall, shopping can be a lot of fun. Not only do you get to buy things to maintain your lifestyle, but you also can discover new items and buy things you hadn't even considered.

This chapter exposes you to the important words and terms that help you shop, whether you're in an Arabic-speaking country or simply interacting with an Arabic-speaking store owner. Discover how to choose the right dress size, how to choose the best item from an electronics store, and even how to shop for nice jewelry! You also find out how to interact with sales staff so that you're sure to find and purchase the item that you want.

Going to the Store

When you want to buy something, you head to the **dukkaan** (*doo-kan;* store). Depending on your shopping list, you can choose from different types of **dakaakiin** (*dah-kah-keen;* stores). If you want to buy some **khubz** (*koo-bez;* bread), then you want to head to the **makhbaza** (*mak-bah-zah;* bakery). If you're trying to find a particular **kitaab** (*kee-tab;* book), then your destination is the **maktaba** (*mak-tah-bah;* bookstore/library). To buy **malaabis** (*mah-lah-bees;* clothes), head to **dukkaan al-malaabis** (*doo-kan al-mah-lah-bees;* clothing store). And if you want to buy a **midyaa'** (*meed-yah;* radio) or **tilifizyoon** (*tee-lee-feez-yoon;* television), the **dukkaan al-iliktroniyaat** (*doo-kan al-ee-leek-troo-nee-yat;* electronics store) is your best bet.

Here are some additional specialty **dakaakiin** you may need to visit:

- **dukkaan al-Halawiyyaat** (*doo-kan al-hah-lah-wee-yat;* pastry shop)
- **dukkaan al-baqqaal** (*doo-kan al-bah-kal;* grocery store)
- **dukkaan as-samak** (*doo-kan ah-sah-mak;* fish store)
- **jawharii** (*jaw-hah-ree;* jeweler)

Not all **dakaakiin** sell only goods or products. Other types of **dakaakiin** provide services, such as haircuts and manicures. Here are some **dakaakiin** that are more service-oriented:

- **maktab as-siyaaHa** (*mak-tab ah-see-yah-hah;* travel agency)
- **Hallaaq** (*hah-lak;* barber/hairdresser)
- **dukkaan al-jamal** (*doo-kan al-jah-mal;* beauty parlor)

If you need to shop for a variety of goods, then your destination is the **dukkaan kabiir** (*doo-kan kah-beer;* department store/mall). At the **dukkaan kabiir,** you can find almost everything and anything you want. Or if you're not sure what to buy, going to the **dukkaan kabiir** is a great idea because you have so many choices that you're bound to find something that you need or want to purchase!

Browsing the merchandise

If you're at the **dukkaan** and aren't quite sure what to purchase, then browsing and checking out the different items is a good idea. You don't have to buy anything, and that's what can be so much fun about window shopping. Feel free to look through the **dukkaan naafida** (*doo-kan nah-fee-dah;* window) for any items that may attract your attention. While you're browsing, a **khaadim ad-dukkaan** (*kah-deem ah-doo-kan;* store clerk) (M) or a **khaadima ad-dukkaan** (*kah-dee-mah ah-doo-kan;* store clerk) (F) may ask:

- **hal yumkin 'an 'usaa'iduka?** (*hal yoom-keen an oo-sah-ee-doo-kah?;* May I help you?) (M)

  hal yumkin 'an 'usaa'iduki? (*hal yoom-keen an oo-sah-ee-doo-kee?;* May I help you?) (F)

- **hal turiidu shay' khaaS?** (*hal too-ree-doo shay kas?;* Are you looking for anything in particular?) (M)

  hal turiidiina shay' khaaS? (*hal too-ree-dee-nah shay kas?;* Are you looking for anything in particular?) (F)

If you need **musaa'ada** (*moo-sah-ah-dah;* help/assistance), simply respond by saying **na'am** (*nah-am;* yes). (For more on how to ask for and get **musaa'ada,** skip to the section "Asking for a Particular Item," later in this chapter.) Otherwise, if you want to continue browsing, **laa shukran** (*lah shook-ran;* no thank you) should do the trick.

Getting around the store

If you visit a **dukkaan kabiir,** you probably need some sort of **musaa'ada** because department stores can be very big and very confusing. If you want **tawjiihaat** (*taw-jee-hat;* directions), head to the **maktab al-'i'laamaat** (*mak-tab al-eeh-lah-mat;* information desk) to have your **'as'ila** (*ass-ee-lah;* questions) answered. Here are some common **'as'ila** you may ask:

- ✓ **hal yumkin 'an tusaa'idunii?** (*hal yoom-keen an too-sah-ee-doo-nee;* Is it possible for you to help me?)

- ✓ **'ayna aT-Tabiq al-'awwal?** (*ay-nah ah-tah-beek al-ah-wal;* Where is the first floor?)

- ✓ **'ayna al-miS'ad?** (*ay-nah al-mees-ad;* Where is the elevator?)

- ✓ **'ayna maHall al-malaabis?** (*ay-nah mah-hal al-mah-lah-bees;* Where is the section for clothes?)

- ✓ **fii 'ay Tabaq al-jawharii?** (*fee ay tah-baq al-jaw-hah-ree;* On which floor is the jeweler located?)

- ✓ **hal hunaaka makhbaza fii ad-dukaan al-kabiir?** (*hal hoo-nah-kah mak-bah-zah fee ah-doo-kan al-kah-beer;* Is there a bakery in the mall?)

Talkin' the Talk

Jessica is at the mall and is trying to figure out where the clothing section is located. She asks the attendant at the information desk for assistance.

Attendant:	**hal yumkin 'an 'usaa'iduki?** *hal yoom-keen an oo-sah-ee-doo-kee?* May I help you?
Jessica:	**na'am. 'anaa 'abhathu 'an maHall al-malaabis.** *nah-am. ah-nah ab-hah-thoo an mah-hall al-mah-lah-bees.* Yes. I'm searching for the clothing section.

Attendant: **hal tabHathiina 'an maHall al-malaabis li an-nisaa' 'aw li ar-rijaal?**
hal tab-hah-thee-nah an mah-hal al-mah-lah-bees lee ah-nee-sah aw lee ah-ree-jal?
Are you searching for the women's or men's clothing section?

Jessica: **'anaa 'abHath 'an maHall al-malaabis li an-nisaa' wa li ar-rijaal.**
ah-nah ab-hath an mah-hall al-mah-lah-bees lee ah-nee-sah wah lee ah-ree-jal.
I'm looking for both the men's and women's clothing sections.

Attendant: **maHall al-malaabis li an-nisaa' fii aT-Tabaq al-khaamis.**
mah-hall al-mah-lah-bees lee ah-nee-sah fee ah-tah-bak al-kah-mees.
The women's clothing section is located on the fifth floor.

Jessica: **hal hunaaka miS'ad 'ilaa aT-Tabaq al-khaamis?**
hal hoo-nah-kah mees-ad ee-lah ah-tah-bak al-kah-mees?
Is there an elevator to the fifth floor?

Attendant: **na'am, 'alaa yamiinuki.**
nah-am, ah-lah yah-mee-noo-kee.
Yes, to your right.

Jessica: **kwayyis, shukran.**
kwah-yees, shook-ran.
Okay, thank you.

Attendant: **wa maHall al-malaabis li ar-rijaal fii aT-Tabiq as-saabi'. hunaaka miS'ad 'alaa yaSaaruki 'ilaa haadha aT-Tabaq 'ayDan.**
wah mah-hall al-mah-lah-bees lee ah-ree-jal fee ah-tah-beek ah-sah-beeh. hoo-nah-kah mees-ad ah-lah yah-sah-roo-kee ee-lah hah-zah ah-tah-bak ay-dan.
And the men's clothing section is on the seventh floor. There's also an elevator to this floor on your left.

Jessica: **shay' 'aakhar. hal hunaaka jawharii daakhil ad-dukaan al-kabiir?**
shay ah-kar. hal hoo-nah-kah jaw-hah-ree dah-keel ah-doo-kan al-kah-beer?
One other thing. Is there a jeweler inside the mall?

Attendant: **laa laysa daakhil ad-dukkaan al-kabiir. wa laakin hunaaka jawharii khaarij min hunaa fii waSat al-madiina.**
lah lay-sah dah-keel ah-doo-kan al-kah-beer. wah lah-keen hoo-nah-kah jaw-hah-ree kah-reej meen hoo-nah fee wah-sat al-mah-dee-nah.
No, there isn't a jeweler inside the mall. But there is a jeweler outside the mall located in the city center.

Jessica: **shukran jaziilan.**
shook-ran jah-zee-lan.
Thank you very much.

Words to Know

yabHathu	yab-hah-thoo	searching
maHall	mah-hal	section
nisaa'	nee-sah	women
rijaal	ree-jal	men
banaat	bah-nat	girls
'awlaad	aw-lad	boys
Tabiq	tah-beek	floor
miS'ad	mees-ad	elevator
yamiin	yah-meen	right
yaSaar	yah-sar	left
yamiinuki	yah-mee-noo-kee	your right (F)
yamiinuka	yah-mee-noo-kah	your right (M)
yaSaaruki	yah-sah-roo-kee	your left (F)
yaSaaruka	yah-sah-roo-kah	your left (M)
daakhil	dah-keel	inside
khaarij	kah-reej	outside

Getting to know the verb "to search"

Shopping usually involves searching for particular items. In order to help with your **baHth** (*bah-heth;* search), you should be familiar with the verbs **baHatha** (*bah-hah-thah;* searched) and **yabHathu** (*yab-hah-thoo;* searching). Luckily, **baHatha** is a regular verb, meaning that it has three consonants and is conjugated in the **maaDii** (*mah-dee;* past) tense and **muDaari'** (*moo-dah-reeh;* present) tense using the same patterns of prefixes and suffixes as most other regular verbs.

Here's the verb **baHatha** in the **maaDii** form:

Form	Pronunciation	Translation
'anaa baHathtu	ah-nah bah-hath-too	I searched
'anta baHathta	ahn-tah bah-hath-tah	You searched (MS)
'anti baHathtii	ahn-tee bah-hath-tee	You searched (FS)
huwa baHatha	hoo-wah bah-hah-thah	He searched
hiya baHathat	hee-yah bah-hah-that	She searched
naHnu baHathnaa	nah-noo bah-hath-nah	We searched
'antum baHathtum	ahn-toom bah-hath-toom	You searched (MP)
'antunna baHathtunna	ahn-too-nah bah-hath-too-nah	You searched (FP)
hum baHathuu	hoom bah-hah-thoo	They searched (MP)
hunna baHathna	hoo-nah bah-hath-nah	They searched (FP)
antumaa baHathtumaa	ahn-too-mah bah-hath-too-mah	You searched (dual/MP/FP)
humaa baHathaa	hoo-mah bah-hath-ah	They searched (dual/MP)
humaa baHathataa	hoo-mah bah-hah-thah-tah	They searched (dual/FP)

In the **muDaari'** form, use the form **yabHathu** (searching):

Form	Pronunciation	Translation
'anaa 'abHathu	ah-nah ab-hah-thoo	I am searching
'anta tabHathu	ahn-tah tab-hah-thoo	You are searching (MS)
'anti tabHathiina	ahn-tee tab-hah-thee-nah	You are searching (FS)
huwa yabHathu	hoo-wah yab-hah-thoo	He is searching
hiya tabHathu	hee-yah tab-hah-thoo	She is searching

Form	Pronunciation	Translation
naHnu nabHathu	nah-noo nab-hah-thoo	We are searching
'antum tabHathuuna	ahn-toom tab-hah-thoo-nah	You are searching (MP)
'antunna tabHathna	ahn-too-nah tab-hath-nah	You are searching (FP)
hum yabHathuuna	hoom yab-hah-thoo-nah	They are searching (MP)
hunna yabHathna	hoo-nah yab-hath-nah	They are searching (FP)
antumaa tabHathaani	ahn-too-mah tab-hah-thah-nee	You are searching (dual/MP/FP)
humaa yabHathaani	hoo-mah yab-hah-thah-nee	They are searching (dual/MP)
humaa tabHathaani	hoo-mah tab-hah-thah-nee	They are searching (dual/FP)

Asking for a Particular Item

Oftentimes, you head to the **dukkaan** not to window shop or browse around the store but because you have a specific item in mind that you want to purchase. When you want to direct a **khaadim ad-dukkaan** to a particular item, you're likely to need a demonstrative word, such as "that one" or "this" or "those over there." *Demonstratives* are the little words we use to specify particular items. Arabic has a number of different demonstratives, depending on the number of items (singular or plural) and gender (in case of human nouns), as well as state (present or absent). Table 6-1 presents the common demonstratives in Arabic:

Table 6-1	Arabic Demonstratives	
Arabic	*Pronunciation*	*Translation*
haadhaa	hah-zah	this (MS)
haadhihi	hah-zee-hee	this (FS)
dhaalika	zah-lee-kah	that (MS)
tilka	teel-kah	that (FS)
haa'ulaa'ii	hah-oo-lah-ee	these (gender neutral)
'ulaa'ika	oo-lah-ee-kah	those (gender neutral)

Notice that the singular demonstratives (**haadhaa, haadhihi, dhaalika,** and **tilka**) are all gender-defined, meaning that you use a specific demonstrative corresponding to whether the object being referred to is masculine or feminine. On the other hand, the plural demonstratives, **haa'ulaa'ii** and **'ulaa'ika,** are gender-neutral, meaning that the gender of the object being pointed to doesn't matter.

In a sentence, you always place the demonstrative word *before* the object being pointed to, which is often a noun. In addition, the noun must be defined using the definite prefix pronoun **al-.** Here are some examples to illustrate the use of the definite prefix pronoun:

- ✔ **haadhaa al-walad** (*hah-zah al-wah-lad;* this boy)

- ✔ **haadhihi al-bint** (*hah-zee-hee al-bee-net;* this girl)

- ✔ **dhaalika ar-rajul** (*zah-lee-kah ah-rah-jool;* that man)

- ✔ **tilka al-mar'a** (*teel-kah al-mar-ah;* that woman)

- ✔ **haa'ulaa'ii al-banaat** (*hah-oo-lah-ee al-bah-nat;* these girls)

- ✔ **'ulaa'ika an-nisaa'** (*oo-lah-ee-kah ah-nee-sah;* those women)

It's important to not only follow the specific order of the demonstrative phrase (demonstrative word followed by the noun) but also to make sure the noun is defined. If the noun isn't defined with the definite article prefix **al-,** the meaning of the demonstrative phrase changes dramatically. Arabic has no verb "to be" in the present tense, but because every language requires "is/are" sentences to function appropriately, "is/are" sentences are created in Arabic by manipulating these little definite articles. If you include a demonstrative followed by an undefined noun, you create a demonstrative "is/are" sentence. Using the examples from the earlier list, look at what happens to the demonstrative phrase when the definite article isn't included:

- ✔ **haadhaa walad** (*hah-zah wah-lad;* this is a boy)

- ✔ **haadhihi bint** (*hah-zee-hee bee-net;* this is a girl)

- ✔ **dhaalika rajul** (*zah-lee-kah rah-jool;* that is a man)

- ✔ **tilka mar'a** (*teel-kah mar-ah;* that is a woman)

- ✔ **haa'ulaa'ii banaat** (*hah-oo-lah-ee bah-nat;* these are girls)

- ✔ **'ulaa'ika nisaa'** (*oo-lah-ee-kah nee-sah;* those are women)

As you can see by comparing these two lists, one small prefix can radically alter the meaning of a sentence.

Talkin' the Talk

Omar is looking to buy a black leather jacket, so he asks the salesperson for this particular item.

Omar: **hal 'indakum jakiiTaat?**
         hal een-dah-koom jah-kee-tat?
         Do you have jackets?

Salesperson: **na'am. 'indanaa 'anwaa' kathiira min aj-jakiiTaat. 'an 'ay naw' tabHathu?**
         nah-am. een-dah-nah an-wah kah-thee-rah meen ah-jah-kee-tat. an ay nah-weh tab-hah-thoo?
         Yes. We have many different kinds of jackets. Which kind are you looking for?

Omar: **'uriidu jakiiTa bi aj-jald.**
         oo-ree-doo jah-kee-tah bee ah-jah-led.
         I want a leather jacket.

Salesperson: **Tayyib. 'itba'nii min faDlik.**
         tah-yeeb. eet-bah-nee meen fad-leek.
         Okay. Follow me please.

Omar follows the salesperson to the jacket section.

Salesperson: **'ulaa'ika kul aj-jakiiTaat 'indanaa.**
         oo-lah-ee-kah kool ah-jah-kee-tat een-dah-nah.
         Those are all the jackets we have.

Omar: **'uHibbu haa'ulaa'ii aj-jakiiTaat.**
         oo-hee-boo hah-oo-lah-ee ah-jah-kee-tat.
         I like these jackets.

Salesperson: **'anaa muwaafiq. 'innahaa jamiila jiddan.**
         ah-nah moo-wah-feek. ee-nah-hah jah-mee-lah jee-dan.
         I agree. They are very beautiful.

Omar: **'uriidu 'an 'ujarrib haadhihi.**
         oo-ree-doo an oo-jah-reeb hah-zee-hee.
         I would like to try on this one.

Salesperson: **fawran. hal turiidu lawn khaaS?**
faw-ran. hal too-ree-doo lah-wen kass?
Right away. Are you looking for any particular color?

Omar: **'uriidu dhaalika al-lawn.**
oo-ree-doo zah-lee-kah ah-lah-wen.
I want that color.

Words to Know

jakiiTa	jah-kee-tah	jacket
naw'	nah-weh	type/kind
jald	jah-led	leather
yatba'u	yat-bah-oo	following
'itba'	eet-bah	follow (imperative)
'itba'nii	eet-bah-nee	follow me
muwaafiq	moo-wah-feek	agree
jamiil	jah-meel	beautiful (M)
jamiila	jah-mee-lah	beautiful (F)
'ujarrib	oo-jah-reeb	to try (I/me)
lawn	lah-wen	color
khaaS	kass	particular (M)
khaaSSa	kah-sah	particular (F)
fawran	faw-ran	right away

Comparing Merchandise

Have you ever been shopping and found yourself debating between two or more comparable items? Perhaps you have a general idea of what you want to buy — a television, for instance — but you aren't sure what year, make, or model you want. In these instances, being able to compare merchandise is important. In this section, you discover how to evaluate comparable (and incomparable) items based on a variety of important criteria, such as price, quality, and durability.

In order to be able to compare different items, it's necessary to have an understanding of degrees of adjectives and superlatives. In English, degrees of adjectives have straightforward applicability. For example, in order to say that something is bigger than another thing, you simply add the suffix **-er** to the adjective; hence "big" becomes "bigger." Furthermore, when you're comparing two or more items, you use comparatives, meaning you use both the degree of adjectives followed by the preposition "than." For instance, "the truck is bigger *than* the car." To say that something is the biggest, you only need to add the suffix **-est** to the adjective; so "big" becomes "biggest," as in "it's the biggest car." This form is called a *superlative.*

Fortunately, the structures of degrees of adjectives, comparatives, and superlatives in Arabic are fairly similar to those in English.

Comparing two or more items

Adjectives are the linguistic backbone that allow for comparisons between different items, products, or goods. Table 6-2 lists some of the most common adjectives followed by their comparative forms.

Table 6-2		Arabic Adjectives and Their Comparative Forms			
Adjective	*Pronunciation*	*Translation*	*Comparative*	*Pronunciation*	*Translation*
kabiir	kah-beer	big	'akbar	ak-bar	bigger
Saghiir	sah-geer	small	'aSghar	ass-gar	smaller
Hasan	hah-san	good	'aHsan	ah-san	better
suu'	sooh	bad	'aswa'	as-wah	worse
rakhiiS	rah-kees	cheap	'arkhas	ar-kas	cheaper
ghalii	gah-lee	expensive	'aghlaa	ag-lah	more expensive

(continued)

Table 6-2 (continued)

Adjective	Pronunciation	Translation	Comparative	Pronunciation	Translation
sarii'	sah-reeh	fast	'asra'	ass-rah	faster
baTii'	bah-teeh	slow	'abTa	ab-tah	slower
thaqiil	tah-keel	heavy	'athqal	at-kal	heavier
khafiif	kah-feef	light	'akhfaa	ak-fah	lighter
jamiil	jah-meel	pretty	'ajmal	aj-mal	prettier
bashii'	bah-sheeh	ugly	'absha'	ab-shah	uglier
ba'iid	bah-eed	far	'ab'ad	ab-ad	farther
qariib	kah-reeb	near	'aqrab	ak-rab	nearer
jadiid	jah-deed	new	'ajadd	ah-jad	newer
qadiim	kah-deem	old	'aqdam	ak-dam	older

Place these adjectives in their appropriate context in the phrase or sentence —
using these adjectives independently changes their meanings. Similar to the
English language structure, the comparative form of adjectives always follows
this pattern:

> noun + adjective comparative form + preposition **min** (*meen;* than) +
> second adjective

It's essential that you include the preposition **min** right after every comparative adjective. In addition, all nouns being compared need to be defined by
attaching to them the definite article prefix **al-**.

Here are some common examples of comparative sentences using the adjective forms:

- ✔ **al-bint 'akbar min al-walad.** (*al-bee-net ak-bar meen al-wah-lad;* The girl
  is bigger than the boy.)

- ✔ **at-tilifizyuun 'aghlaa min al-midyaa'.** (*ah-tee-lee-fee-zee-yoon ag-lah
  meen al-meed-yah;* The television is more expensive than the radio.)

- ✔ **as-sayyaara 'asra' min as-shaaHina.** (*ah-sah-yah-rah as-rah meen ah-shah-
  hee-nah;* The car is faster than the bus.)

- ✔ **aj-jakiiTa 'arkhas min al-qamiis.** (*ah-jah-kee-tah ar-kas meen al-kah-mees;*
  The jacket is cheaper than the shirt.)

When forming these types of sentences, you may add demonstratives to be even more specific. Here are examples of comparative sentences used in conjunction with demonstratives:

- **haadhihi al-bint 'akbar min dhaalika al-walad.** (*hah-zee-hee al-bee-net ak-bar meen zah-lee-kah al-wah-lad;* This girl is bigger than that boy.)

- **haa'ulaa'ii as-sayyaaraat 'asra' min 'ulaa'ika as-shaahinaat.** (*hah-oo-lah-ee ah-sah-yah-rat as-rah meen oo-lah-ee-kah ah-shah-hee-nat;* These cars are faster than those buses.)

- **tilka al-'imra'a 'ajmal min dhaalika ar-rajul.** (*teel-kah al-eem-rah-ah aj-mal meen zah-lee-kah ah-rah-jool;* That woman is prettier than that man.)

- **haadhaa al-walad 'akbar min 'ulaa'ika al-banaat.** (*hah-zah al-wah-lad ak-bar meen oo-lah-ee-kah al-bah-nat;* This boy is bigger than those girls.)

Notice in the examples that the adjective comparative form remains constant whether the nouns being compared are a combination of singular/singular, singular/plural, or plural/plural. In other words, the adjective comparatives are gender-neutral: They remain the same regardless of both gender and number.

Picking out the best item

A *superlative* describes something that is of the highest order, degree, or quality. Some common superlatives in English are "best," "brightest," "fastest," "cleanest," "cheapest," and so on. Superlatives in Arabic are actually very straightforward and shouldn't be hard for you to understand if you have a good grasp of comparatives (see the preceding section).

Basically, a superlative in Arabic is nothing more than the comparative form of the adjective! The only difference is that comparatives include the preposition **min** (than) and superlatives don't include any preposition. For example, to tell someone, "This is the biggest house," you say **haadhaa 'akbar manzil** (*hah-zah ak-bar man-zeel*).

The biggest differences between superlatives and comparatives are:

- The superlative adjective always comes before the noun.
- When expressing a superlative, the noun is always undefined.

Here are some common examples of superlative sentences:

- **haadhihi 'ajmal bint.** (*hah-zee-hee aj-mal bee-net;* This is the prettiest girl.)

- **dhaalika 'ab'ad dukkaan.** (*zah-lee-kah ab-ad doo-kan;* That is the farthest store.)

If you switch the order of the words to demonstrative + noun + superlative, be sure to define the noun. That's the only other way you can construct a superlative sentence. For example:

- **haadhihi al-bint 'ajmal.** (*hah-zee-hee al-bee-net aj-mal;* This girl is the prettiest.)

- **dhaalika ad-dukaan 'ab'ad.** (*zah-lee-kah ah-doo-kan ab-ad;* That store is the farthest.)

Talkin' the Talk

Adam stops by an electronics store to buy a camera. The salesman helps him pick the best one.

Salesman: **SabaaH an-nuur wa marHaba 'ilaa ad-dukkaan al-iliktroniyaat.**
Sah-bah ah-noor wah mar-hah-bah ee-lah ah-doo-kan al-ee-leek-troo-nee-yat.
Good morning and welcome to the electronics store.

Adam: **shukran. 'anaa 'abHathu 'an muSawwira.**
shook-ran. ah-nah ab-hah-thoo an moo-sah-wee-rah.
Thank you. I am looking for a camera.

Salesman: **hal tabHathu 'an naw' mu'ayyin?**
hal tab-hah-thoo an nah-weh moo-ah-yeen?
Are you looking for a particular model?

Adam: **'abHath 'an 'aHsan muSawwira.**
ab-hath an ah-san moo-sah-wee-rah.
I'm looking for the best camera.

Salesman: **Tayyib. 'indanaa haadhaa an-naw' bi alwaan mutaghayyira.**
Tah-yeeb. een-dah-nah hah-zah ah-nah-weh bee al-wan moo-tah-gah-yee-rah.
Okay. We have this model with different colors.

Adam: **hal 'indakum naw' 'aakhar?**
hal een-dah-koom nah-weh ah-kar?
Do you have another model?

Salesman: **na'am. haadhaa an-naw' ath-thaanii mashhuur ma'a az-zabaa'in.**
nah-am. hah-zah ah-nah-weh ah-thah-nee mash-hoor mah-ah ah-zah-bah-een.
Yes. This second model is popular with customers.

Adam: **'ay naw' 'aHsan?**
ay nah-weh ah-san?
Which is the best model?

Salesman: **an-naw' ath-thaanii 'aHsan min an-naw' al-awwal.**
ah-nah-weh ah-thah-nee ah-san meen ah-nah-weh al-ah-wal.
The second model is better than the first model.

Adam: **'uriidu 'an 'ashtarii an-naw' ath-thaanii min faDlik.**
oo-ree-doo an ash-tah-ree ah-nah-weh ah-thah-nee meen fad-leek.
I'd like to buy the second model please.

Salesman: **'ikhtiyaar mumtaaz!**
eek-tee-yar moom-taz!
Excellent selection!

Words to Know

muSawwira	moo-sah-wee-rah	camera
muSawwir	moo-sah-weer	photographer
mu'ayyin	moo-ah-yeen	particular (M)
mu'ayyina	moo-ah-yee-nah	particular (F)
mutaghayyir	moo-tah-gah-yeer	different (M)
mutaghayyira	moo-tah-gah-yee-rah	different (F)
zabaa'in	zah-bah-een	customers
'ikhtiyaar	eek-tee-yar	selection (M)
'ikthiyaara	eek-tee-yah-rah	selection (F)

More Than a Few Words About Buying and Selling

Perhaps the two most important verbs relating to shopping are **yashtarii** (*yash-tah-ree;* to buy) and **yabii'u** (*yah-bee-ooh;* to sell). Unlike other verbs in Arabic, these two critical verbs are irregular, which means they don't follow a particular pattern. Because these verbs are widely used and have their own pattern, you should be familiar with how to conjugate them.

Use the form **baa'a** (*bah-ah;* sold) to conjugate **yabii'u** in the **maaDii** (past):

Form	Pronunciation	Translation
'anaa bi'tu	ah-nah beeh-too	I sold
'anta bi'ta	ahn-tah beeh-tah	You sold (MS)
'anti bi'tii	ahn-tee beeh-tee	You sold (FS)
huwa baa'a	hoo-wah bah-hah	He sold
hiya baa'at	hee-yah bah-at	She sold
naHnu bi'naa	nah-noo beeh-nah	We sold
'antum bi'tum	ahn-toom beeh-toom	You sold (MP)
'antunna bi'tunna	ahn-too-nah beeh-too-nah	You sold (FP)
hum baa'uu	hoom bah-ooh	They sold (MP)
hunna bi'na	hoo-nah beeh-nah	They sold (FP)
antumaa bi'tumaa	ahn-too-mah beeh-too-mah	You sold (dual/MP/FP)
humaa baa'aa	hoo-mah bah-ah	They sold (dual/MP)
humaa baa'ataa	hoo-mah bah-ah-tah	They sold (dual/FP)

The form **yabii'u** (*yah-bee-oo;* selling) is used to conjugate **yabii'u** in the **muDaari'** (present):

Form	Pronunciation	Translation
'anaa 'abii'u	ah-nah ah-bee-oo	I am selling
'anta tabii'u	ahn-tah tah-bee-oo	You are selling (MS)
'anti tabii'iina	ahn-tee tah-bee-ee-nah	You are selling (FS)
huwa yabii'u	hoo-wah yah-bee-oo	He is selling
hiya tabii'u	hee-yah tah-bee-oo	She is selling

Form	Pronunciation	Translation
naHnu nabii'u	nah-noo nah-bee-oo	We are selling
'antum tabii'uuna	ahn-toom tah-bee-oo-nah	You are selling (MP)
'antunna tabi'na	ahn-too-nah tah-beeh-nah	You are selling (FP)
hum yabii'uuna	hoom yah-bee-oo-nah	They are selling (MP)
hunna yabi'na	hoo-nah yah-beeh-nah	They are selling (FP)
antumaa tabii'aani	ahn-too-mah tah-bee-ah-nee	You are selling (dual/MP/FP)
humaa yabii'aani	hoo-mah yah-bee-ah-nee	They are selling (dual/MP)
humaa tabii'aani	hoo-mah tah-bee-ah-nee	They are selling (dual/FP)

The verb form for "bought" in the **maaDii** is **'ishtaraa** (*eesh-tah-rah;* bought). Like **baa'a, 'ishtaraa** is an irregular verb:

Form	Pronunciation	Translation
'anaa 'ishtaraytu	ah-nah eesh-tah-ray-too	I bought
'anta 'ishtarayta	ahn-tah eesh-tah-ray-tah	You bought (MS)
'anti 'ishtarayti	ahn-tee eesh-tah-ray-tee	You bought (FS)
huwa 'ishtaraa	hoo-wah eesh-tah-rah	He bought
hiya 'ishtarat	hee-yah eesh-tah-rat	She bought
naHnu 'ishtaraynaa	nah-noo eesh-tah-ray-nah	We bought
'antum 'ishtaraytum	ahn-toom eesh-tah-ray-toom	You bought (MP)
'antunna 'ishtaraytunna	ahn-too-nah eesh-tah-ray-too-nah	You bought (FP)
hum 'ishtaraw	hoom eesh-tah-raw	They bought (MP)
hunna 'ishtarayna	hoo-nah eesh-tah-ray-nah	They bought (FP)
antumaa 'ishtaraytumaa	ahn-too-mah eesh-tah-ray-too-mah	You bought (dual/MP/FP)
humaa 'ishtarayaa	hoo-mah eesh-tah-rah-yah	They bought (dual/MP)
humaa 'ishtarayataa	hoo-mah eesh-tah-rah-yah-tah	They bought (dual/FP)

In the **muDaari'** form, the verb "buying" is conjugated using the form **yashtarii** (*yash-tah-ree*):

Form	Pronunciation	Translation
'anaa 'ashtarii	ah-nah ash-tah-ree	I am buying
'anta tashtarii	ahn-tah tash-tah-ree	You are buying (MS)
'anti tashtariina	ahn-tee tash-tah-ree-nah	You are buying (FS)
huwa yashtarii	hoo-wah yash-tah-ree	He is buying
hiya tashtarii	hee-yah tash-tah-ree	She is buying
naHnu nashtarii	nah-noo nash-tah-ree	We are buying
'antum tashtaruuna	ahn-toom tash-tah-roo-nah	You are buying (MP)
'antunna tashtariina	ahn-too-nah tash-tah-ree-nah	You are buying (FP)
hum yashtaruuna	hoom yash-tah-roo-nah	They are buying (MP)
hunna yashtariina	hoo-nah yash-tah-ree-nah	They are buying (FP)
antumaa tashta-riyaani	ahn-too-mah tash-tah-ree-ya-nee	You are buying (dual/MP/FP)
humaa yashtariyaani	hoo-mah yash-tah-ree-yah-nee	They are buying (dual/MP)
humaa tashtariyaani	hoo-mah tash-tah-ree-yah-nee	They are buying (dual/FP)

Shopping for Clothes

For many people, one of the most essential items to shop for is **malaabis** (*mah-lah-bees;* clothes). Whether you're in a foreign country or shopping at the local mall, chances are that **malaabis** make it on your shopping list. Table 6-3 lists some basic articles of clothing and accessories you should know.

Table 6-3	Clothing and Accessories	
Arabic	**Pronunciation**	**Translation**
sirwaal	seer-wal	pants (S)
saraawiil	sah-rah-weel	pants (P)
qamiis	kah-mees	shirt
'aqmisa	ak-mee-sah	shirts
mi'Taf	meeh-taf	coat

Arabic	Pronunciation	Translation
ma'aaTif	mah-ah-teef	coats
kaswa	kass-wah	dress
'aksiwa	ak-see-wah	dresses
jallaaba	jah-lah-bah	Arab dress
jallaabaat	jah-lah-bat	Arab dresses
Hizaam	hee-zam	belt
'aHzima	ah-zee-mah	belts
qubba'a	koo-bah-ah	hat
qubba'aat	koo-bah-at	hats
jawrab	jaw-rab	sock
jawaarib	jah-wah-reeb	socks
Hidaa'	hee-dah	shoe
'aHdiya	ah-dee-yah	shoes
khaatim	kah-teem	ring
saa'a	sah-ah	watch

An important consideration when you're out shopping for **malaabis** is **al-Hajem** (*al-hah-jem;* size). The four standard clothes sizes are:

- ✔ **Saghiir** (*sah-geer;* small) (American size [Men's]: 34–36; American size [Women's]: 6–8)

- ✔ **waSat** (*wah-sat;* medium) (American size [Men's]: 38–40; American size [Women's]: 10–12)

- ✔ **kabiir** (*kah-beer;* large) (American size [Men's]: 42–44; American size [Women's]: 14–16)

- ✔ **zaa'id kabiir** (*zah-eed kah-beer;* extra large) (American size [Men's]: 46 and above; American size [Women's]: 18–20)

Another important consideration in clothes shopping is the **lawn** (*lah-wen;* color). Because **'alwaan** (*al-wan;* colors) are adjectives that describe nouns, a **lawn** always must agree with the noun in terms of gender. If you're describing a feminine noun, use the feminine form of the **lawn.** When describing masculine nouns, use the masculine forms. How do you know whether a noun is feminine or masculine? In about 80 percent of the cases, feminine nouns end with a **fatHa,** or the "ah" sound. For the rest, simply look up the word in the **qaamuus** (*kah-moos;* dictionary) to determine its gender. The masculine and feminine forms of some common colors appear in Table 6-4.

Table 6-4		Basic Colors in Arabic		
Color (M)	*Pronunciation*	*Color (F)*	*Pronunciation*	*Translation*
'abyaD	ab-yad	bayDaa'	bay-dah	white
'aswad	ass-wad	sawdaa'	saw-dah	black
'aHmar	ah-mar	Hamraa'	ham-rah	red
'akhDar	ak-dar	khaDraa'	kad-rah	green
'azraq	az-rak	zarqaa'	zar-kah	blue
'aSfar	ass-far	Safraa'	saf-rah	yellow

Fun & Games

Match the following items with their Arabic words.

A. 'aHdiya

B. khaatim

C. kaswa

D. muSawwira

E. saa'a

The answers are in Appendix C.

Chapter 7

Around Town

In This Chapter

▶ Keeping track of the time

▶ Experiencing the culture of a museum

▶ Taking in a movie

▶ Touring religious sites

*P*art of the fun of mastering a new language is putting your growing language skills to good use; one of the best ways to do that is by exploring a **madiina** (*mah-dee-nah;* city). Whether you're visiting a city in your home country or traveling in a Middle Eastern city, this chapter introduces you to key words, phrases, and concepts to help you navigate any **madiina** — from entertainment spots to cultural venues — like a native Arabic speaker!

Telling Time in Arabic

When you're exploring a **madiina,** you're guaranteed to have a difficult time catching buses to get around or buying tickets for specific events if you can't tell or ask the time. And telling **waqt** (*wah-ket;* time) in Arabic is an entirely different proposition than telling time in English. In fact, you have to accept a fundamental difference right off the bat: Arabic doesn't use an a.m./p.m. convention to denote the time of day, nor does it use the 24-hour military clock (according to which, for example, 10:00 p.m. is written as 22:00). So how do you know which part of the day it is if you can't use the 24-hour system *or* the a.m./p.m. convention? It's actually very simple: You specify the time of day! So you say, for example, "It's 10:00 *in the morning,*" or "It's 10:00 *at night.*" Easy enough, don't you think? (For more on this issue, see the section "Specifying the time of day" later in this chapter.)

If you want to ask someone for the time, you ask the following question: **kam as-saa'a?** (*kam ah-sah-ah;* What time is it?). If someone asks you this question, the appropriate response is **as-saa'a** followed by the ordinal of the hour. So you would say, for instance, "It's the second hour" as opposed to saying "It's 2:00." Because **as-saa'a** is a feminine noun, you use the feminine form of the ordinal numbers, which are listed in Table 7-1. (See Chapter 4 for more on numbers.)

Table 7-1	Arabic Ordinals for Telling Time	
Arabic	Pronunciation	Translation
waaHida	wah-hee-dah	first (F)
thaaniya	thah-nee-yah	second (F)
thaalitha	thah-lee-thah	third (F)
raabi'a	rah-bee-ah	fourth (F)
khaamisa	khah-mee-sah	fifth (F)
saadisa	sah-dee-sah	sixth (F)
saabi'a	sah-bee-ah	seventh (F)
thaamina	thah-mee-nah	eighth (F)
taasi'a	tah-see-ah	ninth (F)
'aashira	ah-shee-rah	tenth (F)
Haadiya 'ashra	hah-dee-yah ah-shrah	eleventh (F)
thaaniya 'ashra	thah-nee-yah ah-shrah	twelfth (F)

You need to use the definite prefix article **al-** with the ordinals because you're referring to a specific hour and not just any hour.

The following are some additional key words related to telling time in Arabic:

- ✔ **saa'a** (*sah-ah;* hour)
- ✔ **daqiiqa** (*da-kee-kah;* minute)
- ✔ **thaaniya** (*thah-nee-yah;* second)
- ✔ **ba'da** (*bah-dah;* after)
- ✔ **qabla** (*kab-lah;* before)
- ✔ **al-yawm** (*al-yah-oum;* today)
- ✔ **al-ghad** (*al-gah-d;* tomorrow)
- ✔ **al-baariHa** (*al-bah-ree-hah;* yesterday)
- ✔ **ba'da al-ghad** (*bah-dah al-gah-d;* the day after tomorrow)
- ✔ **qabla al-baariHa** (*kab-lah al-bah-ree-hah;* the day before yesterday)

Specifying the time of day

Because Arabic uses neither the a.m./p.m. system nor the 24-hour military clock, when giving the time, you need to specify the time of day by actually saying what part of the day it is.

Here are the different times of day you're likely to use:

- ✔ **aS-SabaaH** (*ah-sah-bah;* morning, or sunrise to 11:59 a.m.)
- ✔ **aDH-DHuhr** (*ah-zoo-her;* noon, or 12:00 p.m.)
- ✔ **ba'da aDH-DHuhr** (*bah-dah ah-zoo-her;* afternoon, or 12:01 p.m. to 4:00 p.m.)
- ✔ **al-'asr** (*al-ah-ser;* late afternoon, or 4:01 p.m. to sunset)
- ✔ **al-masaa'** (*al-mah-sah;* evening, or sunset to two hours after sunset)
- ✔ **al-layl** (*ah-lah-yel;* night, or sunset to two hours to sunrise)

For example, if the time is 2:00 p.m., then you attach **ba'da aDH-DHuhr** to the proper ordinal. If sunset is at 6:00 p.m. and you want to say the time's 7:00 p.m., then you use **al-masaa'** and the ordinal because **al-masaa'** applies to the two-hour period right after sunset; if sunset is at 6:00 p.m. and you want to say the time's 9:00 p.m., then you use **al-layl** and the ordinal because 9:00 p.m. falls outside the scope of the evening convention (see the preceding list).

The convention used to specify the part of the day is fairly straightforward:

as-saa'a + ordinal number + **fii** (*fee;* in) + part of the day

So when someone asks you **kam as-saa'a,** your literal reply in Arabic is "It's the ninth hour in the morning," for instance. The following are some examples to better illustrate responses to the question **kam as-saa'?**:

- ✔ **as-saa'a al-waaHida fii ba'da aDH-DHuhr.** (*ah-sah-ah al-wah-hee-dah fee bah-dah ah-zoo-her;* It's 1:00 in the afternoon.)
- ✔ **as-saa'a al-khaamisa fii al-'asr.** (*ah-sah-ah al-kah-mee-sah fee al-ah-ser;* It's 5:00 in the late afternoon.)
- ✔ **as-saa'a al-Haadiya 'ashra fii aS-SabaaH.** (*ah-sah-ah al-hah-dee-yah ah-shrah fee ah-sah-bah;* It's 11:00 in the morning.)
- ✔ **as-saa'a at-taasi'a fii al-layl.** (*ah-sah-ah ah-tah-see-ah fee ah-lah-yel;* It's 9:00 in [at] night.)
- ✔ **as-saa'a as-saabi'a fii al-masaa'.** (*ah-sah-ah ah-sah-bee-ah fee al-mah-sah;* It's 7:00 in the evening.)

Specifying minutes

When telling time in Arabic, you can specify minutes in two different ways: noting the fractions of the hour, such as a half, a quarter, and a third, or actually spelling out the minutes. Because these methods have different conventions, this section examines each method separately.

Using fractions of the hour

When using the fraction method of telling minutes, use the following structure:

>   **as-saa'a** + ordinal number + **wa** (*wah;* and) + fraction

So what you're in fact saying is "It's the second hour and a half," for example. In English transliteration, that's the equivalent of "It's half past two."

The main fractions you use are:

- ✔ **an-niSf** (*ah-nee-sef;* half)
- ✔ **ath-thuluth** (*ah-thoo-looth;* third)
- ✔ **ar-rubu'** (*ah-roo-booh;* quarter)
- ✔ **'ashara** (*ah-sha-rah;* tenth)

The following examples show you how to use the fraction method to specify minutes when telling time:

- ✔ **as-saa'a ath-thaaniya wa ar-rubu'.** (*ah-sah-ah ah-thah-nee-yah wah ah-roo-booh;* It's quarter past two.)
- ✔ **as-saa'a at-taasi'a wa an-niSf.** (*ah-sah-ah ah-tah-see-ah wah ah-nee-sef;* It's half past nine.)
- ✔ **as-saa'a al-waaHida wa ath-thuluth.** (*ah-sah-ah al-wah-hee-dah wah ah-thoo-looth;* It's twenty past one.)
- ✔ **as-saa'a al-khaamisa wa ar-rubu'.** (*ah-sah-ah al-kah-mee-sah wah ah-roo-booh;* It's quarter past five.)
- ✔ **as-saa'a al-Haadiya 'ashra wa an-niSf.** (*ah-sah-ah al-hah-dee-yah ah-shrah wah ah-nee-sef;* It's half past eleven.)

Using this system, you can cover ten past the hour, quarter past the hour, twenty past the hour, and half past the hour, which are the major fractions. But what if you want to say "It's quarter of" or "It's twenty of"? In those cases, you need to use the preposition **'ilaa** *(ee-lah),* which means "of" or "to." If you think of the preposition **wa** as adding to the hour then think of **'ilaa** as subtracting from the hour.

Because **'ilaa** subtracts from the hour, you must add one hour to whatever hour you're referring to. For example, if you want to say "It's 5:45," then you must say "It's quarter of six" and not "It's a quarter of five," which would be 4:45. Here are some examples that use **'ilaa**:

- ✔ **as-saa'a as-saadisa 'ilaa ar-rubu'.** (*ah-sah-ah ah-sah-dee-sah ee-lah ah-roo-booh;* It's quarter to six, or 5:45.)

- ✔ **as-saa'a al-waaHida 'ilaa ath-thuluth.** (*ah-sah-ah al-wah-hee-dah ee-lah ah-thoo-looth;* It's twenty to one, or 12:40.)

If you want to express minutes as a fraction and specify which time of day (a.m. or p.m.), you simply add **fii** and the time of day. For example, **as-saa'a al-waaHida wa an-niSf fii ba'da aDH-DHuhr** means "It's 1:30 in the afternoon." Here are other examples:

- ✔ **as-saa'a ath-thaaniya 'ashra wa ar-rubu' fii al-layl.** (*ah-sah-ah ah-thah-nee-yah ah-shrah wah ah-roo-booh fee ah-lah-yel;* It's 12:15 at night, or 12:15 a.m.)

- ✔ **as-saa'a as-saabi'a wa an-niSf fii al masaa'.** (*ah-sah-ah ah-sah-bee-ah wah ah-nee-sef fee al-mah-sah;* It's 7:30 in the evening.)

- ✔ **as-saa'a ath-thaamina wa ar-rubu' fii aS-SabaaH.** (*ah-sah-ah ah-tha-nee-yah wah ah-roo-booh fee ah-sah-bah;* It's 8:15 in the morning.)

- ✔ **as-saa'a al-khaamisa 'ilaa ar-rubu' fii al-'asr.** (*ah-sah-ah al-kah-mee-sah ee-lah ah-roo-booh fee al-ah-ser;* It's quarter to five in the late afternoon, or 4:45 p.m.)

Talkin' the Talk

Salim and Wafaa are trying to figure out at what time to go to the movies.

Salim: **kam as-saa'a?**
           kam ah-sah-ah?
           What time is it?

Wafaa: **as-saa'a al-khaamisa wa an-niSf.**
           ah-sah-ah al-kah-mee-sah wah ah-nee-sef.
           It's 5:30.

Salim: **mataa sayabda'u ash-shariiT?**
           mah-tah sah-yab-dah-oo ah-shah-reet?
           When will the movie begin?

Wafaa:	**'aDHunnu sayabda'u ma'a as-saa'a as-saadisa wa an-niSf.**
	ah-zoo-noo sah-yab-dah-oo mah-ah ah-sah-ah ah-sah-dee-sah wah ah-nee-sef.
	I believe that it will start at 6:30.
Salim:	**kwayyis. hayya binaa 'ilaa al-maSraH ma'a as-saa'a as-saadisa.**
	kuh-wah-yees. hah-yah bee-nah ee-lah al-mah-suh-rah mah-ah ah-sah-ah ah-sah-dee-sah.
	Okay. Let's go to the theater at 6:00 then.
Wafaa:	**'anaa muwaafiq.**
	ah-nah moo-wah-feek.
	I agree.

Words to Know

mataa	mah-tah	when
bidaaya	bee-dah-yah	beginning
yabda'u	yah-buh-dah-oo	to begin
shariiT	sha-reet	movie
maSraH	mass-rah	theater
hayya binaa	hah-yah bee-nah	let's go
muwaafiq	moo-wah-feek	to agree

Spelling out minutes

When expressing time, you can specify the minutes by actually spelling them out. (Check out Chapter 4 for full coverage of cardinal numbers.) Use the following format:

as-saa'a + ordinal/hours + **wa** + cardinal/minutes + **daqiiqa**

So **as-saa'a al-khaamisa wa 'khamsat daqiiqa** (*ah-sah-ah al-kah-mee-sah wah kam-sat dah-kee-kah*) means "It's 5:05." Here are some other examples:

✔ **as-saa'a al-waaHida wa 'ishriin daqiiqa.** (*ah-sah-ah al-wah-hee-dah wah eesh-reen dah-kee-kah;* It's 1:20.)

✔ **as-saa'a ar-raabi'a wa thalaathiin daqiiqa fii al-'asr.** (*ah-sah-ah ar-bah-ah wah tha-lah-theen dah-kee-kah fee al-ah-ser;* It's 4:30 in the afternoon.)

✔ **as-saa'a ath-thaamina wa khamsa wa 'arba'iin daqiiqa fii aS-SabaaH.** (*ah-sah-ah ah-thah-mee-nah wah kam-sah wah ar-bah-een dah-kee-kah;* It's 8:45 in the morning.)

Talkin' the Talk

Ted is trying to figure out which bus to take.

Ted: **mataa satanTaliqu al-Haafila?**
mah-tah sah-tan-tah-lee-koo al-hah-fee-lah?
When does the bus leave?

Cashier: **satanTaliqu al-Haafila ma'a as-saa'a al-khaamisa wa 'ishriin daqiiqa fii al-'asr.**
sah-tan-tah-lee-koo al-hah-fee-lah mah-ah ah-sah-ah al-kah-mee-sah wah eesh-reen dah-kee-kah fee al-ah-ser.
The bus leaves at 5:30 in the (late) afternoon.

Ted: **hal kaanat Haafila tanTaliqu qabla dhaalika?**
hal kah-nat hah-fee-lah tan-tah-lee-koo kab-lah zah-lee-kah?
Is there a bus that leaves earlier than that?

Cashier: **daqiiqa min faDlik.**
dah-kee-kah meen fad-leek.
One minute please.

Ted: **Taba'an.**
tah-bah-an.
Of course.

Cashier: **hunaaka Haafila tanTaliqu ma'a as-saa'a al-khaamisa.**
hoo-nah-kah hah-fee-lah tan-tah-lee-koo mah-ah ah-sah-ah al-kah-mee-sah.
There is a bus that leaves at 5:00.

Ted: **mumtaaz! biTaaqa waaHida li al-Haafila ma'a as-saa'a al-khaamisa min faDlik.**
moom-taz! bee-tah-kah wah-hee-dah lee al-hah-fee-lah mah-ah ah-sah-ah al-kah-mee-sah meen fad-leek.
Excellent! One ticket for the 5:00 bus please.

Words to Know

'inTilaaq	een-tee-lak	departure
tanTaliqu	tan-tah-lee-koo	to leave
Haafila	hah-fee-lah	bus
maHaTTa	mah-hah-tah	station
qabla	kab-lah	before/earlier
biTaaqa	bee-tah-kah	ticket
saa'iH	sah-eeh	tourist (M)
saa'iHa	sah-ee-hah	tourist (F)
Safar	sah-far	trip
riHla	reeh-lah	voyage

Visiting Museums

I love museums because I can learn so much about virtually any topic, from irrigation systems during the Roman Empire to the brush techniques of the Impressionist artists. The **matHaf** (*mat-haf;* museum) plays a central role in the Arab **madiina** (*mah-dee-nah;* city); Arab people have a deep sense of history and their role in it, and one way to preserve some of that history, in the form of great Arab and Islamic works of art and achievements, is in the **matHaf.**

Here are some Middle Eastern museums worth visiting, in both the United States and the Middle East:

- The Dahesh Museum in New York, New York
- The Arab-American Museum in Detroit, Michigan
- al-ahram Museum in Cairo, Egypt
- Baghdad Museum in Baghdad, Iraq

Arabic scholars and Western civilization

Many of the works of the ancient Greek masters, such as Aristotle and Plato, were preserved by Islamic scholars when Europe was plunged into the Dark Ages (from about the Fifth through the Tenth centuries). Islamic scholars throughout the Muslim world, in Cordoba, Spain, and elsewhere translated gargantuan amounts of texts from Greek and Latin into Arabic. They studied these texts extensively and added a significant amount to the pool of knowledge. Thanks to the work of these Islamic scholars, much of the knowledge that serves as the basis of Western thought and civilization was preserved. In fact, while Europe was in the Dark Ages, Islam went through a revival and renaissance period not experienced anywhere else in the world.

A **ziyaara** (*zee-yah-rah;* visit) to a **matHaf** can be a wonderful experience as long as you follow a number of **qawaa'id** (*kah-wah-eed;* rules). These **qawaa'id** ensure that your experience and the experiences of others at the **matHaf** are **jamiila** (*jah-mee-lah;* pleasant).

The word **mamnuu'** *(mam-nooh)* means "prohibited," and the word **Daruurii** *(dah-roo-ree)* means "required"; whenever you see the word **mamnuu'** on a sign, it's usually accompanied by a picture of the item that's prohibited with a red line across it. Make sure to pay attention to the **qawaa'id** so that you don't get into trouble with the **matHaf** management!

When visiting a **matHaf,** you may see signs that say the following:

- ✔ **Suwar mamnuu'a.** (*soo-war mam-noo-ah;* Taking pictures is prohibited.)
- ✔ **dukhuul mamnuu'.** (*doo-kool mam-nooh;* Entering is prohibited.)
- ✔ **sijaara mamnuu'a.** (*see-jah-rah mam-noo-ah;* Smoking is prohibited.)
- ✔ **Ta'aam mamnuu'.** (*tah-am mam-nooh;* Food is prohibited.)
- ✔ **maa' mamnuu'.** (*mah mam-nooh;* Water is prohibited.)
- ✔ **Hidhaa' Daruurii.** (*hee-dah dah-roo-ree;* Shoes required.)
- ✔ **malaabis Daruuriya.** (*mah-lah-bees dah-roo-ree-yah;* Proper attire required.)

Talkin' the Talk

Larry and Samir are trying to decide at what time to go to the museum.

Larry: **hayyaa binaa 'ilaa al-matHaf al-yawm.**
           hah-yah bee-nah ee-lah al-mat-haf al-yah-oum.
           Let's go to the museum today.

Samir: **haadhihi fikra mumtaaza!**
           hah-zee-hee feek-rah moom-tah-zah!
           That's an excellent idea!

Larry: **mataa yaftaHu al-matHaf?**
           mah-tah yaf-tah-hoo al-mat-haf?
           When does the museum open?

Samir: **al-matHaf yaftaHu ma'a as-saa'a ath-thaamina fii
           aS-SabaaH.**
           *al-mat-haf yaf-tah-hoo mah-ah ah-sah-ah ah-thah-
           mee-nah fee ah-sah-bah.*
           The museum opens at 8:00 in the morning.

Larry: **wa kam as-saa'a al-'aan?**
           wah kam ah-sah-ah al-an?
           And what time is it now?

Samir: **as-saa'a ath-thaamina wa ar-bubu' al-'aan.**
           ah-sah-ah ah-thah-mee-nah wah ah-roo-booh.
           It's 8:15 right now.

Larry: **'aDHiim! Hayyaa binaa al-'aan!**
           ah-deem! hah-yah bee-nah al-an!
           Great! Let's go right now!

Samir: **hayyaa binaa!**
           hah-yah bee-nah!
           Let's go!

Words to Know

yawm	yah-oum	day
al-yawm	al-yah-oum	today
fataHa	fah-tah-hah	to open
yaftaHu	yaf-tah-hoo	will open
al-'aan	al-an	now

Although most verbs in Arabic have three consonants — such as **kataba** (*kah-tah-bah;* to write), **jalasa** (*jah-lah-sah;* to sit), or **darasa** (*dah-rah-sah;* to study) — **zaara** (*zah-rah*), the verb form for "to visit," contains only two consonants. This difference makes **zaara** an irregular verb.

If you want to visit a lot of different places around the **madiina,** being able to conjugate the irregular verb **zaara** in both the **maaDii** (past) and the **muDaari'** (present) tenses is particularly helpful. Because **zaara** is irregular, there's no specific form — like the one available for regular verbs in Chapter 2 — where a pattern is apparent.

For the **maaDii** form of visited, use **zaara** *(zah-rah):*

Form	*Pronunciation*	*Translation*
'anaa zurtu	ah-nah zoor-too	I visited
'anta zurta	ahn-tah zoor-tah	You visited (MS)
'anti zurtii	ahn-tee zoor-tee	You visited (FS)
huwa zaara	hoo-wah zah-rah	He visited
hiya zaarat	hee-yah zah-rat	She visited
naHnu zurnaa	nah-noo zoor-na	We visited
'antum zurtum	ahn-toom zoor-toom	You visited (MP)
'antunna zurtunna	ahn-too-nah zoor-too-nah	You visited (FP)
hum zaaruu	hoom zah-roo	They visited (MP)
hunna zurna	hoo-nah zoor-nah	They visited (FP)
antumaa zurtumaa	ahn-too-mah zoor-too-mah	You visited (dual/MP/FP)

Form	Pronunciation	Translation
humaa zaaraa	hoo-mah zah-rah	They visited (dual/MP)
humaa zaarataa	hoo-mah zah-rah-tah	They visited (dual/FP)

For the **muDaari'** form, use **yazuuru** as the basis of the verb:

Form	Pronunciation	Translation
'anaa 'azuuru	ah-nah ah-zoo-roo	I am visiting
'anta tazuuru	ahn-tah tah-zoo-roo	You are visiting (MS)
'anti tazuuriina	ahn-tee tah-zoo-ree-nah	You are visiting (FS)
huwa yazuuru	hoo-wah yah-zoo-roo	He is visiting
hiya tazuuru	hee-yah tah-zoo-roo	She is visiting
naHnu nazuuru	nah-noo nah-zoo-roo	We are visiting
'antum tazuuruuna	ahn-toom tah-zoo-roo-nah	You are visiting (MP)
'antunna tazurna	ahn-too-nah tah-zoor-nah	You are visiting (FP)
hum yazuuruuna	hoom yah-zoo-roo-nah	They are visiting (MP)
hunna yazurna	hoo-nah yah-zoor-nah	They are visiting (FP)
antumaa tazuuraani	ahn-too-mah tah-zoo-rah-nee	You are visiting (dual/MP/FP)
humaa yazuuraani	hoo-mah yah-zoo-rah-nee	They are visiting (dual/MP)
humaa tazuuraani	hoo-mah taz-zoo-rah-nee	They are visiting (dual/FP)

Talkin' the Talk

Lara is telling her friend Mary about her and her family's visit to the museum.

Lara: **zurnaa al-baariHa matHaf al-ahraam.**
zoor-nah al-bah-ree-hah mat-haf al-ah-ram.
We visited the "Museum of Pyramids" yesterday.

Mary: **kayfa kaanat ziyaaratukum?**
kay-fah kah-nat zee-yah-rah-too-koom?
How was your visit?

Lara: **kaanat mutamatti'a jiddan.**
kah-nat moo-tah-mah-tee-ah jee-dan.
It was very entertaining.

Mary: **maadhaa ra'aytum?**
mah-zah rah-ay-toom?
What did you see?

Lara: **ra'aynaa ba'du al-fannu aT-TaSwiir az-ziitii.**
rah-ay-nah bah-doo al-fah-noo ah-tah-sweer
ah-zee-tee.
We saw some oil paintings.

Mary: **shay' 'aakhar?**
shay ah-kar?
What else?

Lara: **wa ra'aynaa rasm 'alaa az-zaliij. kaana jamiil jiddan.**
wah rah-ay-nah rah-sem ah-lah ah-zah-leej. kah-nah
jah-meel jee-dan.
And we saw marble carvings. They were really
beautiful.

Mary: **haadhaa jamiil.**
hah-zah jah-meel.
Sounds beautiful.

Lara: **wa khudhnaa jawla khalfa al-matHaf li muddat niSf
saa'a.**
wah kooz-nah jah-ou-lah kal-fah mat-haf lee moo-dat
nee-sef sah-ah.
And we went on a guided tour around the museum
that lasted a half hour.

Mary: **'anaa 'uriidu 'an 'adhhab al-'aan! 'ayna al-matHaf?**
ah-nah oo-ree-doo an az-hab al-ahn! eh-yeh-nah
al-mat-haf?
Now I want to go! Where is the museum located?

Lara: **al-matHaf fii waSat al-madiina wa yaftaHu ma'a
as-saa'a ath-thaamina fii aS-SabaaH.**
al-mat-haf fee wah-sat al-mah-dee-nah wah
yaf-tah-hoo mah-ah ah-sah-ah ah-thah-mee-nah fee
ah-sah-bah.
The museum is in the downtown area, and it opens at
8:00 in the morning.

Mary: **wa bikam biTaaqat ad-dukhuul?**
wah bee-kam bee-tah-kat ah-doo-kool?
And how much is the entry ticket?

Lara: **'ashrat daraahim.**
ash-rat dah-rah-heem.
Ten dirhams.

Mary: **shukran.**
shook-ran.
Thank you.

Lara: **'afwan. ziyaara sa'iida!**
ah-feh-wan. zee-yah-rah sah-ee-dah!
You're welcome. Have a fun visit!

Words to Know

ziyaaratukum	zee-yah-rah-too-koom	your visit (MP)
tamtii'	tam-teeh	entertainment
mutamatti'a	moo-tah-mah-tee-ah	entertaining
jiddan	jee-dan	very
ra'aa	rah-ah	saw
ba'du	bah-doo	some
fannu	fah-noo	art
taSwiir	tah-sweer	painting
rasm	rah-sem	drawing/carving
zaliij	zah-leej	marble
jamiil	jah-meel	pretty/beautiful
jawla	jah-ou-lah	tour
khalfa	kal-fah	around
waSaT	wah-sat	center/downtown
dukhuul	doo-kool	entrance
khuruuj	koo-rooj	exit

Going to the Movies

Going to see a **shariiT siinimaa'ii** (*sha-reet see-nee-mah-ee;* movie) in a **maSraH siiniima'ii** (*mas-rah see-nee-mah-ee;* movie theater) is a very popular pastime for people in the Middle East. American action movies are a particularly favorite genre — don't be surprised if you walk into a movie theater in a Middle Eastern city and see Clint Eastwood on the big screen! Most of the movies shown in these **maSraH siiniima'ii** are actually the original versions with **tarjamat al-Hiiwaar** (*tar-jah-mat al-hee-war;* subtitles) at the bottom of the screen. Here are some other popular movie genres:

- **mughaamara** (*moo-gah-mah-rah;* action/adventure)
- **maSraHiyya** (*mas-rah-hee-yah;* comedy)
- **draamii** (*drah-mee;* drama)
- **ru'aat al-baqar** (*roo-aht al-bah-kar;* western)
- **wathaa'iqii** (*wah-tha-ee-kee;* documentary)
- **rusuum al-mutaHarrika** (*roo-soom al-moo-tah-hah-ree-kah;* cartoon)

The verb most commonly associated with going to the movies is **dhahaba** (*za-hah-bah;* to go). Using the conjugations that follow, you can say **dhahabtu 'ilaa al-maSraH as-siiniima'ii** (*za-hab-too ee-lah al-mas-rah ah-see-nee-mah-ee;* I went to the movie theater), or **yadhhabu 'ilaa al-maSraH as-siiniima'ii** (*yaz-hah-boo ee-lah al-mas-rah ah-see-nee-mah-ee;* He is going to the movies) and much, much more.

Here's the verb **dhahaba** in the **maaDii** form:

Form	Pronunciation	Translation
'anaa dhahabtu	ah-nah za-hab-too	I went
'anta dhahabta	ahn-tah za-hab-tah	You went (MS)
'anti dhahabtii	ahn-tee za-hab-tee	You went (FS)
huwa dhaaba	hoo-wah za-hah-bah	He went
hiya dhahabat	hee-yah za-hah-bat	She went
naHnu dhahabnaa	nah-noo za-hab-naa	We went
'antum dhahabtum	ahn-toom za-hab-toom	You went (MP)
'antunna dhahabtunna	ahn-too-nah za-hab-too-nah	You went (FP)
hum dhahabuu	hoom za-hah-boo	They went (MP)
hunna dhahabna	hoo-nah za-hah-nah	They went (FP)

Form	Pronunciation	Translation
antumaa dhahabtumaa	ahn-too-mah za-hab-too-mah	You went (dual/MP/FP)
humaa dhahabaa	hoo-mah za-hah-bah	They went (dual/MP)
humaa dhahabataa	hoo-mah za-hah-bah-tah	They went (dual/FP)

Use the form **yadhhabu** to conjugate **dhahaba** in the **muDaari'** form:

Form	Pronunciation	Translation
'anaa 'adhhabu	ah-nah az-hah-boo	I am going
'anta tadhhabu	ahn-tah taz-hah-boo	You are going (MS)
'anti tadhhabiina	ahn-tee taz-hah-bee-nah	You are going (FS)
huwa yadhhabu	hoo-wah yaz-hah-boo	He is going
hiya tadhhabu	hee-yah taz-hah-boo	She is going
naHnu nadhhabu	nah-noo naz-hah-boo	We are going
'antum tadhhabuuna	ahn-toom taz-hah-boo-nah	You are going (MP)
'antunna tadhhabna	ahn-too-nah taz-hab-nah	You are going (FP)
hum yadhhabuuna	hoom yaz-hah-boo-nah	They are going (MP)
hunna yadhhabna	hoo-nah yaz-hab-nah	They are going (FP)
antumaa tadhhabaani	ahn-too-mah taz-hah-bah-nee	You are going (dual/MP/FP)
humaa yadhhabaani	hoo-mah yaz-hah-bah-nee	They are going (dual/MP)
humaa tadhhabaani	hoo-mah taz-hah-bah-nee	They are going (dual/FP)

Talkin' the Talk

Adam and Asmaa are debating whether to go to the movies.

Asmaa: **hal turiidu 'an nadhhab 'ilaa al-matHaf al-yawm?**
hal too-ree-doo ann naz-hab ee-lah al-mat-haf al-yah-oum?
Do you want to go to the museum today?

Adam: **laa. 'anaa 'uriidu 'an 'adhhab 'ilaa al-maSraH as-siiniima'ii.**
lah. ah-nah oo-ree-doo ann az-hab ee-lah al-mas-rah ah-see-nee-mah-ee.
No. I would like to go to the movie theater.

Asmaa: **wa laakin al-maSraH as-siiniima'ii ba'iid min hunaa.**
wah lah-keen al-mas-rah ah-see-nee-mah-ee bah-eed meen hoo-nah.
But the movie theater is far from here.

Adam: **yumkin 'an nadhhab 'ilaa al-maSraH fii al-Haafila.**
yoom-keen ann naz-hab ee-lah al-mas-rah fee al-hah-fee-lah.
We can go to the movies by bus.

Asmaa: **mataa sayabda'u ash-shariiT?**
mah-tah sah-yab-dah-oo ah-sha-reet?
When does the movie begin?

Adam: **fii saa'a wa niSf.**
fee sah-ah wah nee-sef.
In an hour and a half.

Asmaa: **'ay shariiT sayal'abu fii al-maSraH al-yawm?**
aiy sha-reet sah-yal-ah-boo fee al-mas-rah al-yah-oum?
Which movie is going to be playing today?

Adam: **'aakhir shariiT min anjaliina joolii.**
ah-keer sha-reet meen an-jah-lee-nah joo-lee.
The latest Angelina Jolie movie.

Asmaa: **na'am? li-maadhaa lam taqul dhaalika min qabl?**
nah-am? lee-mah-zah lam tah-kool zah-lee-kah meen kah-bel?
Really? Why didn't you say so earlier?

Adam: **li-maadhaa?**
lee-mah-zah?
How come?

Asmaa: **'anaa 'uHibbu haadhihi al-mumathila kathiir!**
ah-nah oo-hee-boo hah-zee-hee al-moo-mah-thee-lah kah-theer.
I like this actress a lot!

Adam: **kwayyis. hayyaa binaa!**
kuh-wah-yees. hah-yah bee-nah!
Okay. Let's go!

Asmaa: **hayyaa binaa!**
hah-yah bee-nah!
Let's go!

Words to Know

turiidu	too-ree-doo	to want
ba'iid	bah-eed	far
qariib	kah-reeb	close
'aakhir	ah-keer	last/latest
kathiir	kah-theer	a lot
qaliil	kah-leel	a little
mumathil	moo-mah-theel	actor
mumathila	moo-mah-thee-lah	actress
mudiir	moo-deer	director
mushaahid	moo-sha-heed	spectator (MS)
mushaahida	hoo-sha-hee-dah	spectator (FS)

Touring Religious Sites

If you ever get a chance to go to the Middle East, I suggest you visit some of the beautiful religious sites that are spread across the land. If you're in a Middle Eastern or Arab city, be sure to check out a **masjid** (*mas-jeed;* mosque). The largest **masaajid** (*mah-sah-jeed;* mosques) in the Muslim world are located in Mecca and Medina, Saudi Arabia, and in Casablanca, Morocco.

A few rules to keep in mind

When visiting **masaajid,** you must follow certain **qawaa'id** (rules):

✔ **If you're Muslim,** you're allowed to walk into any **masjid** you like; but before entering, you must remove your shoes and say the **shahada** (*shah-hah-dah;* religious prayer): **laa 'ilaaha 'illaa allah wa muHammad rasuul allah** (*lah ee-lah-hah ee-lah ah-lah wah moo-hah-mad rah-sool ah-lah;* There is no god but God and Muhammad is his Prophet.).

✔ **If you're non-Muslim,** entry into a **masjid** is generally forbidden, whether you're in the Middle East, the United States, or anywhere around the world. However, certain mosques, such as the **masjid Hassan II** in Casablanca, have designated wings that are open to both Muslims and non-Muslims. These wings are set aside more as exhibition rooms than as religious or prayer rooms, so you're allowed to enter them, but you still must remove your **Hidaa'** (*hee-dah;* shoes).

The word **masjid** comes from the verb **sajada** *(sah-jah-dah),* which means "to prostrate" or "to kneel." Another word for "mosque" is **jaami'** *(jah-meeh),* which comes from the word **jama'a** *(jah-mah-ah;* to gather). So the Arabic words for "mosque" are related to what one actually does in the mosque, which is to gather in a religious setting and pray.

The Hajj

One of the most popular events during the year for Muslims is the **Hajj** *(haj),* which is the pilgrimage to Mecca in Saudi Arabia. The **Hajj,** which generally lasts for five days, takes place once a year and is actually one of the five pillars of Islam. Technically, attending the Hajj is mandatory for Muslims, but because the pilgrimage can be expensive, it's widely accepted that one can be a Muslim without actually having to attend the **Hajj.**

During the **Hajj, Hajjaaj** *(hah-jaj;* pilgrims) must follow a number of **qawaa'id.** As soon as the **Hajjaaj** arrive in Mecca, they must shed all their worldly clothing and possessions and change into sandals and a simple **ihram** *(eeh-ram),* which basically consists of a white cloth wrapped around the body. Other than these two items, the **Hajjaaj** aren't allowed to wear any watches, jewelry, or any other types of clothes. The logic behind wearing only the **ihram** is that every **Hajjaaj** is equal before God, and because no difference exists between a king and a beggar during the **Hajj,** everyone must wear the same thing.

After they don the **ihram,** the **Hajjaaj** begin a ritual known as the **Tawaf** *(tah-waf;* to turn), in which they walk around the **ka'ba** *(kah-bah),* a cubelike structure located in the middle of the **masjid al-Haraam** *(mas-jeed al-hah-ram;* The Sacred Mosque of Mecca). According to the Koran and other religious texts, the **ka'ba** was built by the Prophet Abraham for the purpose of worship. The **Hajjaaj** must circle the **ka'ba** seven times in an anti-clockwise manner. After the **Tawaf,** the **Hajjaaj** walk to the hills of Safa and Marwah before walking to Medina, the city where the Prophet Muhammad is buried. From Medina, the **Hajjaaj** walk to the hill of Arafat, then to the city of Mina, before returning to the **ka'ba** for a final **Tawaf.**

Because the **Hajj** is one of the five pillars of Islam, literally millions upon millions of people make the voyage to Saudi Arabia to participate in this pilgrimage every year, making it by far the largest religious pilgrimage in the world. In fact, it's not uncommon to have at least 5 million **Hajjaaj** in the cities of Mecca and Medina during the **Hajj.** Once a Muslim has performed the **Hajj,** he or she receives a special status in society, complete with a title: A man who has completed the **Hajj** is called **al-Hajj** *(al-haj)*, and a woman who has done the Hajj is called **al-Hajja** *(al-hah-jah)*.

Saudi Arabian law prohibits non-Muslims from entering Mecca during the **'amra** *(am-rah;* the time of year when the **Hajj** takes place). If you're non-Muslim, you may be able to visit Saudi Arabia and some of its other mosques and religious sites during this period, but you won't be permitted to visit the **ka'ba** and some of the other religious sites related to the **Hajj.**

Fun & Games

Match the hours on the left with their Arabic equivalents on the right.

5:30   **as–saa'a as–saadisa wa ar–rubu' fii aS–SabaaH**

7:45   **as–saa'a at–taasi'a fii aS–SabaaH**

9:00 a.m.   **as–saa'a ath–thaamina 'ilaa ar–rubu'**

2:30 p.m.   **as–saa'a al–khaamisa wa an–niSf**

6:15 a.m.   **as–saa'a ath–thaaniya wa an–niSf fii ba'da aDH–DHuhr**

The answers are in Appendix C.

Chapter 8

Enjoying Yourself: Recreation

∙∙

In This Chapter

▶ Getting active

▶ Playing sports

▶ Exploring the beach

▶ Tuning in to musical instruments

∙∙

Language teachers may not want you to hear this, but if you want to practice a new language, move outside the classroom. Doing things you like, such as playing sports, creating music, or playing card games, is one of the best ways to immerse yourself in your chosen language. In this section, I introduce new words and phrases to help you have fun in Arabic!

Starting Out with the Verbs fa'ala (Did) and yaf'alu (To Do)

One of the most frequently used verbs in the Arabic language is **fa'ala** (*fah-ah-lah;* did). In the **maaDii** (*mah-dee;* past tense), use the **fa'ala** form; for the **muDaari'** (*moo-dah-reeh;* present tense), use **yaf'alu** (*yah-feh-ah-loo;* to do/doing). Use the verb **fa'ala** to describe activities or **riyaaDa** (*ree-yah-dah;* sports) you're taking part in.

Here's the verb **fa'ala** conjugated in the **maaDii** form:

Form	Pronunciation	Translation
'anaa fa'altu	ah-nah fah-all-too	I did
'anta fa'alta	ahn-tah fah-all-tah	You did (MS)
'anti fa'alti	ahn-tee fah-all-tee	You did (FS)
huwa fa'ala	hoo-wah fah-ah-lah	He did
hiya fa'alat	hee-yah fah-ah-laht	She did

Form	Pronunciation	Translation
naHnu fa'alnaa	nah-noo fah-ahl-naa	We did
'antum fa'altum	ahn-toom fah-ahl-toom	You did (MP)
'antunna fa'altunna	ahn-too-nah fah-all-too-nah	You did (FP)
hum faa'aluu	hoom fah-ah-loo	They did (MP)
hunna faa'alna	hoo-nah fah-all-nah	They did (FP)
antumaa faa'altumaa	ahn-too-mah fah-all-too-mah	You did (dual/MP/FP)
humaa faa'alaa	hoo-mah fah-ah-lah	They did (dual/MP)
humaa faa'alataa	hoo-mah fah-ah-lah-tah	They did (dual/FP)

Here are a few examples of the verb **fa'ala** in action:

- ✔ **al-walad dhahaba 'ilaa al-maktaba wa fa'ala waajibuhu.** (*al-wah-lad zah-hah-bah ee-lah al-mak-tah-bah wah fah-ah-lah wah-jee-boo-hoo;* The boy went to the library and did his homework.)

- ✔ **fa'alat al-'amal 'alaa aT-Taawila.** (*fah-ah-lat al-ah-mal ah-lah ah-tah-wee-lah;* She did the work on the table.)

- ✔ **fa'altu at-tamriinaat fii al-manzil.** (*fah-all-too ah-tam-ree-nat fee al-man-zeel;* I did the exercises at home.)

Then use the form **yaf'alu** to conjugate "to do" in the **muDaari':**

Form	Pronunciation	Translation
'anaa 'af'alu	ah-nah ah-fah-loo	I am doing
'anta taf'alu	ahn-tah tah-fah-loo	You are doing (MS)
'anti taf'aliina	ahn-tee tah-fah-lee-nah	You are doing (FS)
huwa yaf'alu	hoo-wah yah-fah-loo	He is doing
hiya taf'alu	hee-yah tah-fah-loo	She is doing
naHnu naf'alu	nah-noo nah-fah-loo	We are doing
'antum taf'aluuna	ahn-toom tah-fah-loo-nah	You are doing (MP)
'antunna taf'alna	ahn-too-nah tah-fal-nah	You are doing (FP)

Form	Pronunciation	Translation
hum yaf'aluuna	hoom yah-fah-loo-nah	They are doing (MP)
hunna yaf'alna	hoom yah-fal-nah	They are doing (FP)
antumaa taf'alaani	ahn-too-mah tah-fah-lah-nee	You are doing (dual/MP/FP)
humaa yaf'alaani	hoo-mah yah-fah-lah-nee	They are doing (dual/MP)
humaa taf'alaani	hoo-mah tah-fah-lah-nee	They are doing (dual/FP)

Here are some examples that include the verb **yaf'alu:**

- **naf'alu al-'awraaq al-'aan.** (*nah-fah-loo al-aw-rak al-an;* We are doing the paperwork right now.)
- **taf'alu at-tajriibaat fii al-Hadiiqa.** (*tah-fah-loo ah-taj-ree-bat fee al-hah-dee-kah;* She is doing the experiments in the garden.)
- **hal taf'aluuna al-'amal li al-ghad?** (*hal tah-fah-loo-nah al-ah-mal lee al-gad;* Are you doing the work for tomorrow?)

Sporting an Athletic Side

I don't know about you, but I love playing **riyaaDa,** whether it's an individual sport such as **al-ghuulf** (*al-goo-lef;* golf) or a team sport like **kurat al-qadam** (*koo-rat al-kah-dam;* soccer).

kurat al-qadam is one of the most popular sports among Arabic-speaking people; in the Middle East, it comes as close as any sport to being the "national" sport. One reason why **kurat al-qadam** is so popular is because it's a **riyaaDa mushaahada** (*ree-yah-dah moo-sha-hah-dah;* spectator sport). In a typical **mubaara** (*moo-bah-rah;* game), one **fariiq** (*fah-reek;* team) with 11 players plays another **fariiq** in a **mal'ab** (*mah-lab;* stadium). Fans follow the **natiija** (*nah-tee-jah;* score) closely, hoping that their **fariiq** manages a **fawz** (*fah-wez;* win). Not surprisingly, excited fans react to every **khata'** (*kah-tah;* foul), often disagreeing with the **Hakam** (*hah-kam;* referee).

If you find yourself enjoying **kurat al-qadam** or a number of other team sports with a friend who speaks Arabic, the following terms may come in handy:

- **malaabis riyaaDiyya** (*mah-lah-bees ree-yah-dee-yah;* uniforms)
- **khasar** (*kah-sar;* loss)

- **kura** (*koo-rah;* ball)

- **laa'ib** (*lah-eeb;* player) (MS)

- **laa'iba** (*lah-ee-bah;* player) (FS)

kurat al-qadam is only one of the many sports popular with Arabic speakers and peoples of the Middle East. Here are some other favorite sports:

- **sibaaHa** (*see-bah-hah;* swimming)

- **furusiiyya** (*foo-roo-see-yah;* horseback riding)

- **kurat aT-Taa'ira** (*koo-rat ah-tah-ee-rah;* volleyball)

- **kurat as-salla** (*koo-rat ah-sah-lah;* basketball)

- **kurat al-miDrab** (*koo-rat al-meed-rab;* tennis)

- **daraaja** (*dah-rah-jah;* cycling)

- **tazaHluq** (*tah-zah-look;* skiing)

- **tazalluj** (*tah-zah-looj;* ice skating)

- **jumbaaz** (*joo-meh-baz;* gymnastics)

- **siyaaqat as-sayaara** (*see-yah-kat ah-sah-yah-rah;* racecar driving)

One of the most common verbs used with sports and other recreational activities is **la'aba** (*lah-ah-bah;* play). Because the verb **la'aba** is commonly used and important — much like the verb **fa'ala** — knowing how to conjugate it in both the **maaDii** and the **muDaari'** is a good idea.

Here's the verb **la'aba** in the **maaDii** form:

Form	Pronunciation	Translation
'anaa la'abtu	ah-nah lah-ahb-too	I played
'anta la'abta	ahn-tah lah-ahb-tah	You played (MS)
'anti la'abti	ahn-tee lah-ahb-tee	You played (FS)
huwa la'aba	hoo-wah lah-ah-bah	He played
hiya la'abat	hee-yah lah-ah-bat	She played
naHnu la'abnaa	nah-noo lah-ahb-naa	We played
'antum la'abtum	ahn-toom lah-ahb-toom	You played (MP)
'antunna la'abtunna	ahn-too-nah lah-ahb-too-nah	You played (FP)
hum la'abuu	hoom lah-ah-boo	They played (MP)
hunna la'abna	hoo-nah lah-ah-bah-nah	They played (FP)

Form	Pronunciation	Translation
antumaa la'abtumaa	ahn-too-mah lah-ahb-too-mah	You played (dual/MP/FP)
humaa la'abaa	hoo-mah lah-ah-bah	They played (dual/MP)
humaa la'abataa	hoo-mah lah-ah-bah-tah	They played (dual/FP)

Use the form **yal'abu** to conjugate "to play" in the **muDaari'**:

Form	Pronunciation	Translation
'anaa 'al'abu	ah-nah al-ah-boo	I am playing
'anta tal'abu	ahn-tah tal-ah-boo	You are playing (MS)
'anti tal'abiina	ahn-tee tal-ah-bee-nah	You are playing (FS)
huwa yal'abu	hoo-wah yal-ah-boo	He is playing
hiya tal'abu	hee-yah tal-ah-boo	She is playing
naHnu nal'abu	nah-noo nal-ah-boo	We are playing
'antum tal'abuuna	ahn-toom tal-ah-boo-nah	You are playing (MP)
'antunna tal'abna	ahn-too-nah tal-ahb-nah	You are playing (FP)
hum yal'abuuna	hoom yal-ah-boo-nah	They are playing (MP)
hunna yal'abna	hoom yal-ah-boo-nah	They are playing (FP)
antumaa tal'abaani	ahn-too-mah tal-ah-bah-nee	You are playing (dual/MP/FP)
humaa yal'abaani	hoo-mah yal-ah-bah-nee	They are playing (dual/MP)
humaa tal'abaani	hoo-mah tal-ah-bah-nee	They are playing (dual/FP)

The sentence structure for creating verbs is such that you use the verb **la'aba** or **yal'abu** followed by the sport or activity you're playing. For example, you may say **'anaa 'al'abu kurat as-salla** (I am playing basketball) or **hiya la'abat kurat al-miDrab** (She played tennis). As you can see from these examples, all you do is start with the personal pronoun and verb conjugation, attach the sport you're referring to, and voila!

Another important phrase commonly used relating to sports and other fun activities is **hayyaa binaa** (*hah-yah bee-nah;* Let's go). You'll often hear friends telling each other **hayyaa binaa** followed by the activity or location of the activity, such as **hayyaa binaa 'ilaa mal'ab kurat al-qadam** (*hah-yah bee-nah ee-lah mal-ahb koo-rat al-kah-dam;* Let's go to the soccer field).

Talkin' the Talk

Karim and Kamal are scheduling a soccer game.

Karim: **hayyaa nal'ab kurat al-qadam ghadan.**
hah-yah nah-lab koo-rat al-kah-dam gah-dan.
Let's go play soccer tomorrow.

Kamal: **haadhihi fikra mumtaaza.**
hah-zee-hee feek-rah moom-tah-zah.
That's an excellent idea.

Karim: **'ayy saa'a?**
ay sah-ah?
At what time?

Kamal: **hal as-saa'a al-khaamisa tuwaafiquka?**
hal ah-sah-ah al-kah-mee-sah too-wah-fee-koo-kah?
Does 5:00 work for you?

Karim: **na'am. as-saa'a al-khaamisa muwaafiqa. 'ayna sa-nal'ab?**
nah-am. ah-sah-ah al-kah-mee-sah moo-wah-fee-kah. eh-yeh-nah sa-nah-lab?
Yes. 5:00 works for me. Where are we going to play?

Kamal: **fii mal'ab al-madrasa.**
fee mah-lab al-mad-rah-sah.
In the school stadium.

Karim: **mumtaaz! hal 'indaka kura?**
moom-tahz! hal een-dah-kah koo-rah?
Excellent! Do you have a ball?

Kamal: **na'am 'indii kura. wa laakin laysa 'indii malaabis riyaaDiyya.**
nah-am een-dee koo-rah. wah lah-keen lah-yeh-sah een-dee mah-lah-bees ree-yah-dee-yah.
Yes, I have a ball. But I don't have any uniforms.

Karim: **laa sha'na lanaa bidhaalika. lam naHtaaj bi al-malaabis riyaaDiyya.**
lah sha-nah lah-nah bee-zah-lee-kah. lam nah-taj bee al-mah-lah-bees ree-yah-dee-yah.
That's not a big deal. We really don't need uniforms.

Kamal: **kwayyis. 'ilaa al-ghad.**
keh-wah-yees. ee-lah al-gad.
Okay. See you tomorrow.

Karim: **'ilaa al-ghad.**
ee-lah al-gad.
See you tomorrow.

Words to Know

fikra	feek-rah	idea
ghadan	gah-dan	tomorrow
saa'a	sah-ah	time
madrasa	mad-rah-sah	school
kura	koo-rah	ball
mal'ab	mah-lab	stadium

Going to the Beach

One of my favorite places is the **shaaTi'** (*shah-teeh;* beach); whether you go to the **shaaTi'** with your **'aSdiqaa'** (*ass-dee-kah;* friends) or your **'usra** (*oos-rah;* family), it's a really great place to have a fun time! You can do some **sibaaHa** (*see-bah-hah;* swimming) in the **muHiiT** (*moo-heet;* ocean) or play around in the **ramla** (*rah-meh-lah;* sand).

Talkin' the Talk

 Rita is trying to convince her mother to take her to the beach.

Rita: **hayyaa binaa 'ilaa ash-shaaTi'!**
hah-yah bee-nah ee-lah ah-shah-teeh!
Let's go to the beach!

Mother: **mataa?**
mah-tah?
When?

Rita: **hayyaa binaa 'al-'aan!**
hah-yah bee-nah all-ann!
Let's go now!

Mother: **hal 'indakii malaabis as-sibaaHa?**
hal een-dah-kee mah-lah-bees ah-see-bah-hah?
Do you have your bathing suit?

Rita: **na'am!**
nah-ahm!
Yes!

Mother: **wa hal 'indakii dihaan shamsii?**
wah hal een-dah-kee dee-han shah-meh-see?
And do you have sunscreen?

Rita: **na'am!**
nah-ahm!
Yes!

Mother: **kwayyis. hayyaa binaa.**
keh-wah-yees. Hah-yah bee-nah.
Okay. Then let's go.

Words to Know

malaabis as-sibaaHa	mah-lah-bees ah-see-bah-hah	bathing suit
dihaan shamsii	dee-han shah-meh-see	sunscreen
shams	shah-mes	sun
saHaab	sah-hab	cloud
shaaTi'	shah-teeh	beach
muHiiT	moo-heet	ocean
miDalla	mee-dah-lah	beach umbrella
ramla	rah-meh-lah	sand
mooja	moo-jah	wave

Playing Musical Instruments

I happen to agree with the saying that **moosiiqaa** (*moo-see-kah;* music) is a universal language. No matter where you come from or what languages you speak, **moosiiqaa** has the power to break down barriers and bring people closer together than perhaps any other activity. Popular **aalaat moosiiqiyya** (*ah-lat moo-see-kee-yah;* musical instruments) include:

- ✔ **biiyaano** (*bee-yah-noo;* piano)
- ✔ **qiithaar** (*kee-thar;* guitar)
- ✔ **kamanja** (*kah-mah-neh-jah;* violin)
- ✔ **Tabl** (*tah-bel;* drums)
- ✔ **fluut** (*feh-loot;* flute)
- ✔ **buuq** (*book;* trumpet)
- ✔ **saaksuufuun** (*sak-soo-foon;* saxophone)

In order to say that someone plays a particular instrument, use the **muDaari'** form of the verb **yal'abu.** For example **yal'abu al-qiithaar** means "He plays the guitar" or "He is playing the guitar" because the **muDaari'** describes both an ongoing and a habitual action.

Middle Eastern music is one of the most popular types of music in the world. It is characterized by a special kind of string instrument called the **'uud** (*ood*) that has 12 strings and a round hollow body. The **'uud** is generally accompanied by a number of percussion instruments, such as the regular drum and the special **Tabla** *(tah-beh-lah)* that keeps the beat and adds extra flavor to the serenading of the **'uud.**

A particularly popular kind of Middle Eastern music is **Rai** *(rah-yee),* which originated in the early 90s in Algeria, Morocco, and Tunisia. **Rai** uses a lot of traditional Arabic instruments such as the **'uud** and the **Tabla** but adds modern rock and roll and jazz instruments such as the electric guitar, the saxophone, and the trumpet. One of the most popular singers of **Rai** music is **Sheb Khaled.**

Popular Hobbies

Besides **riyaaDa** and **moosiiqaa,** you may enjoy a number of other types of hobbies. Do you consider **qiraa'a** *(kee-rah-ah;* reading) a **hiwaaya** *(hee-wah-yah;* hobby)? Perhaps you're creative and like **rasm** *(rah-sem;* drawing) or **fakhaar** *(fah-kar;* pottery)?

Some other popular hobbies include:

- **waraq al-la'ib** *(wah-rak ah-lah-eeb;* cards)
- **raqS** *(rah-kes;* dancing)
- **shaTranj** *(sha-teh-rah-nej;* chess)
- **Hiyaaka** *(hee-yah-kah;* knitting)
- **shi'r** *(shee-ar;* poetry)

When you want to discuss hobbies and personal activities, use the verb **la'aba** (for conjugations, check out "Sporting an Athletic Side" earlier in this chapter). For example, you say **la'abtu kurat al-qadam** *(lah-ab-too koo-rat al-kah-dam;* I played soccer) or **la'aba al-kamanja** *(lah-ah-bah al-kah-mah-neh-jah;* He played the violin). Here are some other example sentences that pair activities with the verb **la'aba:**

✔ **la'abat shaTranj.** (*lah-ah-bat sha-teh-rah-nej;* She played chess.)

✔ **la'abnaa kurat as-salla.** (*lah-ab-nah koo-rat ah-sah-lah;* We played basketball.)

✔ **la'abaa waraq al-la'ib.** (*lah-ah-bah wah-rak ah-lah-eeb;* They played cards.) (dual/MP/FP)

However, there are times when you're going to use the verb **fa'ala.** Generally speaking, the verb **fa'ala** is used to discuss activities that are more work-related than hobbies. For instance, you say **fa'altu al-waajib** (*fah-al-too al-wah-jeeb;* I did the homework). As a rule, use the verb **la'aba** when you're discussing hobbies such as sports and playing musical instruments.

Fun & Games

Draw lines connecting the Arabic activities on the left with their English equivalents on the right.

shaTranj	basketball
rasm	guitar
shi'r	swimming
kurat al-miDrab	drawing
sibaaHa	chess
kurat as-salla	tennis
qiithaar	poetry

The answers are in Appendix C.

Chapter 9

Talking on the Phone

In This Chapter

▶ Beginning a phone conversation

▶ Making plans over the phone

▶ Leaving a phone message

Personally, I really enjoy talking on the **haatif** (*haa-teef;* phone). It's a great way to catch up with friends, make social arrangements, and plan other aspects of your life with ease. With just a phone, you can get in touch with anyone in the world and talk about anything you like — from sports to social events and schoolwork to office gossip!

A few decades ago you may have been limited as to where you could hold a **mukaalama haatifiyya** (*moo-kaah-la-mah haa-teef-eeya;* phone conversation). Today, with the ubiquity of cell phones and other portable phone units, you can literally take your conversation anywhere! This flexibility makes knowing how to hold a phone conversation in Arabic even more important. In this chapter, I explain how to properly begin and end a **mukaalama haatifiyya,** how to make plans over the phone, and how to leave a proper phone message in Arabic. With all that information, you can be confident that you're carrying on a proper phone conversation like a native speaker!

Dialing Up the Basics

Before you can chat on the **haatif** (*haa-teef;* telephone) with your friends like a native speaker, you need to be familiar with the following basic terminology:

✔ **haatif 'aam** (*haa-teef aahm;* public phone)

✔ **haatif selulayr** (*haa-teef seh-loo-layer;* cellphone)

✔ **raqm al-haatif** (*rak-em al-haa-teef;* phone number)

✔ **biTaaqat al-haatif** (*bee-taa-kaht al-haa-teef;* phone card)

✔ **mukaalama haatifiyya** (*moo-kaah-la-mah haa-teef-eeya;* phone conversation)

Beginning a phone conversation

You can begin a phone conversation in a number of ways. The most common, whether you're the caller or the person answering the phone, is to simply say **allo** (*all-low;* hello).

It's proper etiquette to state your name right after the person who picks up the phone says **allo,** particularly if you don't know that person. If you're the caller, you may say **'anaa** (*an-nah;* I am) followed by your name. Alternatively, you may say **haadhaa** (M) / **haadhihi** (F) (*haa-zaah / haa-zee-hee;* this is) followed by your name. A familiar phrase you can also use after you say **allo** is **'as-salaamu 'alaykum** (*ass-sa-laam-ou a-lai-koum;* hello) or **'ahlan wa sahlan** (*ahel-lan wah sahel-lan;* hi). Flip to Chapter 3 for more on greetings and making small talk.

Talkin' the Talk

Kamal calls his friend Rita at home.

Kamal:	**allo.** *all-low.* Hello.
Rita:	**allo.** *all-low.* Hello.
Kamal:	**haadhaa kamal.** *haa-zaah kamal.* This is Kamal.
Rita:	**'ahlan wa sahlan kamal!** *ahel-lan wah sahel-lan kamal!* Hi Kamal!
Kamal:	**'ahlan wa sahlan rita!** *ahel-lan wah sahel-lan ree-taa!* Hi Rita!
Rita:	**kayf al-Haal?** *ka-yef al-haal?* How are you doing?
Kamal:	**al-Hamdu li-llah, shukran.** *al-ham-dou lee-llah, shoo-kran.* I'm doing well, thank you.

Asking to speak to someone

Sometimes, a person other than the one you want to talk to answers the phone. A common phrase to help you ask for the person you called to speak with is **hal (insert name here) hunaa?** *(hal [name] hoo-naah)*, which means "Is (name) here?"

Alternatively you can also use the personal pronouns **huwa** (if the person you're looking for is a man) or **hiya** (in the case of a woman) instead of using the person's name.

Talkin' the Talk

Kamal calls his friend Rita at home. Rita's mom, Souad, answers the phone, and Kamal asks to speak with Rita.

Kamal: **allo.**
            all-low.
            Hello.

Souad: **allo.**
            all-low.
            Hello.

Kamal: **as-salaamu 'alaykum. 'anaa Sadiiq rita. hal hiya hunaa?**
            ass-sa-laam-ou a-lai-koum. an-ah sah-deek ree-taa. hal hee-yah hoo-naah?
            Hello. I am a friend of Rita. Is she here?

Souad: **na'am hiya hunaa. Maa 'ismuk?**
            na-em hee-ya hoo-naah. maah ees-muhk?
            Yes, she is here. What's your name?

Kamal: **haadhaa kamal.**
            haa-zaah kamal.
            This is Kamal.

Souad: **intaDHir daqiiqa min faDlik.**
            in-tah-zer dah-kee-kah meen fah-del-ik.
            Wait one minute please.

Rita   **allo kamal.**
            all-low kamal.
            Hello Kamal.

Words to Know

'anaa	an-aah	I
hiya	hee-yah	her/she
huwa	hoo-wah	him/he
Sadiiq	sah-deek	friend (M)
Sadiiqa	sah-dee-kah	friend (F)
hunaa	hoo-naah	here
intaDHir	in-tah-zer	wait
daqiiqa	dah-kee-kah	minute

Making Plans Over the Phone

The phone is useful not only for staying in touch with friends and family but also for making **mawaa'id 'ijtimaa'iiyya** (*mah-waah-eed eej-tee-maah-ee-yah;* social arrangements) as well as **mawaa'id 'amalliya** (*mah-waah-eed ahm-ahl-ee-yah;* business arrangements). This section covers the specific terminology you need for each of these situations.

Making social plans

If you're talking with a friend, you're free to be a bit more informal than if you were calling a business. Some common words to help you make social arrangements with your friends are:

- **hayyaa binaa!** (*hah-yaah bee-naah;* Let's go!)
- **maT'am** (*ma-tam;* restaurant)
- **siiniimaa** (*see-nee-mah;* movie theater)
- **matHaf** (*maht-haf;* museum)
- **waqt faarigh** (*wah-ket faa-ree-gh;* free time)

Talkin' the Talk

 Selma calls her friend Mark on his **haatif selulayr** (cellphone) so that they can make dinner plans.

Selma:	**allo.** *all-low.* Hello.
Mark:	**allo.** *all-low.* Hello.
Selma:	**ahlan mark. haadhihi selma.** *ahel-lan mark. haa-zee-hee selma.* Hi Mark. This is Selma.
Mark:	**ahlan selma! shukran li mukaalamatukii.** *ahel-lan selma! Shook-ran lee moo-kaa-lah-mah-too-kee.* Hi Selma! Thanks for your call.
Selma:	**'afwan. kayf Haalak?** *ah-feh-wan kay-ef haa-lak?* You're welcome. How are you?
Mark:	**al-Hamdu li-llah. wah 'anti?** *al-ham-doo li-llah. wah ahn-tee?* I'm doing well. And you?
Selma:	**al-Hamdu li-llah. hal 'induka waqt faarigh ghadan?** *al-ham-doo lee-lah. hall een-doo-kah wah-ket faa-ree-gh gha-dan?* I'm doing well. Do you have any free time tomorrow?
Kamal:	**na'am. 'anaa mawjood ma'a as-saa'a as-saadisa.** *nah-am. ah-nah maw-juud mah-ah ah-sah-ah ah-sah-dee-sah.* Yes. I'm free around 6:00.
Selma:	**hal turiidu 'an tadh-hab ma'ii 'ilaa al'maT'am ma'a as-saa'a as-saabi'a?** *hall too-ree-du ann taz-hab ma-eeh ee-laah al-ma-tam ma-ah ass-saa-ah ass-saa-bee-ah?* Would you like to go with me to the restaurant at 7:00?

Kamal:	**Tab'an! 'anaa sa uHibbu dhaalika.**
	tah-bah-an! An-aah sah oo-hee-boo zaa-lee-kah.
	Of course! I would like that.
Selma:	**mumtaaz! 'ilaa al-ghad.**
	moom-taaz! ee-laah al-gad.
	Excellent! See you tomorrow.
Kamal:	**'ilaa al-ghad!**
	ee-laah al-gad!
	See you tomorrow!

Words to Know

mukaalamatuka	moo-kaa-lah-mah-too-kah	your call (M)
mukaalamatukii	moo-kaa-lah-mah-too-kee	your call (F)
'induka	een-doo-kah	you have (M)
'induki	een-doo-kee	you have (F)
waqt	wah-ket	time
faarigh	faa-ree-gh	empty
saa'a	saa-ah	hour
uHibbu	oo-hee-boo	I like
dhaalika	zaa-lee-kah	that
al-ghad	al-gad	tomorrow

Making business appointments

Arranging personal get-togethers with friends or family is always fun, but at times you have to conduct business over the **haatif**, whether you're setting up a **maou'id** (*maw-oo-eed;* appointment) with the dentist or arranging a business **'ijtimaa'** (*eej-tee-maah;* meeting) with a client. Interacting with businesses in Arabic requires specific terminology.

Talkin' the Talk

Susan is calling the Rialto, a company in Casablanca. She reaches the **katiba** (*kah-tee-bah;* secretary) and asks to speak with Mr. Ahmed.

Susan: **allo.**
all-low.
Hello.

Katiba: **allo. sharikat rialto. daqiiqa min faDlik?**
all-low. shah-ree-kaht ree-all-toh. dah-kee-kah meen fah-del-ik?
Hello. Rialto Inc. Can you wait one minute please?

Susan: **Tab'an.**
tah-bah-'an.
Of course.

Katiba: **'afwan li-ta'akhur. kayfa 'usaa'iduk?**
ah-feh-wan lee-tah-ah-khur. kay-fah oo-saa-ee-duk?
Sorry to keep you waiting. How may I help you?

Susan: **'uriidu 'an 'atakallam ma'a sayyid 'aHmad.**
oo-ree-doo ann ah-tah-kah-llam ma-ah sah-yed ah-mad.
I would like to speak with Mr. Ahmed.

Katiba: **sayyid 'aHmad mashghul. huwa fii 'ijtimaa'.**
sah-yed ah-mad mash-ghool. hoo-wah fee eej-tee-maah.
Mr. Ahmed is busy. He is in a meeting.

Susan: **mataa sa-yakun mawjood?**
mah-taah sah-yah-koon maw-juud?
When will he be available?

Katiba: **ayy daqiiqa.**
ay dah-kee-kah.
Any minute now.

Susan: **shukran jaziilan. sa-'ab-qaa fii l-khat.**
shook-ran ja-zee-lan. sa-ah-bek-aah fee al-khah-t.
Thank you very much. I'll stay on the line.

Words to Know

maou'id	maw-oo-eed	appointment
'ijtimaa'	eej-tee-maah	meeting
sayyid	say-yehd	Mr./Sir
sayyida	say-yee-dah	Mrs./Ms.
ra'iis	rah-ees	president
katiba	kah-tee-bah	secretary/assistant
sharika	shah-ree-kah	company
'usaa'iduk	oo-saa-ee-duk	help you
'uriidu	oo-ree-doo	I would like
mashghul	mash-ghool	busy

Leaving a Message

Sometimes you just run out of luck and can't get a hold of the person you're trying to reach. You're forced to leave a **khabaran** (*khah-bah-ran;* message) either on a voice mailbox or with a person.

Dealing with voice mail

When you leave a voice mail message on someone's **haatif,** you want to make sure to include the following:

- ✔ Your **'ism** (*ee-seh-m;* name)
- ✔ The **waqt al-mukaalama** (*wah-ket al-muh-kaah-lah-mah;* time of the call)
- ✔ Your **raqm al-haatif** (*rah-kem al-haa-teef;* phone number or callback number)
- ✔ The **ahsan waqt li al-mukaalama** (*ahe-sahn wah-ket lee al-muh-kaah-lah-mah;* best times you're available to talk)

Selma tries to reach Karim by phone but gets this recording instead:

> **'ahlan, haadhaa kareem. 'anaa lastu hunaa wa lakin 'idhaa takallamta 'ismuka wa raqamuka sa-'ukallimuk fii 'asra' waqt**
>
> *ahel-lan, hah-zah kah-reem. ah-nah las-too hoo-nah wah lah-keen ee-zah tah-kah-lam-tah ees-moo-kah wah rah-kah-moo-kah sah-oo-kah-lee-moo-kah fee ass-rah wah-ket.*
>
> Hi, this is Karim. I'm not in right now, but if you leave your name and number, I'll get back to you as soon as possible.

Selma's voice mail message sounds something like this:

> **'ahlan wa sahlan karim. haadhihi selma. as-saa'a al-waaHida wa an-niSf yawm al-khamiis. khaabirnii min faDlik 'inda wuSuulika bi haadha al-khabar ba'ada as-saa'a al-khaamisa. raqmii Sifr waaHid ithnayn thalaatha. shukran!**
>
> *ahel-lan wah sahel-lan kah-reem. haa-zee-hee selma. ass-saa-ah al-waa-hee-dah wa-ann-nee-sef ya-woom al-kha-mees. khaa-bir-nee meen fahd-lik inn-dah wu-soo-li-kah bee haa-zaah al-khah-bar bah-dah as-saa-ah al-khaa-mee-sah. rak-mee see-fer waa-hid ith-nay-en tha-laah-thah. shook-ran!*
>
> Hi Karim. This is Selma. It's 1:30 in the afternoon on Thursday. Please give me a call back when you get this message anytime after 5:00. My number is 0123. Thanks!

Leaving a message with a person

If you have to leave a **khabaran** directly with a person, make sure you include your **'ism** and ask the person who picks up the phone to pass along word that you called.

Talkin' the Talk

Kamal calls his friend Rita at home. Rita isn't home, and Souad, her mom, answers the phone. Kamal leaves a message for Rita with her mother.

Souad: **allo.**
all-low.
Hello.

Kamal: **allo. haadhaa kamal.**
all-low. haa-zaah kamal.
Hello. This is Kamal.

Souad: **ahlan kamal.**
          ahel-lan kamal.
          Hi Kamal.

Kamal: **hal rita fii l-bayt?**
          hal rita fee al-bay-et?
          Is Rita home?

Souad: **laa. dhahabat 'ilaa ad-dukkaan.**
          laah. za-ha-bat ee-laa ad-doo-kaah-n.
          No. She went to the store.

Kamal: **mataa sa-tarj'u?**
          mah-taah sa-tar-jee-oo?
          When will she be back?

Souad: **sa-tarju' ba'da saa'a.**
          sa-tar-joo bah-dah saa-ah.
          She will be back in an hour.

Kamal: **hal yumkin 'an tukhbiriihaa bi mukaalamatii?**
          hal yoo-mek-in ann too-kh-bee-ree-haa bee
          moo-kaah-lah-mah-tee?
          Is it possible for you tell her that I called?

Souad: **Tab'an!**
          tah-bah-an!
          Of course!

Kamal: **shukran! ma'a as-salaama.**
          shook-ran! ma-ah as-sa-laah-mah.
          Thank you! Bye.

Souad: **ma'a as-salaama.**
          ma-ah as-sa-laah-mah.
          Bye.

Words to Know

Bayt	bah-yet	home
dhahaba	zah-hah-ba	he went
dhahabat	zah-hah-bat	she went
dukkaan	doo-kaah-n	store
mataa	mah-taah	when
tarj'u	tar-jee-oo	come back
ba'da	bah-dah	after
hal yumkin	hal yoo-mek-in	is it possible
mukaalamatii	moo-kaah-lah-mah-tee	my call

Most phones in Arabic- speaking countries use the familiar Arabic numerals (1, 2, 3, and so on). Thank goodness you won't have to struggle to identify the Arabic numbers on the keypad while dialing a number!

Fun & Games

Here are some questions commonly asked on the phone. Match the questions with the appropriate answers.

'as-'ila (*ass-ee-lah;* questions)

1. **mataa sa-tarj'u?** (When will she be back?)

2. **hal 'induka waqt faarigh?** (Do you have free time?)

3. **hal huwa hunaa?** (Is he here?)

4. **kayf al-Haal?** (How are you doing?)

5. **maa 'ismuk?** (What's your name?)

al-jawaab (*al-jah-waab;* answers)

A. **na'am. daqiiqa min faDlik.**

B. **laa. 'anaa mashghuul.**

C. **'ismii Souad.**

D. **al-Hamdu li-llah, shukran.**

E. **sa-tarju' ba'da saa'a.**

The answers are in Appendix C.

Chapter 10

At the Office and Around the House

In This Chapter

▶ Finding a job that's right for you

▶ Interacting with co-workers

▶ Using the imperative verb form

▶ Relaxing in your home

If you're like most people living in the modern world, the two places where you spend the most time probably are your **manzil** (*man-zeel;* house) and your **maktab** (*mak-tab;* office). Like many people who are employed by big companies, small businesses, government agencies, or private ventures, you divide your **waqt** (*wah-ket;* time) between **al-'amal** (*al-ah-mal;* work) and **Hayaat al-'aa'iliyya** (*hah-yat al-ah-ee-lee-yah;* family life). Achieving **tawaazun** (*tah-wah-zoon;* balance) between the two is extremely crucial for your happiness, your efficiency at the workplace, and your effectiveness in your home. In this chapter, I cover all the good "work" words you should know and introduce you to all aspects of life at the office and around the house to help you balance life between these two worlds.

Landing the Perfect Job

At some point in your **Hayaat** (*hah-yat;* life), you may want or need to start working and therefore decide to actively start looking for **'amal.** Identifying a **mihna** (*meeh-nah;* profession) that's right for you and then going about securing **'amal** can be a full-time job itself. In this section, you discover the words and phrases to make your job search as efficient as possible!

One of the first things to keep in mind when you go about your job search is that you need to find an **'amal** that suits your particular **maSlaHaat** (*mas-lah-hat;* interests) and **mahaaraat** (*mah-hah-rat;* skills). You may want to start your search by talking to **'aSdiqaa'** (*ass-dee-kah;* friends) or asking around at your local **jam'iyya** (*jam-ee-yah;* university). Also, you're likely to find listings in the following:

- ✔ **jariidaat** (*jah-ree-dat;* newspapers)
- ✔ **ma'luumaat** (*mah-loo-mat;* classified ads)

As you search, make sure you find out as much as possible about a potential **mustakhdim** (*moos-tak-deem;* employer). When you're able to secure an interview with a **sharika** (*shah-ree-kah;* company), here's a list of things you may want to find out about your potential **mustakhdim:**

- ✔ **'adad al-'ummaal** (*ah-dad al-oo-mal;* number of employees)
- ✔ **Damaan aS-SaHHa** (*dah-man ah-sah-hah;* health insurance)
- ✔ **raatib** (*rah-teeb;* salary)
- ✔ **waqt al-'uTla** (*wah-ket al-oot-lah;* vacation time)
- ✔ **ta'aaqud** (*tah-ah-kood;* pension)

Talkin' the Talk

Mark has been looking for a job and has landed a job interview with Mary, a head of human resources. Mark goes in for his interview with Mary.

Mary:	**marHaban bika. tafaDDal min faDlik.**
	mar-hah-bah bee-kah. tah-fah-dal meen fad-leek.
	Welcome. Please come in.

Mark:	**shukran li 'istiqbaalii.**
	shook-ran lee ees-teek-bah-lee.
	Thank you for having me.

Mary:	**khuz maq'ad min faDlik.**
	kooz mak-ad meen fad-leek.
	Please have a seat.

Mark:	**shukran.**
	shook-ran.
	Thank you.

Mary: **hal turiidu 'an tashraba shay'an?**
hal too-ree-doo an tash-rah-bah shay-an?
Would you like anything to drink?

Mark: **maa' min faDlik.**
mah meen fad-leek.
Water please.

Mary: **hal 'indaka 'as'ila 'an haadhihi al-waDHiifa?**
hal een-dah-kah ass-ee-lah an hah-zee-hee
al-wah-dee-fah?
Do you have any questions about this position?

Mark: **na'am. kam min 'ummaal fii ash-sharika?**
nah-am. kam meen oo-mal fee ah-shah-ree-kah?
Yes. How many employees are in the company?

Mary: **'indanaa 'ishriin 'ummaal wa mudiir waaHid.**
een-dah-nah eesh-reen oo-mal wah moo-deer
wah-heed.
We have 20 employees and one director.

Mark: **hal ash-sharika tuqaddim Damaan aS-SaHHa?**
hal ah-shah-ree-kah too-kah-deem dah-man
ah-sah-hah?
Does the company provide health insurance?

Mary: **na'am. nuqaddim Damaan aS-SaHha li kul**
muwaDHaf ba'da muddat thalaath 'ashhur fii
al-'amal.
nah-am. noo-kah-deem dah-man ah-sah-hah lee kool
moo-wah-daf bah-dah moo-dat thah-lath ash-hoor
fee al-ah-mal.
Yes. We provide health insurance to every employee
after a period of three months on the job.

Mark: **raai'! wa hal hunaaka waqt li al-'uTla?**
rah-eeh! wah hal hoo-nah-kah wah-ket lee
al-oot-lah?
Great! And is there any vacation time?

Mary: **Taba'an. hunaaka 'ishriin yawm li al-'uTla fii as-sana**
al-'uulaa. wa fii as-sana ath-thaaniya hunaaka
thalaathiin yawm li al-'uTla.

tah-bah-an. hoo-nah-kah eesh-reen yah-oum lee al-oot-lah fee ah-sah-nah al-oo-lah. wah fee ah-sah-nah ah-thah-nee-yah hoo-nah-kah thah-lah-theen yah-oum lee al-oot-lah.

Of course. There are 20 days for vacation during the first year. And then during the second year there are 30 vacation days.

Mark: **shukran jaziilan li haadhihi al-ma'luumaat.**
shook-ran jah-zee-lan lee hah-zee-hee al-mah-loo-mat.
Thank you very much for this information.

Words to Know

'istiqbaal	ess-teek-bal	host
maq'ad	mak-ad	seat
'as'ila	ass-ee-lah	questions
waDHiifa	wah-dee-fah	position
taqdiim	tak-deem	offering
tuqaddim	too-kah-deem	to offer
'ashhur	ash-hoor	months
ma'luuma	mah-loo-mah	information (S)
ma'luumaat	mah-loo-mat	information (P)

Managing the Office Environment

The **maktab** is an essential part of modern life. In most Arabic-speaking and Muslim countries, **'ummaal** (*ooh-mal;* workers) work from **al-'ithnayn** (*al-eeth-nah-yen;* Monday) until **al-jumu'a** (*al-joo-moo-ah;* Sunday). Most **'ummaal** follow a standard **as-saa'a at-taasi'a 'ilaa al-khaamisa** (*ah-sah-ah ah-tah-see-ah ee-lah al-kah-mee-sah;* 9:00 to 5:00) schedule for workdays.

Although most **makaatib** (*mah-kah-teeb;* offices) around the world give their **'ummaaal** time for **ghadaa'** (*gah-dah;* lunch), the duration depends on the employer and the country. For example, in the United States, it's not uncommon for an **'aamil** (*ah-meel;* worker) to eat her **ghadaa'** while sitting at her **maktab** (*mak-tab;* desk). On the other hand, in most Middle Eastern countries, an **'aamil** gets two hours for **ghadaa'** and is encouraged to eat his **ghadaa'** at his **manzil** (*man-zeel;* house) with his **'usra** (*oos-rah;* family).

Here are some key words and terms to help you navigate the workplace:

- ✔ **'amal** (*ah-mal;* work/job)
- ✔ **mihna** (*meeh-nah;* profession)
- ✔ **sharika** (*shah-ree-kah;* company)
- ✔ **sharika kabiira** (*shah-ree-kah kah-bee-rah;* large company)
- ✔ **sharika Saghiira** (*shah-ree-kah sah-gee-rah;* small company)
- ✔ **ma'mal** (*mah-mal;* factory)
- ✔ **zubuun** (*zoo-boon;* client)
- ✔ **zabaa'in** (*zah-bah-een;* clients)

You can choose from many different kinds of **sharikaat** (*shah-ree-kat;* companies) to work for, including a **maSraf** (*mas-raf;* bank), a **sharikat al-Hisaab** (*shah-ree-kat al-hee-sab;* accounting firm), and a **sharikat al-qaanuun** (*shah-ree-kat al-kah-noon;* law firm). You also have many choices when it comes to **mihan** (*mee-han;* professions). Here are some popular **mihan:**

- ✔ **maSrafii** (*mas-rah-fee;* banker) (M)
- ✔ **maSrafiiya** (*mas-rah-fee-yah;* banker) (F)
- ✔ **rajul al-'a'maal** (*rah-jool al-ah-mal;* businessman)
- ✔ **'imra'at al-'a'maal** (*eem-rah-at al-ah-mal;* businesswoman)
- ✔ **muHaamiiy** (*moo-hah-mee;* lawyer)
- ✔ **shurTa** (*shoor-tah;* police officer)
- ✔ **rajul al-'iTfaa'** (*rah-jool al-eet-fah;* firefighter)

Most **sharikaat** have a lot of **'ummaal** with different responsibilities, and most **'ummaal** find themselves in **daa'iraat** (*dah-ee-rat;* divisions/groups/departments) within the **sharika.** Here are some of the common **daa'iraat** you may find in a **sharika:**

✔ **daa'irat al-Hisaab** (*dah-ee-rat al-hee-sab;* accounting department)

✔ **daa'irat al-'aswaaq** (*dah-ee-rat al-as-wak;* marketing department)

✔ **daa'irat al-qaanuun** (*dah-ee-rat al-kah-noon;* legal department)

✔ **daa'irat al-'ummaal** (*dah-ee-rat al-ooh-mal;* human resources department)

✔ **daa'irat az-zabaa'in** (*dah-ee-rat ah-zah-bah-een;* customer service department)

Interacting with your colleagues

Unless you're in a **mihna** that doesn't require you to interact with people face-to-face (such as being an author), you need to be able to get along with your **zumalaa'** (*zoo-mah-lah;* colleagues) at the **maktab.** This section reveals the terms that will help you get along with everyone at the office so that you can be as productive and efficient as possible.

Before you build good working relationships with your **zumalaa',** you should know the right words for classifying them:

✔ **zamiil** (*zah-meel;* colleague) (MS)

✔ **zamiila** (*zah-mee-lah;* colleague) (FS)

✔ **zumalaat** (*zoo-mah-lat;* colleagues) (FP)

✔ **mudiir** (*moo-deer;* director) (MS)

✔ **mudiira** (*moo-dee-rah;* director) (FS)

✔ **mudiiruun** (*moo-dee-roon;* directors) (MP)

✔ **mudiiraat** (*moo-dee-rat;* directors) (FP)

✔ **ra'iis** (*rah-ees;* president) (MS)

✔ **ra'iisa** (*rah-ee-sah;* president) (FS)

✔ **ru'asaa'** (*roo-ah-sah;* presidents) (MP)

✔ **ru'asaat** (*roo-ah-sat;* presidents) (FP)

Whether you like it or not, your **zumalaa' al-maktab** (*zoo-mah-lah al-mak-tab;* office colleagues) have a big influence over your time at the **maktab;** therefore, getting along with your **zumalaa'** is crucial. You can address people you work with in a number of different ways, such as based on rank, age, or gender. These categorizations may seem discriminatory in an American sense, but these terms actually carry the utmost respect for the person being referenced:

✔ Use **sayyidii** (*sah-yee-dee;* sir) to address the **mudiir** or someone with a higher rank than you.

✔ Use **sayiidatii** (*sah-yee-dah-tee;* madam) to address the **mudiira** or **ra'iisa.**

✔ Use **Sadiiqii** (*sah-dee-kee;* friend) to address a male colleague.

✔ Use **Sadiiqatii** (*sah-dee-kah-tee;* friend) to address a **zamiila.**

✔ Use **al-'akh** (*al-ak;* brother) to address a co-worker or colleague.

✔ Use **al-'ukht** (*al-oo-ket;* sister) to address a **zamiila.**

In Arabic culture, it's okay to address co-workers or people close to you as **'akh** (brother) or **'ukht** (sister) even though they may not be related to you.

Here are some phrases to help you interact cordially and politely with your **zumalaa':**

✔ **hal turiid musaa'ada?** (*hal too-reed moo-sah-ah-dah;* Do you need help?) (M)

✔ **hal turiidiina musaa'ada?** (*hal too-ree-dee-nah moo-sah-ah-dah;* Do you need help?) (F)

✔ **hal yumkin 'an 'usaa'iduka bii dhaalika?** (*hal yoom-keen an oo-sah-ee-doo-kah bee zah-lee-kah;* May I help you with that?) (M)

✔ **hal yumkin 'an 'usaa'idukii bii dhaalika?** (*hal yoom-keen an oo-sah-ee-doo-kee bee zah-lee-kah;* May I help you with that?) (F)

✔ **sa 'adhhab 'ilaa al-maT'am. hal turiid shay'an?** (*sah az-hab ee-lah al-mat-ham. hal too-ree-doo shay-an;* I'm going to the cafeteria. Do you want anything?) (M)

✔ **sa 'adhhab 'ilaa al-maT'am. hal turiidiina shay'an?** (*sah az-hab ee-lah al-mat-ham. hal too-ree-dee-nah shay-an;* I'm going to the cafeteria. Do you want anything?) (F)

✔ **'indanaa 'ijtimaa' fii khams daqaa'iq.** (*een-dah-nah eej-tee-mah fee kah-mes dah-kah-eek;* We have a meeting in five minutes.)

✔ **az-zabuun saya'tii fii saa'a.** (*ah-zah-boon sah-yah-tee fee sah-ah;* The client will arrive in one hour.)

✔ **hal waSaluka bariidii al-'iliktroonii?** (*hal wah-sah-loo-kah bah-ree-dee al-ee-leek-troo-nee;* Did you get my e-mail?)

✔ **hal waSaluka khabaarii al-haatifiiy?** (*hal wah-sah-loo-kah kah-bah-ree al-hah-tee-fee;* Did you get my phone message?)

✔ **hal 'indaka qalam?** (*hal een-dah-kah kah-lam;* Do you have a pen?) (M)

✔ **hal 'indukii qalam?** (*hal een-doo-kee kah-lam;* Do you have a pen?) (F)

Talkin' the Talk

Omar and Samir are colleagues working on a project at the office.

Omar: **hal katabta at-taqriir?**
         hal kah-tab-tah ah-tak-reer?
         Did you write the report?

Samir: **'anaa katabtu niSf at-taqriir, wa laakin 'uriidu musaa'adatuka li kitaabatuh.**
         ah-nah kah-tab-too nee-sef ah-tak-reer, wah lah-keen oo-ree-doo moo-sah-ah-dah-too-kah lee kee-tah-bah-tooh.
         I wrote half of the report, but I need your help to finish writing it.

Omar: **Tayyib, hayyaa binaa li al-'amaal. 'ayna turiidu 'an na'mal?**
         tah-yeeb, hay-yah bee-nah lee al-ah-mal. ay-nah too-ree-doo an nah-mal?
         Okay, let's get to work. Where would you like us to work?

Samir: **hayya binaa 'ilaa qaa'at al-'ijtimaa'.**
         hay-yah bee-nah ee-lah kah-at al-eej-tee-mah.
         Let's go to the conference room.

Omar and Samir head to the conference room to finish the report.

Omar: **hal turiidu haadhihi aS-Suura fii bidaayat 'aw nihaayat at-taqriir?**
         hal too-ree-doo hah-zee-hee ah-soo-rah fee bee-dah-yat aw nee-hah-yat ah-tak-reer?
         Do you want this illustration in the beginning or end of the report?

Samir: **'aDHunnu fii bidaayat at-taqriir 'aHsan.**
         ah-zoo-noo fee bee-dah-yat ah-tak-reer ah-san.
         I believe in the beginning of the report is better.

Omar: **hal naziid SafHa 'ukhraa 'aw haadhaa kaafiiyan?**
         hal nah-zeed saf-hah ook-rah aw hah-zah kah-fee-yan?
         Should we add another page or is this enough?

Samir: **haadhaa kaafiyan li al-'aan.**
hah-zah kah-fee-yan lee al-an.
This is enough for now.

Omar: **mataa turiidu 'an nufarriqa haadhaa at-taqriir?**
*mah-tah too-ree-doo an noo-fah-ree-kah hah-zah
ah-tak-reer?*
When would you like to distribute this report?

Samir: **'indanaa 'ijtimaa' fii saa'a. yajib 'an yakuun at-taqriir
jaahiz li al-'ijtimaa'.**
*een-dah-nah eej-tee-mah fee sah-ah. yah-jeeb an
yah-koon ah-tak-reer jah-heez lee al-eej-tee-mah.*
We have a meeting in one hour. The report must be
ready in time for the meeting.

Omar: **sa yakuun jaahiz fii niSf saa'a. kam min nuskha yajib
'an naTba'?**
*Sah yah-koon jah-heez fee nee-sef sah-ah. kam meen
noos-kah yah-jeeb an nat-bah?*
It'll be ready in half an hour. How many copies do we
need to print?

Samir: **sa yakuun 'ashra mumathiliin fii al-'ijtimaa', wa
laakin 'iTba' khamsat nuskhaat 'iDHaafiyya.**
*sah yah-koon ash-rah moo-mah-thee-leen fee
al-eej-tee-mah, wah lah-keen eet-bah kam-sat
noos-kat ee-dah-fee-yah.*
There will be ten representatives at the meeting, but
print five additional copies just in case.

Omar: **fawran. hal hunaaka shay'un 'aakhar?**
faw-ran. hal hoo-nah-kah shay-oon ah-kar?
Right away. Is there anything else?

Samir: **na'am. 'i'lam kaatibatii min faDlik 'an ta'khudh
mukaalamat al-haatifiyya li 'annanii sa 'akuun fii
al-'ijtimaa'.**
*nah-am. eeh-lam kah-tee-bah-tee meen fad-leek an
tah-kooz moo-kah-lah-mat al-hah-tee-fee-yah lee
ah-nah-nee sah ah-koon fee al-eej-tee-mah.*
Yes. Please inform my assistant to hold all my calls
because I'll be at the meeting.

Omar: **sa 'aquulu lihaa dhallika al-'aan.**
sah ah-koo-loo lee-hah zah-lee-kah al-an.
I will tell her that right now.

Words to Know

taqriir	tak-reer	report
taqriiraat	tak-ree-rat	reports
niSf	nee-sef	half
musaa'ada	moo-sah-ah-dah	help
ghurfa	goor-fah	room
'ijtimaa'	eej-tee-mah	meeting/conference
Suwar	soo-war	pictures
bidaaya	bee-dah-yah	beginning
nihaaya	nee-hah-yah	ending
yaziid	yah-zeed	to add
farraqa	fah-rah-kah	distribute
jaahiz	jah-heez	ready (M)
jaahiza	jah-hee-zah	ready (F)
Taba'a	tah-bah-ah	to print
nuskhaat	noos-kat	copies
mumathil	moo-mah-theel	representative (M)
mumathila	moo-mah-thee-lah	representative (F)
mumathiliin	moo-mah-thee-leen	representatives (MP)
mumathilaat	moo-mah-thee-lat	representatives (FP)
'iDHaafiy	ee-zah-fee	additional (M)
'iDHaafiyya	ee-zah-fee-yah	additional (F)

Giving orders

The *imperative verb form,* also known as the *command form,* is used to give orders or directions. It's an important verb to know in the workplace because that's where you're usually told what to do and where you tell others what to do. The imperative structure is fairly straightforward. This section shares some quick tips to allow you to master the imperative form.

First, because the imperative is a command form, you can use it only with present personal pronouns such as **'anta** (*an-tah;* you) (M) and **'anti** (*an-tee;* you) (F). You can't used the imperative with absent personal pronouns such as **huwa** (*hoo-wah;* him) because you can't give an order to someone who isn't present. The following is a list of the personal pronouns to use with the imperative:

- ✔ **'anta** (*an-tah;* you) (MS)
- ✔ **'anti** (*an-tee;* you) (FS)
- ✔ **'antum** (*an-toom;* you) (MP)
- ✔ **'antunna** (*an-too-nah;* you) (FP)
- ✔ **'antumaa** (*an-too-mah;* you) (dual)

Second, the imperative form is nothing but a derived form of the regular verb in the **maaDii** (*mah-dee;* past) and the **muDaari'** (*moo-dah-reeh;* present) tenses. The following is a list of the most common imperative verbs:

- ✔ **'uktub** (*ook-toob;* write)
- ✔ **'iqra'** (*eek-rah;* read)
- ✔ **'unDHur** (*oon-zoor;* look)
- ✔ **'a'id** (*ah-eed;* repeat)
- ✔ **qull** (*kool;* say)
- ✔ **'u'kul** (*ooh-kool;* eat)
- ✔ **takallam** (*tah-kah-lam;* speak)
- ✔ **qif** (*keef;* stop)
- ✔ **taHarrak** (*tah-hah-rak;* move)

One of the more important verb command forms is the verb **kataba** (*kah-tah-bah;* to write). Table 10-1 shows the imperative (command form) of the verb **kataba.**

Table 10-1	Imperative Form of "Write"		
Pronoun	*Imperative*	*Pronunciation*	*Translation*
'anta (you/MS)	'uktub	ook-toob	write (MS)
'anti (you/FS)	'uktubii	ook-too-bee	write (FS)
'antum (you/MP)	'uktubuu	ook-too-boo	write (MP)
'antunna (you/FP)	'uktubna	ook-toob-nah	write (FP)
'antumaa (dual)	'uktubaani	ook-too-bah-nee	write (dual)

Another verb you should be aware of is the verb **takallama** (*tah-kah-lah-mah;* to speak). Table 10-2 shows the imperative form of the verb **takallama.**

Table 10-2	Imperative Form of "Speak"		
Pronoun	*Imperative*	*Pronunciation*	*Translation*
'anta (you/MS)	takallam	tah-kah-lam	speak (MS)
'anti (you/FS)	takallamii	tah-kah-lah-mee	speak (FS)
'antum (you/MP)	takallamuu	tah-kah-lah-moo	speak (MP)
'antunna (you/FP)	takallamna	tah-kah-lam-nah	speak (FP)
'antumaa (dual)	takallamaa	tah-kah-lah-mah	speak (dual)

Supplying your office

In order to function properly and efficiently at the **maktab,** you need a number of different work-related items. Here are some common supplies you can expect to find at the **maktab:**

- **kursiiy** (*koor-see;* chair)
- **maktab** (*mak-tab;* desk)
- **'aalat al-Hisaab** (*ah-lat al-hee-sab;* computer)
- **haatif** (*hah-teef;* telephone)
- **'aalat al-faks** (*ah-lat al-fah-kes;* fax machine)
- **maTba'a** (*mat-bah-ah;* printer)
- **'aalat al-Tibaa'** (*ah-lat ah-tee-bah;* photocopier)

Besides **'aalaat** (*ah-lat;* machines) and heavy furniture, you also need smaller tools to help you get by at the **maktab:**

- **qalam jaaf** (*kah-lam jaf;* pen)
- **qalam ar-rasaas** (*kah-lam ah-rah-sas;* pencil)
- **mimHaat** (*meem-hat;* eraser)
- **kitaab** (*kee-tab;* book)
- **daftar** (*daf-tar;* notebook)
- **'awraaq** (*aw-rak;* papers)
- **mishbak 'awraaq** (*meesh-bak aw-rak;* paper clip)
- **Dammat 'awraaq** (*dah-mat aw-rak;* stapler)
- **liSaaq** (*lee-sak;* glue)
- **skooch** (*seh-koo-tech;* tape)

If you can't find a **daftar** or **liSaaq,** ask a **zumalaa'** if you can borrow one. Here's how you ask a colleague a question, depending on whether you're speaking to a man or a woman:

- **hal 'indakii daftar?** (*hal een-dah-kee daf-tar;* Do you have a notebook?) (F)
- **hal 'indaka liSaaq?** (*hal een-dah-kah lee-sak;* Do you have glue?) (M)
- **hal 'indakum skooch?** (*hal een-dah-koom seh-koo-tech;* Do you have tape?) (MP)
- **hal 'indahu qalam?** (*hal een-dah-hoo kah-lam;* Does he have a pen?)

The construct "to have" in Arabic isn't a verb (see the preceding list of examples); rather it's a combination of possessive suffix constructions added to the word **'inda** *(een-dah),* which is the best word in the language to denote possession. However, for all intents and purposes, you may use this construct — **'inda** followed by a possessive suffix — in the same way as you would a regular verb. Check out this prepositional phrase using all personal pronoun suffixes:

Pronoun	Form	Pronunciation	Translation
'anaa	'indii	een-dee	I have
'anta	'indaka	een-dah-kah	You have (MS)
'anti	'indakii	een-dah-kee	You have (FS)
huwa	'indahu	een-dah-hoo	He has
hiya	'indahaa	een-dah-hah	She has
naHnu	'indanaa	een-dah-nah	We have

Pronoun	Form	Pronunciation	Translation
'antum	'indakum	een-dah-koom	You have (MP)
'antunna	'indakunna	een-dah-koo-nah	You have (FP)
hum	'indahum	een-dah-hoom	They have (MP)
hunna	'indahunna	een-dah-hoo-nah	They have (FP)
antumaa	'indakumaa	een-dah-koo-mah	You have (dual)
humaa	'indahumaa	een-dah-hoo-mah	They have (dual)

Talkin' the Talk

Samira can't find her eraser. She asks some of her colleagues if they have one available for her to borrow.

Samira: **'afwan tariiq. hal 'indaka mimHaat?**
af-wan tah-reek. hal een-dah-kah meem-hat?
Excuse me Tarik. Do you have an eraser?

Tarik: **laHdha. sa 'araa fii maktabii.**
lah-zah. sah ah-rah fee mak-tah-bee.
One moment. I'll check my desk.

Tarik looks around his desk but can't find the eraser.

Tarik: **'anaa 'aasif. laysa 'indii mimHaat hunaa.**
ah-nah ah-seef. lay-sah een-dee meem-hat hoo-nah.
I'm sorry. I don't have an eraser here.

Samira: **man tadhunn 'indahu mimHaat?**
man tah-zoon een-dah-hoo meem-hat?
Who do you think has an eraser?

Tarik: **'adhunn 'anna frank 'indahu mimHaat.**
ah-zoon ah-nah frank een-dah-hoo meem-hat.
I believe Frank has an eraser.

Samira: **shukran.**
shook-ran.
Thank you.

Samira stops by Frank's desk to ask him for an eraser.

Samira: **'ahlan frank. hal 'indaka mimHaat?**
ah-lan frank. hal een-dah-kah meem-hat?
Hi Frank. Do you have an eraser?

Frank: **na'am. haa hiya.**
nah-am. hah hee-yah.
Yes. Here you go.

Samira: **shukran jaziilan!**
shook-ran jah-zee-lan.
Thank you so much!

Words to Know

laHdha	lah-zah	one moment
'anaa 'aasif	ah-nah ah-seef	I am sorry (M)
'anaa 'aasifa	ah-nah ah-see-fah	I am sorry (F)

Life at Home

If you're like most people, you spend a lot of time at your **manzil** (*man-zeel;* house). The **manzil** is a bit different than the **bayt** (*bah-yet;* home) because a **manzil** can be any old **manzil,** whereas the **bayt** is the space where you feel most comfortable. In many cultures, a **manzil** is a family's or individual's most prized possession or asset. Due to the centrality of the **bayt** and **manzil** in everyday life, knowing how to talk about them in-depth can be very useful. In this section, I tell you all the right words and terms to help you talk about your **manzil!**

As you know, a **manzil** consists of **ghuraf** (*roo-raf;* rooms). In singular form, "room" is known as **ghurfa** (*roor-fah*) in Arabic. This list should help you become familiar with the major types of **ghuraf** in a **manzil:**

- **ghurfat al-juluus** (*goor-fat al-joo-loos;* sitting room)
- **ghurfat al-ma'iisha** (*goor-fat al-mah-ee-shah;* living room)
- **ghurfat al-'akl** (*goor-fat al-ah-kel;* dining room)

- ✔ **ghurfat an-nawm** (*goor-fat ah-nah-wem;* bedroom)

- ✔ **Hammaam** (*hah-mam;* bathroom)

- ✔ **ghurfat al-ghasl** (*goor-fat al-gah-sel;* washing/laundry room)

- ✔ **maTbakh** (*mat-bak;* kitchen)

In addition to **ghuraf,** a **manzil** may also have a **karaaj** (*kah-raj;* garage) where you can park your **sayyaara** (*sah-yah-rah;* car) as well as a **bustaan** (*boos-tan;* garden) where you can play or just relax. Some **manaazil** (*mah-nah-zeel;* houses) even have a **masbaH** (*mas-bah;* swimming pool).

Each **ghurfa** in the **manzil** usually contains different items. For example, you can expect to find a **sariir** (*sah-reer;* bed) in a **ghurfat an-nawm.** Here are some items you can expect to find in the **Hammaam:**

- ✔ **mirHaaD** (*meer-had;* toilet)

- ✔ **duush** (*doosh;* shower)

- ✔ **maghsal** (*mag-sal;* sink)

- ✔ **shawkat al-'asnaan** (*shaw-kat al-ass-nan;* toothbrush)

- ✔ **ghasuul as-sha'r** (*gah-sool ah-shah-er;* shampoo)

- ✔ **Saabuun** (*sah-boon;* soap)

- ✔ **mir'aat** (*meer-at;* mirror)

You can expect to find the following items in the **maTbakh:**

- ✔ **furn** (*foo-ren;* stove)

- ✔ **tannuur** (*tah-noor;* oven)

- ✔ **thallaaja** (*tah-lah-jah;* refrigerator)

- ✔ **zubaala** (*zoo-bah-lah;* trash can)

- ✔ **shawkaat** (*shaw-kat;* forks)

- ✔ **malaa'iq** (*mah-lah-eek;* spoons)

- ✔ **sakaakiin** (*sah-kah-keen;* knives)

- ✔ **ku'uus** (*koo-oos;* glasses)

- ✔ **'aTbaaq** (*at-bak;* dishes)

Family life in a Middle Eastern home

In most Arabic-speaking and Islamic countries, the **bayt** (*bah-yet;* home) plays a very central role in family life. Unlike in Western countries, the **'usra** (*oos-rah;* family) structure in the **bayt** generally consists of more than the parents and children (the typical nuclear family); it extends to other members of the family, such as grandparents, uncles, aunts, and cousins. Therefore, a **bayt** in most Middle Eastern countries houses not only parents and their children but also grandparents, grandchildren, cousins, and other family members.

In countries such as Saudi Arabia, **manaazil** (*mah-nah-zeel;* houses) are built to accommodate up to 10 or 15 family members and sometimes more. Like houses in the United States,

Europe, and other parts of the world, the Middle Eastern home revolves around the **ghurfat al-ma'iisha** (living room). Physically and architecturally, the **ghurfat al-ma'iisha** is the central part of the **manzil**; it's usually surrounded by the **maTbakh** (kitchen) and the **ghurfat al-juluus** (sitting room) and **ghurfat al-'akl** (dining room). Often times, it's the largest room in the **manzil** and is accessible through different **ghuraf**.

During the **'iid** (*eed;* holidays), the **bayt** becomes a place where family members come and celebrate the festivities together. The **ghurfat al-ma'iisha** retains its centrality during these festivities, although other parts of the **manzil** become more significant, such as the **ghurfat al-'akl** and the **bustaan** (garden).

Talkin' the Talk

Hassan can't find the remote control for the living room television. He asks his mother whether she has seen it.

Hassan:	**hal ra'aytii jihaaz at-tilfaaz?** *hal rah-ay-tee jee-haz ah-teel-faz?* Have you seen the remote control?
Mother:	**kaana fawqa aT-Taawila.** *kah-nah faw-kah ah-tah-wee-lah.* It was on the table.
Hassan:	**'ay Taawila?** *ay tah-wee-lah?* Which table?
Mother:	**aT-Taawila fii ghurfat al-'akl.** *ah-tah-wee-lah fee goor-fat al-ah-kel.* The dining room table.

Hassan looks for the remote control on the dining room table but can't find it.

Hassan: **laa, al-jihaaz laysa fawqa aT-Taawila.**
lah, al-jee-haz lay-sah faw-kah ah-tah-wee-lah.
No, the remote is not on the table.

Mother: **hal 'anta muta'akkid?**
hal an-tah moo-tah-ah-keed?
Are you sure?

Hassan: **na'am. huwa laysa hunaa.**
nah-am. hoo-wah lay-sah hoo-nah.
Yes. It's not there.

Mother: **rubbamaa huwa taHta aT-Taawila.**
roo-bah-mah hoo-wah tah-tah ah-tah-wee-lah.
Perhaps it's under the table.

Hassan: **daqiiqa sa'araa taHta aT-Taawila.**
dah-kee-kah sah-ah-rah tah-tah ah-tah-wee-lah.
One minute while I look under the table.

Hassan looks under the table for the remote.

Hassan: **laysa hunaa 'ayDHan. man 'ista'malahu al-'aakhir?**
lay-sah hoo-nah ay-zan. man ees-tah-mah-loo-hoo al-ah-keer?
It's not there either. Who was the last person to use it?

Mother: **'abuuk. 'unDHur fii ghurfat al-juluus. rubbamaa 'akhadhahu hunaaka.**
ah-book. oon-zoor fee goor-fat al-joo-loos. roo-bah-mah ah-kah-dah-hoo hoo-nah-kah.
Your father. Look in the sitting room. Maybe he took it there.

Hassan: **huwa laysa fawqa Taawilat ghurfat al-juluus.**
hoo-wah lay-sah faw-kah tah-wee-lat goor-fat al-joo-loos.
It's not on the sitting room table.

Mother: **hal ra'ayta fii al-kanaba?**
hal rah-ay-tah fee al-kah-nah-bah?
Did you look on the couch?

Hassan: **qimtu 'alayhi!**
           keem-too ah-lay-hee!
           I found it!

Mother: **'ayna kaana?**
           ay-nah kah-nah?
           Where was it?

Hassan: **kaana fawqa aT-Taawila fii al-maTbakh.**
           kah-nah faw-kah ah-tah-wee-lah fee al-mat-bak.
           It was on the kitchen table.

Words to Know

jihaaz at-tilfaaz	jee-haz ah-teel-faz	TV remote control
tilifizyoon	tee-lee-feez-yoon	television
shaasha	shah-shah	screen
miyaa'	mee-yah	radio
kanaba	kah-nah-bah	couch
ra'a	rah-ah	to look/to see
qaama	kah-mah	to find
fawqa	faw-kah	on/on top/over
taHta	tah-tah	under/below
bijaanib	bee-jah-neeb	next to/adjacent
muta'akkid	moo-tah-ah-keed	sure/certain
rubbamaa	roo-bah-mah	perhaps/maybe

From the following list, choose the words that describe the rooms pictured here:

- Hammaam
- maTbakh
- ghurfat an-nawm
- ghurfat al-ma'iisha

The answers are in Appendix C.

Part III
Arabic on the Go

The 5th Wave   By Rich Tennant

AN AWKWARD SILENCE FOLLOWED THE INSTRUCTOR'S SUGGESTION THAT DOUG USE HIS UVULA MORE. WHEN LEARNING TO SPEAK ARABIC.

In this part . . .

You receive the tools you need to take Arabic on the road. Find out how to open a bank account, how to plan a trip, how to make a reservation at a hotel, and how to ask for directions.

Chapter 11

Money, Money, Money

● ●

In This Chapter

▶ Handling financial matters at the bank

▶ Understanding ATM commands

▶ Changing your currency

● ●

al-maal (*al-mal;* money) is an essential part of everyday life. Whether you're in a foreign country or at home, having access to **maal** is necessary in order to do the things you need to do — buy food, buy clothes, pay rent, go to the movies, and so on. Because very few activities in this world are **majjaanan** (*mah-jah-nan;* free), in this chapter you discover the Arabic terminology you need to manage your financial life. Specifically, I tell you how to open and maintain a bank account, how to withdraw money from the bank as well as from an automated teller machine (ATM), and how to exchange currency in case you travel to different countries.

At the Bank

The source of **al-maal** is the **maSraf** (*mas-raf;* bank); conveniently another word for "bank" in Arabic is **al-banka** or simply **banka.** In this section, you become familiar with some of the items you find and transactions that take place at the **maSraf.** Here are some common terms associated with the **maSraf:**

> ✔ **fuluus** (*foo-loos;* cash/physical currency)
>
> ✔ **nuquud** (*noo-kood;* money/coins)
>
> ✔ **naqd** (*nah-ked;* coin)
>
> ✔ **'awraaq** (*aw-rak;* money/paper currencies)
>
> ✔ **biTaaqa al-'i'timaad** (*bee-tah-kah al-eeh-tee-mad;* credit card)
>
> ✔ **biTaaqaat al-'i'timaad** (*bee-tah-kat al-eeh-tee-mad;* credit cards)

✔ **biTaaqa al-'istilaaf** (*bee-tah-kah al-ees-tee-laf;* debit card)

✔ **shiik** (*sheek;* check)

✔ **shiikaat** (*shee-kat;* checks)

✔ **Hisaab maSrafii** (*hee-sab mas-rah-fee;* bank account)

Opening a bank account

One of the most important things you may do in a **maSraf** is open a **Hisaab maSrafii** (bank account). Depending on your current financial situation and your future economic needs, you may open different types of **Husub maSrafiiyya** (*hoo-soob mas-rah-fee-yah;* bank accounts). Here are some of the types of **Husub** (*hoo-soob;* accounts) you may inquire about:

✔ **Hisaab maSrafii 'aadii** (*hee-sab mas-rah-fee ah-dee;* checking account)

✔ **Hisaab maSrafii li at-tawfiir** (*hee-sab mas-rah-fee lee ah-taw-feer;* savings account)

✔ **Hisaab maSrafii li at-tawfiir wa at-taqaa'ud** (*hee-sab mas-rah-fee lee ah-taw-feer wah ah-tah-kah-ood;* retirement savings account)

✔ **Hisaab maSrafii li aT-Tulaab** (*hee-sab mas-rah-fee lee ah-too-lab;* student checking account)

After you determine which type of **Hisaab** is right for you, you're ready to talk to the **'amiin al-maSraf** (*ah-meen al-mas-raf;* bank teller) (M) or the **'amiina al-masraf** (*ah-mee-nah al-mas-raf;* bank teller) (F) to open your **Hisaab.** The **'amiin al-maSraf** or **'amiina al-maSraf** may ask you to step into his or her **maktab** (*mak-tab;* office) in order to ensure your **shakhsiiyya** (*shak-see-yah;* privacy), because **futuuH** (*foo-tooh;* opening) a **Hisaab** must be done securely.

Talkin' the Talk

Said has recently moved to a new city to attend college. One of the first things he does as he's settling into his new hometown is go to the bank to open an account. Sarah, a bank teller, helps Said decide which bank account meets his needs.

Sarah: **SabaaH al-khayr. kayfa yumkin 'an 'usaa'iduka al-yawm?**
sah-bah al-kah-yer. kay-fah yoom-keen ann oo-sah-ee-doo-kah al-yah-oum?
Good morning. How may I help you today?

Said: **SabaaH an-nuur. 'uriidu 'an 'aftaHa Hisaab maSrafii.**
sah-bah ah-noor. oo-ree-doo an af-tah-hah hee-sab mas-rah-fee.
Good morning. I would like to open a bank account.

Sarah: **Tayyib, yumkin 'an 'usaa'iduka. tafaDDal min faDlik 'ilaa maktabii.**
tah-yeeb, yoom-keen an oo-sah-ee-doo-kah. tah-fah-dal meen fad-leek ee-lah mak-tah-bee.
Great, I'll be able to help you with that. Please come in to my office.

Said: **raai', shukran.**
rah-eeh, shook-ran.
Excellent, thank you.

Sarah: **'ay naw' min Hisaab maSrafii tuHibb?**
ay nah-weh meen hee-sab mas-rah-fee too-heeb?
What type of bank account would you like?

Said: **'ay 'anwaa' min al-Husub al-maSrafiiyya 'indakum?**
ay an-wah meen al-hoo-soob al-mas-rah-fee-yah een-dah-koom?
What types of bank accounts do you have?

Sarah: **'indanaa 'anwaa' mutaghayyira. 'indanaa Hisaab maSrafii 'aadii wa Hisaab maSrafii li at-tawfiir. wa 'indanaa Hisaab maSrafii li aT-Tulaab. hal 'anta Taalib?**
een-dah-nah an-wah moo-tah-gah-yee-rah. een-dah-nah hee-sab mas-rah-fee ah-dee wah hee-sab mas-rah-fee lee ah-taw-feer. wah een-dah-nah hee-sab mas-rah-fee lee ah-too-lab. hal an-tah tah-leeb?
We have a lot of different types. We have regular checking accounts as well as savings accounts. And if you're a student, we also provide student checking accounts. Are you a student?

Said: **na'am, 'anaa Taalib.**
nah-am, ah-nah tah-leeb.
Yes, I'm a student.

Sarah: **'aDHunnu 'anna al-Hisaab maSrafii li aT-Tulaab sa-yuwaafiquk.**
ah-zoo-noo ah-nah al-hee-sab mas-rah-fee lee ah-too-lab sah-yoo-wah-fee-kook.
I believe that the student checking account will suit you well.

Said: **maa huwa al-farq bayna al-Hisaab al-maSrafii al-'aadii wa al-Hisaab al-maSrafii li aT-Tulaab?**
mah hoo-wah al-fah-rek bay-nah al-hee-sab al-mas-rah-fee al-ah-dee wah al-hee-sab al-mas-rah-fee lee ah-too-lab?
What's the difference between a regular checking account and a student checking account?

Sarah: **'idhaa 'aradta 'an taftaHa Hisaab maSrafii 'aadii yajib 'an yakuun 'indaka 'alf daraahim fii al-'arbuun. wa laakin yumkin 'an taftaHa Hisaab maSraffi li aT-Tulaab bi 'arbuun bi khamsat mi'a daraahim faqat.**
ee-zah ah-rad-tah an taf-tah-hah hee-sab mas-rah-fee ah-dee yah-jeeb an yah-koon een-dah-kah ah-lef dah-rah-heem fee al-ar-boon. wah lah-keen yoom-keen an taf-tah-hah hee-sab mas-rah-fee lee ah-too-lab bee ar-boon bee kam-sat mee-ah dah-rah-heem fah-kat.
If you want to open a regular checking account, you need a minimum deposit of one thousand dirhams. However, you may open a student checking account with only five hundred dirhams.

Said: **wa hal hunaaka farq 'aakhar baynahumaa?**
wah hal hoo-nah-kah fah-rek ah-kar bay-nah-hoo-mah?
And is there any other difference between the two?

Sarah: **na'am. al-farq al-'aakhar 'anna al-Hisaab al-maSrafii al-'aadii 'indahu faa'ida thalaatha fii al-mi'a wa laakin al-Hisaab al-maSrafii li aT-Tulaab 'indahu faa'ida 'arba'a fii al-mi'a.**
nah-am. al-fah-rek al-ah-kar ah-nah al-hee-sab al-mas-rah-fee al-ah-dee een-dah-hoo fah-ee-dah thah-lah-thah fee al-mee-ah wah lah-keen al-hee-sab al-mas-rah-fee lee ah-too-lab een-dah-hoo fah-ee-dah ar-bah-ah fee al-mee-ah.
Yes. The other difference is that the regular checking account yields three percent interest while the student checking account yields four percent interest.

Said: **shukran. 'uriidu 'an aftaHa Hisaab maSrafii li aT-Tulaab.**
shook-ran. oo-ree-doo an af-tah-hah hee-sab mas-rah-fee lee ah-too-lab.
Thank you. I would like to open a student checking account.

Words to Know

yaftaHu	yaf-tah-hoo	to open
maktab	mak-tab	office
naw'	nah-weh	type
'anwaa'	an-wah	types
yuwaafiq	yoo-wah-feek	to suit (suitable)
farq	fah-rek	difference
'arbuun	ar-boon	deposit
faqat	fah-kat	only
'aakhar	ah-kar	other
faa'ida	fah-ee-dah	interest rate
fii al-mi'a	fee al-mee-ah	percentage

Presenting your ID

After you decide which **Hisaab** is right for you, you need to take care of some initial paperwork. You must present a number of **wathaa'iq** (*wah-tah-eek;* documents) and then answer a few **'as'ila** (*ass-ee-lah;* questions). Here are some of the **wathaa'iq** you should have with you when you want to open a **Hisaab:**

- ✔ **biTaaqa shakhsiyya** (*bee-tah-kah shak-see-yah;* personal identification card)
- ✔ **biTaaqat as-saa'iq** (*bee-tah-kat ah-sah-eek;* driver's license)
- ✔ **jawaaz as-safar** (*jah-waz ah-sah-far;* passport)
- ✔ **biTaaqat at-tilmiidh** (*bee-tah-kat ah-teel-meez;* student identification card)
- ✔ **biTaaqat raqm al-'amn ash-shakhsiiy** (*bee-tah-kat rah-kem al-ah-men ah-shak-see;* social security card)

Providing your contact info

After you establish your identity by presenting various personal identification cards, the **'amiin al-maSraf** will probably ask you for some more **wathaa'iq** so that he can process your application. For example, he may ask for your **'unwaan ar-raahin** (*oon-wan ah-rah-heen;* current address) or your **'unwaan as-saabiq** (*oon-wan ah-sah-beek;* former address). Of course, in order to prove that you actually do live where you say you live, the **'amiin al-maSraf** may ask you for a **risaala** (*ree-sah-lah;* letter) addressed to you at your **'unwaan** (address).

Filling out the forms

After you provide the **wathaa'iq** that the **'amiin al-maSraf** requests, you usually receive an **'istimaarat aT-Talab** (*ees-tee-mah-rat ah-tah-lab;* application form) to fill out. Here are some items you're likely to find on the **'istimaarat aT-Talab:**

- **'ism shakhsii** (*ee-sem shak-see;* first name)
- **'ism 'aa'ilii** (*ee-sem ah-ee-lee;* last name/family name)
- **taariikh al-miilaad** (*tah-reek al-mee-lad;* date of birth)
- **makaan al-miilaad** (*mah-kan al-mee-lad;* place of birth)
- **al-mihna** (*al-meeh-nah;* occupation)
- **al-mustakhdim** (*al-moos-tak-deem;* employer)
- **taariikh al-'amal** (*tah-reek al-ah-mal;* work history)
- **naw' al-Hisaab** (*nah-weh al-hee-sab;* type of account)
- **raqm al-haatif** (*rah-kem al-hah-teef;* telephone number)

After you fill out the **'istimaarat aT-Talab**, the **'amiin al-maSraf** will ask for your **'imdaa'** (*eem-dah;* signature) on the document. When you finish with all the paperwork and have successfully opened your bank account, you're ready to start using it!

Talkin' the Talk

Jennifer is filling out a new bank account application. Adam, the bank manager, helps her with the application form.

Adam: **maa huwa 'ismukii ash-shakshii?**
mah hoo-wah ees-moo-kee ah-shak-see?
What's your first name?

Jennifer: **Jennifer.**
jeh-nee-fer.
Jennifer.

Adam: **wa maa huwa 'ismukii al-'aa'ilii?**
wah mah hoo-wah ees-moo-kee al-ah-ee-lee?
And what's your last name?

Jennifer: **Jones.**
Jones.
Jones.

Adam: **maa huwa taariikh milaadukii?**
mah hoo-wah tah-reek mee-lah-doo-kee?
What's your date of birth?

Jennifer: **yanaayir al-'awwal sanat 'alf wa tis'a mi'a wa thamaaniin.**
yah-nah-yeer al-ah-wal sah-nat ah-lef wah tees-ah mee-ah wah thah-mah-neen.
January 1, 1980.

Adam: **maa hiya mihnatukii?**
mah hee-yah meeh-nah-too-kee?
What's your occupation?

Jennifer: **'anaa mumarriDa.**
ah-nah moo-mah-ree-dah.
I'm a nurse.

Adam: **wa man huwa mustakhdimuk?**
wah man hoo-wah moos-tak-dee-mook?
And who is your employer?

Jennifer: **'anaa 'a'mal fii al-mustashfaa.**
ah-nah ah-mal fee al-moos-tash-fah.
I work at the hospital.

Adam: **shukran. naHnu qarrabnaa 'ilaa 'annihaaya.**
shook-ran. nah-noo kah-rab-nah ee-lah ah-nee-hah-yah.
Thank you. We're almost finished.

Jennifer: **raai'.**
rah-eeh.
Great.

Adam: **'uriidu 'imdaa'uki hunaa.**
oo-ree-doo eem-dah-oo-kee hoo-nah.
I'd like your signature right here.

Jennifer: **Taba'an.**
tah-bah-an.
Of course.

Adam:	**shukran. marHaba biki 'ilaa maSraf al-'arab.**
	shook-ran. mar-hah-bah bee-kee ee-lah mas-raf
	al-ah-rab.
	Thank you. Welcome to Arab Bank.
Jennifer:	**shukran.**
	shook-ran.
	Thank you.

Words to Know

maa huwa	mah hoo-wah	what is (M)
maa hiya	mah hee-yah	what is (F)
mudiir al-maSraf	moo-deer al-mas-raf	bank manager (M)
mudiira al-maSraf	moo-dee-rah al-mas-raf	bank manager (F)
yawm	yah-oom	day
shahr	shah-her	month
sana	sah-nah	year
mumarriDa	moo-mah-ree-dah	nurse (F)
mustashfaa	moos-tash-fah	hospital
nihaaya	nee-hah-yah	finish/ending
al-'i'timaad	al-eeh-tee-mad	credit

Open season on the verb "to open"

You can't open a **Hisaab**, or anything else for that matter, if you don't know how to conjugate the verb **fataHa** (*fah-tah-hah;* opened) in both the **maaDii** (past) and the **muDaari'** (present) forms. Here is the verb "to open" in the **maaDii:**

Form	*Pronunciation*	*Translation*
'anaa fataHtu	ah-nah fah-tah-too	I opened
'anta fataHta	ahn-tah fah-tah-tah	You opened (MS)

Form	Pronunciation	Translation
'anti fataHtii	ahn-tee fah-tah-tee	You opened (FS)
huwa fataHa	hoo-wah fah-tah-hah	He opened
hiya fataHat	hee-yah fah-tah-hat	She opened
naHnu fataHnaa	nah-noo fah-tah-nah	We opened
'antum fataHtum	ahn-toom fah-tah-toom	You opened (MP)
'antunna fataHtunna	ahn-too-nah fah-tah-too-nah	You opened (FP)
hum fataHuu	hoom fah-tah-hoo	They opened (MP)
hunna fataHna	hoo-nah fah-tah-nah	They opened (FP)
antumaa fataHtumaa	ahn-too-mah fah-tah-too-mah	You opened (dual/MP/FP)
humaa fataHaa	hoo-mah fah-tah-hah	They opened (dual/MP)
humaa fataHataa	hoo-mah fah-tah-hah-tah	They opened (dual/FP)

To conjugate **fataHa** in the **muDaari'**, you use the form **yaftaHu** *(yaf-tah-hoo)*:

Form	Pronunciation	Translation
'anaa 'aftaHu	ah-nah af-tah-hoo	I am opening
'anta taftaHu	ahn-tah taf-tah-hoo	You are opening (MS)
'anti taftaHiina	ahn-tee taf-tah-hee-nah	You are opening (FS)
huwa yaftaHu	hoo-wah yaf-tah-hoo	He is opening
hiya taftaHu	hee-yah taf-tah-hoo	She is opening
naHnu naftaHu	nah-noo naf-tah-hoo	We are opening
'antum taftaHuuna	ahn-toom taf-tah-hoo-nah	You are opening (MP)
'antunna taftaHna	ahn-too-nah taf-tah-nah	You are opening (FP)
hum yaftaHuuna	hoom yaf-tah-hoo-nah	They are opening (MP)
hunna yaftaHna	hoo-nah yaf-tah-nah	They are opening (FP)
antumaa taftaHaani	ahn-too-mah taf-tah-hah-nee	You are opening (dual/MP/FP)
humaa yaftaHaani	hoo-mah yaf-tah-hah-nee	They are opening (dual/MP)
humaa taftaHaani	hoo-mah taf-tah-hah-nee	They are opening (dual/FP)

Making deposits and withdrawals

After you open your **Hisaab,** the two most basic transactions you'll probably make are:

- ✔ **wadii'a** (*wah-dee-ah;* deposit)
- ✔ **'insiHaab** (*een-see-hab;* withdrawal)

To make a **wadii'a,** you may deposit into your **Hisaab maSrafii** (bank account) using a **shiik** (check) or **fuluus** (cash). You may go to the **'amiin al-maSraf** to make the **wadii'a** or do it yourself at an ATM, if your bank allows that.

Similarly, you may perform a **'insiHaab** by either going to the **'amiin al-maSraf** or by using the ATM.

Using the ATM

In recent years, the number of ATMs located around the world has mushroomed, and in places like New York City, you can't walk half a block without spotting one. Whether you're in the United States, the Middle East, or other countries or regions of the world, there's a good chance that you'll use an ATM to withdraw **fuluus.** This section covers the terminology you encounter at an ATM to help make this a smooth and efficient transaction.

Most ATMs accept all sorts of cards, whether they're issued by the same **maSraf** that operates the ATM terminal or not. However, some ATMs charge you a **'ujra** (*ooj-rah;* fee) if you use a card not issued by a recognized **maSraf.** In addition, most ATMs accept both **biTaaqaat al-'i'timaad** (credit cards) and **biTaaqaat al-'istilaaf** (debit cards). *Note:* Another word for "credit card" is **biTaaqa diiniiya** (*bee-tah-kah dee-nee-yah*).

Although most ATMs let you choose the language you want to conduct your transaction in, you should still be aware of ATM-related commands and phrases in Arabic:

- ✔ **'udkhul al-biTaaqa** (*ood-kool al-bee-tah-kah;* Insert the card.)
- ✔ **'udkhul ar-raqm as-siriiy.** (*ood-kool ah-rah-kem ah-see-ree;* Enter the PIN/secret number.)
- ✔ **'insiHaab al-fuluus** (*een-see-hab al-foo-loos;* cash withdrawal)
- ✔ **'udkhul al-kammiyya.** (*ood-kool al-kah-mee-yah;* Enter the amount.)
- ✔ **'akkid al-kammiyya.** (*ah-keed al-kah-mee-yah;* Confirm the amount.)
- ✔ **khudh al-fuluus.** (*kooz al-foo-loos;* Take the cash.)

✔ **hal turiidu 'iiSaala?** (*hal too-ree-doo ee-sah-lah;* Do you want a receipt?)

✔ **khudh al-'iiSaala.** (*kooz al-ee-sah-lah;* Take the receipt.)

✔ **Haqqiq ar-raSiid.** (*hah-keek ah-rah-seed;* Check the balance.)

✔ **Hawwil al-amwaal.** (*hah-weel al-am-wal;* Transfer the money.)

✔ **'azil al-biTaaqa min faDlik.** (*ah-zeel al-bee-tah-kah meen fad-leek;* Please remove the card.)

Exchanging Currency

If you're traveling to a foreign **dawla** (*dah-ou-lah;* country), you won't get very far if you don't have the right **'umla mutadaawala** (*oom-lah moo-tah-dah-wah-lah;* currency), or **'umla** (*oom-lah*) for short. (Of course, you could rely on **shiikat al-musaafir** (*shee-kat al-moo-sah-feer;* traveler's checks), but you may find that carrying **'umla** is more convenient.) You can exchange **'umla** at a number of different places. If you like to plan in advance, then stopping by the **maSraf** before your **safar** (*sah-far;* trip) is a good idea. Otherwise, you can go to a **maktab as-sarf** (*mak-tab ah-sah-ref;* exchange desk) located at the **maTaar** (*mah-tar;* airport).

You're likely to get better exchange rates in your home country at your local bank than at an airport in a foreign country. If you're visiting a foreign country and need to change money, then the best way for you to exchange currencies is to go to a reputable bank of international renown and make your transactions there.

Getting to know the currencies around the world

In order to exchange your money, you need to be familiar with the different types of currencies you're dealing with. The following lists feature some of the most common currencies grouped by specific regions around the world.

The following currencies are used in the Middle East:

✔ Algeria: **diinaar jazaa'irii** (*dee-nar jah-zah-ee-ree;* Algerian dinar)

✔ Bahrain: **diinaar baHrainii** (*dee-nar bah-ray-nee;* Bahraini dinar)

✔ Egypt: **junya maSriiyya** (*joon-yah mas-ree-yah;* Egyptian pound)

✔ Iraq: **diinaar 'iraaqii** (*dee-nar ee-rah-kee;* Iraqi dinar)

✔ Jordan: **diinaar 'urduniiy** (*dee-nar oor-doo-nee;* Jordanian dinar)

✔ Kuwait: **diinaar kwaytii** (*dee-nar kuh-way-tee;* Kuwaiti dinar)

✔ Lebanon: **liira lubnaaniiya** (*lee-rah loob-nah-nee-yah;* Lebanese pound)

✔ Libya: **diinaar liibii** (*dee-nar lee-bee;* Libyan dinar)

✔ Morocco: **dirham maghribii** (*deer-ham mag-ree-bee;* Moroccan dirham)

✔ Oman: **riyaal 'ummaanii** (*ree-yal oh-mah-nee;* Omani dinar)

✔ Qatar: **riyaal qaTarii** (*ree-yal kah-tah-ree;* Qatari riyal)

✔ Saudi Arabia: **riyaal sa'uudii** (*ree-yal sah-oo-dee;* Saudi riyal)

✔ Syria: **liira suuriiya** (*lee-rah soo-ree-yah;* Syrian pound)

✔ Tunisia: **diinaar tunsii** (*dee-nar toon-see;* Tunisian dinar)

✔ United Arab Emirates (UAE): **dirham al-'imaaraat** (*deer-ham al-ee-mah-rat;* Emirate dirham)

✔ Yemen: **riyaal yamanii** (*ree-yal yah-mah-nee;* Yemeni riyal)

In North America, you find the following currencies:

✔ Canada: **duulaar kanadiiy** (*doo-lar kah-nah-dee;* Canadian dollar)

✔ Mexico: **biisoo miksiikiiy** (*beh-soo meek-see-kee;* Mexican peso)

✔ USA: **duulaar 'amriikiiy** (*doo-lar am-ree-kee;* American dollar)

Only two currencies are used in Europe:

✔ European Union (EU): **al-yooro** (*al-yoo-roh;* euro)

✔ United Kingdom: **junya briiTaaniiyya** (*joon-yah bree-tah-nee-yah;* British pound)

The following currencies are used in Asia:

✔ Australia: **duulaar 'oosTraliiy** (*doo-lar oos-trah-lee;* Australian dollar)

✔ China: **yooan Siiniiy** (*yoo-an see-nee;* Chinese yuan)

✔ Japan: **yen yabanii** (*yen yah-bah-nee;* Japanese yen)

✔ South Korea: **won al-koorii** (*won al-koo-ree;* Korean won)

Making exchanges

Knowing the names of the currencies is only the first step toward exchanging the currency you hold into the one you need. The following list of questions can help you facilitate this exchange at the **maSraf:**

✔ **'ayna maktab as-sarf?** (*ay-nah mak-tab ah-sah-ref;* Where is the exchange desk?)

✔ **hal maktab as-sarf qariib min hunaa?** (*hal mak-tab ah-sah-ref kah-reeb meen hoo-nah;* Is the exchange desk close to here?)

✔ **mataa yaHull maktab as-sarf?** (*mah-tah yah-hool mak-tab ah-sah-ref;* When does the exchange desk open?)

✔ **maa huwa mu'addal as-sarf al-yawm?** (*mah hoo-wah moo-ah-dal ah-sah-ref al-yah-oum;* What is today's exchange rate?)

✔ **hal mu'addal as-sarf sayakuun 'aHsan ghadan?** (*hal moo-ah-dal ah-sah-ref sah-yah-koon ah-san gah-dan;* Will the exchange rate be better tomorrow?)

✔ **hal hunaaka 'ujra li tasriif al-fuluus?** (*hal hoo-nah-kah ooj-rah lee tas-reef al-foo-loos;* Is there a fee for exchanging money?)

✔ **'uriidu 'an 'aSrifa duularaat 'ilaa daraahim.** (*oo-ree-doo an as-ree-fah doo-lah-rat ee-lah dah-rah-heem;* I would like to exchange dollars into dirhams.)

✔ **kam min diinaar li mi'at duulaar?** (*kam meen dee-nar lee mee-at doo-lar;* How many dinars for one hundred dollars?)

Here are some answers you may hear from the **'amiin maktab as-sarf** (*ah-meen mak-tab ah-sah-ref;* exchange desk representative):

✔ **maktab as-sarf yaHull ma'a as-saa'a ath-thaamina fii aS-SabaaH.** (*mak-tab ah-sah-ref yah-hool mah-ah ah-sah-ah ah-thah-mee-nah fee ah-sah-bah;* The exchange desk opens at 8:00 in the morning.)

✔ **na'am, nusarrif duulaaraat 'ilaa daraahim.** (*nah-am, noo-sah-reef doo-lah-rat ee-lah dah-rah-heem;* Yes, we exchange dollars into dirhams.)

✔ **mu'addal as-sarf al-yawm mithla mu'addal as-sarf al-'ams.** (*moo-ah-dal ah-sah-ref al-yah-oum meet-lah moo-ah-dal ah-sah-ref al-ah-mes;* Today's exchange rate is the same as yesterday's exchange rate.)

✔ **naHnu naqbal duulaaraat faqat.** (*nah-noo nak-bal doo-lah-rat fah-kat;* We only accept dollars.)

✔ **naHnu naqbal nuquud faqat.** (*nah-noo nak-bal noo-kood fah-kat;* We only accept cash.)

✔ **mi'at duulaar tusaawii 'alf riyaal.** (*mee-at doo-lar too-sah-wee ah-lef ree-yal;* One hundred dollars equals one thousand riyals.)

✔ **hunaaka 'ujra 'ashrat duulaar li kul maHDar.** (*hoo-nah-kah ooj-ra ash-rat doo-lar lee kool mah-dar;* There is a ten dollar fee for every transaction.)

✔ **maktab as-sarf daakhil al-maSraf.** (*mak-tab ah-sah-ref dah-keel al-mas-raf;* The exchange desk is inside the bank.)

Talkin' the Talk

Sam stops by a currency exchange desk to exchange dollars into dirhams. The exchange desk teller helps him with this transaction.

Sam: **hal yumkin 'an tusrifa duulaaraat 'ilaa daraahim?**
hal yoom-keen an toos-ree-fah doo-lah-rat ee-lah dah-rah-heem?
Is it possible for you to exchange dollars into dirhams?

Teller: **Tab'an.**
tah-bah-an.
Of course.

Sam: **Tayyib. 'uriidu 'an 'asrifa 'alf duulaar 'ilaa daraahim.**
tah-yeeb. oo-ree-doo an as-ree-fah ah-lef doo-lar ee-lah dah-rah-heem.
Good. I would like to exchange one thousand dollars into dirhams.

Teller: **raa'i'. yumkin 'an 'usaa'iduka.**
rah-eeh. yoom-keen an oo-sah-ee-doo-kah.
Great. I'll be able to help you with that.

Sam: **'awwalan, hal yumkin 'an taquula li maa huwa mu'addal as-sarf al-yawm?**
ah-wah-lan, hal yoom-keen an tah-koo-lah lee mah hoo-wah moo-ah-dal ah-sah-ref al-yah-oum?
First, can you tell me today's exchange rate?

Teller: **mu'addal as-sarf al-yawm 'anna kulla duulaar yusaawii 'ashrat daraahim.**
moo-ah-dal ah-sah-ref al-yah-oum ah-nah koo-lah doo-lar yoo-sah-wee ash-rat dah-rah-heem.
Today's exchange rate is one dollar equals ten dirhams.

Sam: **'idhan 'alf duulaar tusaawii 'ashrat 'alaaf daraahim?**
ee-zan ah-lef doo-lar too-sah-wee ash-rat ah-laf dah-rah-heem?
Therefore one thousand dollars equals ten thousand dirhams?

Teller: **SaHH.**
              sah.
              That's correct.

Sam: **Tayyib. 'israf li min faDlik 'alf duulaar 'ilaa 'ashrat**
              'alaaf daraahim.
              tah-yeeb. ees-raf lee meen fad-leek ah-lef doo-lar
              ee-lah ash-rat ah-laf dah-rah-heem.
              Good. Please exchange one thousand dollars into ten
              thousand dirhams.

Teller: **fawran.**
              faw-ran.
              Right away.

Words to Know

tusrifa	toos-ree-fah	to exchange (M)
tusrifiina	toos-ree-fee-nah	to exchange (F)
'alf	ah-lef	thousand
yusaawii	yoo-sah-wee	equals (M)
tusaawii	too-sah-wee	equals (F)
SaHiiH	sah-heeh	correct

Use the clues below to fill in the words in this Arabic crossword puzzle.

Across

1. dollar

2. check

Down

1. bank

2. coin

3. desk

The answers to this puzzle appear in Appendix C.

Chapter 12

Asking for Directions

. . . .

In This Chapter

▶ Asking and answering "where" questions

▶ Clarifying directions

▶ Exploring ordinal numbers

. . . .

*B*eing able to ask for — and understand — **'ittijaahaat** (*ee-tee-jah-hat;* directions) is an important skill, particularly if you're traveling in an Arabic-speaking country. In order to interact with and get assistance from native Arabic speakers, you need to know how to ask questions that will help you get where you want to be. And you also need to understand the **'ittijaahaat** that are being given to you!

In this chapter, I tell you how to interact with native speakers in order to get relevant information to help you find what you're looking for!

Focusing on the "Where"

In order to ask for and give directions, you need to be able to answer and ask "where" questions. In this section, I tell you how to do just that.

Asking "where" questions

The best way to get directions-related information from Arabic speakers is to ask **'ayna** (*eh-yeh-nah;* where) questions. Luckily, the structure of an **'ayna** question is relatively straightforward: You use **'ayna** followed by the subject. For example:

▶ **'ayna al-funduq?** (*eh-yeh-nah al-foon-dook;* Where is the hotel?)

▶ **'ayna al-haatif?** (*eh-yeh-nah al-haa-teef;* Where is the phone?)

▶ **'ayna al-mirHaaD?** (*eh-yeh-nah al-meer-haad;* Where is the bathroom?)

Be sure to define the subject following **'ayna.** As I explain in Chapter 3, you define a subject by adding the definite article prefix **al-** to the subject noun. For example, **funduq** means "hotel," and **al-funduq** means "the hotel." So if you're asking where the hotel is located, you say, **'ayna al-funduq?** (Where is the hotel?) and not **'ayna funduq?**, which translates to "Where is hotel?"

"Where" questions are useful for more than just asking for directions. You may also apply the **'ayna** question format to human subjects, such as friends or family. For instance:

- ✔ **'ayna maryam?** (*eh-yeh-nah mee-ree-yam;* Where is Myriam?)
- ✔ **'ayna al-'aTfaal?** (*eh-yeh-nah al-aht-faal;* Where are the children?)
- ✔ **'ayna 'ummii?** (*eh-yeh-nah ooh-meey;* Where is my mom?)

You don't need to use the definite article **al-** when referring to a noun that's already defined. For instance, in one of the preceding examples, **maryam** doesn't require the definite article prefix **al-** because she's a specific person. So make sure that you don't go around adding the prefix **al-** to every subject after **'ayna** because sometimes there's no question about what subject you're referring to.

Answering "where" questions

Asking a "where" question is fairly straightforward (see the preceding section), but answering **'ayna** questions isn't always as clear-cut. You can answer an **'ayna** question in a number of different ways, ranging from the simple to the convoluted. In order to answer **'ayna** questions, you have to understand the structure of the **'ayna** question reply, which usually follows this format: subject, preposition, object.

Take a look at some common **'ayna** questions and their corresponding replies:

- ✔ **'ayna al-mustashfaa?** (*eh-yeh-nah al-moos-tash-faah;* Where is the hospital?)
  al-mustashfaa fii al-madiina. (*al-moos-tash-faah fee al-mah-dee-nah;* The hospital is in the city.)
- ✔ **'ayna al-maT'am?** (*eh-yeh-nah al-mah-tam;* Where is the restaurant?)
  al-maT'am qariib min al-funduq. (*al-mah-tam kah-reeb meen al-foon-dook;* The restaurant is close to the hotel.)
- ✔ **'ayna al-kitaab?** (*eh-yeh-nah al-kee-taab;* Where is the book?)
  a-kitaab taHta aT-Taawila. (*al-kee-taab tah-tah at-tah-wee-lah;* The book is underneath the table.)

Notice that in these examples, you use a preposition to establish a connection between the subject (in this case, what or who you're looking for) and the object (the location of the desired subject). In order to establish the desired relationship, it's very important for you to be familiar with some common prepositions:

- ✔ **'alaa** (*ah-laah;* on)
- ✔ **fii** (*fee;* in)
- ✔ **'ilaa** (*ee-laah;* to)
- ✔ **qariib min** (*kah-reeb meen;* close to)
- ✔ **ba'id min** (*bah-eed meen;* far from)
- ✔ **bijaanib** (*bee-jaah-neeb;* next to)
- ✔ **fawqa** (*faw-kah;* on top of)
- ✔ **taHta** (*tah-tah;* underneath/below)
- ✔ **'amaama** (*ah-maah-mah;* in front of)
- ✔ **waraa'a** (*wah-raah-ah;* behind)
- ✔ **yamiin min** (*yah-meen meen;* right of)
- ✔ **yasiir min** (*yah-seer meen;* left of)

Recall that the subject in the **'ayna** interrogatory sentence must be defined (see "Asking 'where' questions" earlier in the chapter for details); similarly, the subject in the reply to an **'ayna** question must also be defined. In addition, the object in the **'ayna** reply statement should be defined as well, either by using the definite article prefix **al-** or by including a predefined object.

Getting Direction About Directions

Understanding the format of the **'ayna** question and reply structures is an important first step toward approaching native Arabic speakers and asking them for directions.

Asking for directions

Of course, you can't just go up to someone and ask them bluntly, **'ayna al-funduq?** (Where is the hotel?). That wouldn't be very polite. The proper etiquette for approaching someone and asking for directions is to first say

as-salaamu 'alaykum (*ah-sah-lah-moo ah-lay-koom;* hello) or **'ahlan wa sahlan** (*ah-hel-an wah sah-hel-an;* hi) and then ask if he or she would permit you to ask a question. For example, you begin the exchange by saying, **'afwan. hal yumkin 'an 'as'alaka su'aalan?** (*ahf-wan. hal yoom-keen an ass-ah-lah-kah soo-aah-lan;* Excuse me. May I ask you a question?).

After the person agrees to take your question, you may proceed to ask for directions. (For more information on greetings and introductions, see Chapter 3.)

Talkin' the Talk

While visiting Casablanca, John is trying to find the museum. He stops Ahmed, a passerby, and asks him for directions.

John:	**'as-salaamu 'alaykum.** *ah-sah-lah-moo ah-lay-koom.* Hello.
Ahmed:	**wa 'alaykum 'as-salaam.** *wah ah-lay-koom ah-sah-laam.* Hello.
John:	**'afwan. hal yumkin 'an 'as'alaka su'aalan?** *ahf-wan. hal yoom-keen ann ass-ah-lah-kah soo-aah-lan?* Excuse me. May I ask you a question?
Ahmed:	**Tab'an.** *tah-bah-an.* Of course.
John:	**'ayna al-matHaf?** *eh-yeh-nah al-met-hef?* Where is the museum?
Ahmed:	**al-matHaf bijaanib al-masjid.** *al-met-hef bee-jaah-neeb al-mas-jeed.* The museum is next to the mosque.
John:	**shukran jazeelan!** *shook-ran jah-zee-lan!* Thank you very much!
Ahmed:	**laa shukran 'alaa waajib.** *laah shook-ran ah-laah waah-jeeb.* You're welcome.

Words to Know

matHaf	met-hef	museum
masjid	mas-jeed	mosque
mustashfaa	moos-tash-faah	hospital
maT'am	mah-tam	restaurant
funduq	foon-dook	hotel
sifaara	see-faah-rah	embassy
madrasa	mah-drah-sah	school
maktaba	mak-tah-bah	library
masraH	mass-rah	theater
suuq	sook	market
makhbaza	mak-bah-zah	bakery
madiina	mah-dee-nah	city
qarya	kah-ree-yah	village
Tariiq	tah-reek	street
shaari'	shah-reeh	avenue
Hay	hay	neighborhood
binaaya	bee-naa-yah	building

Could you repeat that?

Sometimes, when you ask for directions, the person who tries to help you starts talking too fast and you can't quite understand what he or she is saying. Other times, you may be in a loud area, such as near a downtown traffic jam, and you can't make out what the other person is saying. In either case, you have to ask the person who's giving you directions to speak more slowly or to repeat what he or she has just said. These phrases can help you cope with these situations:

- **afwan** (*ahf-wan;* excuse me/pardon me)

- **'ismaH lii** (*ees-maah lee;* excuse me)

- **lan 'afham** (*lann ah-fham;* I don't understand)

- **takallam bi baT'in min faDlik** (*tah-kah-lahm bee bat-een meen fahd-leek;* speak slowly please)

- **hal yumkin 'an ta'id min faDlik?** (*hal yoom-keen an tah-eed meen fahd-leek;* Could you repeat please?)

- **'a'id min faDlik** (*ah-eed meen fahd-leek;* Repeat please)

- **maadhaa qult?** (*maah-zaah koo-let;* What did you say?)

Talkin' the Talk

John is in downtown Casablanca where the traffic is really loud. He stops Maria, a passerby, to ask her for directions but can't make out what she's saying due to the noise. He asks her to repeat what she said.

John:	**'afwan. hal yumkin 'an 'as'alaka su'aalan?** *ahf-wan. hal yoom-keen an ass-ah-lah-kah soo-aah-lan?* Excuse me. May I ask you a question?
Maria:	**na'am.** *nah-ahm.* Yes.
John:	**'ayna al-madrasa?** *eh-yeh-nah al-mah-drah-sah?* Where is the school?
Maria:	**maa 'ismu al-madrasa?** *maah ees-muh al-mah-drah-sah?* What's the name of the school?
John:	**al-madrasa al-amriikiiyya.** *al-mah-drah-sah al-am-ree-kee-yah.* The American school.
Maria:	**al-madrasa ba'iida min hunaa.** *al-mah-drah-sah bah-ee-dah meen hoo-naah.* The school is far from here.

John: **lan 'afham. hal yumkin 'an ta'id min faDlik?**
lann ah-fham. hal yoom-keen an tah-eed meen fahd-leek?
I don't understand. Could you repeat please?

Maria: **al-madrasa laysat qariiba min hunaa. yajib 'an ta'khudh al-haafila 'ilaa waSat al-madiina.**
al-mah-drah-sah lay-saht kah-ree-bah meen hoo-naah. yah-jeeb an tah-khoo-dh al-haa-fee-lah ee-laah wah-saht al-mah-dee-nah.
The school is not close to here. You must take the bus to the center of the city.

John: **fahamt! Shukran jaziilan.**
fah-ha-met! shook-ran jah-zee-lan.
I understand! Thank you very much.

Maria: **'afwan.**
ahf-wan.
You're welcome.

Words to Know

ba'iid	bah-eed	far (M)
ba'iida	bah-eed-ah	far (F)
qariib	kah-reeb	close (M)
qariiba	kah-reeb-ah	close (F)
hunaa	hoo-naah	here
hunaaka	hoo-naah-kah	there
'afham	ahf-ham	understand
haafila	haa-fee-lah	bus
taksii	tah-ksee	taxi
qitaar	kee-taar	train
maHaTTa	mah-hah-tah	station

Using command forms

When you ask someone for directions, the person directs you to a specific location. Essentially, he or she tells you where to go, which qualifies as a *command form.* The command form is uniform, which means it applies to all personal pronouns. However, the command form is gender-defined, which means that you use different commands for men and women. Here are some common command forms:

Masculine Command	Feminine Command
'a'id (*ah-eed;* repeat)	**'a'idii** (*ah-eed-ee;* repeat)
'idhhab (*eez-hab;* go)	**'idhhabii** (*eez-hab-ee;* go)
khudh (*khooz;* take)	**khudhii** (*khooz-ee;* take)
Tuf (*toof;* turn)	**Tufii** (*toof-ee;* turn)
qif (*keef;* stop)	**qifii** (*keef-ee;* stop)

Note: **'imshii** (*eem-shee;* walk) is a special command form that is gender-neutral.

Talkin' the Talk

 Susan is trying to get back to her **funduq** (*foon-dook;* hotel) in Tunis. She stops Rita and asks her how to get there.

Susan: **'afwan. hal yumkin 'an 'as'aluka su'aalan?**
ahf-wan. hal yoom-keen an ass-ah-lah-kah soo-aah-lan?
Excuse me. May I ask you a question?

Rita: **Taba'an.**
tah-bah-an.
Of course.

Susan: **'ayna funduq al-jawhara?**
eh-yeh-nah foon-dook al-jaw-ha-rah?
Where is the Jawhara Hotel?

Rita: **'aDHunnu 'anna haadhaa al-funduq fii waSat al-madiina.**
ah-zuh-nuh an-nah hah-zah al-foon-dook fee wah-sat al-mah-dee-nah.
I believe that this hotel is in the center of the city.

Susan: **na'am. kayfa 'adhhabu hunaaka?**
na-am. kay-fah az-hah-boo hoo-nah-kah?
Yes. How do I get there?

Rita: **'idhhabii 'ilaa shaari' Hassan . . .**
eez-hab-ee ee-lah shah-reeh hah-san . . .
Go to Avenue Hassan . . .

Susan: **'afwan. lan 'afham. takallamii bi baT'in min faDlik.**
ahf-wan. lann ah-fham. tah-kah-lahm-ee bee bat-een meen fahd-leek.
Excuse me. I don't understand. Speak slowly please.

Rita: **Taba'an. 'idhhabii 'ilaa shaari' Hassan thumma Tufii 'ilaa al-yamiin.**
tah-bah-an. eez-hab-ee ee-laah shah-reeh hah-san thoo-mah toof-ee ee-laah al-yah-meen.
Certainly. Go to Avenue Hassan, then turn right.

Susan: **kwayyis.**
kwah-yees.
Okay.

Rita: **thumma 'imshii 'ilaa al-maktaba wa qifii. al-funduq 'amaama al-maktaba. Al-funduq fii ash-shamaal.**
thoo-maah eem-shee ee-laah al-mak-tah-bah wah keef-ee. al-foon-dook ah-maah-mah al-mak-tah-bah. al-foon-dook fee as-shah-maal.
Then walk toward the library and stop. The hotel is in front of the library. The hotel is facing north.

Susan: **shukran li musaa'adatuki.**
shook-ran lee moo-saa-ah-dah-too-kee.
Thank you for your help.

Words to Know

'aDHunnu	ah-zuh-nnuh	I believe
Thumma	thoo-mah	then
kwayyis	kwah-yees	okay
musaa'ada	moo-saa-ah-dah	help
shamaal	shah-maal	north
janoub	jah-noob	south
sharq	shah-rek	east
gharb	ghah-reb	west

Discovering Ordinal Numbers

Ordinal numbers are used to order things in a first-second-third kind of format. Unlike cardinal numbers, which are mostly used for counting, you use ordinals when giving directions. For example, you would tell someone to "turn right on the second street" and not "turn right on two street." Hear the difference?

Ordinal numbers in Arabic are gender-defined, so you need to be familiar with both the masculine and feminine ordinal forms, which I present in Table 12-1.

Table 12-1		Ordinal Numbers		
Ordinal (M)	*Pronunciation*	*Ordinal (F)*	*Pronunciation*	*Translation*
'awwal	ah-wall	'uulaa	ooh-laah	first
thaanii	thah-nee	thaaniya	thah-nee-yah	second
thaalith	thah-leeth	thaalitha	thah-lee-thah	third
raabi'	rah-bee	raabi'a	rah-bee-hah	fourth
khaamis	khah-mees	khaamisa	khah-mee-sah	fifth
saadis	sah-dees	saadisa	sah-dee-sah	sixth
saabi'	sah-bee	saabi'a	sah-bee-ah	seventh
thaamin	thah-meen	thaamina	thah-meen-ah	eighth
taasi'	tah-see	taasi'a	tah-see-ah	ninth
'aashir	ah-sheer	'aashira	ah-shee-rah	tenth
Haadi 'ashar	hah-dee ah-shar	Haadia 'ashra	hah-dee-yah ash-rah	eleventh
thaanii 'ashar	thah-nee ah-shar	thaaniya 'ashra	thah-nee-yah ash-rah	twelfth
thaalith 'ashar	thah-leeth ash-ar	thaalitha 'ashra	thah-lee-thah ash-rah	thirteenth
raabi' 'ashar	rah-bee ah-shar	raabi'a 'ashra	rah-bee-ah ash-rah	fourteenth
khaamis 'ashar	khah-mees ah-shar	khaamisa 'ashra	khah-mee-sah ash-rah	fifteenth
saadis 'ashar	sah-dees ah-shar	saadisa 'ashra	sah-dee-sah ash-rah	sixteenth
saabi' 'ashar	sah-bee ah-shar	saabi'a 'ashra	sah-bee-ah ash-rah	seventeenth
thaamin 'ashar	thah-meen ah-shar	thaamina 'ashra	thah-mee-nah ash-rah	eighteenth

Ordinal (M)	Pronunciation	Ordinal (F)	Pronunciation	Translation
taasi' 'ashar	tah-see ah-shar	taasi'a ash-ra	tah-see-ah ash-rah	nineteenth
'ishriin	eesh-reen	'ishriin	eesh-reen	twentieth
thalaathiin	thah-lah-theen	thalaathiin	thah-lah-theen	thirtieth

If you want to tell a friend that your house is "the fifth house," you say, **al-manzil al-khaamis** (*al-man-zeel al-khah-mees*). Note that you use the masculine ordinal form **khaamis** because **manzil** is a masculine noun subject. To say that you're taking the "eighth bus," you would say, **ash-shaahina ath-thaamina** *(ash-aahee-nah ah-thah-mee-nah).* The ordinal **thaamina** is feminine because **shaahina** (bus) is a feminine noun subject.

So if you want to tell your friend to "turn left on the second street," you say, **Tuf 'ilaa al-yasiir fii aT-Tariiq ath-thaanee** (*toof eel-ah al-yah-seer fee at-tah-reek ah-thah-nee*). Because **Tariiq** (*tah-reek;* street) is a masculine subject, the corresponding ordinal **thaanee** (second) should also be masculine.

Fun & Games

Match the Arabic statements in Section 1 with their English translations in Section 2.

Section 1: al-jumla al-'arabiyya (*al-joom-lah al-ah-rah-bee-yah;* Arabic sentence)

1. **Tuf 'ilaa al-yamiin.**

2. **hal yumkin 'an ta'id min faDlik.**

3. **idhhabii 'ilaa al-gharb.**

4. **al-funduq qariib.**

5. **al-binaaya al-'aashira.**

Section 2: al-jumla al-'injliziyya (*al-joom-lah al-een-jeh-lee-zee-yah;* English sentence)

A. Please repeat that.

B. The hotel is close.

C. It's the tenth building.

D. Turn right.

E. Go west.

The answers are in Appendix C.

Chapter 13

Staying at a Hotel

In This Chapter

▶ Hunting for the right accommodation

▶ Reserving your room

▶ Checking in and out

Picking the right **funduq** (*foon-dook;* hotel) for you and your family or friends can sometimes make or break your **safar** (*sah-far;* trip). During a **safar** or **riHla** (*reeh-lah;* vacation), the **funduq** is your home away from home — it's where you get up in the morning and sleep at night, and it can serve as a base for you to regroup before facing daily adventures. So choosing the **funduq** that's right for you is very important.

In this chapter, I show you the ins and outs of choosing the right **funduq** to meet your travel, budgetary, and personal needs. You find out how to inquire about specific aspects of the **funduq** (such as available amenities and proximity to the city center), how to make a room reservation and check into your room, how to interact with the **funduq** staff, and, last but not least, how to successfully check out of your hotel room! You find out everything you ever wanted to know about **funduq** life, and more!

Choosing the Right Accommodation

When choosing the right **funduq**, you need to consider a number of factors. First and foremost, you must figure out what kind of hotel you want to stay in. With so many options to choose from, how do you know which **funduq** is right for you? Here are some details to consider:

✔ **thaman** (*tah-man;* price)

✔ **ghurfa** (*roor-fah;* room)

✔ **Hajem al-ghurfa** (*hah-jem al-goor-fah;* room size)

✔ **naw' al-ghurfa** (*nah-ouh al-goor-fah;* room type)

✔ **khidmat al-ghurfa** (*keed-mat al-goor-fah;* room service)

✔ **'iiwaa'** (*ee-wah;* accommodations)

Of course, you have many other factors to consider, but these are some of the more popular ones. Not only do you need to find the right **funduq,** one that perhaps includes such **maraafiq** (*mah-rah-feek;* amenities) as a **masbaH** (*mas-bah;* swimming pool) or a **maT'am** (*mat-ham;* restaurant), but you also need to make sure you find the right **ghurfa** (room). After all, that's where you'll spend most of your private time.

An important factor to think about when finding a **ghurfa** is its **Hajem** (size). For example, if you're traveling alone, a **ghurfa li-shakhS waaHid** (*goor-fah lee-sha-kes wah-heed;* single room) is more appropriate than a **ghurfa li-shakhsayn** (*goor-fah lee-shak-sayn;* double room). When inquiring about a **ghurfa,** you may need to use the following terms:

- **sariir** (*sah-reer;* bed)
- **mirHaad** (*meer-had;* toilet)
- **balcoon** (*bal-koon;* balcony)
- **tilifizyoon** (*tee-lee-feez-yoon;* television)
- **Tabaq** (*tah-bak;* floor/level)

To create a possessive noun in the English language, you usually use an apostrophe, such as "the girl's cat" or "the woman's house." It's the same in Arabic, except that you reverse the word order — you use an undefined noun followed by a defined noun, as in **Hajem al-ghurfa. al-ghurfa** (a definite noun because it contains the definite article prefix **al-**) means "the room," and **Hajem** (an undefined noun) means "size." So when you read or hear **Hajem al-ghurfa,** you automatically know that the **ghurfa** is the possessor acting on the **Hajem** (size) to express the "room's size" or, literally, "the size of the room."

Talkin' the Talk

Sarah is planning a trip and wants to find the right hotel for her visit. She calls one of the local hotels to inquire about its facilities.

Desk clerk: **funduq al-baraka.**
foon-dook al-bah-rah-kah.
Al-Baraka Hotel.

Sarah: **masaa' al-khayr. 'uriidu 'an 'a'raf 'idhaa kaana 'indakum ghuraf faarigha.**
mah-sah al-kah-yer. oo-ree-doo ann ah-raf ee-zah kah-nah een-dah-koom goo-raf fah-ree-gah.
Good evening. I would like to know whether you have any rooms available.

Desk clerk: **laHdha.**
lah-zah.
One moment.

Sarah: **Tab'an.**
tah-bah-an.
Certainly.

Desk clerk: **na'am 'indanaa ghuraf faarigha. 'ay naw' min ghurfa turiidiina?**
nah-am. een-dah-nah goo-raf fah-ree-gah. ey nah-ouh meen goor-fah too-ree-dee-nah?
Yes, we have rooms available. What type of room would you like?

Sarah: **hal 'indakum ghuraf li-shakhsayn?**
hal en-dah-koom goo-raf lee-shak-sayn?
Do you have any double rooms?

Desk clerk: **na'am.**
nah-am.
Yes.

Sarah: **kam min sariir fii haadhihi al-ghurfa?**
kam meen sah-reer fee hah-zee-hee al-goor-fah?
How many beds are in this room?

Desk clerk: **'ithnayn.**
eeth-nah-yen.
Two.

Sarah: **wa kam min naafida fii al-ghurfa?**
wah kam meen nah-fee-dah fee al-goor-fah?
And how many windows are in the room?

Desk clerk: **thalaathat naafidaat. Haadhihi al-ghurfa 'indahaa shams kathiir.**
tha-lah-that nah-fee-dat. hah-zee-hee al-goor-fah een-dah-hah shah-mes kah-theer.
Three windows. This room gets plenty of sunlight.

Sarah: **Tayyib. wa hal 'indahaa balcoon?**
tah-yeeb. wah hal een-dah-hah bal-koon?
Okay. And does it have a balcony?

Desk clerk:	**na'am. 'indahaa balcoon ya'Tii 'alaa ash-shaaTi'.**
	nah-am. een-dah-hah bal-koon yah-tee ah-lah ah-shah-teeh.
	Yes. It has a balcony that overlooks the beach.
Sarah:	**mumtaaz! sa-a'khudh haadhihi al-ghurfa.**
	moom-taz! sah-ah-kooz hah-zee-hee al-goor-fah.
	Excellent! I'll take this room.

Words to Know

ghuraf	goo-raf	rooms
faarigha	fah-ree-gah	available
naafida	nah-fee-dah	window
shams	shah-mes	sun
shaaTi'	shah-teeh	beach

Discussing minor room details

I don't know about you, but before I reserve a hotel room, I want to find out as much as possible about what's actually *inside* the **ghurfa**. Your friends, like mine, may call it obsessive-compulsive, but I want to know everything about the room, down to the last detail, such as the kind of bathroom, what channels the TV receives, and even the number of pillows I can expect to find on the bed!

Talkin' the Talk

Amine calls Hotel Salam to inquire about the room he's reserving.

Amine:	**hal haadhihi al-ghurfa li-shakhs waaHid 'aw li-shakhsayn?**
	hal hah-zee-hee al-goor-fah lee-sha-kes wah-deed aw lee-shak-sayn?
	Is this a single room or a double room?
Desk clerk:	**haadhihi ghurfa li-shakhs waaHid.**
	hah-zee-hee goor-fah lee-sha-kes wah-heed.
	This is a single room.

Amine: **wa fii 'ay Tabaq haadhihi al-ghurfa?**
wah fee ay tah-bak hah-zee-hee al-goor-fah?
And on what floor is this room located?

Desk clerk: **fii aT-Tabaq al-khaamis.**
fee ah-tah-bak al-kah-mees.
On the fifth floor.

Amine: **al-ghurfa fiihaa Hammaam, na'am?**
al-goor-fa fee-hah hah-mam, nah-am?
The room comes with a bathroom, correct?

Desk clerk: **na'am yaa sayyidii.**
nah-am yah sah-yee-dee.
Yes sir.

Amine: **hal fii al-Hammaam duush wa banyoo?**
hal fee al-hah-mam doosh wah ban-yoo?
Is there a shower and a bathtub in the bathroom?

Desk clerk: **fiihaa duush faqaT.**
fee-hah doosh fah-kat.
It only comes with a shower.

Amine: **Tayyib. wa hal fii al-ghurfa khizaana?**
tah-yeeb. wah hal fee al-goor-fah kee-zah-nah?
Okay. And is there a safe in the room?

Desk clerk: **na'am. wa 'indanaa khizaana fii maktab al-'istiqbaal 'ayDan.**
nah-am. wah een-dah-nah kee-zah-nah fee mak-tab al-ees-teek-bal ay-zan.
Yes. And we have a safe in the reception desk as well.

Amine: **wa su'aal 'aakhar: hal al-ghurfa 'indahaa mikwaa al-malaabis?**
wah soo-all ah-kar: hal al-goor-fah een-dah-hah meek-wah al-mah-lah-bees?
One final question: Does the room come equipped with a clothes iron?

Desk clerk: **na'am. wa 'idhaa 'aradta, yumkin 'an tu'Tii malaabisuka 'ilaa mushrifat al-ghurfa li-al-ghasl.**
nah-am. wah ee-zah ah-rad-tah, yoom-keen an tooh-teeh mah-lah-bee-soo-kah ee-lah moosh-ree-fat al-goor-fah lee-al-gah-sel.
Yes. And if you'd like, you may give your clothes to the room's staff attendant for dry cleaning.

Words to Know

Hammaam	hah-mam	bathroom
duush	doosh	shower
banyoo	ban-yoo	bathtub
mirHaaD	meer-had	toilet
maghsala	mag-sah-lah	sink
fuuTa	foo-tah	towel
mir'aat	meer-at	mirror
sariir	sah-reer	bed
wisaada	wee-sah-dah	pillow
baTTaniyya	bah-tah-nee-yah	blanket
mikwaa al-malaabis	meek-wah al-mah-lah-bees	clothes iron
miSbaaH	mees-bah	lamp
haatif	hah-teef	phone
tilfaaz	teel-faz	TV
midyaa'	meed-yah	radio
khizaana	kee-zah-nah	safe deposit box
naafida	nah-fee-dah	window
mushrifat al-ghurfa	moosh-ree-fat al-goor-fah	room staff attendant

Getting to know direct object pronouns

Direct object pronouns ascribe possession to a particular individual or group of individuals, as in "his room," "her cat," or "their house." In Arabic, instead of using a separate possessive word such as "his," "her," or "their," you add a possessive direct object pronoun *suffix* to the noun to which you're ascribing possession.

For example, if you want to say "his room" in Arabic, you take the noun for "room" **(ghurfa)** and add the direct object pronoun suffix corresponding to "his," which is the suffix **-hu**. So "his room" in Arabic is **ghurfatuhu.** Note that because **ghurfa** is a feminine singular noun, it automatically ends in a **taa marbuuTa** — the silent "t" located at the end of every feminine singular noun — and you must also add a **Damma** — the *oo* sound **(u)** — to the end of the word before placing the suffix **-hu**. So instead of saying **ghurfahu,** you say **ghurfa*tu*hu.**

If you want to say "her room," follow the same rule except that instead of adding the masculine possessive suffix **-hu,** you add the feminine possessive suffix **-haa.** Hence, "her room" is **ghurfatuhaa.** This rule applies to all singular possessive direct object pronouns, but you must pay close attention when using the possessive suffix in the plural form. For example, to say "their room," you must first determine the gender of "their" — whether it's masculine plural or feminine plural; the plural possessive suffix is gender-defined, meaning it changes based on the gender. "Their room" in the masculine is **ghurfatuhum** (**-hum** is the masculine plural possessive suffix). Alternatively, "their room" in the feminine is **ghurfatuhunna** (you add the feminine plural possessive suffix **-hunna**).

Table 13-1 contains all direct object pronoun possessive suffixes, so feel free to turn to this table whenever you're looking to add a possessive suffix to a particular noun but aren't sure which possessive suffix to use.

Table 13-1	Direct Object Pronoun Possessive Suffixes		
Personal Pronoun	*Translation*	*Possessive Suffix*	*Translation*
'anna	I/me	-ii	my/mine
'anta	you (MS)	-ka	your (MS)
'anti	you (FS)	-ki	your (FS)
huwa	he/him	-hu	his
hiya	she/her	-haa	hers

(continued)

Table 13-1 *(continued)*

Personal Pronoun	Translation	Possessive Suffix	Translation
naHnu	we/us	-naa	ours
'antum	you (MP)	-kum	your (MP)
'antunna	you (FP)	-kunna	your (FP)
hum	they (MP)	-hum	their (MP)
hunna	they (FP)	-hunna	their (FP)
'antumaa	you (dual)	-kumaa	your (dual)
humaa	they (dual)	-humaa	your (dual)

The dual form **humaa** is generally gender-defined, meaning that there's a **humaa** in both the feminine and the masculine. However, in the construction of direct object pronoun suffixes, you use the same possessive suffix **–humaa** regardless of the gender!

Making a Reservation

After you identify the right **funduq** with the right **maraafiq** and **ghurfa,** you're ready to make a **Hajzu** (*haj-zoo;* reservation)! Before you do, though, you have a few considerations to make, such as the duration and length of your stay, the number and type of **ghuraf** you're reserving, the number of people staying, and the cost to stay at the **funduq.** This section explores all these elements in-depth so that you can be prepared to make a smooth **Hajzu** and secure the best accommodation for your **safar!**

Figuring out the price

thaman (*tah-man;* price) is an important factor to think about before you make your **Hajzu.** Fortunately, there are many accommodation options to suit every **mizaaniya** (*mee-zah-nee-yah;* budget). If you can afford it, making a **Hajzu** in a **funduq faakhir** (*foon-dook fah-kheer;* luxury hotel) is nice. These five-star hotels tend to have all sorts of **maraafiq,** and you're sure to get the star treatment from the hotel staff; a **funduq faakhir** almost guarantees a great experience. If you're a **Taalib** (*tah-leeb;* student) or someone with a limited **mizaaniya,** staying at a **daar aT-Talaba** (*dar ah-tah-lah-bah;* youth hostel) is a more-affordable option. Hostels tend to have very basic **maraafiq,** such as communal bathrooms and shared living space, but are fine if you're not planning to spend that much **waqt** (*wah-ket;* time) in the **funduq.**

When making your **Hajzu**, be sure to inquire about any special **tanziilaat** (*tan-zee-lat;* discounts) that the **funduq** might be offering. Here are some **tanzi-ilaat** you can ask about:

- ✔ **tanziilaat al-majmoo'aat** (*tan-zee-lat al-maj-moo-at;* group discounts)

- ✔ **tanziilaat as-saa'aat baTaala** (*tan-zee-lat ah-sah-at bah-tah-lah;* off-peak discounts)

- ✔ **tanziilaat al-fuSul** (*tan-zee-lat al-foo-sol;* seasonal discounts)

When you inquire about the **thaman**, ask about any **rayTaat as-safar** (*ray-tat ah-sah-far;* special travel packages) that the **funduq** may offer, such as local sightseeing expeditions. Many hotels now offer these kinds of packages in addition to basic room and board accommodations. If you don't ask, you may miss out on a good deal!

Talkin' the Talk

Omar wants to make a reservation at Hotel Ramadan. He asks the operator about the price of the rooms and about any applicable discounts.

Omar: **kam thaman ghurfa li-shakhS waaHid li muddat layla waaHida?**
kam tah-man goor-fah lee-sha-kes wah-heed lee moo-dat lay-lah wah-hee-dah?
How much is a single room for one night?

Operator: **mi'a wa khamsiin daraahim li layla waaHida.**
mee-ah wah kam-seen dah-rah-heem lee lay-lah wah-hee-dah.
One hundred and fifty dirhams for one night.

Omar: **wa kam thaman ghurfa li-shakhsayn li muddat layla waaHida?**
wah kam tah-man goor-fah lee-shak-sayn lee moo-dat lay-lah wah-hee-dah?
And how much is a double room for one night?

Operator: **mi'atay daraahim li al-layla.**
mee-ah-tay dah-rah-heem lee ah-lay-lah.
Two hundred dirhams for the night.

Omar: **Tayyib. 'uriidu ghurfa li-waaHid li muddat 'usbuu'.**
tah-yeeb. oo-ree-doo goor-fah lee-wah-heed lee moo-dat oos-booh.
Okay. I'd like a single room for one week.

Operator:	**mumtaaz!** *moom-taz!* Excellent!
Omar:	**hal 'indakum 'ay tanziilaat li al-fuSul?** *hal een-dah-koom ay tan-zee-lat lee al-foo-sool?* Do you have any seasonal discounts?
Operator:	**na'am.** *nah-am.* Yes.
Omar:	**wa maa hiya haadhihi at-tanziilaat?** *wah mah hee-yah hah-zee-hee ah-tan-zee-lat?* And what are these discounts?
Operator:	**'idhaa baqayta li muddat 'ashrat 'ayyam, at-thaman sa-yakuun mi'a wa 'ishriin daraahim badalan min mi'a wa khamsiin li al-layla.** *ee-zah bah-kay-tah lee moo-dat ash-rat ah-yam, ah-tah-man sah-yah-koon mee-ah wah eesh-reen dah-rah-heem bah-dah-lan meen mee-ah wah kam-seen lee ah-lay-lah.* If you stay in the room for ten days, the price goes down to one hundred and twenty dirhams per night instead of one hundred and fifty dirhams.
Omar:	**'uriidu 'an 'ufakkir 'akthar 'an haadha. sa-'ukallimuk ba'da qaliil.** *oo-ree-doo an oo-fah-keer ak-thar an hah-zah. sah-oo-kah-lee-mook bah-dah kah-leel.* I'd like to think about it a little bit longer. I'll call you back in a liitle while.

Omar thinks about the discount and then calls back the operator.

Omar:	**Tayyib. 'uriidu ghurfa waaHida li muddat 'ashrat 'ayyam.** *tah-yeeb. oo-ree-doo goor-fah wah-hee-dah lee moo-dat ash-rat ah-yam.* Okay. I'd like a single room for ten days.
Operator:	**raai'. hal sa-tadfa' nuquud 'aw shiik 'aw biTaaqa diiniiya?** *rah-eeh. hal sah-taz-fah noo-kood aw sheek aw bee-tah-kah dee-nee-yah?* Great. Will you be paying by cash, check, or credit card?

Omar: **bi biTaaqa diiniiya.**
         bee bee-tah-kah dee-nee-yah.
         By credit card.

Words to Know

mudda	moo-dah	period/duration
daraahim	dah-rah-heem	dirham (type of currency)
mi'a	mee-ah	one hundred
mi'atay	mee-ah-tay	two hundred
'usbuu'	oos-booh	week
'asaabi'	ah-sah-beeh	weeks
tanziilaat	tan-zee-lat	discounts
yawm	yah-oum	day
'ayyam	ah-yam	days
baqaa	bah-kah	stayed
baqayta	bah-kay-tah	to stay
bi	bee	with
qaliil	kah-leel	while
dafa'a	dah-fah-ah	paid
tadfa'	tad-fah	to pay
nuquud	noo-kood	cash/coins
shiik	sheek	cashier's check
biTaaqa diiniiya	bee-tah-kah dee-nee-yah	credit card

Indicating the length of your stay

Making sure you get the room you want when you need it is as important as sticking to your **funduq** budget. Securing a **ghurfa** can be difficult, particularly during the **faSl al-'uTla** (*fah-sel al-oot-lah;* holiday season); therefore, it's advisable you make your **Hajzu** ahead of schedule so that you're assured to get the **ghurfa** you want during the **mudda** (*moo-dah;* period) of your choosing.

In order to say you're going to stay at the **funduq** "for a period of" so much time, use the following formula: **li muddat** (*lee moo-dat*) followed by the duration of your stay. For example, to say you're staying "for a period of a week," say **li muddat 'usbuu'** (*lee moo-dat oos-booh*). Here are some other examples:

- ✔ **li muddat yawm** (*lee moo-dat yah-oum;* for a period of one day)

- ✔ **li muddat shahr** (*lee moo-dat shah-her;* for a period of one month)

- ✔ **li muddat 'usbuu'ayn** (*lee moo-dat oos-boo-ayn;* for a period of two weeks)

- ✔ **li muddat khamsat 'ayyam** (*lee moo-dat kam-sat ah-yam;* for a period of five days)

- ✔ **li muddat 'usbuu' wa niSf** (*lee moo-dat oos-booh wah nee-sef;* for a period of one and a half weeks)

To say that you're staying from one date until another date, use the prepositions **min** (*meen;* from) and **'ilaa** (*ee-lah;* until). For example, if you're staying "from Monday until Thursday," you say **min al-'ithnayn 'ilaa al-khamiis** (*meen al-eeth-nayn ee-lah al-kah-mees*). Here are some other examples:

- ✔ **min al-'arbi'aa' 'ilaa al-'aHad** (*meen al-ar-bee-ah ee-lah al-ah-had;* from Thursday until Sunday)

- ✔ **min 'ishriin yulyuu 'ilaa thalaathiin yulyuu** (*meen eesh-reen yool-yoo ee-lah thah-lah-theen yool-yoo;* from July 20 until July 30)

- ✔ **min ghusht 'ilaa sibtambar** (*meen goo-shet ee-lah seeb-tam-bar;* from August until September)

The verb for "to stay" is **baqaa** in the **maaDii** (past) and **yabqaa** in the **muDaari'** (present). To put a **fi'l** (*fee-ehl;* verb) in the **mustaqbal** (*moos-tak-bal;* future), all you do is add the prefix **sa-** to the **fi'l** in the **muDaari'**. For example, to communicate "I will stay for a period of one week," you say **sa-'abqaa li muddat 'usbuu'** (*sah-ab-kah lee moo-dat oos-booh*).

Talkin' the Talk

 Reda calls the Hotel Marrakech to make a room reservation.

Reda: **hal hunaaka ghuraf li-shakhsayn?**
hal hoo-nah-kah goo-raf lee-shak-sayn?
Are there any double rooms?

Clerk: **na'am, 'indanaa ghurfa li-shakhsayn mawjuuda.**
nah-am, een-dah-nah goor-fah lee-shak-sayn mah-joo-dah.
Yes, we have one double room available.

Reda: **hal haadhihi al-ghurfa mawjuuda li 'uTlat nihaayat as-sana?**
hal hah-zee-hee al-goor-fah maw-joo-dah lee oot-lat nee-hah-yat ah-sah-nah?
Is this room available during the end of year holiday?

Clerk: **haadhihi al-mudda mashghuula kathiira wa laakin haadhihi al-ghurfa mawjuuda al-'aan.**
hah-zee-hee al-moo-dah mash-goo-lah kah-thee-rah wah lah-keen hah-zee-hee al-goor-fah maw-joo-dah al-an.
This is a very busy period, but this room is still available.

Reda: **raai'! 'uriidu haadhihi al-ghurfa li-muddat 'usbuu'.**
rah-eeh! oo-ree-doo hah-zee-hee al-goor-fah lee-moo-dat oos-booh.
Great! I'd like this room for a period of one week.

Clerk: **Tayyib. wa maa hiya al-mudda al-mu'ayyana li-al-Hajzu?**
tay-yeeb. wah mah hee-yah al-moo-dah al-moo-ah-yah-nah lee-al-haj-zoo?
Okay. And what is the exact period for the reservation?

Reda: **min dujanbir al-'awwal 'ilaa dujanbir as-saabi'.**
meen doo-jan-beer al-ah-wal ee-lah doo-jan-beer ah-sah-beeh.
From December 1 until December 7.

Words to Know

mawjuuda	mah-joo-dah	available (F)
mawjuud	mah-jood	available (M)
'uTlaat	oot-laht	holidays
sana	sah-nah	year
nihaaya	nee-hah-yah	end
mashghuula	mash-goo-lah	busy (F)
mashguul	mash-gool	busy (M)
mu'ayyana	moo-ah-yah-nah	exact/designated (F)
mu'ayyan	moo-ah-yan	exact/designated (M)
laakin	lah-keen	but/however

Subjecting you to subjunctive verbs

yuriidu *(yoo-ree-doo)* is a special kind of verb — called *subjunctive* — that means "want to." Other verbs that fall into this category include **yajibu** *(yah-jee-boo;* have to), **yastaTii'u** *(yas-tah-tee-ooh;* able to), and **yuHibbu** *(yoo-hee-boo;* like). Unlike other types of verbs, these four verbs fall into the main subjunctive category, which means that they're conjugated in one tense only.

For example, here is the verb **yuriidu** conjugated in the subjunctive form:

Form	Pronunciation	Translation
'anaa 'uriidu	ah-nah oo-ree-doo	I want
'anta turiidu	ahn-tah too-ree-doo	You want (MS)
'anti turidiina	ahn-tee too-ree-dee-nah	You want (FS)
huwa yuriidu	hoo-wah yoo-ree-doo	He wants

hiya turiidu	hee-yah too-ree-doo	She wants
naHnu nuriidu	nah-noo noo-ree-doo	We want
'antum turiiduuna	ahn-toom too-ree-doo-nah	You want (MP)
'antunna turidna	ahn-too-nah too-reed-nah	You want (FP)
hum yuriiduuna	hoom yoo-ree-doo-nah	They want (MP)
hunna yuridna	hoo-nah yoo-reed-nah	They want (FP)
antumaa turiidaana	ahn-too-mah too-ree-dah-nah	You want (dual/MP/FP)
humaa yuriidaani	hoo-mah yoo-ree-dah-nee	They want (dual/MP)
humaa turiidaani	hoo-mah too-ree-dah-nee	They want (dual/FP)

In English, when you use a subjunctive verb to describe an action, you always follow the verb with the preposition "to." For example, you say "I want *to* watch movies" or "I like *to* eat chocolate;" you would never say "I want watch movies" or "I like eat chocolate." Not only is it not proper English, but dropping the "to" doesn't really make that much sense. The same rule applies in Arabic: When you use a subjunctive verb to describe an action, you always add the preposition "to," which is **'an** *(ann)* in Arabic.

To illustrate the subjunctive verbs in action, here are some examples:

- ✔ **'uHibbu 'an adhhaba 'ilaa al-maktaba.** (*oo-hee-boo ann az-hah-bah ee-lah al-mak-tah-bah;* I like to go to the library.)

- ✔ **'astaTii'u 'an 'af'ala al-waajib li-ghadan.** (*as-tah-tee-oo ann af-ah-lah al-wah-jeeb lee-gah-dan;* I'm able to do the homework for tomorrow.)

- ✔ **yajibu 'an taqra'a al-kitaab.** (*yah-jee-boo ann tak-rah al-kee-tab;* You must read the book.)

However, unlike in English where the auxiliary verb — the verb after the main verbs "have to," "like to," "able to," and "want to" — remains the same, the auxiliary verb in Arabic changes and becomes a subjunctive verb. For all intents and purposes, the subjunctive verb in this case is any verb that follows the preposition **'an** after one of the four main verbs. So when you use one of the four main verbs above followed by **'an** and an auxiliary verb, you must conjugate the auxiliary verb in the subjunctive form.

The subjunctive verb form is similar to the **muDaari'** verb tense, except that the verb endings are significantly different. For example, the **muDaari'** form of the verb **kataba** (*kah-tah-bah;* wrote) is **yaktubu** (*yak-too-boo;* to write). The subjunctive form of **yaktubu** is **yaktuba** (*yak-too-bah),* with the **Damma** changed to a **fatHa.** So if you wanted to say "I like to write," you say **'uHibbu 'an 'aktuba** and not **'uHibbiu 'an aktubu.**

To get a better sense of the subjunctive, here is the verb "to write" in the subjunctive form:

Form	Pronunciation	Translation
'anaa 'aktuba	ah-nah ak-too-bah	I write
'anta taktuba	ahn-tah tak-too-bah	You write (MS)
'anti taktubii	ahn-tee tak-too-bee	You write (FS)
huwa yaktuba	hoo-wah yak-too-bah	He writes
hiya taktuba	hee-yah tak-too-bah	She writes
naHnu naktuba	nah-noo nak-too-bah	We write
'antum taktubuu	ahn-toom tak-too-boo	You write (MP)
'antunna taktubna	ahn-too-nah tak-toob-nah	You write (FP)
hum yaktubuu	hoom yak-too-boo	They write (MP)
hunna yaktubna	hoo-nah yak-toob-nah	They write (FP)
antumaa taktubaa	ahn-too-mah tak-too-bah	You write (dual/MP/FP)
humaa yaktubaa	hoo-mah yak-too-bah	They write (dual/MP)
humaa taktubaa	hoo-mah tak-too-bah	They write (dual/FP)

Notice that whereas most of the endings in the subjunctive form change, a few remain the same. These are the personal pronouns whose endings remain the same in both the subjunctive and the **muDaari'** environments — **'antunna** and **hunna**. Also, although a majority of the endings change vowels, a few have endings that change completely: **'anti, 'antum, hum, 'antumaa, humaa** (M), and **humaa** (F). In these endings, you actually drop the suffix. For example, **'antum taktubuuna** becomes **'antum taktubuu.**

Whenever you use an auxiliary verb, make sure you use the subjunctive form of that verb!

Checking In to the Hotel

When you arrive at your **funduq** after a long **safar,** probably the last thing on your mind is going through the formalities of checking in. You probably just want to go up to your **ghurfa,** jump on the **sariir,** and relax for a little while! To help relieve the annoyance of check-in time, this section covers all the necessary words and phrases to help you check in to your room as smoothly as possible.

If you already have a **Hajzu**, ask the **muwaDHaf al-'istiqbaal** (*moo-wah-daf al-ees-teek-bal;* desk clerk) for more **ma'luumaat** (*mah-loo-mat;* information) regarding your **ghurfa.** If you don't have a **Hajzu,** you can inquire about room **mawjooda** (*maw-joo-dah;* availability) at the front desk.

Here are some important terms you may need during check-in:

- **miftaH** (*meef-tah;* key)
- **miftaH al-ghurfa** (*meef-tah al-goor-fah;* room key)
- **'amti'a** (*am-tee-ah;* luggage)
- **shanTa** (*shan-tah;* suitcase)
- **miHfaDHa** (*meeh-fah-dah;* briefcase)
- **Tabiq** (*tah-beek;* floor)
- **miS'ad** (*mees-ad;* elevator)
- **'istiqbaal** (*ees-teek-bal;* reception)
- **maktab al-'istiqbaal** (*mak-tab al-ees-teek-bal;* reception desk)
- **muwaDHaf al-'istiqbaal** (*moo-wah-daf al-ees-teek-bal;* desk clerk) (M)
- **muwaDHafa al-'istiqbaal** (*moo-wah-dah-fah al-ees-teek-bal;* desk clerk) (F)
- **bawwaab** (*bah-wab;* concierge) (M)
- **bawwaaba** (*bah-wah-bah;* concierge) (F)
- **maDmuun** (*mad-moon;* included)

When interacting with the **funduq** staff, the following key phrases are likely to come in handy:

- **hal al-fuTuur maDmuun ma'a al-ghurfa?** (*hal al-foo-toor mad-moon mah-ah al-goor-fah;* Is breakfast included with the room?)
- **mataa yabda'u al-fuTuur?** (*mah-tah yab-dah-oo al-foo-toor;* When does breakfast begin?)
- **mataa yantahii al-fuTuur?** (*mah-tah yan-tah-hee al-foo-toor;* When does breakfast end?)
- **hal hunaaka khabaran lii?** (*hal hoo-nah-kah kah-bah-ran lee;* Are there any messages for me?)
- **'uriidu nahaad bi shakel mukaalama ma'a as-saa'a as-saabi'a.** (*oo-ree-doo nah-had bee shah-kel moo-kah-lah-mah mah-ah ah-sah-ah ah-sah-bee-ah;* I would like a wake-up call at 7:00.)
- **hal 'indakum mushrifat al-ghurfa?** (*hal een-dah-koom moosh-ree-fat al-goor-fah;* Do you have room service?)

Talkin' the Talk

Frank arrives at Hotel Casablanca and begins checking in to his room.

Frank: **'ahlan. 'indii Hajzu li ghurfa li-shakhs waaHid li muddat 'usbuu' bidaa'an al-yawm.**
ah-lan. een-dee haj-zoo lee goor-fah lee-shah-kes wah-heed lee moo-dat oos-booh bee-dah-an al-yah-oum.
Hi. I have a reservation for a single room for one week beginning today.

Clerk: **Tayyib. maa 'ismuka?**
tay-yeeb. mah ees-moo-kah?
Okay. What's your name?

Frank: **frank 'abd-allah.**
frank abed-ah-lah.
Frank Abdallah.

Clerk: **'abd-allah bi haa'?**
abed-ah-lah bee hah?
Abdallah with an H?

Frank: **na'am.**
nah-am.
Yes.

Clerk: **daqiiqa min faDlik.**
dah-kee-kah meen fad-leek.
One minute please.

The clerk checks the reservation log.

Clerk: **marHaba bik sayyid 'abdallah! ghurfatuka fii aT-Tabiq as-saadis.**
mar-hah-bah beek sah-yeed ab-dah-lah! goor-fah-too-kah fee ah-tah-beek ah-sah-dees.
Welcome Mr. Abdallah! Your room is located on the sixth floor.

Frank: **shukran.**
shook-ran.
Thank you.

Clerk:	**haa huwa al-miftaH. hal 'indaka 'amti'a?**
	hah hoo-wah al-meef-tah. hal een-dah-kah am-tee-ah?
	Here is your room key. Do you have any luggage?
Frank:	**na'am, 'indii thalaathat shanTaat.**
	nah-am, een-dee tah-lah-that shan-tat.
	Yes, I have three suitcases.
Clerk:	**Tayyib. al-Hammaal sa-yusaa'iduka 'ilaa al-ghurfa.**
	tah-yeeb. al-hah-mal sah-yoo-sah-ee-doo-kah ee-lah al-goor-fah.
	Okay. The baggage handler will help you to your room.
Frank:	**Kwayyis. wa 'ayna al-miS'ad?**
	kwah-yees. wah ay-nah al-mees-ad?
	Good. And where is the elevator?
Clerk:	**'ilaa al-yasaar.**
	ee-lah al-yah-sar.
	To your left.
Frank:	**shukran.**
	shook-ran.
	Thank you.

Checking Out of the Hotel

After your nice stay at the **funduq**, it's time for **waqt al-khuruuj** (*wah-ket al-koo-rooj;* checkout). Ask the **maktab al-'istiqbaal** for the exact **waqt al-khu-ruuj;** most hotels have a specific **waqt al-khuruuj,** such as noon, and if you go over that time by only a few minutes, some hotels will charge you for a whole extra night! It's your responsibility to know the exact **waqt al-khuruuj** and to be out of your room by then.

Before you leave the **funduq,** make sure you get all your **'amti'a** from your **ghurfa,** and take care of the **faatuura** (*fah-too-rah;* bill). Some common extra charges to watch out for include:

- **faatuura al-haatif** (*fah-too-rah al-hah-teef;* telephone bill)
- **faatuura at-tilfaaz** (*fah-too-rah ah-teel-faz;* TV pay-per-view bill)
- **faatuura aT-Ta'aam** (*fah-too-rah ah-tah-am;* food bill)

When you pay the **faatuura,** it's a good idea to get a **'iiSaala** (*eeh-sah-lah;* receipt) in case you have a problem with the bill later on or can be reimbursed for your travel costs.

Talkin' the Talk

Gabrielle is ready to check out of her room.

Gabrielle:	**mataa waqt al-khuruuj?** *mah-tah wah-ket al-koo-rooj?* When is the checkout time?
Clerk:	**waqt al-khuruuj ma'a as-saa'a al-waaHida.** *wah-ket al-koo-rooj mah-ah ah-sah-ah al-wah-hee-dah.* Checkout time is at 1:00.
Gabrielle:	**Tayyib. maa hiya al-faatuura al-'aama?** *tah-yeeb. mah hee-yah al-fah-too-rah al-ah-mah?* Okay. What's the total bill?
Clerk:	**khamsa mi'at daraahim.** *kamsah mee-at dah-rah-heem.* Five hundred dirhams.
Gabrielle:	**'uriidu 'iiSaala min faDlik.** *oo-ree-doo ee-sah-lah meen fad-leek.* I'd like a receipt please.
Clerk:	**Tab'an. shukran li ziyaaratuki wa 'ilaa al-liqaa'!** *tah-bah-an. shook-ran lee zee-yah-rah-too-kee wah ee-lah al-lee-kah!* Of course. Thank you for your visit, and we look forward to seeing you soon!

Fun & Games

Match the Arabic words and phrases with their English equivalents:

Arabic terms and phrases:

1. **faatuura al-haatif**

2. **hal hunaaka khabaran lii?**

3. **maktab al-'istiqbaal**

4. **maraafiq**

5. **mataa waqt al-khuruuj?**

English terms and phrases:

A. Are there any messages for me?

B. When is the checkout time?

C. Telephone bill

D. Reception desk

E. Amenities

The answers are in Appendix C.

Chapter 14

Getting from Here to There: Transportation

In This Chapter
▶ Taking to the skies
▶ Catching taxis, buses, and trains

When it comes to getting around the block, the city, or the world, you have a lot of different modes of **naql** (*nah-kel;* transportation) to choose from. And making the right choice for you is extremely important, particularly if you're traveling in a foreign country. Modes of transportation differ from region to region and country to country, so it's important you are aware of subtle differences between the transportation methods you're used to and those you discover when you're traveling abroad.

In this chapter, I tell you, in Arabic, not only how to use all major transportation methods but also how to navigate a Middle Eastern city using these modes of transport.

Traveling by Plane

One of the most common methods of **naql** is flying in a **Taa'ira** (*tah-ee-rah;* airplane). The **Taa'ira** is probably the best method of **naql** to help you get to a distant location in the least amount of time. Chances are if you're in North America or Europe and want to go to the Middle East, you'll take a **Taa'ira**.

Making reservations

The first step in air travel is making a **Hajzu** (*haj-zoo;* reservation) and buying a **biTaaqat as-safar** (*bee-tah-kat ah-sah-far;* plane ticket). You may purchase your **biTaaqat as-safar** the traditional way, by simply visiting your **wakiil**

safariyaat (*wah-keel sah-fah-ree-yat;* travel agent). However, in this technological age, more and more people choose to bypass the **wakiil safariyaat** in favor of online travel agents. Even though you get more personalized service from a **wakiil safariyaat,** you can probably get better deals by ordering your plane tickets online. If you're not sure where you want to go, the **wakiil safariyaat** may be able to suggest destinations to suit your specific traveling needs. But if you know exactly where you want to go, using an online travel agent is probably more appropriate.

One of the potential pitfalls of going through online travel agents — particularly if you use a specialized broker that focuses on specific global destinations, such as the Middle East — is making sure that the online site is reputable. In order to not get fooled, I recommend you use one of the more established online travel agents, such as Expedia.com or Travelocity.com.

Talkin' the Talk

Sophia calls her travel agent, Ahmed, to make an airline reservation.

Sophia: **'ahlan wa sahlan 'aHmed. haadhihi sofia.**
ahel-an wah sa-hel-an ah-med. hah-zee-hee so-fee-ah.
Hi Ahmed. This is Sophia.

Ahmed: **'ahlan sofia. kayfa yumkin 'an 'usaa'iduki?**
ahel-an so-fee-yah. kay-fah yoom-keen ann oo-sah-ee-doo-kee?
Hi Sophia. How may I help you?

Sophia: **'uriidu 'an 'adhhab 'ilaa 'ad-daar 'al-bayDaa' ma'a 'ummii li al-'uTla.**
oo-ree-doo an az-hab ee-lah ah-dar al-bay-dah mah-ah oo-mee lee al-oot-lah.
I would like to go to Casablanca for the holidays with my mother.

Ahmed: **raa'i'! haadhihi fikra mumtaaza. wa mataa turiidaani 'an tadhabaani?**
rah-eeh! hah-zee-hee feek-rah moom-tah-zah. wah mah-tah too-ree-dah-nee an taz-hah-bah-nee?
Excellent! That's a great idea. And when would you like to go?

Sophia: **nuriidu 'an nadhhab yawm as-sabt.**
noo-ree-doo an naz-hab yah-oum ah-sabt.
We would like to go on Saturday.

Ahmed: **kwayyis. ma'a 'ay saa'a?**
kuh-wah-yees. mah-ah ay sah-ah?
Okay. At what time would you like to leave?

Sophia: **hal 'indaka Tayaraan ma'a 'as-saa'a al-khaamisa?**
hal een-dah-kah tay-yah-ran mah-ah ah-sah-ah al-kah-mee-sah?
Do you have any flights at 5:00?

Ahmed: **na'am.**
nah-am.
Yes.

Sophia: **Tayyib. sana'khudh biTaaqatayn min faDlik.**
tah-yeeb. sah-nah-kooz bee-tah-kah-tayn meen fad-leek.
Good. We'll take two tickets please.

Ahmed: **hal turiidaani maqaa'id 'amaama 'an-naafida 'aw bayna al-maqaa'id?**
hal too-ree-dah-nee mah-kah-eed ah-mah-mah ah-nah-fee-dah ah-ou bay-nah al-mah-kah-eed?
Would you like window or aisle seats?

Sophia: **maqaa'id 'amaama 'an-naafida min faDlik.**
mah-kah-eed ah-mah-mah ah-nah-fee-dah meen fad-leek.
Window seats please.

Ahmed: **'indii biTaaqatayn li maqaa'id 'amaama 'an-naafida li Tayaarin li daar al-bayDaa' yawm as-sabt ma'a 'as-saa'a al-khaamisa.**
een-dee bee-tah-kah-tayn lee mah-kah-eed ah-mah-mah ah-nah-fee-dah lee tah-yah-reen lee dar al-bay-dah ya-oum ah-sah-bet ma-ah ah-sah-ah al-kah-mee-sah.
So I have two tickets for window seats for a flight to Casablanca on Saturday at 5:00.

Sophia: **mumtaaz!**
moom-taz!
Excellent!

Ahmed:	**riHla sa'eeda!**
	reeh-lah sah-ee-dah!
	Have a nice trip!
Sophia:	**shukran!**
	shook-ran!
	Thank you!

Words to Know

'uTla	oot-lah	holiday/vacation
biTaaqa	bee-tah-kah	ticket
biTaaqatayn	bee-tah-kah-tayn	2 tickets
biTaaqaat	bee-tah-kaht	tickets (3 or more)
Tayaraan	tah-yah-ran	flight
maq'ad	mak-had	seat
maqaa'id	mah-kah-eed	seats (3 or more)
bayna al-maqaa'id	bay-nah al-mah-kah-eed	aisle seat(s)
maq'ad an-naafida	mak-had ah-nah-fee-dah	window seat
riHla	reeh-lah	voyage
safar	sah-far	trip
musaafir	moo-sah-feer	traveler (M)
mussafira	moo-sah-fee-rah	traveler (F)
musaafiruun	moo-sah-fee-ruun	travelers (M)
musaafiraat	moo-sah-fee-rat	travelers (F)

Getting some legwork out of the verb "to travel"

If there's one verb you need to be familiar with relating to travel, it's the verb **saafara** *(sah-fah-rah)*, which conveniently means "to travel." Even though **saafara** has four consonants instead of the usual three, it's nevertheless considered to be a regular verb because the fourth consonant, the **'alif**, is actually a consonant that acts as a long vowel elongating the **siin**. (For more on regular verbs, flip to Chapter 2.) So **saafara** is conjugated in the **maaDii** (past) and the **muDaari'** (present) the same way as most other regular verbs. Here is the verb **saafara** in the **maaDii** form:

Form	Pronunciation	Translation
'anaa saafartu	ah-nah sah-far-too	I traveled
'anta saafarta	ahn-tah sah-far-tah	You traveled (MS)
'anti saafartii	ahn-tee sah-far-tee	You traveled (FS)
huwa saafara	hoo-wah sah-fah-rah	He traveled
hiya saafarat	hee-yah sah-fah-rat	She traveled
naHnu saafarnaa	nah-noo sah-far-nah	We traveled
'antum saafartum	ahn-toom sah-far-toom	You traveled (MP)
'antunna saafartunna	ahn-too-nah sah-far-too-nah	You traveled (FP)
hum saafaruu	hoom sah-fah-roo	They traveled (MP)
hunna saafarna	hoo-nah sah-far-nah	They traveled (FP)
antumaa safartumaa	ahn-too-mah sah-far-too-mah	You traveled (dual/MP/FP)
humaa saafaraa	hoo-mah sah-fah-rah	They traveled (dual/MP)
humaa saafarataa	hoo-mah sah-fah-rah-tah	They traveled (dual/FP)

Use the form **yusaafiru** to conjugate "traveling" in the **muDaari'**:

Form	Pronunciation	Translation
'anaa 'usaafiru	ah-nah oo-sah-fee-roo	I am traveling
'anta tusaafiru	ahn-tah too-sah-fee-roo	You are traveling (MS)
'anti tusaafiriina	ahn-tee too-sah-fee-ree-nah	You are traveling (FS)
huwa yusaafiru	hoo-wah yoo-sah-fee-roo	He is traveling

hiya tusaafiru	hee-yah too-sah-fee-roo	She is traveling
naHnu nussafiru	nah-noo noo-sah-fee-roo	We are traveling
'antum tusaafiruuna	ahn-toom too-sah-fee-roo-nah	You are traveling (MP)
'antunna tusaafirna	ahn-too-nah too-sah-feer-nah	You are traveling (FP)
hum yusaafiruuna	hoom yoo-sah-fee-roo-nah	They are traveling (MP)
hunna yusaafirna	hoo-nah yoo-sah-feer-nah	They are traveling (FP)
antumaa tusaafiraani	ahn-too-mah too-sah-fee-rah-nee	You are traveling (dual/MP/FP)
humaa yusaafiraani	hoo-mah yoo-sah-fee-rah-nee	They are traveling (dual/MP)
humaa tusaafiraani	hoo-mah too-sah-fee-rah-nee	They are traveling (dual/FP)

Registering at the airport

With a **biTaaqat as-safar,** you're ready to head off to the **maTaar** (*mah-tar;* airport) and board the **Taa'ira.** But before you actually get on the **Taa'ira,** you need to take care of a few logistical things. First, you must present your **jawaaz as-safar** (*jah-waz ah-sah-far;* passport) and your **biTaaqat as-safar** at the airport **tasjiil** (*tass-jeel;* registration) desk, which is located in the **maHaTTat al-khuTuut al-jawwiya** (*mah-hah-tah al-koo-toot al-jah-wee-yah;* airport terminal). Second, you must also answer some **'as'ila** (*ass-ee-lah;* questions) about your **safar** and your **'amti'a** (*am-tee-ah;* luggage).

Talkin' the Talk

At the airport, Zayneb is registering her luggage.

Attendant: **kam min 'amti'a 'induki?**
kam meen am-tee-ah een-doo-kee?
How many pieces of luggage do you have?

Zayneb: **'indii thalaathat 'amti'a: shanTatayn wa miHfaDHa waaHida.**
een-dee tha-lah-that am-tee-ah: shan-tah-tayn wah meeh-fah-dah wah-hee-dah.
I have three pieces of luggage: two suitcases and a briefcase.

Attendant: **kam min 'amti'a satusajjiliina?**
kam meen am-tee-ah sah-too-sah-jee-lee-nah?
How many pieces of luggage are you going to register?

Zayneb: **sa'usajjilu ash-shanTatayn wa sa'aakhudu al-miHfaDHa ma'ii fii 'aT-Taa'ira.**
sah-oo-sah-jee-loo ah-shan-tah-tayn wah sah-ah-khoo-zoo al-meeh-fah-dah mah-ee fee ah-tah-ee-rah.
I'm going to register the two suitcases, and I will take the briefcase with me on the plane.

Attendant: **kwayyis. hal naDHamti al-'amti'a binafsuki?**
keh-wah-yees. hal nah-zam-tee al-am-tee-ah bee-naf-soo-kee?
Okay. Did you pack your bags by yourself?

Zayneb: **na'am.**
nah-am.
Yes.

Attendant: **lam yunaDHDHim shakhsun 'aakhar al-'amti'a?**
lam yoo-nah-zim shak-soon ah-kar al-am-tee-ah?
No one else packed the bags?

Zayneb: **laa'. 'anaa binafsii.**
lah. ah-nah bee-naf-see.
No. By myself.

Attendant: **hal kul shay' fii al-'amti'a milkuki?**
hal kool shay fee al-am-tee-ah meel-koo-kee?
Is everything in the bags yours?

Zayneb: **na'am.**
nah-am.
Yes.

Attendant: **hal kaanat al-'amti'a ma'akii fii kul al-waqt?**
hal kah-nat al-am-tee-ah mah-ah-kee fee kool al-wah-ket?
Have you had the bags in your possession at all times?

Zayneb: **na'am.**
nah-am.
Yes.

Attendant: **shukran. Tayaraan sa'iid.**
shook-ran. tah-yah-ran sah-eed.
Thank you. Have a nice flight.

Zayneb:	**shukran.**
	shook-ran.
	Thank you.

Words to Know

'amti'a	am-tee-ah	luggage
shanTa	shan-tah	suitcase
shanTatayn	shan-tah-tayh	two suitcases
shanTaat	shan-taht	suitcases (3 or more)
miHfaDHa	meeh-fah-dah	briefcase
miHfaDHatayn	meeh-fah-dah-tayn	two briefcases
miHfaDHaat	meeh-fah-daht	briefcases (3 or more)
yusajjilu	yoo-sah-jee-loo	to register
ma'ii	mah-ee	with me
naDHama	nah-zah-mah	to organize
shakhsun	shak-soon	individual
'aakhar	ah-kar	other
binafsii	bee-naf-see	by myself
ta'shiira	tah-shee-rah	visa
madkhal	mad-kal	gate

Boarding the plane

So you're ready to board the **Taa'ira!** After you check your **'amti'a** and present your **biTaaqat as-safar** and your **jawaaz as-safar** to the airline attendant, be sure to follow all **ta'liimaat** (*tah-lee-mat;* instructions) very carefully. Stay in the **Saff** (*saf;* line) with your fellow **rukkaab** (*roo-kab;* passengers), and follow any requests made by airport officials.

When you reach the **madkhal** (*mad-kal;* gate) and board the **Taa'ira**, present your **biTaaqat as-safar** to the **muwaafiq aT-Taa'ira** (*moo-wah-feek ah-tah-ee-rah;* flight attendant), who will show you your **maq'ad** (*mak-had;* seat). The following terms are related to the **Taa'ira** and your flight:

- **raakib** (*rah-keeb;* passenger)
- **rukkaab** (*roo-kab;* passengers)
- **muwaafiq** (*moo-wah-feek;* attendant) (M)
- **muwaafiqa** (*moo-wah-fee-kah;* attendant) (F)
- **Tayyaar** (*tah-yar;* pilot) (M)
- **Tayyaara** (*tah-yah-rah;* pilot) (F)
- **ghurfat al-qiyaada** (*goor-fah al-kee-yah-dah;* cockpit)
- **mirHaad** (*meer-had;* bathroom)
- **mirHaad mashghuul** (*meer-had mash-gool;* bathroom occupied)
- **'araba fii 'a'laa** (*ah-rah-bah fee ah-lah;* overhead compartment)
- **qism al-'awwal** (*kee-sem al-ah-wal;* first class)
- **qism al-'a'maal** (*kee-sem al-ah-mal;* business class)
- **qism 'iqtiSaadii** (*kee-sem eek-tee-sah-dee;* "economy" class)
- **sur'a** (*soor-ah;* speed)
- **'irtifaa'** (*eer-tee-fah;* altitude)
- **'inTilaaq** (*een-tee-lak;* departure)
- **wuSuul** (*woo-sool;* arrival)

A brief departure on the verb "to arrive"

A helpful verb to know when you're traveling is **waSala** (*wah-sah-lah;* to arrive). (You can also use the verb **waSala** to express "to arrive," "to land," or "to come.") Even though **waSala** has three consonants and therefore should fall into the mold of regular verb forms, it's nevertheless classified as an irregular verb. It's irregular because it includes the consonant **waaw;** verbs with **waaw** are classified as irregular because their **muDaari'** forms are radically different than the regular **muDaari'** verb forms. As a result, whereas the **maaDii** form of **waSala** follows a regular pattern, the **muDaari'** does not.

Here's the verb **waSala** conjugated in the **maaDii:**

Form	Pronunciation	Translation
'anaa waSaltu	ah-nah wah-sal-too	I arrived
'anta waSalta	ahn-tah wah-sal-tah	You arrived (MS)

'anti waSaltii	ahn-tee wah-sal-tee	You arrived (FS)
huwa waSala	hoo-wah wah-sah-lah	He arrived
hiya waSalat	hee-yah wah-sah-lat	She arrived
naHnu waSalnaa	nah-noo wah-sal-naa	We arrived
'antum waSaltum	ahn-toom wah-sal-toom	You arrived (MP)
'antunna waSaltunna	ahn-too-nah wah-sal-too-nah	You arrived (FP)
hum waSaluu	hoom wah-sah-loo	They arrived (MP)
hunna waSalna	hoo-nah wah-sal-nah	They arrived (FP)
antumaa waSaltumaa	ahn-too-mah wah-sal-too-mah	You arrived (dual/MP/FP)
humaa waSalaa	hoo-mah wah-sah-lah	They arrived (dual/MP)
humaa waSalataa	hoo-mah wah-sah-lah-tah	They arrived (dual/FP)

Use the irregular form **yaSilu** to conjugate "arriving" in the **muDaari'**:

Form	*Pronunciation*	*Translation*
'anaa 'aSilu	ah-nah ah-see-loo	I am arriving
'anta taSilu	ahn-tah tah-see-loo	You are arriving (MS)
'anti taSiliina	ahn-tee tah-see-lee-nah	You are arriving (FS)
huwa yaSilu	hoo-wah yah-see-loo	He is arriving
hiya taSilu	hee-yah tah-see-loo	She is arriving
naHnu naSilu	nah-noo nah-see-loo	We are arriving
'antum taSiluuna	ahn-toom tah-see-loo-nah	You are arriving (MP)
'antunna taSilna	ahn-too-nah tah-seel-nah	You are arriving (FP)
hum yaSiluuna	hoom yah-see-loo-nah	They are arriving (MP)
hunna yaSilna	hoo-nah yah-seel-nah	They are arriving (FP)
antumaa taSilaani	ahn-too-mah tah-see-lah-nee	You are arriving (dual/MP/FP)
humaa yaSilaani	hoo-mah yah-see-lah-nee	They are arriving (dual/MP)
humaa taSilaani	hoo-mah tah-see-lah-nee	They are arriving (dual/FP)

Going through immigration and customs

When your **Taa'ira** lands and you arrive at your chosen destination, it's time to deal with the **hijra** (*heej-rah;* immigration) and **diwaana** (*dee-wah-nah;* customs) officials. In recent years, airports have established more stringent requirements on **musaafiruun** (travelers), so be prepared to answer a number of **'as'ila** regarding the details and purpose of your **safar.** Here are some common questions a **hijra** or **diwaana** official may ask you:

✔ **maa 'ismuk?** (*mah ees-mook;* What's your name?)

✔ **kam 'umruk?** (*kam um-rook;* How old are you?)

✔ **'ayna taskun?** (*eh-yeh-nah tass-koon;* Where do you live?)

✔ **maa hiya mihnatuk?** (*mah meeh-nah-took;* What do you do?)

✔ **kam muddat safaruk?** (*kam moo-dah sah-fah-rook;* How long is your trip?)

✔ **maa hadaf safaruk?** (*mah hah-daf sah-fah-rook;* What's the purpose of your trip?)

✔ **'ayna sataskun li muddat as-safar?** (*eh-yeh-nah sah-tass-koon lee moo-dat ah-sah-far;* Where will you be staying during the trip?)

✔ **hal tusaafir biwaHdik?** (*hal too-sah-feer bee-wah-deek;* Are you traveling alone?)

Provide clear and accurate answers to these questions. Providing false statements to an official from **hijra** or **diwaana** is a serious offense, so make sure you're truthful throughout the questioning.

If you're visiting a Muslim country, check with your travel agent or consular official about restrictions certain countries may have regarding bringing particular items into the country. For example, if you're traveling to Saudi Arabia, you can't bring alcohol with you into the country; and if you're a woman, you may have to wear specific clothing, such as the **Hijaab** (*hee-jab;* veil) in order to comply with local religious laws. You want to be certain you are aware of all the rules and laws before you face someone from **hijra** or **diwaana.**

Talkin' the Talk

Jennifer has just landed at the Mohammed V Airport in Casablanca, Morocco, and she answers some questions at the immigration booth.

Officer: **tafaDDalii min faDlik.**
             tah-fah-dah-lee meen fad-leek.
             Step forward please.

Jennifer: **'ahlan yaa sayyidii.**
ahel-an yah sah-yee-dee.
Hello sir.

Officer: **jawaaz as-safar min faDlik.**
jah-waz ah-sah-far meen fad-leek.
Your passport please.

Jennifer: **haa huwa.**
hah hoo-wah.
Here it is.

Officer: **jinsiyya?**
jeen-see-yah?
Nationality?

Jennifer: **'amriikiiyya.**
am-ree-kee-yah.
American.

Officer: **sanat al-miilaad?**
sah-nat al-mee-lad?
Date of birth?

Jennifer: **1980.**
1980.
1980.

Officer: **maa hadaf safaruk?**
mah hah-daf sah-fah-rook?
What's the purpose of your trip?

Jennifer: **'anaa saa'iHa.**
ah-nah sah-ee-ha.
I'm a tourist.

Officer: **'ayna sataskunii li muddat as-safar?**
eh-yeh-nah sah-tas-koo-nee lee moo-dat ah-sah-far?
Where will you be staying during the trip?

Jennifer: **funduq booshentoof.**
foon-dook boo-shen-toof.
The Bouchentouf hotel.

Officer: **maa huwa taariikh al-khuruuj?**
mah hoo-wah tah-reek al-koo-rooj?
When is your date of departure?

Jennifer:	**'ishriin yunyoo.** *eesh-reen yoon-yoo.* June 20.	

Officer:	**shukran. marHaba 'ilaa al-maghrib.** *shook-ran. mar-hah-bah ee-lah al-mag-reeb.* Thank you. Step forward please.	

Jennifer:	**shukran!** *shook-ran!* Thank you!	

Words to Know

jinsiyya	jeen-see-yah	nationality
sanat al-miilaad	sah-nat al-mee-lad	date of birth
'iid al-miilaad	eed al-mee-lad	birthday
hadaf	hah-daf	purpose/goal
taariikh	tah-reek	date
khuruuj	koo-rooj	exit/departure
dukhuul	doo-kool	entry
siyaaHa	see-yah-hah	tourism
saa'iH	sah-eeh	tourist (M)
saa'iHa	sah-ee-hah	tourist (F)
muhaajir	moo-hah-jeer	immigrant (M)
muhaajira	moo-hah-jee-rah	immigrant (F)
muhaajiruun	moo-hah-jee-roon	immigrants (M)
muhaajiraat	moo-hah-jee-rat	immigrants (F)

Getting through the **hijra** post puts you one step closer to leaving the **maTaar** and discovering the wonders of the exotic country you're visiting! After your interview with the **hijra,** you may proceed to pick up your **'amti'a.** You may use the help of a **Hammaal** (*hah-mal;* baggage handler/porter), or you may simply use an **'ariiba** (*ah-ree-bah;* cart) to haul your own luggage.

Before you actually leave the **maTaar,** you must go through **diwaana** (customs). Use the following phrases when speaking with **diwaana** officials:

- ✔ **laa shay' li al-'i'laan.** (*lah shay lee al-eeh-lan;* Nothing to declare.)
- ✔ **'indii shay' li al-'i'laan.** (*een-dee shay lee al-eeh-lan;* I have something to declare.)

Check with your travel agent, consular officer, or embassy official to find out about any products or restrictions imposed by countries you're traveling to. You should know what's prohibited from entering or leaving a specific country because the consequences of not knowing may be quite high. In addition, certain countries have limits on the amount of cash you can bring in and take out. Knowing these currency restrictions is equally important.

Talkin' the Talk

Before leaving the airport, Hassan needs to stop by the customs department.

Officer:	**hal 'indaka shay'un li-l'i'laan?** *hal een-dah-kah shay-oon leel-eeh-lan?* Do you have anything to declare?
Hassan:	**laa.** *lah.* No.
Officer:	**maa fii daakhil ash-shanTa?** *mah fee dah-keel ah-shan-tah?* What's inside the suitcase?
Hassan:	**malaabisii.** *Mah-lah-bee-see.* My clothes.
Officer:	**'iftaH ash-shanTa min faDlik.** *eef-tah ah-shan-tah meen fad-leek.* Open the suitcase please.
Hassan:	**Tab'an. TafaDDal.** *tah-bah-an. tah-fah-dal.* Certainly. Here you go.

Officer:	**shukran. yumkin 'an takhruj al-'aan.**
	shook-ran. yoom-keen an tak-rooj al-an.
	Thank you. You may proceed now.

Words to Know

'i'laan	eeh-lan	declare
daakhil	dah-keel	inside
khaarij	kah-reej	outside
'iftaH	eef-tah	open (command form)

Getting Around on Land

Major metropolitan areas and most small towns have a number of transportation methods you can choose from. Table 14-1 lists some of the most common forms of transportation you're likely to use.

Table 14-1	Major Forms of Transportation	
Arabic	*Pronunciation*	*Translation*
taaksii	tak-see	taxi
Haafila	hah-fee-lah	bus
qiTaar	kee-tar	train
nafaq 'arDiiy	nah-fak ar-dee	subway
safiina	sah-fee-nah	ship
Sayyaara	sah-yah-rah	car
Sayyaara 'ijaariya	sah-yah-rah ee-jah-ree-yah	rental car
darraaja	dah-rah-jah	bicycle
darraaja naariyya	dah-rah-jah nah-ree-yah	motorcycle

Hailing a taxi

If you're in a large or medium-sized city and need to get from one location to another quickly and relatively inexpensively, then hailing a taxi is probably the best option for you. When hailing a cab in a foreign country, keep the following advice in mind:

✔ **Make sure that the taxi you hail is fully licensed and authorized by the local agencies to operate as a taxi.** A number of companies operate illegal taxis and take advantage of unsuspecting tourists — make sure you're not one of them! Usually, most legitimate taxi operators have licensing information on display somewhere inside the cab or even on the car's exterior.

✔ **Be aware that most taxis that run to and from the airport charge a flat rate. Inquire about the flat rate before you get into the taxi.**

✔ **If you're in the city, make sure the taxi saa'iq (*sah-eek;* driver) turns on the Hasuub (*hah-soob;* meter).** A common occurrence is that a driver forgets (either accidentally or intentionally) to turn on the meter and ends up charging you, the passenger, an exorbitant amount of money for a short ride.

In most Arab and Middle Eastern countries, tipping the **saa'iq** is not required. However, I'm sure the **saa'iq** won't argue if you decide to give him a little tip!

Talkin' the Talk

Larry hails a taxi in downtown Casablanca.

Driver: **'ayna turiid 'an tadhhab?**
eh-yeh-nah too-reed an taz-hab?
Where do you want to go?

Larry: **'ilaa al-funduq.**
ee-lah al-foon-dook.
To the hotel.

Driver: **maa 'ism al-funduq?**
mah ee-sem al-foon-dook?
What's the name of the hotel?

Larry: **funduq maryam.**
foon-dook mar-yam.
Hotel Myriam.

Driver:	**Tayyib. tafaDDal.**
	tah-yeeb. tah-fah-dal.
	Okay. Come in.

The taxi arrives at the hotel.

Driver:	**waSalnaa 'ilaa al-funduq.**
	wah-sal-nah ee-lah al-foon-dook.
	We've arrived at the hotel.

Larry:	**bikam?**
	bee-kam?
	How much?

Driver:	**'ishriin daraahim.**
	eesh-reen dah-rah-heem.
	Twenty dirhams.

Larry:	**khudh. 'iHtafiDH 'an al-baaqii.**
	kooz. eeh-tah-feez an al-bah-kee.
	Here you go. Keep the change.

Driver:	**shukran jaziilan!**
	shook-ran jah-zee-lan!
	Thank you very much!

Words to Know

'iHtafiDH	eeh-tah-feed	keep (command form)
baaqii	bah-kee	change (money)
thaman tadhkiira	tah-man taz-kee-rah	fare
Hasuub	hah-soob	counter/meter

Taking a bus

The **Haafila** (bus) is a convenient mode of transportation whether you're traveling across town or across the country. If you're in a city and traveling within city limits, taking the bus is a good option because it usually costs less than a taxi. If you're traveling across the country, not only is taking a bus an economical option, but you also get to enjoy the beautiful scenery up close and personal!

Most **Haafilaat** (buses) accept prepaid **biTaaqaat** (tickets). If you take the **Haafila** frequently, refill your **biTaaqa** regularly. Otherwise, if you only take a bus occasionally, you'll be glad to know that most **Haafilaat** also accept **fuluus** (*foo-loos;* cash) as long as it's small bills. Here are some common terms you may need or encounter if you decide to take a **Haafila:**

- ✔ **biTaaqat al-Haafila** (*bee-tah-kat al-hah-fee-lah;* bus ticket)

- ✔ **maHaTTat al-Haafila** (*mah-hah-tat al-hah-fee-lah;* bus station/bus stop)

- ✔ **saa'iq al-Haafila** (*sah-eek al-hah-fee-lah;* bus driver)

- ✔ **tawqiit al-Haafila** (*taw-keet al-hah-fee-lah;* bus schedule)

If you want to say "every" as in "every day" or "every hour," all you do is add the work **kul** (*kool;* every) before the noun that describes the time you're referring to. For example:

- ✔ **kul al-yawm** (*kool al-yawm;* every day)

- ✔ **kul saa'a** (*kool sah-ah;* every hour)

- ✔ **kul niSf saa'a** (*kool nee-sef sah-ah;* every half hour)

- ✔ **kul rubu' saa'a** (*kool roo-booh sah-ah;* every fifteen minutes)

Talkin' the Talk

Malika is waiting at the bus stop. She's trying to figure out which bus to take, so she asks a fellow commuter for information.

Malika: **'afwan, hal haadhihi al-Haafila tadhhab 'ilaa waSat al-madiina?**
af-wan, hal hah-zee-hee al-hah-fee-lah taz-hab ee-lah wah-sat al-mah-dee-nah?
Excuse me, does this bus go downtown?

Commuter: **laa. Haadhihi al-Haafila tadhhab 'ilaa khaarij al-madiina.**
lah. hah-zee-hee al-hah-fee-lah taz-hab ee-lah kah-reej al-mah-dee-nah.
No. This bus goes outside of the city.

Malika:	'ayna al-Haafila 'ilaa waSat al-madiina?
	eh-yeh-nah al-hah-fee-lah ee-lah wah-sat al-mah-dee-nah?
	Which bus goes downtown?
Commuter:	al-Haafila raqm 'ashra.
	al-hah-fee-lah rah-kem ash-rah.
	Bus number 10.
Malika:	mataa sataSil al-Haafila raqm 'ashra?
	mah-tah sah-tah-sil al-hah-fee-lah rah-kem ash-rah?
	When does bus number 10 arrive?
Commuter:	fii 'ishriin daqiiqa.
	fee eesh-reen dah-kee-kah.
	In 20 minutes.
Malika:	shukran.
	shook-ran.
	Thank you.
Commuter:	'afwan.
	af-wan.
	You're welcome.

Boarding a train

The **qiTaar** (train) is a popular alternative if you're looking for transportation that's convenient, fast, affordable, and allows you to do a little sightseeing while you're on the go. When you board the **qiTaar,** be ready to provide your **biTaaqa** to the **qiTaar** attendant. Although boarding most **qiTaar** doesn't require a **biTaaqa shakhSiyya** (*bee-tah-kah shak-see-yah;* personal ID card), you should be ready to present one if an attendant asks you for it.

Talkin' the Talk

Fatima is purchasing a ticket at the train station.

Fatima:	'uriidu biTaaqa li muraakush.
	oo-ree-doo bee-tah-kah lee moo-rah-koosh.
	I would like a ticket to Marrakech.

Clerk:	**riHla waaHida 'aw riHla dhahaab wa 'iyaab?**
	reeh-lah wah-hee-dah aw reeh-lah za-hab wah ee-yab?
	One-way or round-trip?
Fatima:	**riHla waaHida min faDlik.**
	reeh-lah wah-hee-dah meen fad-leek.
	One-way please.
Clerk:	**haa huwa.**
	hah hoo-wah.
	Here you go.
Fatima:	**shukran. mataa yanTaliq al-qiTaar?**
	shook-ran. mah-tah yan-tah-leek al-kee-tar?
	Thank you. When does the train leave?
Clerk:	**al-qiTaar yanTaliq fii niSf saa'a fii raSiif raqm khamsa.**
	al-kee-tar yan-tah-leek fee nee-sef sah-ah fee rah-seef rah-kem kam-sah.
	The train leaves in a half hour from platform number 5.
Fatima:	**shukran.**
	shook-ran.
	Thank you.

Words to Know

riHla waaHida	reeh-lah wah-hee-dah	one-way trip
riHla dhahaab wa 'iyaab	reeh-lah za-hab wah ee-yab	round-trip
raSiif	rah-seef	platform

Fun & Games

Identify the following modes of transportation in Arabic:

1. _____

2. _____

3. _____

4. _____

The answers are in Appendix C.

Chapter 15

Planning a Trip

. . . .

In This Chapter

▶ Deciding where and when to go

▶ Packing your bags

▶ Dealing with travel documents

▶ Consulting a travel agent

. . . .

1 don't know about you, but I simply love traveling. I enjoy visiting exotic locations around the world, meeting new people from different backgrounds, and discovering new cultures. This chapter tells you everything you need to know about planning, organizing, and going on a **riHla** (*reeh-lah;* trip) — in Arabic, of course.

Choosing Your Destination

When you decide to take a trip, **'ayna** (*ay-nah;* where) to go is probably the biggest decision you face. For **'afkaar** (*af-kar;* ideas) on a possible travel **wujha** (*wooj-hah;* destination), you may want to consult a **wakiil safariyaat** (*wah-keel sah-fah-ree-yat;* travel agent). Table 15-1 lists the Arabic names of some popular travel destinations you can choose from.

Table 15-1	Names of Countries	
Arabic	*Pronunciation*	*Translation*
al-maghrib	al-mag-reeb	Morocco
al-jazaa'ir	al-jah-zah-eer	Algeria
tuunis	too-nees	Tunisia

(continued)

Table 15-1 (continued)

Arabic	Pronunciation	Translation
liibiya	lee-bee-yah	Libya
maSr	mah-ser	Egypt
'isra'iil	ees-rah-eel	Israel
falastiin	fah-las-teen	Palestine
lubnaan	loob-nan	Lebanon
'urdun	oor-doon	Jordan
suuriya	soo-ree-yah	Syria
sa'uudiiya	sah-oo-dee-yah	Saudi Arabia
'iraaq	ee-rak	Iraq
kuuwayt	koo-wah-yet	Kuwait
baHrayn	bah-rain	Bahrain
qaTar	kah-tar	Qatar
'imaaraat	ee-mah-rat	United Arab Emirates
yamaan	yah-man	Yemen
'ummaan	oh-man	Oman
suudaan	soo-dan	Sudan
soomaal	so-mal	Somalia
'iraan	ee-ran	Iran
'amriikaa	am-ree-kah	United States of America
kanaadaa	kah-nah-dah	Canada
miksiikuu	meek-see-koo	Mexico
'injlaTirra	ee-nej-lah-teh-rah	England
faransaa	fah-ran-sah	France
'isbaaniya	ees-ban-yah	Spain
'iTaaliyaa	ee-tah-lee-yah	Italy

Arabic	Pronunciation	Translation
'almaaniyaa	al-man-yah	Germany
baraaziil	bah-rah-zeel	Brazil
'arjentiinah	ar-jen-tee-nah	Argentina
yabaan	yah-bah	Japan
Siin	seen	China
kooryaa	koo-ree-yah	Korea
hind	hind	India
paqisTaan	pah-kess-tan	Pakistan
'afghanisTaan	af-gah-nees-tan	Afghanistan

'as'ila (*ass-ee-lah;* questions) you should ask when choosing your **wujha** include:

- ✔ **kayfa aT-Taqs fii haadhaa al-balad?** (*kay-fah ah-tah-kes fee hah-zah al-bah-lad;* How is the weather in this country?)

- ✔ **kayfa aT-Taqs fii haadha al-waqt fii as-sana?** (*kay-fah ah-tah-kes fee hah-zah al-wah-ket fee ah-sah-nah;* How is the weather during this time of year?)

- ✔ **hal hunaaka kathiir min as-suyyaaH hunaaka?** (*hal hoo-nah-kah kah-theer meen ah-soo-yah hoo-nah-kah;* Are there a lot of tourists there?)

- ✔ **hal haadhaa al-makaan muwaafiq li as-'sura wa al-'aTfaal?** (*hal hah-zah al-mah-kan moo-wah-feek lee ah-soo-rah wah al-at-fal;* Is this place suitable for the family and for children?)

- ✔ **hal hunaaka tamtii' li al-'aTfaal?** (*hal hoo-nah-kah tam-teeh lee al-at-fal;* Is there entertainment for the children?)

- ✔ **hal al-madiina naDHiifa?** (*hal al-mah-dee-nah nah-zee-fah;* Is the city clean?)

- ✔ **hal al-qarya qarriba min al-madiina?** (*hal al-kar-yah kah-ree-bah meen al-mah-dee-nah;* Is the town close to the city?)

- ✔ **mataa tashriqu ash-shams?** (*mah-tah tash-ree-koo ah-shah-mes;* When does the sun rise?)

✔ **'ay waqt al-gharb?** (*ay wah-ket al-gah-reb;* What time is sunset?)

✔ **hal ash-shaaTi' qariib min al-funduq?** (*hal ah-shah-teeh kah-reeb meen al-foon-dook;* Is the beach close to the hotel?)

✔ **hal hunaaka matHaf fii al-madiina?** (*hal hoo-nah-kah mat-haf fee al-mah-dee-nah;* Is there a museum in the city?)

Talkin' the Talk

Stephanie calls her travel agent, Murad, to get his recommendations on where she should go on vacation this year.

Stephanie:	**'ahlan muraad. haadhihi stefanii.** *ah-lan moo-rad. hah-zee-hee steh-fah-nee.* Hi Murad. This is Stephanie.
Murad:	**'ahlan stefanii! Kayfa yumkin 'an 'usaa'iduki?** *ah-lan steh-fah-nee! kay-fah yoom-keen ann oo-sah-ee-doo-kee?* Hi Stephanie! How may I help you?
Stephanie:	**'anaa 'uriidu 'an 'adhhab ma'a 'usratii li riHla fii nihaayat as-sana.** *ah-nah oo-ree-doo an az-hab mah-ah oos-rah-tee lee reeh-lah fee nee-hah-yat ah-sah-nah.* I want to go on a trip with my family at the end of the year.
Murad:	**haadhihi fikra raa'i'a.** *hah-zee-hee feek-rah rah-ee-ah.* This is an excellent idea.
Stephanie:	**hal 'indaka 'ay naSiiHaat?** *hal een-dah-kah ay nah-see-hat?* Do you have any recommendations?
Murad:	**hal turiidiina 'an tadhhabii 'ilaa makaan daafi'?** *hal too-ree-dee-nah an taz-hah-bee ee-lah mah-kan dah-feeh?* Do you want to go someplace warm?

Stephanie: **na'am, min al-'afDal.**
nah-am, meen al-af-dal.
Yes, preferably.

Murad: **hal dhahabti 'ilaa al-maghrib min qabl?**
hal zah-hab-tee ee-lah al-mag-reeb meen kah-bel?
Have you gone to Morocco before?

Stephanie: **laa. lam 'adhhab 'ilaa al-magrib min qabl wa laakin
'uHibbu 'an 'azuurahu.**
*lah. lam az-hab ee-lah al-mag-reeb meen kah-bel
wah lah-keen oo-hee-boo an ah-zoo-rah-hoo.*
No. I have never visited Morocco before, but I would
love to visit it.

Murad: **mumtaaz! haadhaa al-balad daafi' mundhu kul waqt
fii as-sana.**
*moom-taz! hah-zah al-bah-lad dah-fee moon-zoo
kool wah-ket fee ah-sah-nah.*
Excellent! This country is warm during the whole
year.

Stephanie: **haadhaa raa'i'!**
hah-zah rah-eeh!
That's great!

Murad: **hunaaka mudun kathiira yumkin 'an tazuurihaa.**
*hoo-nah-kah moo-doon kah-thee-rah yoom-keen an
tah-zoo-ree-hah.*
There are a lot of cities you can visit.

Stephanie: **maa hiya?**
mah hee-yah?
Which ones?

Murad: **murraakush wa ad-dar al-bayDaa' madiinatayn
jamiilatayn.**
*moo-rah-koosh wah ah-dar al-bay-dah
mah-dee-nah-tayn jah-mee-lah-tayn.*
Marrakech and Casablanca are two beautiful cities.

Stephanie: **maa huwa al-farq bayna humaa?**
mah hoo-wah al-fah-rek bay-nah hoo-mah?
What's the difference between the two?

Murad: **hunaaka shaaTi' fii ad-daar al-bayDaa' li 'anna
al-madiina qariiba min al-muHiiT al-'aTlassii.**
*hoo-nah-kah shah-teeh fee ah-dar al-bay-dah
lee ah-nah al-mah-dee-nah kah-ree-bah meen
al-moo-heet al-at-lah-see.*
There is a beach in Casablanca because the city is
located near the Atlantic Ocean.

Stephanie: **jamiil.**
jah-meel.
Beautiful.

Murad: **wa murrakush laysa fiihaa shaaTi' wa laakin
hunaaka jabal al-'aTlas qariib minhaa.**
*wah moo-rah-koosh lay-sah fee-hah shah-teeh wah
lah-keen hoo-nah-kah jah-bal al-at-las kah-reeb
meen-hah.*
There is no beach in Marrakech, but it is located near
the Atlas Mountains.

Stephanie: **wa hal yumkin 'an natazallaj fii jabal al-'aTlas?**
*wah hal yoom-keen an nah-tah-zah-laj fee jah-bal
al-at-las?*
And is it possible to ski in the Atlas Mountains?

Murad: **na'am. jabal al-'aTlas 'akbar jabal fii shamaal
'afriiqiyaa wa fii as-sharq al-'awSaT. hunaaka
kathiir min ath-thalj fiih.**
*nah-am. jah-bal al-at-las ak-bar jah-bal fee
shah-mal af-ree-kee-yah wah fee ah-shah-rek
al-aw-sat. hoo-nah-kah kah-theer meen
ah-thah-lej feeh.*
Yes. The Atlas Mountains is the biggest mountain
range in North Africa and in the Middle East. There
is plenty of snow there.

Stephanie: **haadhaa 'ikhtiyaar Sa'b jiddan.**
hah-zah eek-tee-yar sahb jee-dan.
This is a very difficult choice.

Murad: **hal sa-tadhhabiina ma'a usratuki?**
hal sah-taz-hah-bee-nah mah-ah oos-rah-too-kee?
Are you going to go with your family?

Stephanie: **na'am. ma'a zawjii wa 'ibnii.**
nah-am. mah-ah zaw-jee wah eeb-nee.
Yes. With my husband and son.

Murad: **kam 'amr 'ibnukii?**
kam ah-mer eeb-noo-kee?
How old is your son?

Stephanie: **'ashr sanawaat.**
ah-sher sah-nah-wat.
Ten years old.

Murad: **'aDHunn 'anna murraakush tuwaafiq riHla li al-'usra. 'ibnukii sayuHibbuhaa.**
ah-zoon ah-nah moo-rah-koosh too-wah-feek reeh-lah lee al-oos-rah. eeb-noo-kee sah-yoo-hee-boo-hah.
I believe that Marrakech is suitable for a family trip. Your son will like it.

Stephanie: **Tayyib sa nadhhab 'ilaa murrakush. wa laakin 'uriidu 'an 'adhhab 'ilaa ad-daar al-bayDaa' 'ayDHan. hal haadha mumkin?**
tah-yeeb sah naz-hab ee-lah moo-rah-koosh. wah lah-keen oo-ree-doo an az-hab ee-lah ah-dar al-bay-dah ay-dan. hal hah-zah moom-keen?
Okay, we'll go to Marrakech. But I'd like to go to Casablanca as well. Is this possible?

Murad: **na'am. haadhaa 'aHsan 'idhaa zurtum murrakush wa ad-dar al-bayDaa'.**
nah-am. hah-zah ah-san ee-zah zoor-room moo-rah-koosh wah ah-dar al-bay-dah.
Yes. It's better if you visit both Marrakech and Casablanca.

Words to Know

zawj	zah-wej	husband
zawja	zaw-jah	wife
fikra	feek-rah	idea
naSiiHa	nah-see-hah	recommendation
daafi'	dah-feeh	warm
baarid	bah-reed	cold
makaan	mah-kan	place
'afDal	af-dal	preferable
ziyaara	zee-yah-rah	visit
mundhu	moon-zoo	during/throughout
madiina	mah-dee-nah	city
mudun	moo-doon	cities
shaaTi'	shah-teeh	beach
muHiiT	moo-heet	ocean
sibaaHa	see-bah-hah	swimming
jabal	jah-bal	mountain
jibaal	jee-bal	mountains
thalj	tah-lej	snow
tazalluj	tah-zah-looj	skiing
shamaal	shah-mal	north
januub	jah-noob	south
gharb	gah-reb	west
sharq	shah-rek	east

Picking the Right Time for Your Trip

A major part of travel planning is timing. When you have an idea of what you want to do or where you want to go, you need to consider the most appropriate time to take the trip. An obvious example is deciding to go skiing and making sure your mountain destination will have snow when you're there. However, things can get trickier if you're traveling to a Middle Eastern or Islamic country; during some months of the year, such as the holy month of Ramadan, traveling to these countries probably isn't a good idea because the time is sacred to Muslims.

The months of the year

Look at the **taqwiim** (*tak-weem;* calendar) and choose the **shahr** (*shah-her;* month) most suitable not only to your travel plans but also to the **dawla** (*daw-lah;* country) you're visiting. Table 15-1 identifies the months in Arabic.

Table 15-2	Months in Arabic	
Arabic	*Pronunciation*	*Translation*
yanaayir	yah-nah-yeer	January
fibraayir	feeb-rah-yeer	February
maaris	mah-rees	March
'abriil	ah-beh-reel	April
maayuu	mah-yoo	May
yunyu	yoo-neh-yoo	June
yulyu	yoo-leh-yoo	July
'aghusTus	ah-goo-seh-toos	August
sibtambar	see-beh-tam-bar	September
'uktuubar	oo-key-too-bar	October
nufambar	noo-fahm-bar	November
disambar	dee-sahm-bar	December

There are in fact two methods of transcribing months in Arabic. The one in Table 15-2 is based on the Gregorian calendar, which is widely used in the West. The second way of identifying months is based on the Islamic lunar system. Flip to Chapter 4 to see the months listed according to the Islamic calendar.

For travel purposes, the Gregorian calendar convention is most widely used, so if you're making a reservation, you can use the months listed in Table 15-2 to communicate the time of your **riHla.**

Dates and ordinal numbers

After you narrow down the **shahr** in which you want to take your **riHla,** you must specify the dates of your **riHla** by using numbers. Arabic numbers fall into two categories: cardinals and ordinals. *Cardinals* are regular counting numbers, like "one," "two," or "three;" *ordinals* are the adjective forms of numbers, like "first," "second," and "third." Arabic ordinals differ from cardinals in that every ordinal number has both a masculine and feminine form. Because ordinals are treated as adjectives, they must be in gender agreement with their corresponding nouns.

When you specify a date, you say "December fifth" or "January eighth." Because **shahr** is a masculine noun (the terms for months are masculine), you must use masculine ordinals to identify specific dates. For example, you say **disambar al-khaamis** (*dee-sam-bar al-kah-mees;* December fifth) or **yanaayir ath-thaamin** (*yah-nah-yeer ah-thah-meen;* January eighth). In addition, because the ordinal acts as a possessive adjective, you must include the possessive prefix **al-.** For more on cardinals and ordinals, flip to Chapter 4. For a comprehensive list of ordinals, flip to Chapter 12.

Talkin' the Talk

George and his wife Selma are trying to figure out when to visit their favorite country, Morocco.

George: **mataa turiidiina 'an nadhhab 'ilaa al-maghrib haadhihi as-sana?**
mah-tah too-ree-dee-nah an naz-hab ee-lah al-mag-reeb hah-zee-hee ah-sah-nah?
When would you like us to go to Morocco this year?

Selma: **fii nihaayat as-sana, kam al-'aada.**
fee nee-hah-yat ah-sah-nah, kam al-ah-dah.
At the end of the year, as usual.

George: **disambar? hal yumkin 'an tadhhabii fii disambar al-khaamis?**
dee-sam-bar? hal yoom-keen an taz-hah-bee fee dee-sam-bar al-kah-mees?
December? Can you go on December fifth?

Selma: **'intaDHir daqiiqa. sa 'araa taqwiimii.**
een-tah-zeer dah-kee-kah. sah ah-rah tak-wee-mee.
Hold on one minute. I'll check my calendar.

Selma checks her calendar.

Selma: **lisuu'i al-HaDH laa yumkin 'an 'adhhab disambar al-khaamis. 'indii 'ijtimaa' muhimm haadhaa al-yawm.**
lee-soo-ee al-haz lah yoom-keen an az-hab dee-sam-bar al-kah-mees. een-dee eej-tee-mah moo-heem hah-zah al-yah-oum.
Unfortunately I'm not able to leave on December fifth. I have an important meeting that day.

George: **hal yumkin 'an tadhhabii fii disambar ath-thaamin?**
hal yoom-keen an taz-hah-bee fee dee-sam-bar ah-thah-meen?
Can you go on December eighth?

Selma: **na'am. disambar ath-thaamin tamaam!**
nah-am. dee-sam-bar ah-thah-meen tah-mam!
Yes. December eighth is perfect!

George: **mumtaaz! wa hal narja' fii disambar 'ishriin?**
moom-taz! wah hal nar-jah fee dee-sam-bar eesh-reen?
Excellent! And should we come back on December twentieth?

Selma: **na'am haadhaa mumkin. wa laakin 'anaa 'uriidu 'an 'abqaa waqt 'akthar. hal yumkin 'an nabqaa 'ilaa disambar raabi' 'ishriin?**
nah-am hah-zah moom-keen. wah lah-keen ah-nah oo-ree-doo an ab-kah wah-ket ak-thar. hal yoom-keen an nab-kah ee-lah dee-sam-bar rah-beeh eesh-reen?
Yes that's possible. But I'd like to stay a bit longer. Can we stay until December twenty-fourth?

George:	**Tayyib. nabqaa 'ilaa raabi' 'ishriin.**
	tah-yeeb. nab-kah ee-lah rah-beeh eesh-reen.
	Okay. Let's stay until the twenty-fourth.
Selma:	**shukran. sa takuun riHla mutamatti'a!**
	shook-ran. sah tah-koon reeh-lah
	moo-tah-mah-tee-ah!
	Thank you. It's going to be an entertaining trip!

Words to Know

dhahaba	zah-hah-bah	to go
nadhhab	naz-hab	we go
shahr	shah-her	month
'ashhaar	ash-har	months
nihaaya	nee-hah-yah	end
bidaaya	bee-dah-yah	beginning
waSat	wah-sat	middle
waqt	wah-ket	time
taraka	tah-rah-kah	to leave
raja'a	rah-jah-ah	to return/come back
'amal	ah-mal	work
daqiiqa	dah-kee-kah	minute
taqwiim	tak-weem	calendar
'ijtimaa'	eej-tee-mah	meeting
muhimm	moo-heem	important (M)
muhimma	moo-hee-mah	important (F)
tamaam	tah-mam	perfect

Tackling Packing

Packing the right items for your **riHla** is a crucial step toward enjoying your travel experience. First, you must gather the **'amti'a** (*am-tee-ah;* luggage) you need. Here are some possibilities:

- **shanTa** (*shan-tah;* suitcase)
- **shanTaat** (*shan-tat;* suitcases)
- **miHfaDHa** (*meeh-fah-dah;* briefcase)
- **miHfaDHaat** (*meeh-fah-dat;* briefcases)
- **kiis** (*kees;* bag)
- **'akyaas** (*ak-yas;* bags)
- **kiis al-Hammamm** (*kees al-hah-mam;* toiletry bag)
- **'akyaas al-Hammaam** (*ak-yas al-hah-mam;* toiletry bags)
- **Haqiiba** (*hah-kee-bah;* small bag)
- **Haqaa'ib** (*hah-kah-eeb;* small bags)

With your **'amti'a** selected, it's time to choose what to put in the **'amti'a**. Here are some essential items you should carry with you regardless of your **wujha:**

- **malaabis** (*mah-lah-bees;* clothes)
- **'aqmisa** (*ak-mee-sah;* shirts)
- **sirwaal** (*seer-wal;* pants)
- **mi'Taf** (*meeh-taf;* coat)
- **'aHdiya** (*ah-dee-yah;* shoes)
- **'aHzima** (*ah-zee-mah;* belts)
- **jawaarib** (*jah-wah-reeb;* socks)
- **naDHaraat** (*nah-zah-rat;* glasses)
- **naDHaraat ash-shams** (*nah-zah-rat ah-shah-mes;* sunglasses)
- **qubba'a** (*koo-bah-ah;* hat)

In addition to clothing and accessories, you also need grooming items. Here are some toiletries you may pack for your **riHla:**

- **shawkat al-'asnaan** (*shaw-kat al-ass-nan;* toothbrush)
- **ma'juun al-'asnaan** (*mah-joon al-ass-nan;* toothpaste)
- **mushT** (*moo-shet;* comb)

- **ghasuul as-sha'r** (*gah-sool ah-shah-er;* shampoo)
- **Saabuun** (*sah-boon;* soap)
- **muziil ar-rawaa'iH** (*moo-zeel ah-rah-wah-eeh;* deodorant)
- **fuuTa** (*foo-tah;* towel)
- **'aalat al-Hilaaqa** (*ah-lat al-hee-lah-kah;* shaving razor)
- **ma'juun al-Hilaaqa** (*mah-joon al-hee-lah-kah;* shaving cream)

Preparing Your Travel Documents

The logistics of travel can get pretty complicated, especially when you're traveling internationally. In recent years, travel restrictions have grown more stringent due to growing concern over security. In this section, you can find all the key terms you need to know in order to gather the appropriate **wathaa'iq as-safar** (*wah-thah-eek ah-sah-far;* travel documents) to make your **riHla** go as smoothly as possible.

Before you leave on a **riHla,** you need to have at least one **biTaaqa shakhsiyya** (*bee-tah-kah shak-see-yah;* personal identification card); to be safe, you should probably have two or more. In case you need further confirmation of your identity, carrying three forms of identification is ideal. Here are some **biTaaqaat shaksiyya** (*bee-tah-kat shak-see-yah;* personal identification cards) you could carry with you:

- **biTaaqat as-saa'iq** (*bee-tah-kat ah-sah-eek;* driver's license)
- **biTaaqa min al-Hukuuma** (*bee-tah-kah meen al-hoo-koo-mah;* government-issued ID)
- **biTaaqa min al-jaysh** (*bee-tah-kah meen al-jah-yesh;* military-issued ID)
- **jawaaz as-safar** (*jah-waz ah-sah-far;* passport)
- **biTaaqat al-'amal** (*bee-tah-kat al-ah-mal;* work permit)

The word **biTaaqa** *(bee-tah-kah)* literally means "card." However, its meaning may change depending on the context of the phrase in which it's used. For instance, in the terms just listed, the word, **biTaaqa** means "license" as well as "permit."

In addition to personal identification documents, if you're traveling overseas, many countries require that you also have a **ta'shiira** (*tah-shee-rah;* visa) stamped on your **jawaaz as-safar.** Every **dawla** (*daw-lah;* country) has different procedures and requirements for obtaining **ta'shiiraat** (*tah-shee-rat;* visas), so it's your responsibility to find out whether the **dawla** you're planning to visit requires a **ta'shiira** and, if so, how to go about obtaining one. The categories of **ta'shiiraat** include:

> ✔ **ta'shiirat aT-Taalib** (*tah-shee-rat ah-tah-leeb;* student visa)
>
> ✔ **ta'shiirat al-'amal** (*tah-shee-rat al-ah-mal;* work visa)
>
> ✔ **ta'shiirat as-saa'iH** (*tah-shee-rat ah-sah-eeh;* tourist visa)
>
> ✔ **ta'shiirat al-'usra** (*tah-shee-rat al-oos-rah;* family visa)

In order to determine which **naw'** (*nah-weh;* type) of **ta'shiira** you need and how to go about getting one, you should contact the **qunSuliiyya** (*kon-soh-lee-yah;* consulate) of your **sifaaraat** (*see-fah-rat;* embassy). If possible, arrange to speak with a **muwDHaf al-qunSulliiyya** (*moo-wah-daf al-kon-soh-lee-yah;* consular officer); he or she should be able to provide you with all the **ma'lumaat** (*mah-loo-mat;* information) you need about **ta'shiiraat.**

Talkin' the Talk

Alan stops by the American consulate and speaks to a consular officer to get information about traveling to the Middle East.

Alan: **sa 'usaafir 'ilaa ash-sharq al-'awSaT wa 'aHtaaju 'ilaa ma'luumaat 'an as-safar.**
sah oo-sah-feer ee-lah ah-shah-rek al-aw-sat wah ah-tah-joo ee-lah mah-loo-mat an ah-sah-far.
I'm going to be traveling to the Middle East, and I need some travel information.

Officer: **Tayyib. yumkin 'an 'usaa'iduka. mataa sa-tadhhab?**
tah-yeeb. yoom-keen an oo-sah-ee-doo-kah. mah-tah sah-taz-hab?
Okay. I'm able to help you. When will you be going?

Alan: **'uriidu 'an 'adhhab fii nihaayat as-sana.**
oo-ree-doo an az-hab fee nee-hah-yat ah-sah-nah.
I would like to go at the end of the year.

Officer: **wa li kam waqt?**
wah lee kam wah-ket?
And for how long?

Alan:	**thalaath 'asaabii'.**
	thah-lath ah-sah-beeh.
	Three weeks.

Officer:	**'ay balad sa-tazuur?**
	ay bah-lad sah-tah-zoor?
	Which country will you be visiting?

Alan:	**'uriidu 'an 'azuur maSr wa lubnaan.**
	oo-ree-doo an ah-zoor mah-ser wah loob-nan.
	I want to visit Egypt and Lebanon.

Officer:	**Tayyib. laysa Daruurii 'an taHSul 'alaa ta'shiira li maSr.**
	tah-yeeb. lay-sah dah-roo-ree an tah-sool ah-lah
	tah-shee-rah lee mah-ser.
	Okay. It's not necessary to obtain a visa for Egypt.

Alan:	**wa li lubnaan?**
	wah lee loob-nan?
	And for Lebanon?

Officer:	**'idhaa satazuur lubnaan li 'akthar min 'usbuu' Daruurii 'an taHSul 'alaa ta'shiira.**
	ee-zah sah-tah-zoor loob-nan lee ak-that meen
	oos-booh dah-roo-ree an tah-sool ah-lah
	tah-shee-rah.
	If you're going to visit Lebanon for more than two weeks, then it's necessary for you to obtain a visa.

Alan:	**'ayna yumkin 'an 'aHSul 'alaa ta'shiira li lubnaan?**
	ay-nah yoom-keen ah ah-sool ah-lah tah-shee-rah lee loob-nan?
	Where can I obtain a visa for Lebanon?

Officer:	**fii al-qunSuliiyya al-lubnaaniiya. hiya fii waSat al-madiina.**
	fee al-kon-soo-lee-yah ah-loob-nah-nee-yah. hee-yah fee wah-sat al-mah-dee-nah.
	At the Lebanese consulate. It's located at the center of the city.

Alan:	**shukran li musaa'adatuka.**
	shook-ran lee moo-sah-ah-dah-too-kah.
	Thank you for your help.

Officer:	**'afwan.**
	af-wan.
	You're welcome.

Words to Know

'aHtaaj	ah-taj	I need
balad	bah-lad	country
buldaan	bool-dan	countries
Daruurii	dah-roo-ree	necessary
Hasala	hah-sah-lah	to obtain
'akthar	ak-thar	more than
'aqqall	ah-kal	less than
ma'luumaat	mah-loo-mat	information
musaa'ada	moo-sah-ah-dah	help

TIP

What's the difference between an embassy and a consulate?

The *consulate* and the *embassy* are foreign government outposts located in a host or target country. For example, the United States has both embassies and consulates in many countries around the world. A consulate is generally located in a busy tourist destination, and its officials and employees take care of minor diplomatic tasks such as issuing visas and sponsoring educational seminars. An embassy is usually located in a nation's capital and has a more policy-oriented approach. It's slightly less bureaucratic than a consulate, and it usually represents its country's official diplomatic stance in the host country.

A consulate is headed by a *consul,* the person in charge of issuing visas and promoting better relations with the people of a host country; in contrast, an embassy is run by an ambassador whose general responsibility is to make sure that diplomatic ties — on a government-to-government basis — remain strong and healthy.

If you're in a foreign country and need to ask a quick bureaucratic question (such as, "How can I extend my visa?"), you should head to the consulate. However, if something serious happens (you're put in jail, for instance), then contacting the embassy is more appropriate.

If you're an American citizen traveling abroad, to find answers to any questions you have regarding preparing your **wathaa'iq as-safar** prior to your **riHla,** visit the State Department's Bureau of Consular Affairs Web site at `travel.state.gov`.

Using a Travel Agency

Although you can turn to a number of different sources for **ma'luumaat** on organizing your **riHla,** few can provide you with the degree of top-notch service and personal attention that a **wakiil as-safariyaat** (*wah-keel ah-sah-fah-ree-yat;* travel agent) can provide.

A good **wakiil as-safariyaat** can recommend the most suitable places for your **riHla** and provide you with logistical information and assistance to make your **riHla** a success. A **wakiil as-safariyaat** can provide you with **ma'luumaat** concerning:

- ✔ **fanaadiq** (*fah-nah-deek;* hotels)
- ✔ **'amwaal an-naql** (*am-wal ah-nah-kel;* modes of transportation)
- ✔ **Taa'iraat** (*tah-ee-rat;* airplanes)
- ✔ **Sayyaaraat** (*sah-yah-rat;* cars)
- ✔ **Haafilaat** (*hah-fee-lat;* buses)
- ✔ **'ijaazaat** (*ee-jah-zat;* plans)
- ✔ **Hujuuzaat** (*hoo-joo-zat;* reservations)
- ✔ **tanziilaat** (*tan-zee-lat;* discounts)
- ✔ **tanziilaat al-majmoo'a** (*tan-zee-lat al-maj-moo-ah;* group discounts)

For example, the **wakiil as-safariyaat** can tell you about **tanziilaat** that you're eligible for if you're traveling in a **majmoo'a** (*maj-moo-ah;* group) or special rates you can obtain on transportation.

Many **wakiil as-safariyaat** provide special rates and packages that include not only airfare but also hotel **Hujuuzaat.** Here are some travel packages you should ask about:

- ✔ **layla wa yawmayn** (*lay-lah wah yaw-mayn;* one night and two days)
- ✔ **laylatayn wa thalaath 'ayyaam** (*lay-lah-tayn wah thah-lath ah-yam;* two nights and three days)
- ✔ **sittat layla wa sab'at 'ayyaam** (*see-tat lay-lah wah sab-at ah-yam;* six nights and seven days)

When reviewing information from your **wakiil as-safariyaat,** keep a lookout for the following deals:

✔ **al-funduq maDmuun.** (*al-foon-dook mad-moon;* Hotel is included.)

✔ **ziyaara fii al-madiina maDmuuna.** (*zee-yah-rah fee al-mah-dee-nah mad-moo-nah;* Sightseeing around the city is included.)

✔ **al-fuTuur wa al-ghidaa' maDmuuniin.** (*al-foo-toor wah al-gee-dah mad-moo-neen;* Breakfast and lunch are included.)

✔ **al-funduq wa aT-Taa'ira maDmuuniin.** (*al-foon-dook wah ah-tah-ee-rah mad-moo-neen;* Hotel and airfare are included.)

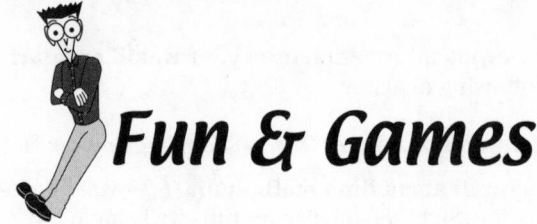

Fun & Games

Name the items in Arabic.

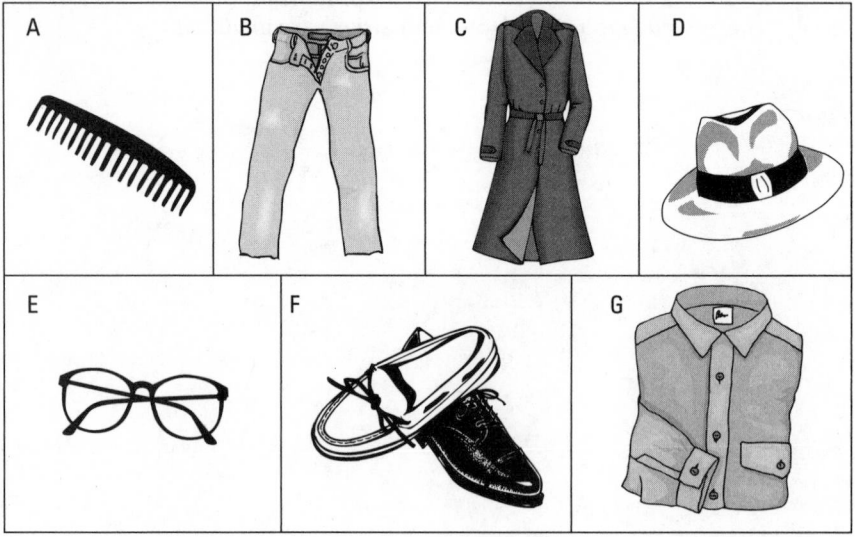

A. _____

B. _____

C. _____

D. _____

E. _____

F. _____

G. _____

The answers are in Appendix C.

Chapter 16

Handling an Emergency

. . . .

In This Chapter

▶ Finding help when you need it

▶ Talking with a doctor

▶ Getting legal help

. . . .

*N*o one can deny the power of positive thinking. However, there are times when negative situations arise, and you must be able to rise to the occasion and help not only yourself but those around you if necessary. So even though remaining positive is always a good thing, you should also know how to handle negative situations if you find yourself faced with them.

Handling an emergency in your native tongue can be quite hard to begin with, given the adrenaline rush and possible feelings of panic, so dealing with a situation in a foreign language such as Arabic may seem daunting. But don't panic! In this chapter, I give you the right words, phrases, and procedures to help you overcome any emergency situation — whether medical, legal, or political — just like a native speaker.

Shouting Out for Help

When you're witnessing or experiencing an emergency such as a theft, a fire, or even someone having a heart attack, your first instinct is to start yelling and shouting. That's the right instinct. But you also need to be able to communicate coherently so that you can get **musaa'ada** (*moo-sah-ah-dah;* help). This section tells you which words to use to express your sense of emergency verbally in order to get the right kind of **musaa'ada**.

Essentially, Arabic has two words that mean "help": **musaa'ada** *(moo-sah-ah-dah)* and **mu'aawana** *(moo-ah-wah-nah)*. Both words are used interchangeably to ask for help in an emergency. You can attract help by shouting **musaa'ada** or **mu'aawana** once, but you attract more attention when you shout the words consecutively:

> ✔ **musaa'ada musaa'ada!** *(moo-sah-ah-dah moo-sah-ah-dah;* Help help!)

> ✔ **mu'aawana mu'aawana!** *(moo-ah-wah-nah moo-ah-wah-nah;* Help help!)

Arabic actually has a third word that means "help": **najda** *(nah-jeh-dah)*. You can use **najda** to call for help, but be aware that screaming **najda** means that someone is in a severe, extremely dangerous, life-and-death situation. (If there were degrees to words for "help" — where level 3 is high and level 5 is extreme — **musaa'ada** and **mu'aawana** would be level 3s and **najda** would be a level 5.)

It may be difficult to understand this classification of "help" because when you're in an emergency, you tend not to think about your situation on a scale of seriousness. Your reaction is usually, "I'm in trouble, and I need help now." The Arabic vocabulary for emergencies is structured in such a way as to differentiate between life-and-death emergencies and non–life-and-death situations.

The basic rule for expressing that you need help is that if you're involved in a life-and-death situation, you should scream out **najda.** Think of **najda** as the code red of distress signals, only to be used if your life or the life of others is in danger. For example, screaming **najda** isn't appropriate if you sprain your ankle while playing soccer. However, if you're witnessing or experiencing a drowning, a heart attack, or a suicide attempt, you should scream **najda** like this:

> **an-najda an-najda!** *(ahn-nah-jeh-dah ahn-nah-jeh-dah;* Help help!)

Here are some other important words and phrases to help you cope with an emergency:

> ✔ **saa'iduunii!** *(sah-ee-doo-nee;* Help me!)

> ✔ **'aawinuunii!** *(ah-wee-noo-nee;* Help me!)

> ✔ **shurTa!** *(shoo-reh-tah;* Police!)

> ✔ **'uriidu Tabiib!** *(oo-ree-doo tah-beeb;* I need a doctor!)

> ✔ **liSS!** *(lehs;* Thief!)

> ✔ **naar!** *(nahr;* Fire!)

A little help with the verb "to help"

The word **musaa'ada** is derived from the verb **saa'ada** *(sah-ah-dah)*, which means "to help." Although screaming **musaa'ada** is an important first step to attract attention to an emergency, you also need to be able to coherently formulate a sentence in order to get the right kind of help. Use the form **saa'ada** to conjugate the verb "to help" in the **maaDii** *(mah-dee;* past tense) and **yusaa'idu** *(yoo-sah-ee-doo)* to conjugate it in the **muDaari'** *(moo-dah-reeh;* present tense). (Check out Chapter 2 for a quick reminder of the **maaDii** and **muDaari'** forms.)

Here's the verb **saa'ada** conjugated in the **maaDii** form:

Form	Pronunciation	Meaning
'anaa saa'adtu	ah-nah sah-ahd-too	I helped
'anta saa'adta	ahn-tah sah-ahd-tah	You helped (MS)
'anti saa'adti	ahn-tee sah-ahd-tee	You helped (FS)
huwa saa'ada	hoo-wah sah-ah-dah	He helped
hiya saa'adat	hee-yah sah-ah-daht	She helped
naHnu saa'adnaa	nah-noo sah-ahd-naa	We helped
'antum saa'adtum	ahn-toom sah-ahd-toom	You helped (MP)
'antunna saa'adtunna	ahn-too-nah sah-ahd-too-nah	You helped (FP)
hum saa'aduu	hoom sah-ah-doo	They helped (MP)
hunna saa'adna	hoo-nah sah-ahd-nah	They helped (FP)
antumaa saa'adtumaa	ahn-too-mah sah-ahd-too-mah	You helped (dual/MP/FP)
humaa saa'adaa	hoo-mah sah-ah-dah	They helped (dual/MP)
humaa saa'adataa	hoo-mah sah-ah-dah-tah	They helped (dual/FP)

Use the form **yusaa'idu** to conjugate "to help" in the **muDaari'**. Recall that the present tense in Arabic describes both a habitual action, such as "I help," and an ongoing action, such as "I am helping."

Form	Pronunciation	Meaning
'anaa 'usaa'idu	ah-nah oo-sah-ee-doo	I am helping
'anta tusaa'idu	ahn-tah too-sah-ee-doo	You are helping (MS)
'anti tusaa'idiina	ahn-tee too-sah-ee-dee-nah	You are helping (FS)
huwa yusaa'idu	hoo-wah yoo-sah-ee-doo	He is helping
hiya tusaa'idu	hee-yah too-sah-ee-doo	She is helping
naHnu nusaa'idu	nah-noo noo-sah-ee-doo	We are helping
'antum tusaa'iduuna	ahn-toom too-sah-ee-doo-nah	You are helping (MP)
'antunna tusaa'idna	ahn-too-nah too-sah-eed-nah	You are helping (FP)
hum yusaa'iduuna	hoom yoo-sah-ee-doo-nah	They are helping (MP)
hunna yusaa'idna	hoo-nah yoo-sah-eed-nah	They are helping (FP)
antumaa tusaa'idaani	ahn-too-mah too-sah-ee-dah-nee	You are helping (dual/MP/FP)
humaa yusaa'idaani	hoo-mah yoo-sah-ee-dah-nee	They are helping (dual/MP)
humaa tusaa'idaani	hoo-mah too-sah-ee-dah-nee	They are helping (dual/FP)

Although Arabic has more than one word for "help," only **musaa'ada** is the most conjugated verb form. **mu'aawana** may also be conjugated using the form **'aawana** in the **maaDii** and **yu'aawinu** in the **muDaari'**, but it's more of an archaic and arcane verb that isn't widely used in everyday Arabic. Because **najda** is more of a code word for distress, it doesn't have a verb equivalent form.

Lending a hand

Being in an emergency doesn't always mean that you're the one who needs help. You may be faced with a situation where you're actually the person who's in a position to offer help. In this case, you need to know words and phrases of an altogether different nature. The words and phrases in this section help you better respond to a situation in which you're the helper and not the one being helped.

The first thing you do in such a situation is ask questions to assess the damage and determine what course of action to take:

✔ **maadhaa waqa'a?** (*mah-zah wah-kah-ah;* What happened?)

✔ **hal kul shay' bikhayr?** (*hal kool shah-yeh bee-kayr;* Is everything alright?)

✔ **hal turiidu musaa'ada?** (*hal too-ree-doo moo-sah-ah-dah;* Do you need help?)

✔ **'ay naw' min musaa'ada turiidu?** (*ay nah-weh meen moo-sah-ah-dah too-ree-doo;* What kind of help do you need?)

✔ **hal yajibu 'an tadhhab 'ilaa al-mustashfaa?** (*hal yah-jee-boo ann taz-hab ee-laa al-moos-tash-fah;* Do you need to go to the hospital?)

✔ **hal turiidu Tabiib?** (*hal too-ree-doo tah-beeb;* Do you need a doctor?)

If you're in a situation in which injuries are serious and the person appears to be disoriented, then you must take further steps, such as contacting the **shurTa** (*shoo-reh-tah;* police) or other first responders.

If you're ever in a situation where you need to call the police, you may say the following on the phone: **'aHtaaju bi musaa'ada fawran** (*ah-tah-joo bee moo-sah-ah-dah faw-ran;* I need help right away).

Talkin' the Talk

 Lamia is walking down the street when, all of a sudden, the woman walking in front of her falls on the ground. Lamia approaches the woman to see how she can be of help.

Lamia: **'afwan. hal kul shay' bikhayr?**
ah-feh-wan. hal kool shah-yeh bee-kayr?
Excuse me. Is everything alright?

Woman: **na'am. kul shay' bikhayr.**
nah-am. kool shah-yeh bee-kayr.
Yes. Everything is alright.

Lamia: **maadhaa waqa'a?**
mah-zah wah-kah-ah?
What happened?

Woman: **laa shay'. laqad saqaTtu.**
lah shah-yeh. lah-kad sah-kah-too.
Nothing. I fell.

Lamia: **hal turiidiina musaa'ada?**
hal too-ree-dee-nah moo-sah-ah-dah?
Do you need help?

Woman: **laa shukran. kul shay' sayakun bikhayr.**
lah shook-ran. kool shah-yeh sah-yah-koon bee-kayr.
No thank you. I will be alright.

Getting Medical Help

If you're like me, you may find that even though going to the doctor's office is necessary and important, it isn't always the most fun part of your day. But visiting the doctor is essential for each and every one of us. This section introduces you to important medical terms to help you interact effectively with medical staff.

Locating the appropriate doctor

In case of a medical urgency, your first stop should be the **mustashfaa** (*moos-tash-fah;* hospital) to see a **Tabiib** (*tah-beeb;* doctor). If you simply need a checkup, go see a **Tabiib 'aam** (*tah-beeb ahm;* general doctor). If your needs are more specific, look for one of these specialist doctors:

- **Tabiib 'asnaan** (*tah-beeb ahs-nan;* dentist)
- **Tabiib 'aynayn** (*tah-beeb ah-yeh-nayn;* ophthalmologist)
- **Tabiib rijl** (*tah-beeb ree-jel;* orthopedist)
- **Tabiib 'aTfaal** (*tah-beeb aht-fal;* pediatrician)

Talking about your body

Locating the right doctor is only the first step toward getting treatment. In order to interact with the **Tabiib,** you need to be able to identify your different body parts in Arabic, explaining which parts hurt and which are fine. Table 16-1 lists all your major body parts.

Table 16-1	Body Parts	
Arabic	*Pronunciation*	*Translation*
jasad	jah-sad	body
ra's	rahs	head
fam	fahm	mouth
lisaan	lee-sahn	tongue
'asnaan	ass-nahn	teeth
wajh	wah-jeh	face

Arabic	Pronunciation	Translation
jild	jee-led	skin
'anf	ah-nef	nose
'udhunayn	oo-zoo-nayn	ears
'aynayn	ah-yeh-nayn	eyes
dimaagh	dee-mag	brain
qalb	kah-leb	heart
ri'a	ree-ah	lung
katef	kah-tef	shoulder
Sadr	sah-der	chest
ma'iida	mah-ee-dah	stomach
diraa'	dee-rah	arm
yad	yahd	hand
'aSaabi'	ah-sah-beh	fingers
rijl	ree-jel	leg
qadam	kah-dam	foot
'aSaabi' al-qadam	ah-sah-beh al-kah-dam	toes
rukba	roo-keh-bah	knee
'aDHm	ah-zem	bone
damm	deh-m	blood
Dhahr	zah-her	back

Explaining your symptoms

The **Tabiib** can't provide you with the proper treatment unless you communicate the kind of pain you're experiencing. How **mariiD** (*mah-reed;* sick) do you feel? Do you have a **SuDaa'** (*soo-dah;* headache)? Or perhaps a **Haraara** (*hah-rah-rah;* fever)? Table 16-2 lists common symptoms.

Table 16-2	Common Symptoms	
Arabic	**Pronunciation**	**Translation**
maraD	mah-rad	sickness
waja'	wah-jah	ache/ailment
su'aal	soo-ahl	cough
bard	bah-red	cold
Harq	hah-rek	burn
raDDa	rah-dah	bruise
waja' 'aDHahr	wah-jah ah-zah-her	backache
maraD al-Hasaasiya	mah-rad al-hah-sah-see-yah	allergy

When you go to the **Tabiib,** he or she may ask you, **maadha yu'limuka?** (*mah-zah yoo-lee-moo-kah;* What hurts you?). The most common way to respond to this question is to name the body part that hurts followed by **yu'limunii** (*yoo-lee-moo-nee;* hurts me). So when the **Tabiib** asks **maadha yu'limuka?,** you may say:

  ✔ **ra'sii yu'limunii.** (*rah-see yoo-lee-moo-nee;* My head hurts me.)

  ✔ **'udhunayn tu'limunii.** (*oo-zoo-nay-nee too-lee-moo-nee;* My ears hurt me.)

  ✔ **Sadrii yu'limunii.** (*sah-der-ee yoo-lee-moo-nee;* My chest hurts me.)

  ✔ **diraa'ii yu'imunii.** (*dee-rah-ee yoo-lee-moo-nee;* My arm hurts me.)

Getting treatment

After the **Tabiib** analyzes your symptoms, he or she is able to offer you **'ilaaj** (*ee-laj;* treatment). Following the **Tabiib**'s orders is important for both getting and remaining **saliim** (*sah-leem;* healthy), so pay attention. Here are treatment-related words you may encounter:

  ✔ **dawaa'** (*dah-wah;* medicine)

  ✔ **SayDaliiyya** (*sah-yeh-dah-lee-yah;* pharmacy)

  ✔ **'iyaada** (*ee-yah-dah;* clinic)

Talkin' the Talk

 Omar has been feeling nauseous all day long, so he decides to go see his doctor in the afternoon.

Doctor: **maadha yu'limuka?**
mah-zah yoo-lee-moo-kah?
What hurts you?

Omar: **ra'sii yu'limunii.**
rah-see yoo-lee-moo-nee.
My head hurts.

Doctor: **shay' 'aakhar?**
shah-y ah-kar?
Anything else?

Omar: **na'am. 'indii Haraara.**
nah-am. een-dee hah-rah-rah.
Yes. I have a fever.

Doctor: **khudh haadhaa 'asbiriin wa satakuun bikhayr.**
kooz hah-zah ass-pee-reen wah sah-tah-koon bee-kah-yer.
Take this aspirin, and you will be alright.

Words to Know

sharaab su'aal	shah-rahb soo-all	cough medicine
Suurat 'ashi'a	soo-rat ah-shee-ah	X-ray
'asbiriin	ass-pee-reen	aspirin

Acquiring Legal Help

Let's hope it's never the case, but you may have a run-in with the law and need the services of a **muHaamiiy** (*moo-hah-mee;* lawyer). The **muHaamiiy** has a good understanding of the **qaanuun** (*kah-noon;* law) and is in a position to help you if you're ever charged with committing a **mujrima** (*mooj-ree-mah;* crime).

If you happen to be in a foreign country and need legal representation, the best route is to contact your country's **qunSuliyya** (*koon-soo-lee-yah;* consulate) and ask to speak to the **qunSul** (*koon-sool;* consul). Because consular officers have a very good understanding of the laws of their host countries, you may be better off getting help directly from them rather than finding your own **muHaamiiy**. Especially if it looks like you have to go to **maHkama** (*mah-kah-mah;* court) and face a **qaadiiy** (*kah-dee;* judge), the help a **qunSuliyya** can provide is invaluable.

You may also want to call your country's **sifaara** (*see-fah-rah;* embassy) if you're in a really serious situation. Even if you're unable to talk to the **safiir** (*sah-feer;* ambassador) directly, your **sifaara** may take the appropriate steps to provide you with assistance.

Fun & Games

Identify the following body parts in Arabic:

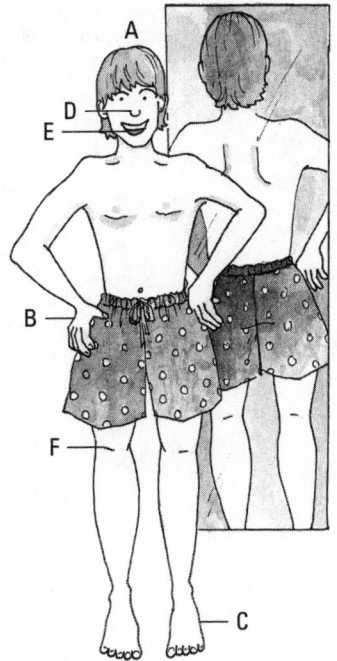

A. _____

B. _____

C. _____

D. _____

E. _____

F. _____

Answers are in Appendix C.

Part IV
The Part of Tens

In this part . . .

*Y*ou discover ten of the greatest Arabic proverbs, and you find out proper ways to interact with people if you're in an Arabic-speaking country. I also share my recommendations on the best ways to acquire Arabic as quickly as possible.

Chapter 17

Ten Ways to Pick Up Arabic Quickly

In This Chapter

▶ Explore Arabic media offerings online and in print

▶ Practice on Arabic speakers

▶ Get musical

Arabic is a language that needs to be constantly spoken, heard, and practiced. Even many native speakers try to read an Arabic newspaper every day or watch a **majalla 'ikhbaariya** (*mah-jah-lah eek-bah-ree-yah;* news broadcast) in order to maintain their level of fluency. So to get the best grasp of the language, you should try to immerse yourself in an environment where Arabic is the prevalent language. This chapter has recommendations on some key ways to help you not only pick up Arabic but also maintain a good degree of understanding of the language after you're comfortable with it.

Watch Arabic Television

Since the late 1990s, the Arabic audiovisual landscape has experienced a seismic shift. With the advent of satellite TV across the Arab world and the Middle East, Arab TV stations have spread across the world. Besides the well-known satellite news outlets **al-jaziira** (*al-jah-zee-rah;* the island) and **al-'arabiyya** (*al-ah-rah-bee-ya;* the Arabic), there are a number of other TV stations you can watch to help you fine-tune your accent and intonation. The news channels offer valuable exposure to spoken Modern Standard Arabic, which is the Arabic used in this book. Because this version's more formal than others, watching Arabic news channels will give you a better grasp of the grammatical rules — and your Arabic will be greatly improved as a result.

Another option for Arabic TV is MBC (Middle East Broadcast Corporation), which airs movies, soap operas, and talk shows that showcase some of the local spoken dialects such as Lebanese and Egyptian. If you're in the United States, you can order Arabic channels from your local cable provider or satellite TV operator; these channels have subtitles in English so you can follow along. Believe it or not, watching TV is one of the best ways to pick up a language. Personally, I didn't start speaking English until I was 10 years old, and one of the most effective tools that helped me grasp the language was watching sitcoms like *The Simpsons*.

Use the Dictionary

The **qaamoos** (*kah-moos;* dictionary) contains a wealth of information about Arabic words, phrases, and expressions. Simply picking up the dictionary once a day and memorizing a single word can have a huge effect on your Arabic vocabulary. Once you reach fluency in reading and writing Arabic, you'll realize that vowels aren't included in most of the Arabic texts you read, such as newspapers, books, and magazines. At first, trying to read without the vocalizations takes practice, but with the help of the **qaamoos,** you should be able to overcome this hurdle.

If reading the **qaamoos** is simply too low-tech for your taste, go online and find a word-a-day generating program that sends you an e-mail every morning with a new Arabic word; its pronunciation, meaning, and origins; and the context in which you use it. What a great way for you to build your vocabulary without actually opening the **qaamoos!** The Web site www.ectaco.com offers such a service.

Read Arabic Newspapers

The Arabic **SaHaafa** (*sah-hah-fah;* press) is very vibrant and offers many different publications covering a wide array of perspectives. Newspapers across the Arab world cater to all sorts of points-of-view, from the ultraliberal to the ultra-conservative. Reading Arabic newspapers is a good way to not only practice reading the language but also become more familiar with the issues concerning the Arab world.

You can purchase Arabic newspapers at most major newsstands in major metropolitan areas, such as New York City. Also, many Arabic newspapers now have online editions that you can access anytime, from anywhere. For more on Arabic newspapers and where to locate them, visit www.al-baab.com.

Surf the Internet

I believe that the Internet is one of the greatest inventions of all time — you have practically all the world's information at your fingertips! Plus, it's an amazing tool that can help you master Arabic quickly and efficiently. Simply visit any search engine — such as Google or Yahoo! — type the search word "Arabic," and start surfing. Or you can browse media Web sites, such as www.aljazeera.net or www.arabicworldnews.com. Most media sites have a Links section where you generally find a list of other Web sites that are similar in nature. Perusing these sites in Arabic should greatly improve your reading comprehension.

Use a Language Tape or CD

If you're a person who picks up a language by hearing it over and over, then you can't afford not to buy a few instructional Arabic CDs. Start by listening to the CD that came with this book; you'll find that the conversations are extremely helpful in helping you identify the speed, intonation, and pronunciation that makes you sound more like a native speaker. For more resources, investigate Arabic libraries in your city that offer instructional tapes and CDs, or check out your regular library to see what Arabic audio tools it offers — you may be surprised at what's available.

Listen to Arabic Music

Arabic music is one of the liveliest, most melodic, and fun types of music in the world. Because Arabic music is so energetic and fun, you'll pick up new phrases and words without even realizing it! You can choose from a lot of popular Arabic musicians, including:

- **Sheb Khaled** from Algeria, who plays **Rai** music. **Rai** music is the equivalent of Arabic hip-hop. The singer freestyles over a musical beat or rhythm.
- **Farid Al-atrache,** a master of the **'uud.** The **'uud** is a musical instrument that's similar to the guitar; but unlike a regular guitar, it has a wide, hollow body.
- **Najat 'atabou,** a popular folk singer from Morocco.

Check out any of these artists online, or go to your local music store and browse through the Middle East section for even more possiblities.

Make Arabic-Speaking Friends

It's really hard to find a substitute for human contact and human interactions. Making friends who are native or fluent Arabic speakers and carrying on conversations with them in Arabic dramatically improves your speaking and comprehension skills. After all, your friends are in a position to correct you gently and help you use the right expressions, phrases, and sentences in the appropriate contexts. Part of the challenge of picking up a language, especially one like Arabic, lies in the fact that you need to put your language skills — especially vocabulary and expressions — in the right context. Speaking with friends is the best way to do that!

Watch Arabic Movies

Watching Arabic movies can be a lot more fun than watching TV because you aren't interrupted by commercials and you generally have subtitles to follow. Most local movie stores and libraries carry popular Arabic movies on DVD or VHS tape, so you're sure to find something that interests you. Just be sure to get a movie with English subtitles so that you can follow along!

A movie that's worth watching is the Arabic version of Lawrence of Arabia. Another classic movie is The Messenger (ar-risaala).

Eat at a Middle Eastern Restaurant

Almost every city in the world has at least one Middle Eastern **maT'am** (*mat-ham;* restaurant), so let your fingers do the walking and find one in your area. Eating at a Middle Eastern restaurant provides you with a safe, fun, and engaging atmosphere in which to practice your language skills by interacting with the waitstaff in Arabic. Order drinks, food, and ask questions about the food preparation in Arabic, and you'll be amazed at how much you'll improve your Arabic reading and comprehension skills. And the restaurant staff are sure to be impressed with both your skill and interest in the language!

Sing Arabic Songs

Singing an **'ughniiya** (*oog-nee-yah;* song) is a fun, interactive, and effective way to pick up Arabic. Arabic songs tend to be extremely melodic and soulful, so not only will you enjoy singing an **'ughniiya,** but you'll also encounter new vocabulary and identify some of the intonations and beats that make Arabic such a unique language.

Chapter 18

Ten Things You Should Never Do in an Arab Country

....

In This Chapter

▶ Following proper greeting etiquette

▶ Respecting places that are off-limits

▶ Displaying appropriate behavior during the holy month of Ramadan

▶ Being a good guest

....

Cross-cultural dialogue isn't only spoken; nonlanguage signs are equally important in communicating and building bridges between cultures. By definition, a culture has a different set of values, principles, and social customs than other cultures. This chapter covers the unspoken rules to follow to help you avoid making faux-pas with native Arabic speakers or peoples from Arab countries.

Don't Shake Hands with a Firm Grip

In the United States, Europe, and throughout most of the Western world, people are encouraged to shake hands with a firm grip. Having a good, solid grip conveys a healthy dose of confidence in the West. In the Middle East, however, shaking hands with a tight or firm grip is considered impolite. Sometimes, it may even be interpreted as an openly hostile act! The logic behind this social custom is as follows: You use force and strength against your enemies, so shaking someone's hand with extreme force or strength may be interpreted as considering that person an enemy. The best way to shake hands if you're traveling in the Arab world is to present a friendly, not-too-firm grip — that way you're sure not to make any unnecessary foes!

Don't Enter a Room Full of People Without Saying "'as-salaamu 'alaykum"

As a general rule, you should get into the habit of saying **'as-salaamu 'alaykum** (*ah-sah-lah-moo ah-lay-koom*) whenever you enter a room, regardless of whether the people in the room are acquaintances or strangers. The phrase literally means "May peace be upon you" but is the equivalent of saying "Hello" in English.

Many people believe this saying has special significance because of religious and historical connotations. More than just a simple greeting, the phrase is used to convey a sense of respect and camaraderie; it's the equivalent of saying "I come in peace." Saying **'as-salaamu 'alaykum** signals to all that your intentions are honorable and pure. Rather than direct this greeting at a single person, **'as-salaamu 'alaykum** should be directed at everyone in the room. After you say it, you will hear a reply in unison: **wa 'alaykum as-salaam** (*wah ah-lay-koom ah-sah-lam;* and upon you peace).

Don't Start Eating Before Saying "bismi allah"

If you're invited to eat at a friend's house for dinner or lunch, or if you're sitting with co-workers at the cafeteria, make sure that you say **bismi allah** (*bees-mee ah-lah;* In the name of Allah [God]) before you start eating. Arabs and Muslims believe that before you eat, you should give thanks to God for the food you're about to put in your mouth. It doesn't matter whether you're Muslim or non-Muslim; **bismi allah** is an important phrase to use. (You don't have to say **bismi allah** before every bite, just before you begin the meal.)

Keep in mind that this phrase isn't used exclusively to bless food; you may hear someone say **bismi allah** before drinking water, starting a car, getting on a plane, and even before beginning to speak.

If You're Not Muslim, Don't Enter a Mosque Without Explicit Authorization

For Muslims, the **masjid** (*mas-jeed;* mosque) is one of the holiest places on earth. It's where Muslims go to pray, both individually and communally, and where most Muslims feel the closest bond to **allah.** Therefore, if you're non-Muslim, entering a mosque — any mosque — is strictly prohibited. There are exceptions to this rigidly enforced rule, but they're few and far between. For example, the Hassan II mosque in Casablanca, Morocco, has a special section for non-Muslims who are interested in discovering the beautiful architecture of the **masjid.** Visitors are allowed to walk through parts of the **masjid** — excluding the main prayer room, which is reserved for Muslims only — with a properly certified guide. Even in these exceptions, however, strict rules must be followed, such as removing your shoes (see the next section) and performing absolution before entering parts of the **masjid.**

Don't Enter a Mosque with Your Shoes On

Whereas non-Muslims are generally restricted from entering the **masjid,** Muslims aren't allowed to enter the **masjid** with their shoes on. Muslims strongly believe the **masjid** is a holy place that must be treated with considerable respect and cleanliness. If you're Muslim and want to go to the **masjid** for prayer, it's absolutely necessary you remove your **Hidaa'** (*hee-dah;* shoes). Similarly, if you're non-Muslim but are granted permission to visit parts of the **masjid,** you must remove your shoes as well.

Don't Eat or Drink During Ramadan

The holy month of Ramadan is the most sacred time for Muslims around the world. During this month, Muslims fast from sunrise to sunset in an attempt to cleanse themselves from the impurities of the world. The fasting is usually very strict — no food, no drink (including water), and no smoking. If you're non-Muslim and happen to visit an Islamic country during the month of Ramadan, it's really important that you don't eat or drink while the rest of the population is fasting. If you want to eat, you may do so within the confines of your own lodging. But under no circumstances should you go out and have a cigarette on the street corner while Ramadan is taking place. However, after sunset, when the fast is over and people are allowed to eat, smoke, and drink (nonalcoholic beverages), feel free to partake in these activities with everyone else.

Don't Drink Alcohol During Ramadan

Although you may drink water, soda, or juice in public after the breaking of the fast during Ramadan, you may not under any circumstances drink alcoholic beverages in public during the holy month of Ramadan. In most Islamic countries, if you're non-Muslim, you can have alcohol in designated public areas, such as a hotel bar or restaurant. However, during Ramadan, the sale and consumption of alcohol is prohibited. To be safe, you're advised to avoid any alcoholic drinks during the whole month of Ramadan, whether publicly or privately.

Don't Drink Alcohol in Public

Legally speaking, alcohol use by Muslims is prohibited in most, if not all, Arab and Islamic countries. Although enforcement of these laws isn't always consistent, you probably should err on the side of caution and not attract any negative attention to yourself if you're a non-Muslim visiting a Muslim country.

If you're a Muslim, most bars, restaurants, and hotels offer alcoholic beverages. If you're inside your hotel room or visiting friends at their house, you should feel free to enjoy an alcoholic drink (in moderation, of course). If you're out in public, then possession and consumption of alcoholic beverages is strictly prohibited. Make sure you keep this in mind before deciding to open a can of beer out on the beach or in another public space.

Don't Engage in Public Displays of Affection

Most Arab and Muslim countries follow strict Islamic social guidelines. These guidelines change from country to country, but it's smart to be aware of them in order to avoid any potentially troubling situations. As a general rule, public displays of affection are frowned upon in most Islamic countries. In countries such as Saudi Arabia and Indonesia, most women wear the **Hijaab** (*hee-jab;* veil) and must limit their interactions with the opposite sex. It's therefore not a good idea to kiss your girlfriend, boyfriend, fiancé, or even your spouse out in public. Keep outward affection for your significant other in the comforts of your own home. If you "accidentally" engage in public displays of affection, don't be surprised to receive some disapproving looks.

Don't Refuse a Gift If One Is Offered to You

People in the Middle East are known around the world for their incredible hospitality. If you ever get a chance to visit the region, you'll be surprised at how welcoming people are. An incredible social fabric encourages hospitality, and as a result, people love to share their food and their homes with others. If you're invited to a Middle Eastern home and are offered a gift — a piece of jewelry, clothes, food, or other item — it's considered impolite to refuse such a gift, no matter how extravagant you may think it is. However, when you accept a gift, you enter into a social contract: It's accepted and understood that you reciprocate by offering another gift in response. But don't worry, you don't have to match gifts in value. As the saying goes, it's the thought that counts.

Chapter 19

Ten Favorite Arabic Expressions

In This Chapter

▶ Welcoming someone with open arms

▶ Using religious expressions appropriately

▶ Sending your regards

Arabic uses a lot of very colorful expressions and words, which is to be expected because Arabic is in fact a very poetic language. Arabic speakers speak Arabic with a burning passion because the words, phrases, and expressions are so descriptive and conjure up strong visual images.

Linguists have studied the language in order to figure out why Arabic tends to be much more flowery and descriptive than most languages. One theory explains this phenomenon by examining the structure of the language itself; unlike in English and most Romance languages, adjectives in Arabic always come *after* the noun. This simple linguistic construct encourages speakers to use adjectives — some would argue they're the main ingredients of poetic sentences — which in turn creates very descriptive sentences. In English, because adjectives come before the noun, you're forced to use a limited number of adjectives before you have to get to the point, the noun.

Whatever the explanation, the passion with which speakers speak Arabic is sometimes hard to translate. However, if you familiarize yourself with some common expressions that make Arabic one of the most poetic languages in the world, you can come close to capturing that spirit! The expressions I cover in this chapter help you get acquainted with popular phrases in Arabic.

marHaba bikum!

mahr-hah-bah bee-koom; Welcome to all of you!

This term of welcoming is extremely popular with Arabic speakers. It's usually said with a lot of zest and enthusiasm and is often accompanied by very animated hand gestures. It's not uncommon for someone to say **marHaba bikum** and then proceed to hug you or give you a kiss on the cheek! This expression is a very affectionate form of greeting someone, such as an old friend, a very special guest, or a close family relative. But the relationship doesn't necessarily have to be a close one — if you're ever invited into a Middle Eastern home for a dinner or a lunch, don't be surprised if the host jovially shouts **marHaba bikum** and gives you a great big bear hug!

The shortened form of **marHaba bikum** is to simply say **marHaba,** which literally means "welcome." You may also say **marHaba bika** *(mahr-hah-bah bee-kah)*, which is the masculine singular form of **marHaba bikum.** (So you use **marHaba bika** when greeting a male friend and **marHaba biki** *(mahr-hah-bah bee-kee)* to greet a female friend because **biki** is the feminine singular form of **bikum.**) Finally, if you have a very close relationship with the person you're greeting, you may even use a variation of the following expression: **marHaba ya habibi** *(mahr-hah-bah yah hah-bee-bee;* Welcome my darling [M]) or **marHaba ya Habibtii** *(mahr-hah-bah yah hah-bee-beh-tee;* Welcome my darling [F]).

mumtaaz!

moom-tahz; Excellent!

This expression is used much like "excellent" is used in English: It's a way to note that something is going very well. For instance, a teacher may tell her students **mumtaaz** if they conjugate a difficult Arabic verb in the past tense, or a fan may yell **mumtaaz** if his hometown team scores a goal against an opponent. **mumtaaz** is used during joyous events or as a sign of encouragement. It's a very positive word that Arabic speakers like to use because it connotes a positive attitude. If you're having a conversation with a native speaker, it's very likely that he or she will use the word **mumtaaz** a lot for the duration of the conversation. You should do the same!

al-Hamdu li-llah

al-hahm-doo lee-lah; Praise to God

A number of expressions in the Arabic language make reference to **allah** for a very simple reason: As a spoken language, Arabic evolved from the writings of the Koran — Islam's Holy Book — which was recorded soon after the death of the Prophet Muhammad. Muslims believe that the Koran is actually God's words transmitted by the Angel Gabriel to the Prophet Muhammad.

According to Muslim tradition and belief, the Koran is literally God's message to His followers. Therefore, a lot of references to **allah** come directly from the Koran. Although spoken Arabic evolved from a religious language based on the Koran toward one with a more secular and everyday usage, it nevertheless retained many of its references to **allah.** Although they're based on a direct reference to **allah,** many of these phrases are actually used quite casually nowadays.

al-Hamdu li-llah, which has very wide usage, is a part of everyday Arabic. Arabic speakers say **al-Hamdu li-llah** after performing almost any single task, including finishing a meal, drinking water, finishing a project at work, and running an errand. The expression's extensive application goes beyond completing tasks; for example, if someone asks you, **kayf al-Haal?** (*kah-yef al-hal;* How are you doing?) you may reply, **al-Hamdu li-llah** and mean "Praise to God; I'm doing well." Because of its versatility, it's customary to hear **al-Hamdu li-llah** quite often when native speakers are talking to each other.

inshaa' allah

een-shah-ah ah-lah; If God wishes it

If you've ever watched Arabic speakers on Arabic TV, you've probably heard them use the expression **inshaa' allah.** This expression, which literally means "If God wishes it" or "If God wills it," is very popular among Arabic speakers when discussing future events. It's almost a rule that whenever someone brings up an event that will take place in the future, the expression **inshaa' allah** follows soon after. For example, when someone asks you how you think you're going to do on your next exam, you say, **'atamannaa 'an 'anjaH inshaa' allah** (*ah-tah-mah-nah ann an-jaheen-shah-ah ah-lah;* I hope I do well, if God wishes it). Or if someone asks you if your sister is going to start working soon, you say, **sa-tabda'u al-'ithnayn inshaa' allah** (*sa-tab-dah-oo al-eeth-nah-yen een-shah-ah ah-lah;* she starts on Monday, if God wishes it). Politicians in particular like to use this expression when someone asks them when they're going to hold elections. They say, **waqt qariib inshaa' allah** (*wah-ket kah-reeb een-shah-ah ah-lah;* Sometime soon, if God wishes it).

mabruk!

mahb-rook; Blessing upon you!

The root of the word **mabruk** is the noun **baraka** (*bah-rah-kah*), which means "blessing." **mabruk** is used at joyous occasions, such as the birth of a baby, a wedding, a graduation ceremony, or another festive event. Though its strict interpretation is "Blessing upon you," **mabruk** is just like saying "Congratulations." When you say **mabruk,** make sure you say it with a lot of energy and enthusiasm!

bi 'idni allah

bee eed-nee ah-lah; With God's guidance

This expression is meant to motivate and offer support and guidance, and although this expression contains a reference to God, it's actually a lot less common than expressions such as **inshaa' allah** or **al-Hamdu li-llah. bii 'idni allah** is used only during very special occasions, when one is facing serious challenges or is having difficulty in life, marriage, work, or school. Whenever someone's facing hardship, it's common for him or her to say **sa-'uwaajihu haadhihi as-su'uubu bi 'idni allah** (*sah-oo-wah-jee-hoo hah-zee-hee ah-so-oo-bah bee eed-nee ah-lah;* I will face this difficulty, with God's guidance). You can also use **bii 'idni allah** to encourage a friend who's having troubles. You may tell her, **kul shay' sa-yakun ki-khayr bi'idniallah** (*kool shah-yeh sah-yah-koon kee-kah-yer bee eed-nee ah-lah;* All will go well, with God's guidance).

bi SaHHa

bee sah-hah; With strength

Even though this expression literally means "with strength," it's not necessarily used in a context of encouragement or support like **bi 'idni allah** is (see the preceding section). Rather, **bi SaHHa** is an appropriate thing to say after someone has finished a difficult task and can relax and enjoy himself. For example, if a friend has wrapped up writing a book, closed a big deal, or ended a difficult case, you may say to him **bi SaHHa,** which signifies that your friend will be stronger as a result of accomplishing what he's accomplished and now can rest a bit.

taHiyyaat

tah-hee-yat; Regards

taHiyyaat is a religious term that Muslims use when they're praying. After a Muslim finishes praying, he performs the **taHiyyaat** by turning once to the right and once to the left, acknowledging the two angels that Muslims believe guard each person.

In addition to its religious affiliation, Arabic speakers commonly use **taHiyyaat** to send their regards. For instance, a friend may say to you, **salaam 'an 'abuuka** (*sah-lam ann ah-boo-kah;* Say hello to your father for me.) Similarly, to send your regards to a friend, you say, **taHiyyaat.**

muballagh

moo-bah-lag; Equally

muballagh is an expression that's similar to **taHiyyaat** in that you use it to send regards. However, unlike **taHiyyaat, muballagh** is a response; that is, you use it *after* someone sends their regards to you. So if someone says to you, **salaam 'an 'ukhtuk** (*sah-lam ann ook-took;* Say hello to your sister for me), you respond, **muballagh.** Responding with this expression means that you acknowledge the message and thank the person for it on behalf of your sister. So make sure to only say **muballagh** after someone sends their regards — not before!

tabaaraka allah

tah-bah-rah-kah ah-lah; With God's blessing

This expression is the equivalent of "God bless you" in English; it's most commonly used among close friends or family members to congratulate each other on accomplishments, achievements, or other happy events. For instance, if a son or daughter receives a good grade on an exam, the parents would say, **tabaaraka allah.** Another very popular use for this expression is to express warmth and joy toward kids.

Chapter 20

Ten Great Arabic Proverbs

In This Chapter
▶ Illuminating the meaning of modesty
▶ Seeking knowledge
▶ Expressing the importance of teamwork

*E*ven if you've read only a few chapters of this book, you've probably fig-
ured out that Arabic is a very poetic language. One aspect of the language that reinforces its poetic nature is the use of **'amthila** (*am-thee-lah;*
proverbs). Proverbs play an important role in the Arabic language. If you're
having a conversation with an Arabic speaker or listening to Arabic speakers
converse among themselves, don't be surprised to hear proverbs peppered
throughout the conversation. This chapter introduces you to some of the
more common and flowery proverbs of the Arabic language.

al-'amthaal noor al-kalaam.

al-am-thal noor al-kah-lam; Proverbs are the light of speech.

The role of proverbs in Arabic is so important that there's a proverb on the
importance of proverbs!

'a'mal khayr wa 'ilqahu fii al-baHr.

ah-mal kah-yer wah eel-kah-hoo fee al-bah-her; Do good and cast it into the sea.

Arab culture emphasizes humility and modesty. This proverb means that
when you commit a charitable act, you shouldn't go around boasting about it;
rather, you should "cast it into the sea" where no one can find out about it.

'uTlubuu al-'ilm min al-mahd 'ilaa al-laHd.

oot-loo-boo al-ee-lem meen al-mahd ee-lah al-lah-hed; Seek knowledge from the cradle to the grave.

al-'ilm (*al-ee-lem;* knowledge) is an important virtue in Arabic culture. Arabs have produced some of the greatest legal, medical, and scientific minds in history, in no small part because Arabs like to instill in their children a life-long desire to learn and continue learning every single day of one's existence.

yad waaHida maa tusaffiq.

yad wah-hee-dah mah too-sah-feek; A hand by itself cannot clap.

This proverb, which is common in the West but originates in Arab culture, underscores the importance of teamwork, cooperation, and collaboration.

al-Harbaa' laa Yughaadir shajaratuh hattaa yakun mu'akkid 'an shajara 'ukhraa.

al-har-bah lah yoo-gah-deer shah-jah-rah-tooh hah-tah yah-koon moo-ah-keed ann shah-jah-rah ook-rah; The chameleon does not leave his tree until he is sure of another.

This proverb stresses the importance of foresight, planning, and looking ahead. A chameleon that is mindful of predators won't change trees until it knows that it'll be safe in the next tree it goes to.

khaTa' ma'roof 'aHsan min Haqiiqa ghayr ma'roofa.

kah-tah mah-roof ah-san meen hah-kee-kah gah-yer mah-roo-fah; A known mistake is better than an unknown truth.

This metaphysical proverb has a deep meaning: It's better for you to identify and learn from a mistake than to not know a truth at all. In the debate of known versus unknown knowledge, this proverb indicates that knowing is better than not knowing, even if what you know is not an absolute truth.

as-sirr mithel al-Hamaama: 'indamaa yughaadir yadii yaTiir.

ah-seer mee-thel al-hah-mah-mah: een-dah-mah yoo-gah-deer yah-dee yah-teer; A secret is like a dove: When it leaves my hand, it flies away.

A secret is meant to be kept close to your chest — in other words, you shouldn't divulge a secret. As soon as you let a secret out of your "hand," it flies away and spreads around. Just as a dove won't leave unless you release it, a secret won't become known unless you divulge it.

al-'aql li an-niDHaar wa al-kalb li as-simaa'.

al-ah-kel lee ah-nee-zar wah al-kah-leb lee ah-see-mah; The mind is for seeing, and the heart is for hearing.

The mind is to be used for analytical purposes: observation and analysis. The heart, on the other hand, is for emotions; you should listen and feel with your heart.

kul yawm min Hayaatuk SafHa min taariikhuk.

kool yah-oum meen hah-yah-took saf-hah meen tah-ree-kook; Every day of your life is a page of your history.

You only live one life, so you should enjoy every single day. At the end, each day's experiences are what make up your history.

li faatik bi liila faatik bi Hiila.

lee fah-tek bee lee-lah fah-tek bee hee-lah; He who surpasses (is older than) you by one night surpasses you by one idea.

In Arabic culture and society, maturity and respect for elders is a highly regarded virtue. This proverb reinforces the idea that elders are respected, and their counsel is sought often.

Part V
Appendixes

The 5th Wave   By Rich Tennant

"I'm listening to a golden oldie.
Recitations of the Koran."

In this part . . .

Appendix A lists regular and irregular verbs to help you conjugate verbs in the past, present, and future tenses. Appendix B offers two mini-dictionaries — Arabic–English and English–Arabic — for quick reference. Appendix C provides the answers to all of the Fun & Games quizzes throughout the book, and Appendix D guides you through the audio tracks on the CD.

Appendix A
Verb Tables

Regular Arabic Verbs in the Past Tense

kataba (*kah-tah-bah;* wrote)		
Form	*Pronunciation*	*Translation*
'anaa katabtu	ah-nah kah-tab-too	I wrote
'anta katabta	an-tah kah-tab-tah	You wrote (M)
'anti katabtii	an-tee kah-tab-tee	You wrote (F)
huwa kataba	hoo-wah kah-tah-bah	He wrote
hiya katabat	hee-yah kah-tah-bat	She wrote
naHnu katabnaa	nah-noo kah-tab-nah	We wrote
'antum katabtum	an-toom kah-tab-toom	You wrote (MP)
'antunna katabtunna	an-too-nah kah-tab-too-nah	You wrote (FP)
hum katabuu	hoom kah-tah-boo	They wrote (MP)
hunna katabna	hoo-nah kah-tab-nah	They wrote (FP)
antumaa katabtumaa	an-too-mah kah-tab-too-mah	You wrote (dual/ MP/FP)
humaa katabaa	hoo-mah kah-tah-bah	They wrote (dual/MP)
humaa katabataa	hoo-mah kah-tah-bah-tah	They wrote (dual/FP)

darasa (*dah-rah-sah;* studied)

Form	Pronunciation	Translation
'anaa darastu	ah-nah dah-ras-too	I studied
'anta darasta	an-tah dah-ras-tah	You studied (M)
'anti darastii	an-tee dah-ras-tee	You studied (F)
huwa darasa	hoo-wah dah-rah-sah	He studied
hiya darasat	hee-yah dah-rah-sat	She studied
naHnu darasnaa	nah-noo dah-ras-nah	We studied
'antum darastum	an-toom dah-ras-toom	You studied (MP)
'antunna darastunna	an-too-nah dah-ras-too-nah	You studied (FP)
hum darasuu	hoom dah-rah-soo	They studied (MP)
hunna darasna	hoo-nah dah-ras-nah	They studied (FP)
antumaa darastumaa	an-too-mah dah-ras-too-mah	You studied (dual/ MP/FP)
humaa darasaa	hoo-mah dah-rah-sah	They studied (dual/MP)
humaa darasataa	hoo-mah dah-rah-sah-tah	They studied (dual/FP)

'akala (*ah-kah-lah;* ate)

Form	Pronunciation	Translation
'anaa 'akaltu	ah-nah ah-kal-too	I ate
'anta 'akalta	ahn-tah ah-kal-tah	You ate (M)
'anti 'akalti	ahn-tee ah-kal-tee	You ate (F)
huwa 'akala	hoo-wah ah-kah-lah	He ate
hiya 'akalat	hee-yah ah-kah-lat	She ate
naHnu 'akalnaa	nah-noo ah-kal-nah	We ate
'antum 'akaltum	ahn-toom ah-kal-toom	You ate (MP)
'antunna 'akaltunna	ahn-too-nah ah-kal-too-nah	You ate (FP)

Form	Pronunciation	Translation
hum 'akaluu	hoom ah-kah-loo	They ate (MP)
hunna 'akalna	hoo-nah ah-kal-nah	They ate (FP)
antumaa 'akaltumaa	ahn-too-mah ah-kal-too-mah	You ate (dual/MP/FP)
humaa 'akalaa	hoo-mah ah-kah-lah	They ate (dual/MP)
humaa 'akalataa	hoo-mah ah-kah-lah-tah	They ate (dual/FP)

Regular Arabic Verbs in the Present Tense

yaktubu (*yak-too-boo;* to write)		
Form	**Pronunciation**	**Translation**
'anaa 'aktubu	ah-nah ak-too-boo	I am writing
'anta taktubu	an-tah tak-too-boo	You are writing (M)
'anti taktubiina	an-tee tak-too-bee-nah	You are writing (F)
huwa yaktubu	hoo-wah yak-too-boo	He is writing
hiya taktubu	hee-yah tak-too-boo	She is writing
naHnu naktubu	nah-noo nak-too-boo	We are writing
'antum taktubuuna	an-toom tak-too-boo-nah	You are writing (MP)
'antunna taktubna	an-too-nah tak-toob-nah	You are writing (FP)
hum yaktubuuna	hoom yak-too-boo-nah	They are writing (MP)
hunna yaktubna	hoo-nah yak-toob-nah	They are writing (FP)
antumaa taktubaani	an-too-mah tak-too-bah-nee	You are writing (dual/MP/FP)
humaa yaktubaani	hoo-mah yak-too-bah-nee	They are writing (dual/MP)
humaa taktubaani	hoo-mah tak-too-bah-nee	They are writing (dual/FP)

yadrusu (*yad-roo-soo;* to study)		
Form	**Pronunciation**	**Translation**
'anaa 'adrusu	ah-nah ad-roo-soo	I am studying
'anta tadrusu	an-tah tad-roo-soo	You are studying (M)
'anti tadrusiina	an-tee tad-roo-see-nah	You are studying (F)
huwa yadrusu	hoo-wah yad-roo-soo	He is studying
hiya tadrusu	hee-yah tad-roo-soo	She is studying
naHnu nadrusu	nah-noo nad-roo-soo	We are studying
'antum tadrusuuna	an-toom tad-roo-soo-nah	You are studying (MP)
'antunna tadrusna	an-too-nah tad-roos-nah	You are studying (FP)
hum yadrusuuna	hoom yad-roo-soo-nah	They are studying (MP)
hunna yadrusna	hoo-nah yad-roos-nah	They are studying (FP)
antumaa tadrusaani	an-too-mah tad-roo-sah-nee	You are studying (dual/ MP/FP)
humaa yadrusaani	hoo-mah yad-roo-sah-nee	They are studying (dual/MP)
humaa tadrusaani	hoo-mah tad-roo-sah-nee	They are studying (dual/FP)

ya'kulu (*yah-koo-loo;* to eat)		
Form	**Pronunciation**	**Translation**
'anaa 'a'kulu	ah-nah ah-koo-loo	I am eating
'anta ta'kulu	ahn-tah tah-koo-loo	You are eating (M)
'anti ta'kuliina	ahn-tee tah-koo-lee-nah	You are eating (F)
huwa ya'kulu	hoo-wah yah-koo-loo	He is eating
hiya ta'kulu	hee-yah tah-koo-loo	She is eating
naHnu na'kulu	nah-noo nah-koo-loo	We are eating
'antum ta'kuluuna	ahn-toom tah-koo-loo-nah	You are eating (MP)
'antunna ta'kulna	ahn-too-nah tah-kool-nah	You are eating (FP)

Form	Pronunciation	Translation
hum ya'kuluuna	hoom yah-koo-loo-nah	They are eating (MP)
hunna ya'kulna	hoo-nah yah-kool-nah	They are eating (FP)
antumaa ta'kulaani	ahn-too-mah tah-koo-lah-nee	You are eating (dual/MP/FP)
humaa ya'kulaani	hoo-mah yah-koo-lah-nee	They are eating (dual/MP)
humaa ta'kulaani	hoo-mah tah-koo-lah-nee	They are eating (dual/FP)

Regular Arabic Verbs in the Future Tense

sa-yaktubu (*sah-yak-too-boo;* will write)		
Form	Pronunciation	Translation
'anaa sa-'aktubu	ah-nah sah-ak-too-boo	I will write
'anta sa-taktubu	an-tah sah-tak-too-boo	You will write (M)
'anti sa-taktubiina	an-tee sah-tak-too-bee-nah	You will write (F)
huwa sa-yaktubu	hoo-wah sah-yak-too-boo	He will write
hiya sa-taktubu	hee-yah sah-tak-too-boo	She will write
naHnu sa-naktubu	nah-noo sah-nak-too-boo	We will write
'antum sa-taktubuuna	an-toom sah-tak-too-boo-nah	You will write (MP)
'antunna sa-taktubna	an-too-nah sah-tak-toob-nah	You will write (FP)
hum sa-yaktubuuna	hoom sah-yak-too-boo-nah	They will write (MP)
hunna sa-yaktubna	hoo-nah sah-yak-toob-nah	They will write (FP)
antumaa sa-taktubaani	an-too-mah sah-tak-too-bah-nee	You will write (dual/MP/FP)
humaa sa-yaktubaani	hoo-mah sah-yak-too-bah-nee	They will write (dual/MP)
humaa sa-taktubaani	hoo-mah sah-tak-too-bah-nee	They will write (dual/FP)

sa-yadrusu (*sah-yad-roo-soo;* will study)

Form	Pronunciation	Translation
'anaa sa-'adrusu	ah-nah sah-ad-roo-soo	I will study
'anta sa-tadrusu	an-tah sah-tad-roo-soo	You will study (M)
'anti sa-tadrusiina	an-tee sah-tad-roo-see-nah	You will study (F)
huwa sa-yadrusu	hoo-wah sah-yad-roo-soo	He will study
hiya sa-tadrusu	hee-yah sah-tad-roo-soo	She will study
naHnu sa-nadrusu	nah-noo sah-nad-roo-soo	We will study
'antum sa-tadrusuuna	an-toom sah-tad-roo-soo-nah	You will study (MP)
'antunna sa-tadrusna	an-too-nah sah-tad-roos-nah	You will study (FP)
hum sa-yadrusuuna	hoom sah-yad-roo-soo-nah	They will study (MP)
hunna sa-yadrusna	hoo-nah sah-yad-roos-nah	They will study (FP)
antumaa sa-tadrusaani	an-too-mah sah-tad-roo-sah-nee	You will study (dual/MP/FP)
humaa sa-yadrusaani	hoo-mah sah-yad-roo-sah-nee	They will study (dual/MP)
humaa sa-tadrusaani	hoo-mah sah-tad-roo-sah-nee	They will study (dual/FP)

sa-ya'kulu (*sah-yah-koo-loo;* will eat)

Form	Pronunciation	Translation
'anaa sa-'a'kulu	ah-nah sah-ah-koo-loo	I will eat
'anta sa-ta'kulu	ahn-tah sah-tah-koo-loo	You will eat (M)
'anti sa-ta'kuliina	ahn-tee sah-tah-koo-lee-nah	You will eat (F)
huwa sa-ya'kulu	hoo-wah sah-yah-koo-loo	He will eat
hiya sa-ta'kulu	hee-yah sah-tah-koo-loo	She will eat
naHnu sa-na'kulu	nah-noo sah-nah-koo-loo	We will eat
'antum sa-ta'kuluuna	ahn-toom sah-tah-koo-loo-nah	You will eat (MP)
'antunna sa-ta'kulna	ahn-too-nah sah-tah-kool-nah	You will eat (FP)

Form	Pronunciation	Translation
hum sa-ya'kuluuna	hoom sah-yah-koo-loo-nah	They will eat (MP)
hunna sa-ya'kulna	hoo-nah sah-yah-kool-nah	They will eat (FP)
antumaa sa-ta'kulaani	ahn-too-mah sah-tah-koo-lah-nee	You will eat (dual/MP/FP)
humaa sa-ya'kulaani	hoo-mah sah-yah-koo-lah-nee	They will eat (dual/MP)
humaa sa-ta'kulaani	hoo-mah sah-tah-koo-lah-nee	They will eat (dual/FP)

Irregular Arabic Verbs in the Past Tense

baa'a (*bah-ah;* sold)		
Form	Pronunciation	Translation
'anaa bi'tu	ah-nah beeh-too	I sold
'anta bi'ta	ahn-tah beeh-tah	You sold (M)
'anti bi'tii	ahn-tee beeh-tee	You sold (F)
huwa baa'a	hoo-wah bah-hah	He sold
hiya baa'at	hee-yah bah-at	She sold
naHnu bi'naa	nah-noo beeh-nah	We sold
'antum bi'tum	ahn-toom beeh-toom	You sold (MP)
'antunna bi'tunna	ahn-too-nah beeh-too-nah	You sold (FP)
hum baa'uu	hoom bah-ooh	They sold (MP)
hunna bi'na	hoo-nah beeh-nah	They sold (FP)
antumaa bi'tumaa	ahn-too-mah beeh-too-mah	You sold (dual/MP/FP)
humaa baa'aa	hoo-mah bah-ah	They sold (dual/MP)
humaa baa'ataa	hoo-mah bah-ah-tah	They sold (dual/FP)

'ishtaraa (*eesh-tah-rah;* bought)

Form	Pronunciation	Translation
'anaa 'ishtaraytu	ah-nah eesh-tah-ray-too	I bought
'anta 'ishtarayta	ahn-tah eesh-tah-ray-tah	You bought (M)
'anti 'ishtarayti	ahn-tee eesh-tah-ray-tee	You bought (F)
huwa 'ishtaraa	hoo-wah eesh-tah-rah	He bought
hiya 'ishtarat	hee-yah eesh-tah-rat	She bought
naHnu 'ishtaraynaa	nah-noo eesh-tah-ray-nah	We bought
'antum 'ishtaraytum	ahn-toom eesh-tah-ray-toom	You bought (MP)
'antunna 'ishtaraytunna	ahn-too-nah eesh-tah-ray-too-nah	You bought (FP)
hum 'ishtaraw	hoom eesh-tah-raw	They bought (MP)
hunna 'ishtarayna	hoo-nah eesh-tah-ray-nah	They bought (FP)
antumaa 'ishtaraytumaa	ahn-too-mah eesh-tah-ray-too-mah	You bought (dual/ MP/FP)
humaa 'ishtarayaa	hoo-mah eesh-tah-rah-yah	They bought (dual/MP)
humaa 'ishtarayataa	hoo-mah eesh-tah-rah-yah-tah	They bought (dual/FP)

zaara (*zah-rah;* visited)

Form	Pronunciation	Translation
'anaa zurtu	ah-nah zoor-too	I visited
'anta zurta	ahn-tah zoor-tah	You visited (M)
'anti zurtii	ahn-tee zoor-tee	You visited (F)
huwa zaara	hoo-wah zah-rah	He visited
hiya zaarat	hee-yah zah-rat	She visited
naHnu zurnaa	nah-noo zoor-nah	We visited
'antum zurtum	ahn-toom zoor-toom	You visited (FP)

Form	Pronunciation	Translation
'antunna zurtunna	ahn-too-nah zoor-too-nah	You visited (MP)
hum zaaruu	hoom zah-roo	They visited (MP)
hunna zurna	hoo-nah zoor-nah	They visited (FP)
antumaa zurtumaa	ahn-too-mah zoor-too-mah	You visited (dual/MP/FP)
humaa zaaraa	hoo-mah zah-rah	They visited (dual/MP)
humaa zaarataa	hoo-mah zah-rah-tah	They visited (dual/FP)

Irregular Arabic Verbs in the Present Tense

yabii'u (*yah-bee-oo;* to sell)		
Form	**Pronunciation**	**Translation**
'anaa 'abii'u	ah-nah ah-bee-oo	I am selling
'anta tabii'u	ahn-tah tah-bee-oo	You are selling (M)
'anti tabii'iina	ahn-tee tah-bee-ee-nah	You are selling (F)
huwa yabii'u	hoo-wah yah-bee-oo	He is selling
hiya tabii'u	hee-yah tah-bee-oo	She is selling
naHnu nabii'u	nah-noo nah-bee-oo	We are selling
'antum tabii'uuna	ahn-toom tah-bee-oo-nah	You are selling (MP)
'antunna tabi'na	ahn-too-nah tah-beeh-nah	You are selling (FP)
hum yabii'uuna	hoom yah-bee-oo-nah	They are selling (MP)
hunna yabi'na	hoo-nah yah-beeh-nah	They are selling (FP)
antumaa tabii'aani	ahn-too-mah tah-bee-ah-nee	You are selling (dual/MP/FP)
humaa yabii'aani	hoo-mah yah-bee-ah-nee	They are selling (dual/MP)
humaa tabii'aani	hoo-mah tah-bee-ah-nee	They are selling (dual/FP)

yashtarii (*yash-tah-ree;* to buy)

Form	Pronunciation	Translation
'anaa 'ashtarii	ah-nah ash-tah-ree	I am buying
'anta tashtarii	ahn-tah tash-tah-ree	You are buying (M)
'anti tashtariina	ahn-tee tash-tah-ree-nah	You are buying (F)
huwa yashtarii	hoo-wah yash-tah-ree	He is buying
hiya tashtarii	hee-yah tash-tah-ree	She is buying
naHnu nashtarii	nah-noo nash-tah-ree	We are buying
'antum tashtaruuna	ahn-toom tash-tah-roo-nah	You are buying (MP)
'antunna tashtariina	ahn-too-nah tash-tah-ree-nah	You are buying (FP)
hum yashtaruuna	hoom yash-tah-roo-nah	They are buying (MP)
hunna yashtariina	hoo-nah yash-tah-ree-nah	They are buying (FP)
antumaa tashtariyaani	ahn-too-mah tash-tah-ree-yah-nee	You are buying (dual/MP/FP)
humaa yashtariyaani	hoo-mah yash-tah-ree-yah-nee	They are buying (dual/MP)
humaa tashtariyaani	hoo-mah tash-tah-ree-yah-nee	They are buying (dual/FP)

yazuuru (*yah-zoo-roo;* to visit)

Form	Pronunciation	Translation
'anaa 'azuuru	ah-nah ah-zoo-roo	I am visiting
'anta tazuuru	ahn-tah tah-zoo-roo	You are visiting (M)
'anti tazuuriina	ahn-tee tah-zoo-ree-nah	You are visiting (F)
huwa yazuuru	hoo-wah yah-zoo-roo	He is visiting
hiya tazuuru	hee-yah tah-zoo-roo	She is visiting
naHnu nazuuru	nah-noo nah-zoo-roo	We are visiting
'antum tazuuruuna	ahn-toom tah-zoo-roo-nah	You are visiting (MP)

Form	Pronunciation	Translation
'antunna tazurna	ahn-too-nah tah-zoor-nah	You are visiting (FP)
hum yazuuruuna	hoom yah-zoo-roo-nah	They are visiting (MP)
hunna yazurna	hoo-nah yah-zoor-nah	They are visiting (FP)
antumaa tazuuraani	ahn-too-mah tah-zoo-rah-nee	You are visiting (dual/MP/FP)
humaa yazuuraani	hoo-mah yah-zoo-rah-nee	They are visiting (dual/MP)
humaa tazuuraani	hoo-mah taz-zoo-rah-nee	They are visiting (dual/FP)

Irregular Arabic Verbs in the Future Tense

sa-yabii'u (*sah-yah-bee-oo;* will sell)		
Form	**Pronunciation**	**Translation**
'anaa sa-'abii'u	ah-nah sah-ah-bee-oo	I will sell
'anta sa-tabii'u	ahn-tah sah-tah-bee-oo	You will sell (M)
'anti sa-tabii'iina	ahn-tee sah-tah-bee-ee-nah	You will sell (F)
huwa sa-yabii'u	hoo-wah sah-yah-bee-oo	He will sell
hiya sa-tabii'u	hee-yah sah-tah-bee-oo	She will sell
naHnu sa-nabii'u	nah-noo sah-nah-bee-oo	We will sell
'antum sa-tabii'uuna	ahn-toom sah-tah-bee-oo-nah	You will sell (MP)
'antunna sa-tabi'na	ahn-too-nah sah-tah-beeh-nah	You will sell (FP)
hum sa-yabii'uuna	hoom sah-yah-bee-oo-nah	They will sell (MP)
hunna sa-yabi'na	hoo-nah sah-yah-beeh-nah	They will sell (FP)
antumaa sa-tabii'aani	ahn-too-mah sah-tah-bee-ah-nee	You will sell (dual/MP/FP)
humaa sa-yabii'aani	hoo-mah sah-yah-bee-ah-nee	They will sell (dual/MP)
humaa sa-tabii'aani	hoo-mah sah-tah-bee-ah-nee	They will sell (dual/FP)

sa-yashtarii (*sah-yash-tah-ree;* will buy)

Form	Pronunciation	Translation
'anaa sa-'ashtarii	ah-nah sah-ash-tah-ree	I will buy
'anta sa-tashtarii	ahn-tah sah-tash-tah-ree	You will buy (M)
'anti sa-tashtariina	ahn-tee sah-tash-tah-ree-nah	You will buy (F)
huwa sa-yashtarii	hoo-wah sah-yash-tah-ree	He will buy
hiya sa-tashtarii	hee-yah sah-tash-tah-ree	She will buy
naHnu sa-nashtarii	nah-noo sah-nash-tah-ree	We will buy
'antum sa-tashtaruuna	ahn-toom sah-tash-tah-roo-nah	You will buy (MP)
'antunna sa-tashtariina	ahn-too-nah sah-tash-tah-ree-nah	You will buy (FP)
hum sa-yashtaruuna	hoom sah-yash-tah-roo-nah	They will buy (MP)
hunna sa-yashtariina	hoo-nah sah-yash-tah-ree-nah	They will buy (FP)
antumaa sa-tashtariyaani	ahn-too-mah sah-tash-tah-ree-yah-nee	You will buy (dual/MP/FP)
humaa sa-yashtariyaani	hoo-mah sah-yash-tah-ree-yah-nee	They will buy (dual/MP)
humaa sa-tashtariyaani	hoo-mah sah-tash-tah-ree-yah-nee	They will buy (dual/FP)

sa-yazuuru (*sah-yah-zoo-roo;* will visit)

Form	Pronunciation	Translation
'anaa sa-'azuuru	ah-nah sah-ah-zoo-roo	I will visit
'anta sa-tazuuru	ahn-tah sah-tah-zoo-roo	You will visit (M)
'anti sa-tazuuriina	ahn-tee sah-tah-zoo-ree-nah	You will visit (F)
huwa sa-yazuuru	hoo-wah sah-yah-zoo-roo	He will visit
hiya sa-tazuuru	hee-yah sah-tah-zoo-roo	She will visit

Form	Pronunciation	Translation
naHnu sa-nazuuru	nah-noo sah-nah-zoo-roo	We will visit
'antum sa-tazuuruuna	ahn-toom sah-tah-zoo-roo-nah	You will visit (MP)
'antunna sa-tazurna	ahn-too-nah sah-tah-zoor-nah	You will visit (FP)
hum sa-yazuuruuna	hoom sah-yah-zoo-roo-nah	They will visit (MP)
hunna sa-yazurna	hoo-nah sah-yah-zoor-nah	They will visit (FP)
antumaa sa-tazuuraani	ahn-too-mah sah-tah-zoo-rah-nee	You will visit (dual/MP/FP)
humaa sa-yazuuraani	hoo-mah sah-yah-zoo-rah-nee	They will visit (dual/MP)
humaa sa-tazuuraani	hoo-mah sah-tah-zoo-rah-nee	They will visit (dual/FP)

Arabic-English Mini-Dictionary

A

'aala (*ah-lah*) F: machine

'aalat al-faks (*ah-lat al-fah-kes*) F: fax machine

'aalat al-Hisaab (*ah-lat al-hee-sab*) F: computer

'aalat al-Tibaa' (*ah-lat ah-tee-bah*) F: photocopy machine

'aaSifa (*ah-see-fah*) F: storm

'abriil (*ah-beh-reel*): April

'adas (*ah-das*) M: lentils

aDH-DHuhr (*ah-zoo-her*): noon

'afookaat (*ah-foo-kat*) M: avocado

'aghusTus (*ah-goo-seh-toos*): August

'ajiib (*ah-jeeb*): amazing

'akala (*ah-kah-lah*): ate

al-'aHad (*al-ah-had*): Sunday

al-anbaj (*al-ann-baj*): mango

al-'arbi'aa' (*al-ah-reh-bee-ah*): Wednesday

al-'asr (*al-ah-ser*): late afternoon

al-ghuulf (*al-goo-lef*) M: golf

al-'ithnayn (*al-eeth-nah-yen*): Monday

al-jubun (*al-joo-boon*) M: cheese

al-jumu'a (*al-joo-moo-ah*): Friday

al-khamiis (*al-khah-mees*): Thursday

al-maal (*al-mal*) M: money

al-masaa' (*al-mah-sah*) M: evening

al-mustakhdim (*al-moos-tak-deem*): employer

'amal (*ah-mal*) M: work, job

'amti'a (*am-tee-ah*) F: luggage

'anf (*ah-nef*) M: nose

'ariiD (*ah-reed*): wide

'arqaam (*ah-reh-kam*) M: numbers

'asal (*ah-sal*) M: honey

'aSdiqaa' (*ass-dee-kah*): friends

'ashaa' (*ah-shah*) M: dinner

'asnaan (*ass-nahn*) M: teeth

aS-SabaaH (*ah-sah-bah*) M: morning

as-sabt (*ass-sah-bet*): Saturday

ath-thulathaa' (*ah-thoo-lah-thah*): Tuesday

'awaan fiDDiyya (*ah-wan fee-dee-yah*): silverware

'ayn (*ah-yen*) F: eye

'ayna (*eh-yeh-nah*): where

'aynayn (*ah-yeh-nayn*) M: eyes

'ayshu al-ghuraab (*ay-shoo al-goo-rab*) M: mushrooms

'aziima (*ah-zee-mah*) F: determination

B

baab (*bahb*) F: door

baadhinjaan (*bah-zeen-jan*) F: eggplant

ba'da (*bah-dah*): after

ba'da aDH-DHuhr (*bah-dah ah-zoo-her*): afternoon

balcoon (*bal-koon*) M: balcony

bard (*bah-red*): cold

barq (*bah-rek*) M: lightning

baSla (*bass-lah*) F: onions

baTaaTa (*bah-tah-tah*) F: potato

baTTiikh (*bah-teek*) M: cantaloupe

bayD (*bah-yed*) M: eggs

bayt (*bah-yet*) M: house

baziilya (*bah-zee-lee-yah*) F: peas

biiyaano (*bee-yah-noo*) M: piano

bikam (*bee-kam*): how much

bint (*bee-neht*) F: girl

biTaaqat as-saa'iq (*bee-tah-kat ah-sah-eek*) F: driver's license

buuq (*book*) M: trumpet

D

daftar (*daf-tar*) M: notebook

dajaaj (*dah-jaj*) M: chicken

dallaaHa (*dah-lah-hah*) F: watermelon

Dammat 'awraaq (*dah-mat aw-rak*) F: stapler

daqiiqa (*da-kee-kah*) F: minute

daraaja/darraaja (*dah-rah-jah*) F: cycling

daraja (*dah-rah-jah*) F: degrees

darasa (*dah-rah-sah*): studied

darraaja (*dah-rah-jah*) F: bicycle

darraaja naariyya (*dah-rah-jah nah-ree-yah*) F: motorcycle

dawaa' (*dah-wah*) M: medicine

dhaalika (*zah-lee-kah*) M: that

dhahaba (*zah-hah-bah*): went

Dhahr (*zah-her*) M: back

DHuhr (*do-her*): noon

dhurra (*zoo-rah*): corn

diraa' (*dee-rah*) M: arm

Disambar (*dee-sahm-bar*): December

dukkaan (*doo-kan*) M: store

duush (*doosh*) F: shower

F

fa'ala (*fah-ah-lah*): did

fakhaar (*fah-kar*) M: pottery

fam (*fahm*) M: mouth

farraan (*fah-ran*) M: oven

fawz (*fah-wez*) M: win

fibraayir (*feeb-rah-yeer*): February

fluut (*feh-loot*) M: flute

fulful (*fool-fool*) M: pepper

funduq (*foon-dook*) M: hotel

furusiiyya (*foo-roo-see-yah*) F: horseback riding

fuTuur (*foo-toor*) M: breakfast

fuul (*fool*): beans

G

ghadan (*rah-dan*): tomorrow

ghaDbaan (*rad-bahn*): angry

ghasuul as-sha'r (*gah-sool ah-shah-er*) M: shampoo

ghidaa' (*gee-dah*) M: lunch

ghinaa' (*ree-nah*): singing

ghurfa (*roor-fah*) F: room

ghuul (*roohl*) M: ghost

H

haadhaa (*hah-zah*) M: this

haadhihi (*hah-zee-hee*) F: this

Haafila (*hah-fee-lah*) F: bus

haatif (*haa-teef*) M: telephone

haa'ulaa'i (*hah-oo-lah-ee*) MP/FP: these

Hajzu (*haj-zoo*): reservation

Hakam (*hah-kam*) M: referee

Haliib (*hah-leeb*) M: milk

Hallaaq (*hah-lak*) M: barber, hairdresser

Halwa al-jaliidiiya (*hal-wah al-jah-lee-dee-yah*) F: ice cream

Harara (*hah-rah-rah*) F: temperature

Hariira (*hah-ree-rah*) F: Middle Eastern soup

Hasaa' (*hah-sah*) F: soup

Haziin (*hah-zeen*): sad

Hidaa' (*hee-dah*): shoe

hilyoon (*heel-yoon*) M: asparagus

Hiwaar (*hee-war*) M: conversation

hiwaaya (*hee-waa-yah*) F: hobby

Hiyaaka (*hee-yah-kah*) F: knitting

Hizaam (*hee-zam*) M: belt

Hubuub al-fuTuur (*hoo-boob al-foo-toor*) M: breakfast cereal

I

'iiwaa' (*ee-wah*) F: accommodations

'ijaaSa (*ee-jah-sah*) F: pear

'ilaaj (*ee-laj*) M: treatment

'inab (*ee-nab*) M: grapes

'insiHaab (*een-see-hab*) M: withdrawal

'isfaanaakh (*ees-fah-nak*) M: spinach

'islaam (*ees-lahm*): Islam

'asm 'aa'ilii (*ah-sem ah-ee-lee*) M: last name, family name

'ism shakhsii (*ee-sem shak-see*) M: first name

'istiqbaal (*ees-teek-bal*) M: reception

'iyaada (*ee-yah-dah*) F: clinic

J

jallaaba (*jah-lah-bah*) F: Arab dress

jam'iyya (*jam-ee-yah*) F: university

jariida (*jah-ree-dah*) F: newspaper

jasad (*jah-sad*) M: body

jawaarib (*jah-wah-reeb*) F: socks

jawaaz as-safar (*jah-waz ah-sah-far*) M: passport

jawharii (*jaw-hah-ree*) M: jeweler

jumbaaz (*joo-meh-baz*) M: gymnastics

jumla (*joom-lah*) F: sentence

K

ka'k (*kahk*) M: cake

ka'k ash-shuukuulaat (*kahk ah-shoo-koo-lat*) M: chocolate cake

ka's (*kahs*) M: glass

kabiir (*kah-beer*): big

kalb (*kah-leb*) M: dog

kalima (*kah-lee-mah*) F: word

kam min (*kam meen*): how many

kam'a (*kam-ah*) F: truffles

kamanja (*kah-mah-neh-jah*) F: violin

kaswa (*kass-wah*) F: dress

kataba (*kah-tah-bah*): wrote

kayfa (*keh-yeh-fah*): how

khariif (*kah-reef*): fall

khasar (*kah-sar*) F: loss

khass (*kass*) M: lettuce

khata' (*kah-tah*) M: foul

khawkha (*kaw-kah*) F: peach

khiyaar (*kee-yar*) M: cucumber

khizaana (*kee-zah-nah*) F: cupboard

khurshuuf (*koor-shoof*) M: artichokes

kitaab (*kee-tab*) M: book

kura (*koo-rah*) F: ball

kurat al-miDrab (*koo-rat al-meed-rab*) F: tennis

kurat al-qadam (*koo-raht al-kah-dam*) F: soccer

kurat as-salla (*koo-rat ah-sah-lah*) F: basketball

kurat aT-Taa'ira (*koo-rat ah-tah-ee-rah*) F: volleyball

kursiiy (*koor-see*) M: chair

kuub (*koob*) M: tumbler

ku'uus (*koo-oos*): glasses

L

laa'ib (*lah-eeb*) M: player

laa'iba (*lah-ee-bah*) F: player

laHam (*lah-ham*) M: meat

laHam al-'ajal (*lah-ham al-ah-jel*) M: veal

laHam al-baqar (*lah-ham al-bah-kar*) M: beef

laHam al-ghanam (*lah-ham al-gah-nam*) M: lamb

layla (*lah-ye-lah*) F: night

laymoon (*lay-moon*) M: lemon

laymoon hindii (*lay-moon heen-dee*) M: grapefruit

laymoon maaliH (*lay-moon mah-leeh*) M: lime

lii maadhaa (*lee maah-zaah*): why

lisaan (*lee-sahn*) M: tongue

liSaaq (*lee-sak*) M: glue

lougha (*loo-rah*) F: language

M

maadhaa (*maah-zaah*): what

maaris (*mah-rees*): March

maayuu (*mah-yoo*): May

madiina (*mah-dee-nah*) F: city

maDmuun (*mad-moon*): included

madrasa (*mad-rah-sah*) F: school

maghsal (*mag-sal*) M: sink

maghsala (*mag-sah-lah*) F: sink

maHkama (*mah-kah-mah*) F: court

ma'iida (*mah-ee-dah*) F: stomach

makaan al-miilaad (*mah-kan al-mee-lad*) M: place of birth

makhbaza (*mak-bah-zah*) F: bakery

maktab as-siyaaHa (*mak-tab ah-see-yah-hah*) M: travel agency

maktaba (*mak-tah-bah*) F: bookstore, library

malaabis (*mah-lah-bees*) M: clothes

malaabis riyaaDiyya (*mah-lah-bees ree-yah-dee-yah*) M: uniforms

mal'ab (*mah-lab*) M: stadium

ma'luuma (*mah-loo-mah*) F: classified ads

ma'mal (*mah-mal*) M: factory

man (*meh-n*): who

manzil (*man-zeel*) M: house

maraafiq (*mah-rah-feek*) M: amenities

mariiD (*mah-reed*): sick

masaa' (*mah-sah*) M: evening

masbaH (*mas-bah*) M: swimming pool

masjid (*mas-jeed*) M: mosque

maSraf (*mas-raf*) M: bank

maSrafii (*mas-rah-fee*) M: banker

mataa (*mah-taah*): when

maT'am (*mat-ham*) M: restaurant

maTar (*mah-tar*): rain

maTba'a (*mat-bah-ah*) F: printer

matHaf (*mat-haf*) M: museum

miftaH (*meef-tah*) M: key

miHfaDHa (*meeh-fah-dah*) F: briefcase

mihna (*meeh-nah*) F: job, profession

mil'aqa (*meel-ah-kah*): spoon

milH (*mee-leh*) M: salt

mimHaat (*meem-hat*) F: eraser

mindiil (*meen-deel*) M: napkin

mir'aat (*meer-at*) F: mirror

mirHaaD (*meer-had*) M: toilet

miS'ad (*mees-ad*) M: elevator

mishbak 'awraaq (*meesh-bak aw-rak*) M: paper clip

mi'Taf (*meeh-taf*) M: coat

mu'ajjanaat (*moo-ah-jah-nat*) F: pastries

mubaara (*moo-bah-rah*) F: game

mudda (*moo-dah*) F: period

muHaamiiy (*moo-hah-mee*): lawyer

mujrima (*mooj-ree-mah*) F: crime

musaa'ada (*moo-sah-ah-dah*) F: help, assistance

N

naqd (*nah-ked*) M: coin

naql (*nah-kel*): transportation

natiija (*nah-tee-jah*) F: score

naw' al-Hisaab (*nah-weh al-hee-sab*) M: type of account

nawm (*nah-oom*): sleep

Nufambar (*noo-fahm-bar*): November

nuur (*noohr*) M: light

Q

qaadiiy (*kah-dee*) M: judge

qaamuus (*kah-moos*) M: dictionary

qabla (*kab-lah*): before

qahwa (*kah-wah*) F: coffee

qalam ar-rasaas (*kah-lam ah-rah-sas*) M: pencil

qalam jaaf (*kah-lam jaf*) M: pen

qalb (*kah-leb*) M: heart

qamiis (*kah-mees*) M: shirt

qara'a (*kah-rah-ah*): read

qarnabiiT (*kar-nah-beet*) M: broccoli

qaws (*kah-wes*) M: bow

qawsu quzaH (*kah-wuh-suh koo-zah*) M: rainbow

qif (*kee-f*): stop

qiithaar (*kee-thar*) F: guitar

qiraa'a (*kee-rah-ah*) F: reading

qird (*kee-red*) M: monkey

qiTaar (*kee-tar*) M: train

qubba'a (*koo-bah-ah*) F: hat

qunnabiiT (*koo-nah-beet*) M: cauliflower

R

raatib (*rah-teeb*) M: salary

rabii' (*rah-beeh*): spring

ra'D (*rah-ed*) M: thunder

rajul al-'iTfaa' (*rah-jool al-eet-fah*): firefighter

raqm (*rah-kem*) M: number

raqm al-haatif (*rah-kem al-hah-teef*) M: telephone number

raqs (*rah-kes*) M: dancing

ra's (*rahs*) M: head

rasm (*rah-sem*) M: drawing

ri'a (*ree-ah*) F: lung

riHla (*reeh-lah*) F: vacation

riiH (*ree-eh*) M: wind

rijl (*ree-jel*) F: leg

rubyaan (*roob-yan*) M: shrimp

rukba (*roo-keh-bah*) F: knee

ruTuuba (*roo-too-bah*): humidity

ruz (*rooz*) M: rice

S

saa'a (*sah-ah*) F: hour

Saabuun (*sah-boon*) M: soap

saaksuufuun (*sak-soo-foon*) M: saxophone

SabaaH (*sah-bah*) M: morning

safar (*sah-far*) M: trip

safiina (*sah-fee-nah*) F: ship

Saghiir (*sah-reer*): small

saHaab (*sah-hab*) M: cloud

SaHen (*sah-hen*) M: plate

saliim (*sah-leem*): healthy

samak (*sah-mak*) M: fish

sariir (*sah-reer*) M: bed

Sawt (*sah-oot*): noise

SayDaliiyya (*sah-yeh-dah-lee-yah*) F: pharmacy

Sayf (*sah-yef*): summer

shams (*shah-mes*): sun

shanTa (*shan-tah*) F: suitcase

shariiT siinimaa'ii (*sha-reet see-nee-mah-ee*) M: movie

sharika (*shah-ree-kah*) F: company

sharikat al-Hisaab (*shah-ree-kat al-hee-sab*) F: accounting firm

sharikat al-qaanuun (*shah-ree-kat al-kah-noon*) F: law firm

shaTranj (*sha-teh-rah-nej*) M: chess

shawka (*shaw-kah*) F: fork

shawkat al-'asnaan (*shaw-kat al-ass-nan*) F: toothbrush

shefanj (*sheh-fanj*) M: donuts

shiik (*sheek*) M: check

shi'r (*shee-ar*) M: poetry

shitaa' (*shee-tah*): winter

shurTa (*shoor-tah*): police officer

shuukuulaat (*shoo-koo-lat*) M: chocolate

sibaaHa (*see-bah-hah*) F: swimming

Sibtambar (*see-beh-tam-bar*): September

siiniimaa (*see-nee-mah*) F: movie theater

sikkiin (*see-keen*) M: knife

sirwaal (*seer-wal*) M: pants

siyaaqat aS-Sayaara (*see-yah-kat ah-sah-yah-rah*) F: racecar driving

skhoun (*suh-koon*): hot

su'aal (*soo-aahl*) M: question

SubH (*soo-beh*): morning

suHub (*soo-hoob*) M: clouds

sukkar (*soo-kar*) M: sugar

T

Ta'aam (*tah-am*): food

ta'aaqud (*tah-ah-kood*) M: pension

Taaksii (*tak-see*) M: taxi

taariikh al-'amal (*tah-reek al-ah-mal*) M: work history

taariikh al-miilaad (*tah-reek al-mee-lad*) M: date of birth

Tabaq (*tah-bak*): dish

Tabaq (*tah-bak*) M: floor

Tabl (*tah-bel*) M: drums

tafarraja (*tah-fah-rah-jah*): watched

takallama (*tah-kah-lah-mah*): spoke

TamaaTim (*tah-mah-teem*) F: tomatoes

Taqs (*tah-kes*) M: weather

tawaazun (*tah-wah-zoon*) M: balance

Tayyaarat waraq (*tah-yah-raht wah-rak*): kite-flying

tazaHluq (*tah-zah-look*) M: skiing

tazalluj (*tah-zah-looj*) M: ice skating

thaaniya (*tha-nee-yah*) F: second

thalj (*thah-lej*) M: snow

thallaaja (*thah-la-jah*) F: refrigerator

thaman (*tah-man*) M: price

thuum muHammar (*toom moo-hah-mar*) M: roasted garlic

tilifizyoon (*tee-lee-feez-yoon*) M: television

tilka (*teel-kah*) F: that

tuuta (*too-tah*) F: strawberry

U

'udhunayn (*oo-zoo-nayn*) M: ears

'ujra (*ooj-rah*) F: fee

'uktuubar (*oo-key-too-bar*): October

'ulaa'ika (*oo-lah-ee-kah*) MP/FP: those

'ummaal (*ooh-mal*) M: workers

'usra (*oos-rah*) F: family

W

wadii'a (*wah-dee-ah*) F: deposit

walad (*wah-lahd*) M: boy

waraq al-la'ib (*wah-rak ah-lah-eeb*) F: cards

waraq 'ay-nab (*wah-rak ay-nab*) M: stuffed vine leaves

Y

yad (*yahd*) F: hand

yadhhabu (*yaz-hah-boo*): to go

yadrusu (*yad-roo-soo*): to study

yaf'alu (*yaf-ah-loo*): to do

yaftaHu (*yaf-tah-hoo*): to open

yaktubu (*yak-too-boo*): to write

ya'kulu (*yah-koo-loo*): to eat

yanaayir (*yah-nah-yeer*): January

yaqra'u (*yak-rah-oo*): to read

ya'rifu (*yah-ree-foo*): to know

yarji'u (*yar-jee-oo*): to return

yaskunu (*yas-koo-noo*): to live

yawm (*yah-oom*) M: day

yulyu (*yoo-leh-yoo*): July

yunyu (*yoo-neh-yoo*): June

Z

zayt (*zah-yet*) M: oil

zayt az-zaytuun (*zah-yet ah-zay-toon*) M: olive oil

zaytuuna (*zay-too-nah*) F: olive

ziyaara (*zee-yah-rah*) F: visit

zubuun (*zoo-boon*): client

English-Arabic Mini-Dictionary

A

accommodations: **'iiwaa'** (*ee-wah*) F

accounting firm: **sharikat al-Hisaab** (*shah-ree-kat al-hee-sab*) F

after: **ba'da** (*bah-dah*)

afternoon: **ba'da aDH-DHuhr** (*bah-dah ah-zoo-her*)

amazing: **'ajiib** (*ah-jeeb*)

amenities: **maraafiq** (*mah-rah-feek*) M

angry: **ghaDbaan** (*rad-bahn*)

April: **'abriil** (*ah-beh-reel*)

Arab dress: **jallaaba** (*jah-lah-bah*) F

arm: **diraa'** (*dee-rah*) M

artichokes: **khurshuuf** (*koor-shoof*) M

asparagus: **hilyoon** (*heel-yoon*) M

ate: **'akala** (*ah-kah-lah*)

August: **'aghusTus** (*ah-goo-seh-toos*)

avocado: **'afookaat** (*ah-foo-kat*) M

B

back: **Dhahr** (*zah-her*) M

bakery: **makhbaza** (*mak-bah-zah*) F

balance: **tawaazun** (*tah-wah-zoon*) M

balcony: **balcoon** (*bal-koon*) M

ball: **kura** (*koo-rah*) F

bank: **maSraf** (*mas-raf*) M

banker: **maSrafii** (*mas-rah-fee*) M

barber: **Hallaaq** (*hah-lak*) M

C

basketball: **kurat as-salla** (*koo-rat ah-sah-lah*) F

beans: **fuul** (*fool*)

bed: **sariir** (*sah-reer*) M

beef: **laHam al-baqar** (*lah-ham al-bah-kar*) M

before: **qabla** (*kab-lah*

belt: **Hizaam** (*hee-zam*) M

bicycle: **darraaja** (*dah-rah-jah*) F

big: **kabiir** (*kah-beer*)

body: **jasad** (*jah-sad*) M

book: **kitaab** (*kee-tab*) M

bow: **qaws** (*kah-wes*) M

boy: **walad** (*wah-lahd*) M

breakfast: **fuTuur** (*foo-toor*) M

breakfast cereal: **Hubuub al-fuTuur** (*hoo-boob al-foo-toor*) M

briefcase: **miHfaDHa** (*meeh-fah-dah*) F

broccoli: **qarnabiiT** (*kar-nah-beet*) M

bus: **Haafila** (*hah-fee-lah*) F

cake: **ka'k** (*kahk*) M

cantaloupe: **baTTiikh** (*bah-teek*) M

cards: **waraq al-la'ib** (*wah-rak ah-lah-eeb*) F

cauliflower: **qunnabiiT** (*koo-nah-beet*) M

chair: **kursiiy** (*koor-see*) M

check: **shiik** (*sheek*) M

cheese: **al-jubun** (*al-joo-boon*) M

chess: **shaTranj** (*sha-teh-rah-nej*) M

chicken: **dajaaj** (*dah-jaj*) M

chocolate: **shuukuulaat** (*shoo-koo-lat*) M

chocolate cake: **ka'k ash-shuukuulaat** (*kahk ah-shoo-koo-lat*) M

city: **madiina** (*mah-dee-nah*) F

classified ads: **ma'luuma** (*mah-loo-mah*) F

client: **zubuun** (*zoo-boon*)

clinic: **'iyaada** (*ee-yah-dah*) F

clothes: **malaabis** (*mah-lah-bees*) M

cloud: **saHaab** (*sah-hab*) M

clouds: **suHub** (*soo-hoob*) M

coat: **mi'Taf** (*meeh-taf*) M

coffee: **qahwa** (*kah-wah*) F

coin: **naqd** (*nah-ked*) M

cold: **bard** (*bah-red*)

company: **sharika** (*shah-ree-kah*) F

computer: **'aalat al-Hisaab** (*ah-lat al-hee-sab*) F

conversation: **Hiwaar** (*hee-war*) M

corn: **dhurra** (*zoo-rah*)

court: **maHkama** (*mah-kah-mah*) F

crime: **mujrima** (*mooj-ree-mah*) F

cucumber: **khiyaar** (*kee-yar*) M

cupboard: **khizaana** (*kee-zah-nah*) F

cycling: **daraaja/darraaja** (*dah-rah-jah*) F

D

dancing: **raqs** (*rah-kes*)

date of birth: **taariikh al-miilaad** (*tah-reek al-mee-lad*) M

day: **yawm** (*yah-oom*) M

December: **Disambar** (*dee-sahm-bar*)

degrees: **daraja** (*dah-rah-jah*) F

deposit: **wadii'a** (*wah-dee-ah*) F

determination: **'aziima** (*ah-zee-mah*) F

dictionary: **qaamuus** (*kah-moos*) M

did: **fa'ala** (*fah-ah-lah*)

dinner: **'ishaa'** (*ee-shah*) M

dish: **Tabaq** (*tah-bak*)

do: **yaf'alu** (*yaf-ah-loo*)

dog: **kalb** (*kah-leb*) M

donuts: **shefanj** (*sheh-fanj*) M

door: **baab** (*bahb*) F

drawing: **rasm** (*rah-sem*) M

dress: **kaswa** (*kass-wah*) F

driver's license: **biTaaqat as-saa'iq** (*bee-tah-kat ah-sah-eek*) F

drums: **Tabl** (*tah-bel*) M

E

ears: **'udhunayn** (*oo-zoo-nayn*) M

eat: **ya'kulu** (*yah-koo-loo*)

eggplant: **baadhinjaan** (*bah-zeen-jan*) F

eggs: **bayD** (*bah-yed*) M

elevator: **miS'ad** (*mees-ad*) M

employer: **al-mustakhdim** (*al-moos-tak-deem*) M

eraser: **mimHaat** (*meem-hat*) F

evening: **al-masaa'** (*al-mah-sah*) M

evening: **masaa'** (*mah-sah*) M

eye: **'ayn** (*ah-yen*) F

eyes: **'aynayn** (*ah-yeh-nayn*) M

F

factory: **ma'mal** (*mah-mal*) M

fall: **Khariif** (*kah-reef*)

family: **'usra** (*oos-rah*) F

fax machine: **'aalat al-faks** (*ah-lat al-fah-kes*) F

February: **fibraayir** (*feeb-rah-yeer*

fee: **'ujra** (*ooj-rah*) F

firefighter: **rajul al-'iTfaa'** (*rah-jool al-eet-fah*)

first name: **'ism shakhsii** (*ee-sem shak-see*) M

fish: **samak** (*sah-mak*) M

floor: **Tabaq** (*tah-bak*) M

flute: **fluut** (*feh-loot*) M

food: **Ta'aam** (*tah-am*)

fork: **shawka** (*shaw-kah*) F

foul: **khata'** (*kah-tah*) M

Friday: **al-jumu'a** (*al-joo-moo-ah*)

friends: **'aSdiqaa'** (*ass-dee-kah*)

G

game: **mubaara** (*moo-bah-rah*) F

ghost: **ghoul** (*roohl*) M

girl: **bint** (*bee-neht*) F

glass: **ka's** (*kahs*) M

glasses: **ku'uus** (*koo-oos*)

glue: **liSaaq** (*lee-sak*) M

go: **yadhhabu** (*yaz-hah-boo*)

golf: **al-ghuulf** (*al-goo-lef*) M

grapefruit: **laymoon hindii** (*lay-moon heen-dee*) M

grapes: **'inab** (*ee-nab*) M

guitar: **qiithaar** (*kee-thar*) F

gymnastics: **jumbaaz** (*joo-meh-baz*) M

H

hand: **yad** (*yahd*) F

hat: **qubba'a** (*koo-bah-ah*) F

head: **ra's** (*rahs*) M

healthy: **saliim** (*sah-leem*)

heart: **qalb** (*kah-leb*) M

help: **musaa'ada** (*moo-sah-ah-dah*) F

hobby: **hiwaaya** (*hee-waa-yah*) F

honey: **'asal** (*ah-sal*) M

horseback riding: **furusiiyya** (*foo-roo-see-yah*) F

hot: **skhoun** (*suh-koon*)

hotel: **funduq** (*foon-dook*) M

hour: **saa'a** (*sah-ah*) F

house: **bayt** (*bah-yet*) M

house: **manzil** (*man-zeel*) M

how: **kayfa** (*keh-yeh-fah*)

how many: **kam min** (*kam meen*)

how much: **bikam** (*bee-kam*)

humidity: **ruTuuba** (*roo-too-bah*)

I

ice cream: **Halwa al-jaliidiiya** (*hal-wah al-jah-lee-dee-yah*) F

ice skating: **tazalluj** (*tah-zah-looj*) M

included: **maDmuun** (*mad-moon*)

Islam: **'islaam** (*ees-lahm*)

J

January: **yanaayir** (*yah-nah-yeer*)

jeweler: **jawharii** (*jaw-hah-ree*) M

job: **mihna** (*meeh-nah*) F

judge: **qaadiiy** (*kah-dee*) M

July: **yulyu** (*yoo-leh-yoo*)

June: **yunyu** (*yoo-neh-yoo*)

K

key: **miftaH** (*meef-tah*) M

kite-flying: **Tayyaarat waraq** (*tah-yah-raht wah-rak*)

knee: **rukba** (*roo-keh-bah*) F

knife: **sikkiin** (*see-keen*) M

knitting: **Hiyaaka** (*hee-yah-kah*) F

know: **ya'rifu** (*yah-ree-foo*)

L

lamb: **laHam al-ghanam** (*lah-ham al-gah-nam*) M

language: **lougha** (*loo-rah*) F

last name: **'ism 'aa'ilii** (*ee-sem ah-ee-lee*) M

late afternoon: **al-'asr** (*al-ah-ser*)

law firm: **sharikat al-qaanuun** (*shah-ree-kat al-kah-noon*) F

lawyer: **muHaamiiy** (*moo-hah-mee*)

leg: **rijl** (*ree-jel*) F

lemon: **laymoon** (*lay-moon*) M

lentils: **'adas** (*ah-das*) M

lettuce: **kass** (*khass*) M

library: **maktaba** (*mak-tah-bah*) F

light: **nuur** (*noohr*) M

lightning: **barq** (*bah-rek*) M

lime: **laymoon maaliH** (*lay-moon mah-leeh*) M

live: **yaskunu** (*yas-koo-noo*)

loss: **khasar** (*kah-sar*) F

luggage: **'amti'a** (*am-tee-ah*) F

lunch: **ghidaa'** (*gee-dah*) M

lung: **ri'a** (*ree-ah*) F

M

machine: **'aala** (*ah-lah*) F

mango: **al-anbaj** (*al-ann-baj*)

March: **maaris** (*mah-rees*)

May: **maayuu** (*mah-yoo*)

meat: **laHam** (*lah-ham*) M

medicine: **dawaa'** (*dah-wah*) M

Middle Eastern soup: **Hariira** (*hah-ree-rah*) F

milk: **Haliib** (*hah-leeb*) M

minute: **daqiiqa** (*da-kee-kah*) F

mirror: **mir'aat** (*meer-at*) F

Monday: **al-'ithnayn** (*al-eeth-nah-yen*)

money: **al-maal** (*al-mal*) M

monkey: **qird** (*kee-red*) M

morning: **aS-SabaaH** (*ah-sah-bah*) M

mosque: **masjid** (*mas-jeed*) M

motorcycle: **darraaja naariyya** (*dah-rah-jah nah-ree-yah*) F

mouth: **fam** (*fahm*) M

movie: **shariiT siinimaa'ii** (*sha-reet see-nee-mah-ee*) M

movie theater: **siiniimaa** (*see-nee-mah*) F

museum: **matHaf** (*mat-haf*) M

mushrooms: **'ayshu al-ghuraab** (*ay-shoo al-goo-rab*) M

N

napkin: **mindiil** (*meen-deel*) M

newspaper: **jariida** (*jah-ree-dah*) F

night: **layla** (*lah-ye-lah*) F

noise: **Sawt** (*sah-oot*)

noon: **aDH-DHuhr** (*ah-zoo-her*)

noon: **DHuhr** (*do-her*)

nose: **'anf** (*ah-nef*) M

notebook: **daftar** (*daf-tar*) M

November: **Nufambar** (*noo-fahm-bar*)

number: **raqm** (*rah-kem*) M

numbers: **'arqaam** (*ah-reh-kam*) M

O

October: **'uktuubar** (*oo-key-too-bar*)

oil: **zayt** (*zah-yet*) M

olive: **zaytuuna** (*zay-too-nah*) F

olive oil: **zayt az-zaytuun** (*zah-yet ah-zay-toon*) M

onions: **baSla** (*bass-lah*) F

open: **yaftaHu** (*yaf-tah-hoo*)

oven: **farraan** (*fah-ran*) M

P

pants: **sirwaal** (*seer-wal*) M

paper clip: **mishbak 'awraaq** (*meesh-bak aw-rak*) M

passport: **jawaaz as-safar** (*jah-waz ah-sah-far*) M

pastries: **mu'ajjanaat** (*moo-ah-jah-nat*) F

peach: **khawkha** (*kaw-kah*) F

pear: **'ijaaSa** (*ee-jah-sah*) F

peas: **baziilya** (*bah-zee-lee-yah*) F

pen: **qalam jaaf** (*kah-lam jaf*) M

pencil: **qalam ar-rasaas** (*kah-lam ah-rah-sas*) M

pension: **ta'aaqud** (*tah-ah-kood*) M

pepper: **fulful** (*fool-fool*) M

period: **mudda** (*moo-dah*) F

pharmacy: **SayDaliiyya** (*sah-yeh-dah-lee-yah*) F

photocopy machine: **'aalat al-Tibaa'** (*ah-lat ah-tee-bah*) F

piano: **biiyaano** (*bee-yah-noo*) M

place of birth: **makaan al-miilaad** (*mah-kan al-mee-lad*) M

plate: **SaHen** (*sah-hen*) M

player: **laa'ib** (*lah-eeb*) M

player: **laa'iba** (*lah-ee-bah*) F

poetry: **shi'r** (*shee-ar*) M

police officer: **shurTa** (*shoor-tah*)

potato: **baTaaTa** (*bah-tah-tah*) F

pottery: **fakhaar** (*fah-kar*) M

price: **thaman** (*tah-man*) M

printer: **maTba'a** (*mat-bah-ah*) F

profession: **mihna** (*meeh-nah*) F

Q

question: **su'aal** (*soo-aahl*) M

R

racecar driving: **siyaaqat aS-Sayaara** (*see-yah-kat ah-sah-yah-rah*) F

rain: **maTar** (*mah-tar*

rainbow: **qawsu quzaH** (*kah-wuh-suh koo-zah*) M

read: **yaqra'u** (*yak-rah-oo*)

reading: **qiraa'a** (*kee-rah-ah*) F

reception: **'istiqbaal** (*ees-teek-bal*) M

referee: **Hakam** (*hah-kam*) M

refrigerator: **thallaaja** (*thah-la-jah*) F

reservation: **Hajzu** (*haj-zoo*)

restaurant: **maT'am** (*mat-ham*) M

return: **yarji'u** (*yar-jee-oo*)

rice: **ruz** (*rooz*) M

roasted garlic: **thuum muHammar** (*toom moo-hah-mar*) M

room: **ghurfa** (*roor-fah*) F

S

sad: **Haziin** (*hah-zeen*

salary: **raatib** (*rah-teeb*) M

salt: **milH** (*mee-leh*) M

Saturday: **as-sabt** (*ass-sah-bet*)

saxophone: **saaksuufuun** (*sak-soo-foon*) M

school: **madrasa** (*mad-rah-sah*) F

score: **natiija** (*nah-tee-jah*) F

second: **thaaniya** (*tha-nee-yah*) F

sentence: **jumla** (*joom-lah*) F

September: **Sibtambar** (*see-beh-tam-bar*)

shampoo: **ghasuul as-sha'r** (*gah-sool ah-shah-er*) M

ship: **safiina** (*sah-fee-nah*) F

shirt: **qamiis** (*kah-mees*) M

shoe: **Hidaa'** (*hee-dah*) M

shower: **duush** (*doosh*) F

shrimp: **rubyaan** (*roob-yan*) M

sick: **mariiD** (*mah-reed*)

silverware: **'awaan fiDDiyya** (*ah-wan fee-dee-yah*)

singing: **ghinaa'** (*ree-nah*)

sink: **maghsala** (*mag-sah-lah*) F

sink: **maghsal** (*mag-sal*) M

skiing: **tazaHluq** (*tah-zah-look*) M

sleep: **nawm** (*nah-oom*)

small: **Saghiir** (*sah-reer*)

snow: **thalj** (*thah-lef*) M

soap: **Saabuun** (*sah-boon*) M

soccer: **kurat al-qadam** (*koo-raht al-kah-dam*) F

socks: **jawaarib** (*jah-wah-reeb*) F

soup: **Hasaa'** (*hah-sah*) F

spinach: **'isfaanaakh** (*ees-fah-nak*) M

spoke: **takallama** (*tah-kah-lah-mah*)

spoon: **mil'aqa** (*meel-ah-kah*)

spring: **rabii'** (*rah-bee*)

stadium: **mal'ab** (*mah-lab*) M

stapler: **Dammat 'awraaq** (*dah-mat aw-rak*) F

stomach: **ma'iida** (*mah-ee-dah*) F

stop: **qif** (*kee-f*)

store: **dukkaan** (*doo-kan*) M

storm: **'aaTifa** (*ah-tee-fah*) F

strawberry: **tuuta** (*too-tah*) F

studied: **darasa** (*dah-rah-sah*)

study: **yadrusu** (*yad-roo-soo*)

stuffed vine leaves: **waraq 'ay-nab** (*wah-rak ay-nab*) M

sugar: **sukkar** (*soo-kar*) M

suitcase: **shanTa** (*shan-tah*) F

summer: **Sayf** (*sah-yef*)

sun: **shams** (*shah-mes*)

Sunday: **al-'aHad** (*al-ah-had*)

swimming: **sibaaHa** (*see-bah-hah*) F

swimming pool: **masbaH** (*mas-bah*) M

T

taxi: **Taaksii** (*tak-see*) M

teeth: **'asnaan** (*ass-nahn*) M

telephone: **haatif** (*haa-teef*) M

telephone number: **raqm al-haatif** (*rah-kem al-hah-teef*) M

television: **tilifizyoon** (*tee-lee-feez-yoon*) M

temperature: **Harara** (*hah-rah-rah*) F

tennis: **kurat al-miDrab** (*koo-rat al-meed-rab*) F

that: **tilka** (*teel-kah*) F

that: **dhaalika** (*zah-lee-kah*) M

these: **haa'ulaa'I** (*hah-oo-lah-ee*) MP/FP

this: **haadhaa** (*hah-zah*) M

this: **haadhihi** (*hah-zee-hee*) F

those: **'ulaa'ika** (*oo-lah-ee-kah*) MP/FP

thunder: **ra'D** (*rah-ed*) M

Thursday: **al-khamiis** (*al-khah-mees*)

toilet: **mirHaaD** (*meer-had*) M

tomatoes: **TamaaTim** (*tah-mah-teem*) F

tomorrow: **ghadan** (*rah-dan*)

tongue: **lisaan** (*lee-sahn*) M

toothbrush: **shawkat al-'asnaan** (*shaw-kat al-ass-nan*) F

train: **qiTaar** (*kee-tar*) M

transportation: **naql** (*nah-kel*)

travel agency: **maktab as-siyaaHa** (*mak-tab ah-see-yah-hah*) M

treatment: **'ilaaj** (*ee-laj*) M

trip: **safar** (*sah-far*) M

truffles: **kam'a** (*kam-ah*) F

trumpet: **buuq** (*book*) M

Tuesday: **ath-thulathaa'** (*ah-thoo-lah-thah*)

tumbler: **kuub** (*koob*) M

type of account: **naw' al-Hisaab** (*nah-weh al-hee-sab*) M

U

uniforms: **malaabis riyaaDiyya** (*mah-lah-bees ree-yah-dee-yah*) M

university: **jam'iyya** (*jam-ee-yah*) F

V

vacation: **riHla** (*reeh-lah*) F

veal: **laHam al-'ajal** (*lah-ham al-ah-jel*) M

violin: **kamanja** (*kah-mah-neh-jah*) F

visit: **ziyaara** (*zee-yah-rah*) F

volleyball: **kurat aT-Taa'ira** (*koo-rat ah-tah-ee-rah*) F

W

watched: **tafarraja** (*tah-fah-rah-jah*)

watermelon: **dallaaHa** (*dah-lah-hah*) F

weather: **Taqs** (*tah-kes*) M

Wednesday: **al-'arbi'aa'** (*al-ah-reh-bee-ah*)

went: **dhahaba** (*zah-hah-bah*)

what: **maadhaa** (*maah-zaah*)

when: **mataa** (*mah-taah*)

where: **'ayna** (*eh-yeh-nah*)

who: **man** (*meh-n*)

why: **lii maadhaa** (*lee maah-zaah*)

wide: **'ariiD** (*ah-reed*)

win: **fawz** (*fah-wez*) M

wind: **riiH** (*ree-eh*) M

winter: **shitaa'** (*shee-tah*)

withdrawal: **'insiHaab** (*een-see-hab*) M

word: **kalima** (*kah-lee-mah*) F

work: **'amal** (*ah-mal*) M

work history: **taariikh al-'amal** (*tah-reek al-ah-mal*) M

workers: **'ummaal** (*ooh-mal*) M

write: **yaktubu** (*yak-too-boo*)

wrote: **kataba** (*kah-tah-bah*)

Appendix C

Answer Key

Here are all the answers to the Fun & Games quizzes.

Chapter 2

you (M): 'anta

we: naHnu

they (F): hunna

you (F): 'anti

he: huwa

I: 'anaa

Chapter 3

'alaykum as-salaam

al-Haal

'anta kayf al-Haal

'ismuka

'ismii

'ismuki

'ismii

tasharrafnaa

'ayna

min

min

al-ghad

Chapter 4

A. shitaa'

B. Sayf

C. rabii'

D. Khariif

Chapter 5

1. lettuce: khass

2. tomatoes: TamaaTim

3. potatoes: baTaaTis

4. broccoli: qarnabiiT

5. corn: dhurra

6. cucumber: khiyaar

7. mushrooms: 'ayshu al-ghuraab

Chapter 6

1. D (muSawwira)

2. A ('attdiya)

3. E (saa'a)

4. C (kaswa)

5. D (Khaatim)

Chapter 7

5:30: as-saa'a al-khaamisa wa an-niSf

7:45: as-saa'a ath-thaamina 'ilaa ar-rubu'

9:00 a.m.: as-saa'a at-taasi'a fii aS-SabaaH

2:30 p.m.: as-saa'a ath-thaaniya wa an-niSf fii ba'da aDH-DHuhr

6:15 a.m.: as-saa'a as-saadisa wa ar-rubu' fii aS-SabaaH

Chapter 8

shaTranj: chess

rasm: drawing

shi'r: poetry

kurat al-miDrab: tennis

sibaaHa: swimming

kurat as-salla: basketball

qiithaar: guitar

Chapter 9

1. E (sa-tarju' ba'da saa'a.)
2. B (laa. 'anaa mashghuul.)
3. A (na'am. daqiiqa min faDlik.)
4. D (al-Hamdu li-llah, shukran.)
5. C ('ismii Souad.)

Chapter 10

1. Hammaam
2. ghurfat an-nawm
3. maTbakh
4. ghurfat al-ma'iisha

Chapter 11

Across

1. duulaar
2. shiik

Down

1. maSraf
2. naqd
3. maktab

Chapter 12

1. D (Turn right.)
2. A (Please repeat that.)
3. E (Go west.)
4. B (The hotel is close.)
5. C (It's the tenth building.)

Chapter 13

1. C (Telephone bill)
2. A (Are there any messages for me?)
3. D (Reception desk)
4. E (Amenities)
5. B (When is the checkout time?)

Chapter 14

1. Sayyaara
2. qiTaar
3. Haafila
4. Taa'ira

Chapter 15

A. mushT
B. sirwaal
C. mi'Taf
D. qubba'a
E. naDHaraat
F. attdiya
G. qamiis

Chapter 16

A. ra's (head)
B. yad (hand)
C. qadam (foot)
D. 'anf (nose)
E. fam (mouth)
F. rukba (knee)

Appendix D

About the CD

*T*he following is a list of tracks that appear on the book's audio CD.

Track 1: Introduction

Track 2: Pronunciation Guide (Chapter 1)

Track 3: Greetings at school (Chapter 3)

Track 4: Meeting at the coffee shop (Chapter 3)

Track 5: A conversation in the cafeteria (Chapter 4)

Track 6: Chatting about the weather (Chapter 4)

Track 7: Ordering breakfast (Chapter 5)

Track 8: Picking up a sandwich (Chapter 5)

Track 9: Finding the clothing section of a store (Chapter 6)

Track 10: Shopping for a camera (Chapter 6)

Track 11: Planning to see a movie (Chapter 7)

Track 12: Figuring out the bus schedule (Chapter 7)

Track 13: Scheduling a soccer game (Chapter 8)

Track 14: Going to the beach (Chapter 8)

Track 15: Making dinner plans over the phone (Chapter 9)

Track 16: Leaving a message (Chapter 9)

Track 17: A job interview (Chapter 10)

Track 18: Borrowing an eraser (Chapter 10)

Track 19: Filling out a bank account application (Chapter 11)

Track 20: Exchanging currency (Chapter 11)

Track 21: Asking for directions (Chapter 12)

Track 22: Getting directions to a hotel (Chapter 12)

Track 23: Inquiring about hotel facilities (Chapter 13)

Track 24: Making a hotel reservation (Chapter 13)

Track 25: Making an airline reservation (Chapter 14)

Track 26: Speaking to an immigration agent (Chapter 14)

Track 27: Making plans to visit Morocco (Chapter 15)

Track 28: Speaking to a consular officer (Chapter 15)

Track 29: Helping someone who's fallen (Chapter 16)

Track 30: Describing symptoms to a doctor (Chapter 16)

Index

• A •

a- prefix, 25
'aalaat (machines), 179
'aalat al-Hisaab (computer), 178
aawinuunii! (Help me!), 282
'ab (father), 64
'abnaa' (children), 65
'abriil (April), 77, 269
accounts, bank, 190–197
'aDHm (bone), 287
adjectives
  comparative form, 109–110
  defined, 20
  definite, 27–28
  feminine forms, 23
  identifying, 21–24
  indefinite, 26–27
  irregular, 23
  masculine forms, 23
  multiple, with subject/object nouns, 32
  nature, changing, 29
  noun interactions, 24, 26–28
  position, 24, 26
'af'aal. See verbs
affection, public displays, 302
'afghanisTaan (Afghanistan), 263
'afham (understand), 211
'afwan. hal yumkin 'an 'as'alaka su'aalan?
    (Excuse me. May I ask you a
    question?), 208
'aghusTus (August), 77, 269
aHdiya (shoes), 273
'ahlan wa sahlan (hi), 50, 54, 57, 156
'aHtaaju bi musaa'ada fawran. (I need help
    right away.), 285
'a'id/'a'idii (repeat), 212
airport. See also flying; transportation
  exchange desk, 199
  registering at, 244–246
'ajiib/'ajiiba (amazing), 22
'akala, 90–91

'akala (ate), 318–319
'akh (brother), 65, 173
al- prefix, 22, 24, 25–26, 27, 106
'alaa (on), 31, 207
al-'aHad (Sunday), 76, 77
al-'amal (work), 167
al-'amthaal noor al-kalaam. (Proverbs are
    the light of speech.), 311
al-'aql li an-niDHaar wa al-kalb li as-simaa'.
    (The mind is for seeing, and the heart
    is for hearing.), 313
al-'arabiyya (the Arabic), 295
al-'arbi'aa' (Wednesday), 76, 77
al-'azaq (the blue (one)), 26
al-baariHa (yesterday), 122
al-bint (the girl), 26
alcohol, not drinking, 302
al-ghad (tomorrow), 122
al-ghuulf (golf), 145
al-Hajem (size), 117
al-Hamdu li-llah. (Praise to God./I'm doing
    well.), 51–52, 57, 306–307
al-Harbaa' laa Yughaadir shajaratuh hattaa
    yakun mu'akkid 'an shajara 'ukhraa.
    (The chameleon does not leave his
    tree until he is sure of another.), 312
'alif, 13, 14
al-'imra'a (the woman), 26
al-'iraaq (Iraq), 56
al-'ithnayn (Monday), 76
al-jazaa'ir (Algeria), 56, 261
al-jaziira (the island), 295
al-jumu'a (Friday), 76
al-kabiir (the big (one)), 26
al-khamiis (Thursday), 76, 77
al-kitaab (the book), 25, 29
al-ladhiidh (the delicious (one)), 26
'almaaniyaa (Germany), 263
al-maal (money), 189
al-madrasa (the school), 25
al-maghrib (Morocco), 56, 261
alphabet, 11–17

al-qamar (the moon), 26
'alwaan (colors), 23, 117–118
al-walad (the boy), 25
al-yawm (today), 122
al-yooro (euro), 200
'amaama (in front of), 31, 207
'amal (work/job), 171, 272
'a'mal khayr wa 'ilqahu fii al-baHr. (Do good and cast it into the sea), 311
'amm/'amma (uncle/aunt), 65
'amriikaa (America/USA), 56, 262
'amthila (proverbs), 311
'amti'a (luggage), 233, 246, 273
'anaa (I am/me), 34, 57, 156, 223
'anf (nose), 287
'annaii (my/mine), 223
answer key, Fun & Games quizzes, 345–349
'anta (you), 34, 57, 177, 223
'anti (you), 34, 57, 177, 223
'antumaa (you dual), 35, 177, 224
'antum (you MP), 34, 177, 224
'antunna (you FP), 34, 177, 224
appetizers, 93
appointments, business, 160–161
Arabic
  English word origins, 10–11
  expressions, 305–309
  historical significance, 10
  Koranic, 2
  learning, quickly, 295–298
  Modern Standard (MSA), 1, 2
  movies, 298
  music, 297
  newspapers, 296
  proverbs, 311–314
  regional dialects, 2
  scholars, 129
  songs, 298
  speaking, 18
  television, 295–296
  transcription, 18
Arabic SaHaafa (press), 296
Arabic-English mini-dictionary, 331–337
'arba'a (4), 75
'arba'ata 'ashar (14), 75
'arba'iin (40), 76
'arjentiinah (Argentina), 263
'arqaam (numbers), 74–76
ar-rajul (the man), 26

articles
  common, 25–26
  defined, 24
  definite, 24, 25–26
  exceptions, 24–25
  indefinite, 24
  rule, 24
'aSaabi' (fingers), 287
'aSaabi' al-qadam (toes), 287
'aSdiqaa' (friends), 149
'ashra (10), 75
ash-sham (the sun), 26
Asian currencies, 200
'as'ila (questions), 101, 244
'asnaan (teeth), 286
aS-SabaaH (the morning), 26
as-sabt (Saturday), 76
aS-Safraa' (the yellow (one)), 26
aS-Saghiir (the small (one)), 26
'as-salaamu 'alaykum (hello), 50, 156, 300
aS-Samraa' (the brown (one)), 26
as-sarii' (the fast (one)), 26
as-sa'uudiiyya (Saudi Arabia), 56
as-sirr mithel al-Hamaama: 'indamaa yughaadir yadii yaTiir. (A secret is like a dove: When it leaves my hand, it flies away.), 313
ath-thulathaa' (Tuesday), 76, 77
ATMs, using, 198–199
aT-Taqs (weather), 61
audience, assumptions, 3
auxiliary verbs, 231, 232
'awlaad (boys), 20, 103
'awraaq (money/paper currency), 189
'awraaq (papers), 179
'awwal (first), 64
'ayna? (where?), 62, 205–207
'ayn, 14, 16, 18
'anyayn (eyes), 287
'ayyam (days), 227
'azuuru (I visit), 68
az-zarqaa' (the blue (one)), 26

• *B* •

baa', 14
baa'a (sold), 45, 46, 114, 323
baarid (cold), 268
baHatha (searched), 104

baHrayn (Bahrain), 262
baHth (search), 104
ba'iid min (far from), 31, 207
ba'iid/ba'iida (far), 211
balad (country), 277
banaat (girls), 20, 103
banks
    accounts, opening, 190–197
    ATMs, 198–199
    contact info, 193–194
    deposits, 198
    forms, filling out, 194
    identification, 193
    terminology, 189–190
    withdrawals, 198
banyoo (bathtub), 222
baqsheeh (tip), 97
baraaziil (Brazil), 263
bard (cold), 288
baTii'/baTii'a (slow), 22
baTTaniyya (blanket), 222
bawwaab/bawwaaba (concierge), 233
bayt (home), 14, 165, 181, 183
beach, 149–151, 268
beverages, 94–95
bi 'idni allah (With God's guidance), 308
bi SaHHa (with strength), 308
biisoo miksiikiiy (Mexican peso), 200
biiyaano (piano), 151
bijaanibi (next to), 31, 207
bikam? (How much?), 62
binaaya (building), 209
bint
    Gregorian, 77
    Islamic, 77
bint (daughter), 65
bint (girl), 12, 20
bismi allah (In the name of Allah), 300
biTaaqa (ticket), 242
biTaaqa al-'istilaaf (debit card), 190, 198
biTaaqa al-'i'timaad (credit card),
        189, 198
biTaaqa shakhsiyya (personal
        identification), 193
biTaaqaat (tickets), 256
biTaaqaat shaksiyya (identification cards),
        274
biTaaqat as-saa'iq (driver's license),
        193, 274

body parts, 286–287
breakfast. *See also* meals
    fruit, 86–87
    at home, 82
    items, 82
    terminology, 84
buldaan (countries), 277
Bureau of Consular Affairs Web site, 277
buses. *See also* transportation
    frequency, 256
    taking, 255–256
    talk, 256–257
    terminology, 256
business appointments, 160–161
buuq (trumpet), 151

• C •

calendar
    days of the week, 76
    lunar, 77
    speaking about, 76–78
CD, this book, 351–352
check-in, hotel. *See also* hotels
    staff interaction phrases, 233
    talk, 234–235
    terminology, 233
check-out, hotel, 235–236
clothes
    accessories, 117
    colors, 117–118
    shopping for, 116–118
    sizes, 117
    types of, 116–117
colors, 23, 117–118
command forms, 212
comparative adjectives, 109–110
comparative sentences
    with demonstratives, 111
    examples, 109
    superlatives versus, 111
comparing merchandise, 109–113
consonants, 14–17
consulates, 275, 277, 290
contact info, 193–194
conventions, this book, 2
country names, 56

currencies
Asian, 200
European, 200
exchange, 199–203
exchange, making, 200–201
Middle East, 199–200
North America, 200
types, 199–200
customs, 249–253

• D •

Daad, 16, 25
daafi' (warm), 268
daal, 15, 25
daar aT-Talaba (youth hostel), 224
Da'iif/Da'iifa (weak), 21
dakiiy/dakiiya (smart), 22
damm (blood), 287
damma
common verbs, 43
defined, 12
double, 12
long vowel form, 13
daqiiqa (minute), 122, 272
daraaja (cycling), 146
darasa (studied), 39–40, 318
darraaja (bicycle), 71, 253
darraaja naariyya (motorcycle), 253
dates, 270–272
dawaa' (medicine), 288
dawla (country), 199, 269, 274, 275
day, time of, 123
definite articles, 24, 25–26
definite phrases, 27–28
demonstratives
comparative sentences with, 111
defined, 32, 105
with definite noun/definite adjective, 34
with definite noun/indefinite
adjective, 33
list, 105
phrase meaning and, 33
plural, 33, 106
singular, 32, 106
using, 32–34
deposits, bank, 198
desserts, 94

destinations. *See also* trips
choosing, 261–268
countries, 261–263
terminology, 268
DHaa', 16, 25
dhaal, 15, 25
dhaalika (that), 32, 105
dhahaba (to go), 135–136, 272
Dhahr (back), 287
dialects, 2
dictionary
Arabic-English, 331–337
English-Arabic, 338–344
using, 296
diinaar baHrainii (Bahraini dinar), 199
diinaar 'iraaqii (Iraqi dinar), 199
diinaar jazaa'irii (Algerian dinar), 199
diinaar kwaytii (Kuwaiti dinar), 200
diinaar liibii (Libyan dinar), 200
diinaar tunsii (Tunisian dinar), 200
diinaar 'urduniiy (Jordanian dinar), 199
dimaagh (brain), 287
diphthongs. *See also* vowels
defined, 13
examples, 14
sounds, 13
as vowel category, 11
diraa' (arm), 287
directions
asking for, 205–215
repeating, 209–211
subject/object relationship, 207
"where" questions, 205–207
dirham al-'imaaraat (Emirate
dirham), 200
dirham maghribii (Moroccan
dirham), 200
disambar (December), 77, 269
diwaana (customs), 249–253
doctors
body terminology and, 286–287
locating, 286
symptoms, explaining to, 287–288
treatment, getting from, 288
dominant vowels. *See also* vowels
common verbs by, 43–44
defined, 43
double vowels, 11, 12

dukhuul (entrance), 134
dukkaan (store), 99–105, 165
dukkaan al-iliktroniyaat (electronics store), 99
dukkaan al-malaabis (clothing store), 99
duulaar 'amriikiiy (American dollar), 200
duulaar kanadiiy (Canadian dollar), 200
duulaar 'oosTraliiy (Australian dollar), 200
duush (shower), 222

● *E* ●

embassies, 209, 277, 290
emergencies
  handling, 281–290
  help, 281–285
  legal, 290
  medical help, 286–289
English-Arabic mini-dictionary, 338–344
entrees, 94
-est suffix, 109
European currencies, 200
exchange, currency, 199–203
expressions, favorite Arabic, 305–309

● *F* ●

faa', 16
faakiha (fruit), 86–87
fa'ala (did), 143–144, 153
faatuura (bill), 235, 236
fakhaar (pottery), 152
falastiin (Palestine), 262
fallaaH (farmer), 69
fam (mouth), 286
family
  role, 66
  speaking about, 64–66
  words, 64–66
fannaan (artist), 69
faransaa (France), 262
faSl al-'uTla (holiday season), 228
fataHa (opened), 196–197
fatHa, 11
  common verbs, 43
  defined, 12
  double, 12

long vowel form, 13
  past tense and, 38
fawqa (above), 31, 207
fibraayir (February), 77, 269
fii (in), 31, 207
fi'l (verb), 228
finances. *See* money
fluut (flute), 151
flying. *See also* transportation
  airport registration, 244–246
  customs, 249–253
  immigration, 249–253
  plane boarding, 246–247
  reservations, 239–242
formal greeting, 49
friends, Arabic-speaking, 298
fruit, 86–87
fuluus (cash), 189, 256
Fun & Games answer key, 345–349
funduq (hotel), 12, 209, 217–236
furusiiyya (horseback riding), 146
fuSuul (seasons), 72
future tense. *See also* past tense verbs; present tense verbs; verbs
  conjugation in, 44–45
  defined, 44–45
  irregular verbs, 327–329
  regular verbs, 321–323
fuuTa (towel), 222

● *G* ●

ghabiiy/ghabiiya (dumb), 22
gharb (west), 213, 268
ghayn, 16, 18
ghidaa' (lunch), 81, 87–91
ghinaa' (singing), 70
ghuraf (rooms), 181–182
ghurfa (room), 176, 217, 232
ghurfat al-ma'iisha (living room), 181, 183
gifts, excepting, 303
goodbye, 51
greetings, 49–52
Gregorian calendar, 77

• *H* •

Haa', 15, 17, 18
haadhaa/haadihi (this), 32, 33, 105
haafila (bus), 211, 253, 255
-haa suffix, 223
haatif (telephone), 178
haatif 'aam (public phone), 155
haatif selulayr (cellphone), 155
haa'ulaa'i (these), 33, 105
haDHan sa'iidan (good luck), 49
Hafiid/Hafiida (grandson/
    granddaughter), 65
Hajj, 139–140
Hajzu (reservation), 224, 225, 233, 239
hal (name) hunaa? (Is (name) here?), 157
Hallaaq (barber/hairdresser), 69, 100
Hammaal (baggage handler/porter), 252
Hammaam (bathroom), 182, 222
handshakes, 299
Haraara (fever), 287
Harq (burn), 288
Hay (neighborhood), 209
Hayaat (life), 167
hayyaa binaa. (Let's go.), 147, 158
hello greeting, 50
help
  getting, 281–290
  legal, 290
  levels of, 282
  medical, 286–289
  offering, 284–285
  shouting out for, 281–285
  terminology, 281–282
Hidaa' (shoes), 301
Hijaab (veil), 249, 302
hijra (immigration), 249–253
hind (India), 263
Hisaab (bill), 97
Hisaab maSrafii (bank account), 190,
    190–197
hiwaayaat (hobbies), 61, 152–153
hiya (she/it), 34, 157, 223
Hiyaaka (knitting), 152
hobbies, 70–71, 152–153
home
  bathroom, 182
  family life, 183
  kitchen, 182
    life at, 181–185
    rooms, 181–182
    talk, 183–185
hospitality, 303
hotels
  bills, 235
  checking into, 232–235
  checking out of, 235–236
  length of stay, 228–229
  price, 224–227
  reservations, 224–232
  room details, 220–222
  selecting, 217–224
  staying at, 217–236
  terminology, 217–218
-hu suffix, 223
Hujuuzaat (reservations), 278
hum (they MP), 34, 224
humaa (they dual), 35, 224
-humaa suffix, 224
-hum suffix, 224
hunaa (here), 211
hunaaka (there), 211
hunna (they FP), 35, 224
-hunna suffix, 224
Husub (accounts), 190
huwa (he), 34, 38, 157, 223

• *1* •

'ibn (son), 65
icons, this book, 4–5
Identification, 193
'idhhab/'idhhabii (go), 212
iHdaa 'ashar (11), 75
'iid (holidays), 183
-ii suffix, 54, 223
-iin suffix, 76
'iiSaala (receipt), 236
'iiwaa' (accommodations), 217
'ijtimaa' (meeting), 160
'ilaa (to), 31, 124, 125, 207
'ilaa al-ghad (see you tomorrow), 51
'ilaa al-liqaa' (until next time), 51, 57
'ilaaj (treatment), 288
'i'laan (declare), 253
'imaaraat (United Arab Emirates), 262
'imdaa' (signature), 194
immigration, 249–253

imperative verbs, 177
'imra'a (woman), 20
'imshii (walk), 212
'inda (possession), 179
indefinite phrases, 26–27
informal greeting, 49
'injlaTirra (England), 262
inshaa' allah. (If God wishes it.), 307
Internet, surfing, 297
'inTilaaq (departure), 247
introductions
    "It's a pleasure to meet you," 54
    speaking, 54–55
    "What's your name?," 53
'iraan (Iran), 262
'iraaq (Iraq), 262
irregular adjectives, 23
irregular verbs
    common, 47
    conjugation, 45–47
    in future tense, 327–329
    in past tense, 323–325
    in present tense, 325–327
'isbaaniya (Spain), 262
'ishaa' (dinner), 81, 92
'ishriin (20), 75, 76
'ishtaraa (bought), 115, 324
Islamic calendar, 78
'ismii (my name), 54, 57
'ism (name), 54, 57, 162, 163
'isra'iil (Israel), 262
'istimaarat aT-Talab (application
        form), 194
'iTaaliyaa (Italy), 262
'iTfaa'ii (fireman), 69
'ithnaa 'ashar (12), 75
'ithnayn (2), 74
'ittijaahaat (directions), 205–215
'iyaada (clinic), 288

• J •

jaahiz/jaahiza (ready), 176
jaai' (hungry), 81
jaami'a (university), 20, 64
jabal (mountain), 268
jadd/jadda (grandfather/grandmother), 65
jamiil/jamiila (beautiful), 21
janoub (south), 213, 268

jariidaat (newspapers), 168
jasad (body), 286
jawaaz as-safar (passport), 193, 244, 274
jiim, 15
jinsiyya (nationality), 251
jobs
    finding, 167–170
    gender distinction, 68
    types of, 68–69
jumbaaz (gymnastics), 146
jumla (sentence), 29
junya briiTaaniiyya (British pound), 200
junya maSriiyya (Egyptian pound), 199

• K •

kaaf, 17
kaana (was/were), 37–38
kaatib (writer), 68
kabiir/kabiira (big), 21, 29
kadhaalika (same/similar), 68
-ka suffix, 223
kalaam khafiif. See small talk
kalimaat (words), 9
kam as-saa'a? (What time is it?), 121, 123
kam min? (How many?), 62
kamanja (violin), 151
kanaadaa (Canada), 262
kasra, 11
    common verbs, 44
    double, 12
    long vowel form, 13
kataba (write)
    conjugation with personal pronouns,
        38–39
    imperative, 177–178
    past tense (wrote), 38, 317
katef (shoulder), 287
kayf al-Haal, 51
kayfa? (How?), 62
khaa', 15
khaadim/khaadima al-maT'am (waiter/
        waitress), 95
khabaran (message), 162, 163
khafiif/khafiifa (light), 22
khamsa (5), 75
khamsata 'ashar (15), 75
khamsiin (50), 76

khaTa' ma'roof 'aHsan min Haqiiqa ghayr ma'roofa. (A known mistake is better than an unknown truth.), 312–313
khudh/khudii (take), 212
khuruuj (exit), 134
kiis (bag), 273
-ki suffix, 223
kitaab (book), 21, 179
kooryaa (Korea), 263
Koranic Arabic, 2
kouratoun (ball), 12
kul yawm min Hayaatuk SafHa min taariikhuk. (Every day of your life is a page of your history.), 313
kulliyya (college), 20, 64
-kumaa suffix, 224
-kum suffix, 224
-kunna suffix, 224
kura (ball), 149
kurat al-miDrab (tennis), 146
kurat al-qadam (soccer), 71, 145
kurat as-salla (basketball), 146
kurat aT-Taa'ira (volleyball), 146
kuuwayt (Kuwait), 262

• *L* •

la'aba (play), 146–147, 152
laam, 17
ladhiidh/ladhiida (delicious), 22
language tapes/CDs, 297
laTiif/laTiifa (nice/kind), 22
lawn (color), 117
layla (night), 14
laysa ("to be"), 36
legal help, 290
length of stay, 228–229
li faatik bi liila faatik bi Hiila. (He who surpasses you by one night surpasses you by one idea.), 314
lii maadhaa? (Why?), 62
liibiya (Libya), 262
liira lubnaaniiya (Lebanese pound), 200
liira suuriiya (Syrian pound), 200
lisaan (tongue), 286
liSS! (Thief!), 282
long vowels, 11, 12–13
lougha (language), 9
lubnaan (Lebanon), 262

lunar calendar, 77
lunch. *See also* meals
  items, 87–88
  time for, 87

• *M* •

ma'a (with), 31
ma'a as-salaama (go with peace), 51
maa 'ismuk (What's your name?), 53
maa? (What?), 62
maadhaa? (What?), 62
maaDii (past), 177
maa'ida (dining table) items, 92–93
maaris (March), 77, 269
maayuu (May), 77, 269
mabruk! (Blessing upon you!), 308
madiina (city), 209, 268
madrasa (school), 20, 209
maghsala (sink), 222
maHaTTa (station), 211
ma'iida (stomach), 287
majalla 'ikhbaariya (news broadcast), 295
makaatib (offices), 170, 171
makhbaza (bakery), 99, 209
maktab as-sarf (exchange desk), 199
maktab as-siyaaHa (travel agency), 100
maktaba (bookstore), 99, 209
malaabis (clothes), 99, 116–117, 273
mal'ab (stadium), 149
ma'luuma/ma'luumaat (information), 170
ma'mal (factory), 171
man? (Who?), 62
manzil (house), 167, 181, 183
maou'id (appointment), 160
maq'ad (seat), 242
maraD (sickness), 288
maraD al-Hasaasiya (allergy), 288
marHaba (welcome), 9
marHaba bikum (Welcome to all of you.), 305–306
mariiD/mariiDa (sick), 22, 287
masaa' al-khayr (good evening), 57
mashghuula/mashguul (busy), 230
mashruubaat (drinks), 94–95
masjid (mosque), 138–139, 209, 300–301
maSlaHaat (interests), 168
maSraf (bank), 189

maSrafii (banker), 68
masraH (theater), 209
mataa? (When?), 62
maTaar (airport), 199, 244–246
maT'am (restaurant), 93, 97, 158, 209
maTbakh (kitchen), 92, 182
matHaf (museum), 128–134, 158, 209
mawjooda (availability), 233
mawjuuda/mawjuud (available), 230
MBC (Middle East Broadcast Corporation), 296
meals
   appetizers, 93–94
   basic, 81
   breakfast, 81, 82–87
   desserts, 94
   dining out, 93–95
   dinner, 81, 92
   drinks, 94–95
   entrees, 94
   at home, 92–93
   lunch, 81, 87–91
medical help
   body terminology, 286–287
   doctor, locating, 286
   symptoms, explaining, 287–288
   treatment, 288
merchandise. *See also* stores
   asking for, 105–108
   best, choosing, 111–112
   browsing, 100–101
   comparing, 109–113
messages, phone
   leaving, 162–164
   with person, 163–164
   with voice mail, 162–163
mi'a (100), 76
Middle East currencies, 199–200
Middle Eastern restaurants, 298
midyaa' (radio), 222
miftaH (key), 233
miHfaDHa (briefcase), 233, 246, 273
mihna (profession), 61, 167, 171
miim, 17
miksiikuu (Mexico), 262
min (from), 31, 110
min 'ayna 'anta (Where are you from?), 55
minutes. *See also* time

as fractions of the hour, 124–126
   specifying, 124–127
   spelling out, 126–127
mir'aat (mirror), 222
mirHaaD (toilet), 222
miSr (Egypt), 56, 262
Modern Standard Arabic (MSA), 1, 2
money
   ATM for, 198–199
   bank and, 189–198
   exchange, 199–203
   terminology, 189–190
months, 269–270
moosiiqaa (music), 151
mosques
   not entering with shoes, 301
   not entering without authorization, 300–301
movies
   genres, 135
   going to, 135–138
   talk, 136–137
   terminology, 138
movies, Arabic, 298
mu'aawana (help), 282, 284
muballagh (equally), 309
muDaari' (present), 177
mudarris/mudarrisa (teacher), 20, 64
mudiir/mudiira (director), 172
mudun (cities), 268
mughannii (singer), 69
muhaajir/muhaajira (immigrant), 251
muHaamii (lawyer), 69, 290
muHaasib (accountant), 69
muhandis (architect), 69
muHiiT (ocean), 149, 151, 268
mujrima (crime), 290
mukaalama haatifiyya (phone conversation), 155
mumarriD (nurse), 69
mumathil (actor), 69
mumtaaz (excellent), 306
muqabbilaat (appetizers), 93–94
musaa'ada (help), 277, 281, 283–284
musaafir/mussafira (traveler), 242
musaafiruun/musaafiraat (travelers), 242
museums
   Middle Eastern, 128
   rules, 129

museums *(continued)*
  signs, 129
  talk, 130
  terminology, 131
  visiting, 128–134
music, Arabic, 297
musical instruments, 151–152
mustakhdim (employer), 168
mustashfaa (hospital), 209
muTarjim (translator), 69

• N •

naafida (window), 222
-naa suffix, 224
naar! (Fire!), 282
naDHaraat (glasses), 273
nadhhab (we go), 272
nafaq 'arDiiy (subway), 253
naHnu (we), 34, 224
najda (help), 282
naql (transportation), 239
nationalities, 56
nawm (sleep), 14
newspapers, Arabic, 296
nisaa' (women), 20, 103
nonverbal signs, 53
North American currencies, 200
nouns
  adjective interactions, 24, 26–28
  common, 20–21
  defined, 19
  definite, 25–26, 27–28
  indefinite, 26–27
  position, 24, 26
nufambar (November), 77, 269
numbers
  0-10, 74–75
  11-20, 75
  20-100, 76
  ordinal, 214–215, 270–272
  patterns, 75
nuquud (money/coins), 189
nuun, 17, 25

• O •

object pronouns, 223–224
offices
  colleagues, interacting with, 172
  departments, 171–172
  environment, 170–181
  lunch, 171
  orders, giving, 177–178
  professions, 171
  schedule, 170
  supplying, 178–180
  talk, 174–175
  terminology, 171
ordinal numbers
  dates and, 270–272
  defined, 214
  as gender-defined, 214
  list of, 214–215
  for telling time, 122
  use examples, 215
organization, this book, 3–4

• P •

paqisTaan (Pakistan), 263
past tense verbs. *See also* verbs
  conjugation, 38–39, 40–41
  consonants, more than three, 40
  irregular, 323–325
  personal pronoun suffixes, 40
  regular, 317–319
  structural form, 38
personal pronouns
  defined, 34
  list of, 34–35
  position, 35
  prefixes/suffixes for present tense verbs, 42–43
  suffixes for past tense verbs, 40
  use examples, 35
phone conversations
  asking to speak to someone, 157
  beginning, 156
  business appointments, making, 160–161
  messages, leaving, 162–164
  plans, making, 158–161
  social plans, making, 158–160
  terminology, 155

phone numbers, 165
phrases
    definite, 27–28
    hotel staff interaction, 233
    indefinite, 26–27
    with prepositions, 31–32
planes. *See also* transportation
    boarding, 246–247
    reservations, making, 239–242
prefixes. *See also* suffixes
    a-, 25
    al-, 22, 24, 25–26, 27, 106
    definite, pronouns, 106
    sa-, 44, 228
    sentence meaning and, 106
prepositions
    building sentences with, 30–32
    common, 31
    defined, 30
    use examples, 31–32
present tense verbs. *See also* verbs
    conjugation, 42–43
    dominant vowel and, 43–44
    irregular, 325–327
    past tense verb differences, 42
    personal pronoun prefixes/suffixes, 42–43
    regular, 319–321
professions, 68–69, 171
pronouns
    definite prefix, 106
    object, 223–224
    personal, "to be" sentences with, 34–35
pronunciation, 18
proverbs, Arabic
    al-'amthaal noor al-kalaam. (Proverbs are the light of speech.), 311
    al-'aql li an-niDHaar wa al-kalb li as-simaa'. (The mind is for seeing, and the heart is for hearing.), 313
    al-Harbaa' laa Yughaadir shajaratuh hattaa yakun mu'akkid 'an shajara 'ukhraa. (The chameleon does not leave his tree until he is sure of another.), 312
    'a'mal khayr wa 'ilqahu fii al-baHr. (Do good and cast it into the sea), 311
    as-sirr mithel al-Hamaama: 'indamaa yughaadir yadii yaTiir. (A secret is like a dove: When it leaves my hand, it flies away.), 313
    khaTa' ma'roof 'aHsan min Haqiiqa ghayr ma'roofa. (A known mistake is better than an unknown truth.), 312–313
    kul yawm min Hayaatuk SafHa min taariikhuk. (Every day of your life is a page of your history.), 313
    li faatik bi liila faatik bi Hiila. (He who surpasses you by one night surpasses you by one idea.), 314
    use of, 311
    'uTlubuu al-'ilm min al-mahd 'ilaa al-laHd. (Seek knowledge from the cradle to the grave.), 312
    yad waaHida maa tusaffiq. (A hand by itself cannot clap.), 312

• *Q* •

qaaf, 16, 18
qaamuus (dictionary), 117, 296
qaanuun (law), 290
qabiiH/qabiiHa (cruel), 22
qadam (foot), 287
qahwa (coffee chop), 84
qalam ar-rasaas (pencil), 179
qalam jaaf (pen), 179
qalb (heart), 287
qariib min (close to), 31, 207
qariib/qariiba (close), 211
qarya (village), 209
qaSiir/qaSiira (short), 21
qaTar (Qatar), 262
qawaa'id (rules), 138–139
qawiiy/qawiiya (strong), 21
qif/qiffi (stop), 212
qiithaar (guitar), 151
qiraa'a (reading), 71, 152
qitaar (train), 211, 253, 257
questions
    examples, 62–63
    speaking, 63
    "where," 205–207
    words, 62
qunSul (consul), 290
qunSuliiyya (consulate), 275, 290

• R •

raa', 15, 25
raaqis (dancer), 69
raDDa (bruise), 288
Rai, 152, 297
ra'iis/ra'iisa (president), 172
rain, 74
rajul (man), 20
rajul 'a'maal (businessman), 69
Ramadan
  defined, 301
  fasting during, 301
  no alcohol during, 302
ramla (sand), 149, 151
raqm al-haatif (phone number), 155, 162
raqs (dancing), 70, 152
ra's (head), 286
rasm (drawing), 152
recreation
  athletic sports, 145–149
  beach, 149–151, 268
  hobbies, 152–153
  musical instruments, 151–152
  verbs, 143–145
regional dialects, 2
regular verbs. *See also* verbs
  defined, 45
  in future tense, 321–323
  in past tense, 317–319
  in present tense, 319–321
religious sites
  Hajj, 139–140
  rules, 138–139
  touring, 138–140
repeat, asking for, 209–210
reservations, hotel. *See also* hotels
  length of stay, 228–229
  price, 224–227
reservations, plane, 239–242
restaurants. *See also* meals
  appetizers, 93–94
  beverages, 94–95
  bill, paying, 97
  desserts, 94
  drinks, 94–95
  entrees, 94
  menus, 93
  orders, placing, 95

tip, 97
waiter/waitress, 95
ri'a (lung), 287
rijaal (men), 20, 103
rijl (leg), 287
riyaaDa (sports), 145
riyaal qaTarii (Qatari riyal), 200
riyaal sa'uudii (Saudi riyal), 200
riyaal 'ummaanii (Omani dinar), 200
riyaal yamanii (Yemeni riyal), 200
rooms, hotel
  details, discussing, 220–221
  elements, 218, 222
rukba (knee), 287
rukkaab (passengers), 246, 247
rules
  museum, 129
  religious sites, 138–139
  unspoken, 299, 303

• S •

sa- prefix, 44, 228
saa'a (hour), 122
Saad, 15, 25
saafara (to travel), 243
saa'iduunii! (Help me!), 282
saa'iH/saa'iHa (tourist), 251
saaksuufuun (saxophone), 151
sab'a (7), 75
SabaaH al-khayr (good morning), 57
sab'ata 'ashar (17), 75
sab'iin (70), 76
Sa'b/Sa'ba (difficult), 22
Sadr (chest), 287
sa'eed (safe/happy), 68
Safar (trip), 68
SafHatin (page), 12
safiina (ship), 253
Saghiir/Saghiira (small), 21
SaHafii (journalist), 68
SaHiiH/SaHiiHa (healthy), 21
sahl/sahla (easy), 22
sana (year), 64, 230
sandwiish (sandwich), 87, 88
sariir (bed), 222, 232
sarii'/sarii'a (fast), 22
sa'uudiiya (Saudi Arabia), 262
Sawt (noise), 14

sa-yabii'u (will sell), 327
sa-yadrusu (will study), 322
sa-yaktubu (will write), 321
sa-ya'kulu (will eat), 322–323
sa-yashtarii (will buy), 328
sa-yazuuru (will visit), 328–329
SayDaliiyya (pharmacy), 288
Sayyaara (car), 21, 182, 253
Sayyaara 'ijaariya (rental car), 253
scholars, Arabic, 129
search, 104–105
seasons, 72
sentences
  with common prepositions, 30–32
  comparative, 110
  demonstratives and, 32–34
  "is/are," 29
  prefixes and, 106
  "to be," 34–35
  without verbs, 28–30
shaari' (avenue), 209
shaaTi' (beach), 149–151, 268
shahr (month), 269–270, 272
shamaal (north), 213, 268
shanTa (suitcase), 233, 246, 273
shariiT siinimaa'ii (movie), 135–138
sharika (company), 171
sharq (east), 213, 268
shaTranj (chess), 152
shiik (check), 190
shiin, 15, 25
shi'r (poetry), 152
shopping
  buying/selling words, 114–116
  clothes, 116–118
  items, asking for, 105–108
  merchandise, comparing, 109–113
  stores, 99–105
  terminology, 108
shukran (thank you), 51–52
shurTa (police), 282, 285
shurtii (police officer), 69
sibaaHa (swimming), 146, 149, 268
sibtambar (September), 77, 269
sifaara (embassy), 209, 290
Sifr (0), 74
siin, 15, 25
Siin (China), 263
siiniimaa (movie theater), 158

simsaar (broker), 69
sitta (6), 75
sittata 'ashar (16), 75
sittiin (60), 76
siyaaqat aS-Sayaara (racecar driving), 146
small talk
  calendar, 76–78
  family, 64–67
  hobbies, 70–71
  importance, 61
  jobs, 68–69
  key questions, 62–63
  numbers, 74–76
  weather, 71–73
social plans, 158–160
songs, Arabic, 298
soomaal (Somalia), 262
speaking Arabic, 18
sports
  sentence structure, 147
  soccer, 145–146
  talk, 148–149
  terms, 145–146
  types of, 146
  verb, 146–147
stores. *See also* merchandise
  bakeries, 99
  clothing, 99
  directions, 101
  electronics, 99
  getting around, 101–103
  information desk, 101
  items, asking for, 105–108
  searching in, 104–105
  service-oriented, 100
  specialty, 100
  terminology, 103
su'aal (cough), 288
subjunctive verbs
  conjugation, 230–231
  defined, 230
  endings, 231, 232
  examples, 231
  rules, 231
SuDaa' (headache), 287
suffixes
  -est, 109
  -haa, 223
  -hu, 223

suffixes *(continued)*
 -hum, 224
 -humaa, 224
 -hunna, 224
 -ii, 54, 223
 -iin, 76
 -ka, 223
 -ki, 223
 -kum, 224
 -kumaa, 224
 -kunna, 224
 -naa, 224
 object pronouns, 223–224
 past tense verbs, 40
 personal pronoun, 42–43
 possessive, 223–224
 present tense verbs, 42–43
suHub (clouds), 12
sukun, 13, 14
sun letters, 25
superlatives
 comparatives versus, 111
 defined, 111
 sentence examples, 111
 talk example, 112–113
 word order and, 112
suudaan (Sudan), 262
suuq (market), 209
suuriya (Syria), 262

• T •

taa', 14, 25
Taa', 16, 25
Ta'aam (food), 81, 87
Ta'aam ra'iisii (entrees), 94
Taa'ira (airplane), 239
taajir (merchant), 69
taaksii (taxi), 253, 254–255
Taalib/Taaliba (college student),
 20, 64, 224
Taawila (table), 21
tabaaraka allah (With God's
 blessing.), 309
Tabbaakh (cook), 69
Tabiib (doctor), 69, 286
Tabiib 'asnaan (dentist), 286
Tabiib 'aTfaal (pediatrician), 286
Tabiib 'aynayn (ophthalmologist), 286

Tabiib rijl (orthopedist), 286
Tabl (drums), 151
Tabla, 152
tables, verb, 317–329
tadfa' (to pay), 227
taHiyyaat (regards), 309
taHliya (dessert), 94
taHta, (underneath), 31, 207
takallama (speak)
 imperative form, 178
 past tense conjugation, 40–41
taksii (taxi), 211
ta'liimaat (instructions), 246
tamtii' (entertainment), 134
tanwiin. *See* double vowels
tanziilaat (discounts), 225, 227, 278
Taqs (weather), 71, 72
taqwiim (calendar), 272
Tariiq (street), 209
tasbaH'alaa khayr (good night), 57
tasharrafnaa (It's a pleasure to meet you.),
 54
ta'shiira (visa), 246, 274
tasjiil (registration), 244
Tawiil/Tawiila (tall), 21
tawjiihaat (directions), 101
taxi
 hailing, 254–255
 licensing, 254
 rates, 254
 talk, 254–255
Tayyaarat waraq (kite flying), 71
tazaHluq (skiing), 146
tazalluj (ice skating), 146
television, Arabic, 295–296
temperature, 72, 73
thaa', 14, 25
thaaniya (second), 122
thalaatha (3), 74
thalaathata 'ashar (13), 75
thalaathiin (30), 76
thamaaniin (80), 76
thamaaniya (8), 75
thamaaniyata 'ashar (18), 75
thaman (price), 224
thaman tadhkiira (fare), 255
thaqiil/thaqiila (heavy), 22
Tibaakha (cooking), 92
tilfaaz (TV), 222

tilifizyuun (television), 11
tilka (that), 32, 105
tilmiidh/tilmiidha (student), 20, 64
time
  Arabic ordinals, 122
  asking for, 121–122
  of day, 123
  key words, 22
  minutes, specifying, 124–127
  telling, 121–128
tis'a (9), 75
tis'ata 'ashar (19), 75
tis'iin (90), 76
"to be" sentences
  forming, 34–35
  negative, creating, 36
  in past tense, 37–38
toiletries, 273–274
trains. *See also* transportation
  boarding, 257
  talk, 257–258
transcription, Arabic, 18
transportation
  bus, 255–257
  land, 253–258
  plane, 239–253
  taxi, 254–255
  train, 257–258
travel agencies, 278–279
travel agents, 239–240, 278, 279
trips
  destinations, 261–268
  packing for, 273–274
  picking time for, 269–272
  planning, 261–279
  travel agencies for, 278–279
  travel documents, 274–277
Tuf/Tufii (turn), 212
tuunis (Tunisia), 56, 261

• *U* •

'udhanayn (ears), 287
'ughniiya (song), 298
'ukht (sister), 65, 173
'uktuubar (October), 77, 269
'ulaa'ika (those), 33, 105
'umla (currency), 199–203
'ummaan (Oman), 262

'um (mother), 64
unspoken rules, 299–303
'unwaan (address), 194
'urdun (Jordan), 262
'uriidu Tabiib! (I need a doctor!), 282
'usra (family), 61, 64–66, 149
'ustaadh/'ustaadha (professor), 20, 64
'uTlubuu al-'ilm min al-mahd 'ilaa al-laHd.
  (Seek knowledge from the cradle to the
  grave.), 312
'uud, 152, 297
'uulaa (first), 64

• *V* •

verb-free sentences, 28–30
verbs
  auxiliary, 231, 232
  common, by dominant vowel, 43–44
  consonants, 131
  future tense, 44–45, 321–323, 327–329
  imperative, 177
  irregular, 45–47
  irregular, in future tense, 327–329
  irregular, in past tense, 323–325
  irregular, in present tense, 325–327
  past tense, 38–41, 317–319, 323–325
  present tense, 41–44, 319–321, 325–327
  regular, 45
  regular, in future tense, 321–323
  regular, in past tense, 317–319
  regular, in present tense, 319–321
  subjunctive, 230–232
  tables, 317–329
  "to search," 104–105
  working with, 38–47
voice mail messages, 162–163
vowels
  characters, 13
  damma, 12
  derivatives, 11
  diphthongs, 11, 12, 13–14
  dominant, 43–44
  double, 11, 12
  fatHa, 11, 12
  kasra, 12
  long, 11, 12–13
  main, 12
  "silent," 12

• W •

wa 'alaykum as-salaam (hello), 57
wa conjunction, 29
waaHid (1), 74
waalidayn (parents), 64
waaw, 13, 17
waja' (ache/ailment), 288
waja' 'aDHahr (backache), 288
wajbaat (breakfast), 81–87
wajh (face), 286
wakiil safariyaat (travel agent), 239–240,
    278, 279
walad (boy), 12, 20
waqt (time), 121
waqt faarigh (free time), 158
waraa'a (behind), 31, 207
waraq al-la'ib (cards), 152
waSala (to arrive), 247–248
wathaa'iq (documents), 193
wathaa'iq as-safar (travel documents),
    274–277
weather
  rain, 74
  seasons, 72
  talking about, 71–73
  temperature, 72, 73
  words, 72
"where" questions. *See also* questions
  answering, 206–207
  asking, 205–206
wisaada (pillow), 222
withdrawals, bank, 198
won al-koorii (Korean won), 200
wujha (destination), 261
wuSuul (arrival), 247

• Y •

yaa', 13, 17
yabaan (Japan), 263
yabHathu (searching), 103, 104–105

yabii'u (to sell), 46, 114–115, 325
yad (hand), 287
yad waaHida maa tusaffiq. (A hand by itself
    cannot clap.), 312
yadrusu (to study), 320
yaf'alu (to do/doing)
  conjugation, 144–145
  defined, 143
  example use, 145
yajibu (have to), 230
yaktubu (to write), 42, 43, 44–45, 231, 232,
    319
ya'kulu (to eat), 91, 320–321
yal'abu (to play), 147
yamaan (Yemen), 262
yamiin min (right of), 207
yanaayir (January), 77, 269
yashtarii (to buy), 326
yasiir min (left of), 207
yastaTii'u (able to), 230
yawm (day), 14, 227
yazuuru (to visit), 132, 326–327
yen yabanii (Japanese yen), 200
yooan Siiniiy (Chinese yuan), 200
yuHibbu (like), 230
yulyu (July), 77, 269
yunyu (June), 77, 269
yuriidu, 230–231

• Z •

zaara (visit), 131–132, 324–325
zaay, 15
zabaa'in (clients), 171
zamiil/zamiila (colleague), 172
zawj (husband), 65, 268
zawja (wife), 65, 268
zay, 25
ziyaara (visit), 68, 268

BUSINESS, CAREERS & PERSONAL FINANCE

0-7645-5307-0

0-7645-5331-3 *†

Also available:
- Accounting For Dummies †
  0-7645-5314-3
- Business Plans Kit For Dummies †
  0-7645-5365-8
- Cover Letters For Dummies
  0-7645-5224-4
- Frugal Living For Dummies
  0-7645-5403-4
- Leadership For Dummies
  0-7645-5176-0
- Managing For Dummies
  0-7645-1771-6

- Marketing For Dummies
  0-7645-5600-2
- Personal Finance For Dummies *
  0-7645-2590-5
- Project Management For Dummies
  0-7645-5283-X
- Resumes For Dummies †
  0-7645-5471-9
- Selling For Dummies
  0-7645-5363-1
- Small Business Kit For Dummies *†
  0-7645-5093-4

HOME & BUSINESS COMPUTER BASICS

0-7645-4074-2

0-7645-3758-X

Also available:
- ACT! 6 For Dummies
  0-7645-2645-6
- iLife '04 All-in-One Desk Reference
  For Dummies
  0-7645-7347-0
- iPAQ For Dummies
  0-7645-6769-1
- Mac OS X Panther Timesaving
  Techniques For Dummies
  0-7645-5812-9
- Macs For Dummies
  0-7645-5656-8

- Microsoft Money 2004 For Dummies
  0-7645-4195-1
- Office 2003 All-in-One Desk Reference
  For Dummies
  0-7645-3883-7
- Outlook 2003 For Dummies
  0-7645-3759-8
- PCs For Dummies
  0-7645-4074-2
- TiVo For Dummies
  0-7645-6923-6
- Upgrading and Fixing PCs For Dummies
  0-7645-1665-5
- Windows XP Timesaving Techniques
  For Dummies
  0-7645-3748-2

FOOD, HOME, GARDEN, HOBBIES, MUSIC & PETS

0-7645-5295-3

0-7645-5232-5

Also available:
- Bass Guitar For Dummies
  0-7645-2487-9
- Diabetes Cookbook For Dummies
  0-7645-5230-9
- Gardening For Dummies *
  0-7645-5130-2
- Guitar For Dummies
  0-7645-5106-X
- Holiday Decorating For Dummies
  0-7645-2570-0
- Home Improvement All-in-One
  For Dummies
  0-7645-5680-0

- Knitting For Dummies
  0-7645-5395-X
- Piano For Dummies
  0-7645-5105-1
- Puppies For Dummies
  0-7645-5255-4
- Scrapbooking For Dummies
  0-7645-7208-3
- Senior Dogs For Dummies
  0-7645-5818-8
- Singing For Dummies
  0-7645-2475-5
- 30-Minute Meals For Dummies
  0-7645-2589-1

INTERNET & DIGITAL MEDIA

0-7645-1664-7

0-7645-6924-4

Also available:
- 2005 Online Shopping Directory
  For Dummies
  0-7645-7495-7
- CD & DVD Recording For Dummies
  0-7645-5956-7
- eBay For Dummies
  0-7645-5654-1
- Fighting Spam For Dummies
  0-7645-5965-6
- Genealogy Online For Dummies
  0-7645-5964-8
- Google For Dummies
  0-7645-4420-9

- Home Recording For Musicians
  For Dummies
  0-7645-1634-5
- The Internet For Dummies
  0-7645-4173-0
- iPod & iTunes For Dummies
  0-7645-7772-7
- Preventing Identity Theft For Dummies
  0-7645-7336-5
- Pro Tools All-in-One Desk Reference
  For Dummies
  0-7645-5714-9
- Roxio Easy Media Creator For Dummies
  0-7645-7131-1

* Separate Canadian edition also available
† Separate U.K. edition also available

Available wherever books are sold. For more information or to order direct: U.S. customers visit www.dummies.com or call 1-877-762-2974.
U.K. customers visit www.wileyeurope.com or call 0800 243407. Canadian customers visit www.wiley.ca or call 1-800-567-4797.

SPORTS, FITNESS, PARENTING, RELIGION & SPIRITUALITY

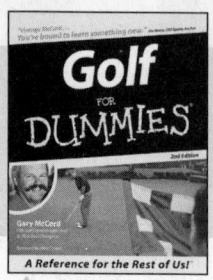

0-7645-5146-9

0-7645-5418-2

Also available:

- Adoption For Dummies
  0-7645-5488-3
- Basketball For Dummies
  0-7645-5248-1
- The Bible For Dummies
  0-7645-5296-1
- Buddhism For Dummies
  0-7645-5359-3
- Catholicism For Dummies
  0-7645-5391-7
- Hockey For Dummies
  0-7645-5228-7

- Judaism For Dummies
  0-7645-5299-6
- Martial Arts For Dummies
  0-7645-5358-5
- Pilates For Dummies
  0-7645-5397-6
- Religion For Dummies
  0-7645-5264-3
- Teaching Kids to Read For Dummies
  0-7645-4043-2
- Weight Training For Dummies
  0-7645-5168-X
- Yoga For Dummies
  0-7645-5117-5

TRAVEL

0-7645-5438-7

0-7645-5453-0

Also available:

- Alaska For Dummies
  0-7645-1761-9
- Arizona For Dummies
  0-7645-6938-4
- Cancún and the Yucatán For Dummies
  0-7645-2437-2
- Cruise Vacations For Dummies
  0-7645-6941-4
- Europe For Dummies
  0-7645-5456-5
- Ireland For Dummies
  0-7645-5455-7

- Las Vegas For Dummies
  0-7645-5448-4
- London For Dummies
  0-7645-4277-X
- New York City For Dummies
  0-7645-6945-7
- Paris For Dummies
  0-7645-5494-8
- RV Vacations For Dummies
  0-7645-5443-3
- Walt Disney World & Orlando For Dummies
  0-7645-6943-0

GRAPHICS, DESIGN & WEB DEVELOPMENT

0-7645-4345-8

0-7645-5589-8

Also available:

- Adobe Acrobat 6 PDF For Dummies
  0-7645-3760-1
- Building a Web Site For Dummies
  0-7645-7144-3
- Dreamweaver MX 2004 For Dummies
  0-7645-4342-3
- FrontPage 2003 For Dummies
  0-7645-3882-9
- HTML 4 For Dummies
  0-7645-1995-6
- Illustrator CS For Dummies
  0-7645-4084-X

- Macromedia Flash MX 2004 For Dummies
  0-7645-4358-X
- Photoshop 7 All-in-One Desk Reference For Dummies
  0-7645-1667-1
- Photoshop CS Timesaving Techniques For Dummies
  0-7645-6782-9
- PHP 5 For Dummies
  0-7645-4166-8
- PowerPoint 2003 For Dummies
  0-7645-3908-6
- QuarkXPress 6 For Dummies
  0-7645-2593-X

NETWORKING, SECURITY, PROGRAMMING & DATABASES

0-7645-6852-3

0-7645-5784-X

Also available:

- A+ Certification For Dummies
  0-7645-4187-0
- Access 2003 All-in-One Desk Reference For Dummies
  0-7645-3988-4
- Beginning Programming For Dummies
  0-7645-4997-9
- C For Dummies
  0-7645-7068-4
- Firewalls For Dummies
  0-7645-4048-3
- Home Networking For Dummies
  0-7645-42796

- Network Security For Dummies
  0-7645-1679-5
- Networking For Dummies
  0-7645-1677-9
- TCP/IP For Dummies
  0-7645-1760-0
- VBA For Dummies
  0-7645-3989-2
- Wireless All In-One Desk Reference For Dummies
  0-7645-7496-5
- Wireless Home Networking For Dummies
  0-7645-3910-8